STUDIES IN
LATE ANTIQUITY AND EARLY ISLAM

5

THE EYE OF THE BEHOLDER

THE LIFE OF MUḤAMMAD AS VIEWED BY THE EARLY MUSLIMS

A Textual Analysis

SLAEI

STUDIES IN
LATE ANTIQUITY AND EARLY ISLAM
5

THE EYE OF THE BEHOLDER

THE LIFE OF MUḤAMMAD AS VIEWED BY THE EARLY MUSLIMS

A TEXTUAL ANALYSIS

URI RUBIN

THE DARWIN PRESS, INC.
PRINCETON, NEW JERSEY
1995

Library of Congress Cataloging-in-Publication Data

Rubin, Uri, 1944–.
The eye of the beholder : the life of Muḥammad as viewed by the early Muslims : a textual analysis / Uri Rubin.
p. cm. – (Studies in late antiquity and early Islam : 5)
Includes bibliographical references (to p.) and index.
ISBN 0-87850-110-X : $27.50
1. Muḥammad, Prophet, d. 632–Biography–History and criticism.
I. Title. II. Series.
BP75.3.R83 1995
297'.63–dc20 94-49175
CIP

Second printing, 1997.

The paper in this book is acid-free neutral pH stock and meets the guidelines for permanence and durability of the Committee on Production Guidelines for Book Longevity of the Council on Library Resources.

Printed in the United States of America

[redacted]

For Tamar

Contents

Preface

ALL PARTS OF THIS BOOK are published here for the first time. A preliminary version of Chapter 4 was read in the Sixth Colloquium "From Jāhiliyya to Islam", held at the Hebrew University of Jerusalem in 1993. The first draft of Chapter 11 was part of a paper I read in the Colloquium on Ḥadīth and Historiography, held in Oxford in 1988. I have benefited much from the notes and comments of the participants in these two conferences. An excellent opportunity for reviewing and improving on various aspects of my findings was given to me during discussions with my students at Tel Aviv University over the past few years.

Special thanks are due to Dr. Lawrence I. Conrad, Co-Director of the *Late Antiquity and Early Islam* project, for his painstaking editorial work on several drafts of this book, as well as for his corrections of style, and invaluable suggestions concerning the book's final form and contents. I am particularly grateful to him for talking me into adding a summary (Chapter 13) which—to use his words—would serve "to focus and draw together all the various trends of thought and argument in the book."

* * *

The very nature of the source materials, and what I have sought to derive from them, makes it inevitable that this book will be full of Arabic personal names and terms. While this will pose no difficulty for those conversant with early Islamic studies, for students and colleagues in other fields it may prove daunting. This very common problem is of course an obstacle to communication across traditional disciplinary boundaries, and I have tried to take it into account here. As a further aid, persons and terms are briefly identified in the Index.

The translation of Quranic verses throughout the book is my own, drawing occasionally on Arthur J. Arberry, *The Koran Interpreted* (Oxford, 1964).

The numbering of *kitāb*s ("Books") and *bāb*s ("Chapters") in *ḥadīth* compilations arranged by topics (*muṣannaf*) are given in parentheses after the indication of the volume and page; e.g. Bukhārī, *Ṣaḥīḥ*, IV, 225 (61:17).

Introduction

THIS BOOK IS ABOUT TEXTS, and the texts are about Muḥammad, the prophet of Islam. The texts—found in the earliest Islamic sources which have come down to us—are studied in this book for the sake of the stories recorded in them, not for the sake of the events described in these stories. The question "what really happened" in Muḥammad's times is not the one asked in this book, which instead is concerned with the manner in which the texts tell the story of Muḥammad's life, and is aimed to discover how the various evolving versions of this story tell us about the image of the Prophet as perceived by the believers among whom these texts were created and circulated.

Many Islamicists who have already studied the story of Muḥammad's life have focussed their attention not only on the story itself, but also and mainly on the historical events which this story is supposed to record; they have conducted their research on the story with a view to revealing what the Prophet was "really" like, and what his enterprise "actually" was. They have noticed the existence of tendentious elaborations and legendary inventions in the early Islamic biographies of the Prophet, but have always regarded them as a secondary element, distinct from what they have considered to be the "early" and most "authentic" and "human" presentation of Muḥammad. They have believed that the "genuine" display of Muḥammad could and should be distinguished from the "later" legendary and tendentious one. This conviction is evident to various degrees of intensity in the studies of many leading Islamicists.

Already Ignaz Goldziher surveyed in some detail the legendary elements which found their way into the biographies of Muḥammad.[1] In his view, these elements were only produced after the popular veneration of saints had already developed during the first decades of Islam. Originally, the Prophet was perceived as an ordinary human being; his legendary image was only established as a later development in contrast to the initial Islamic concepts. To use Goldziher's own words: "The power of *ijmāʿ* here scored one of its biggest triumphs in the whole system of Islam, insofar as the belief of the people succeeded in penetrating into the canonical conception of the Prophet and, so to speak, forcing it to make him into a fortune-teller, worker of miracles, and magician."[2]

---

[1] Ignaz Goldziher, *Muslim Studies* (London, 1967–71), II, 255–62 ("Veneration of Saints in Islam").

[2] *Ibid.*, II, 261.

A similar approach was adopted by Josef Horovitz, who tried to establish the earliest possible date for the "beginning" of legendary elaborations in the biography of the Prophet. This implies that for him too, the legendary presentation is a secondary—albeit early—element in the traditions about the prophet Muḥammad.[3]

Tor Andræ, in his *Die Person Muhammeds in Lehre und Glauben seiner Gemeinde*,[4] surveys the views of later Islamic theologians and their treatment of the Prophet as a subject of veneration. He too treats the legendary image of Muḥammad as a product of later development which deviated considerably from the earliest conception of the Prophet. He believed he could distinguish between the legendary and the real Prophet, and in another book he tried to understand how Muḥammad really thought and acted. The latter is entitled *Mohammed, sein Leben und sein Glaube*.[5]

Rudolf Sellheim has more recently published a thorough literary study of the early biography of the Prophet composed by Ibn Isḥāq (d. AH 150).[6] Here the discrimination between the real and fabricated is very clear-cut. Sellheim is able to detect three major stages in the literary development of the story of Muḥammad's life, each represented in a different "layer" ("Schicht"). The "ground layer" is the most authentic. Here, according to Sellheim, are contained traditions which lead us more or less directly into the actual events. They are closely related to the milieu of Muḥammad's homeland (i.e. Mecca and Medina). Next there is the "first layer", in which the legendary image of Muḥammad presents itself. Here the presence of non-Arab material from Jewish, Christian and Persian origins is evident. Next there is the "second layer" in which manipulations of the text in accordance with political interests of various Islamic groups are embedded.

The conviction that the "sound" information and the tendentious elaborations and inventions in Muḥammad's biography should and could be isolated from each other has been shared by Islamicists who have made an attempt at using the texts for an historical reconstruction of the entire life of the Prophet. Most characteristic of these studies are the numerous works of W. Montgomery Watt.[7] Watt actually followed in the footsteps of his more eminent predecessors, especially Leone Caetani and Frants Buhl.

---

[3] Josef Horovitz, "Zur Muḥammadlegende", *Der Islam* 5 (1914), 41–53.

[4] Published in Uppsala in 1917.

[5] Published in Göttingen in 1932. The English translation by Theophil Menzel is entitled *Mohammed, the Man and his Faith* (London, 1936).

[6] Rudolf Sellheim, "Prophet, Chalif und Geschichte", *Oriens* 18–19 (1965–66), 33–91.

[7] E.g. his *Muhammad at Mecca* (Oxford, 1953); *Muhammad at Medina* (Oxford, 1956); *Muhammad's Mecca* (Edinburgh, 1988).

In the works of all the above-mentioned scholars, as well as in studies by others, including my own,[8] traces are noticeable of the belief in a "hard core" of historical facts existing objectively and independently of the interpretation of Muḥammad's early Muslim biographers. This belief has its origin in what is defined by E.H. Carr as the "nineteenth-century fetishism of facts", which was completed and justified by "a fetishism of documents".[9] In fact, orientalists have continued to preoccupy themselves till this very day with problems of historical reconstruction of the life of the Prophet.[10] In the following chapters, however, the effort to isolate the "historical" from the "fictional" in the early Islamic texts is given up entirely. The bulk of the texts about the Prophet embody the literary product of Islamic religious devotion, and therefore they will be treated in this book not as a door opening onto the "historical" events which are described in them, but rather as a mirror reflecting the state of mind of the believers among whom these texts were created, preserved, and circulated through the ages.

A purely "source analysis" of the early Islamic texts has already been declared to be the purpose of John Wansbrough's *The Sectarian Milieu.*[11] For him the texts represent a "salvation history" that comprises an Arabian version of biblical models. However, the range of source material used by Wansbrough seems to have been too limited to yield any comprehensive idea of the structure of the Prophet's early biographies, and his actual analysis of Muḥammad's life is only focussed on its "interconfessional" polemical aspects, and no systematic analysis of the inner textual dynamics of the stories is undertaken. In carrying out my own research, I shall try to implement the techniques of my great master, M.J. Kister, whose numerous studies have made it perfectly clear that unless the broadest possible range of sources is examined, no real idea about the status of a certain theme in Islamic tradition can be gained.

In the chapters to follow I shall concentrate on the textual analysis of the story of Muḥammad's prophetic emergence in Mecca. The main purpose will be to demonstrate how this story reflects the self-image of medieval Islamic society. Medieval Islam was preoccupied with its own status in the world's history, trying to establish itself as a worthy successor to other monotheistic communities which came under its control, mainly the Jews and the Christians. The

---

[8] See, for example, my "Muḥammad's Curse of Muḍar and the Boycott of Mecca", *Journal of the Economic and Social History of the Orient* 31 (1988), 249–64; also my "The Assassination of Ka'b b. al-Ashraf", *Oriens* 32 (1990), 65–71.

[9] E.H. Carr, *What is History* (repr. Penguin Books, 1980), 16.

[10] For a recent discussion of these problems see F.E. Peters, "The Quest of the Historical Muhammad", *International Journal of Middle East Studies* 23 (1991), 291–315.

[11] Published in Oxford in 1978.

Muslims portrayed the life of their own prophet with the same view in mind. In fact, they sought to provide their prophet with a biography no less glamorous than that of previous prophets; and in order to do so, they applied to it biblical themes inherent in the stories about those prophets. This thematic borrowing is indeed a well-known fact exposed already by scholars mentioned above, but the ensuing chapters survey the process in which these themes were adapted to specific Arabian conditions, as well as to clear Quranic models which were supposed to provide them with Islamic authorization. The chapters to follow also examine the extent to which the adaptation of the universal themes actually succeeded in terms of circulation in the sources, and show that sometimes the process failed with certain themes which were denied wide circulation. Mainstream Islam could not absorb them, due to dogmatic inhibitions.

The themes whose process of conversion to Islamic models is studied are: attestation, preparation, revelation, persecution, and salvation. These themes add up to the story of Muḥammad's prophetic emergence in Mecca. The Medinan period, which tells the story of Muḥammad's triumphant leadership, deserves another book.

The study of these five themes is followed by an epilogue which touches upon the subject of the chronology of Muḥammad's career. This theme places Muḥammad's Meccan period within a larger framework covering his entire life. Finally, there are three chapters of conclusions. The first is a summary of the study of the five themes, highlighting the main findings concerning each theme. In the second chapter, the role of the Quran in the traditions discussed in the previous chapters is examined. This section actually deals with the history of the *asbāb al-nuzūl* ("occasions of revelation") material. The final chapter tackles a specific aspect of the preceding discussion, namely, the *isnāds*, i.e. the chains of transmitters through whom stories about Muḥammad were—or were claimed to have been—transmitted. Throughout the book the *isnād* of each tradition is always indicated when given in the sources. However, only that part of the *isnād* is recorded which contains the earliest transmitters; in "Schachtian" terms—from the common link backwards. According to the school of Schacht, this is the least authentic part of the entire *isnād*, but some of Schacht's basic observations will here be invalidated. The entire study is preceded by a detailed survey of the sources upon which it is based.

The Sources

I

OUR KNOWLEDGE OF THE VIEWS and thoughts of the early Muslims about the life and career of their prophet is derived from Muslim traditions recorded in numerous and often voluminous compilations. These traditions are focussed on one man: the Prophet Muḥammad, and contain stories about his sayings and acts which were transmitted through the ages from his Companions to their Successors. Each individual tradition is called a *ḥadīth*; it is normally preceded by a list, called an *isnād*, which contains the names of the various transmitters of the tradition. The list begins with the latest authority and reaches back to the earliest, which is, ideally, the Prophet himself.

Many of the *ḥadīth* compilations are arranged by chapters, each called a *kitāb*, or "book". The titles of the chapters encompass a vast variety of topics revealing the multifarious fields of interest of the Muslim scholars, and the chapters themselves amount to what the scholars call the *sunan*. In its broader sense this term covers all aspects of Muslim law and dogma.[1] In its stricter meaning it only signifies the practical aspects of the law. For the sake of convenience, we shall follow Goldziher in referring to the compilations arranged according to the topics of the *sunan* as the *muṣannaf* collections.[2] The verb *ṣannafa* means to arrange by chapters, so that a book thus arranged is *muṣannaf*. There are numerous such *muṣannaf* collections, and most noteworthy of these are the so-called "Six Books" which acquired canonical status: the *al-Jāmi' al-ṣaḥīḥ* of al-Bukhārī (d. AH 256), the *al-Jāmi' al-ṣaḥīḥ* of Muslim (d. AH 261), the *Sunan* of Ibn Māja (d. AH 275), the *Sunan* of Abū Dāwūd (d. AH 275), the *Jāmi'* of al-Tirmidhī (d. AH 279), and the *Sunan* of al-Nasā'ī (d. AH 303). The term *jāmi'* signifies the wide range of subjects compiled in the work thus named, whereas the title *sunan* means that the compilation is dedicated mainly to the practical aspects of *ḥadīth*. The most authoritative of the Six are the *Jāmi'* of al-Bukhārī and Muslim, each of which came to be known as *al-Ṣaḥīḥ* ("Sound"). Apart from the "Six Books" there are many other compilations organized as *muṣannaf*. It should be observed in passing that not only *ḥadīth* proper was arranged by chapters. Many books of *fiqh*, i.e. of purely

[1] For a scrutiny of the various aspects of the *sunan*, see e.g. Ibn Ḥibbān, *Ṣaḥīḥ*, I, 105–51.
[2] Goldziher, *Muslim Studies*, II, 214–16.

theoretical discussions of the law, were compiled according to the same system.[3]

Several topics of the "books" in the *muṣannaf* compilations reveal various aspects of the Prophet's status in the Islamic community. Some of them are devoted to the mere obligation to follow the example of the Prophet. His model, or way of conduct, is referred to as the *sunna* (sing. of *sunan*), and the *sunna* of the Prophet, together with the rulings of the Quran, provide the legal foundation for the everyday life of the Muslims.[4] Special chapters about the duty to adhere to the *sunna* of the Prophet (as well as to the *sunna* of the Rāshidūn, the first four "righteous" caliphs) are included in the Introduction of al-Dārimī (d. AH 255) to his *Sunan*.[5] In the *Ṣaḥīḥ* of al-Bukhārī, there is a *kitāb* (no. 96) entitled *al-I'tiṣām bi-l-kitāb wa-l-sunna*, "Adherence to the Quran and the Sunna".[6] A special section was devoted to the same topic by Abū Dāwūd as well.[7] It is also dealt with in the first chapter of the *Jāmi'* of Ibn Abī Zayd al-Qayrawānī (d. AH 386),[8] and in the very first "book" in the rearranged compilation of Ibn Ḥibbān (d. AH 354).[9] The traditions assembled in these chapters praise the examples of the Book of God and of His Prophet, urge the Muslims to stick to them, denounce the reliance on independent judgement (*ra'y*), and attack heretics like the Khawārij, etc., who deviated from them. These very traditions were recorded by some compilers in the section named *Īmān*, "Faith", where various aspects of Islamic dogma are treated.[10]

Being the primary prototype for all aspects of living and thinking, the Prophet is the actual law-giver and judge.[11] His function as a judge is illustrated in one of the sections in the compilation of Ibn Abī Shayba (d. AH 235), called

---

[3] For example, Shaybānī (d. AH 189/805), *Ḥujja*; Saḥnūn (d. AH 240), *Mudawwana*; Aḥmad ibn Ḥanbal (d. AH 241), *Masā'il;* al-Shaykh al-Ṣadūq (d. AH 381), *Man lā yaḥḍuruhu l-faqīh*; Sarakhsī (d. AH 482), *Mabsūṭ*.

[4] See, for example, the chapter "Ḥadīth and Sunna", in Goldziher, *Muslim Studies*, II, 17–37. And see also Meir M. Bravmann, *The Spiritual Background of Early Islam* (Leiden, 1972), 123–98; G.H.A. Juynboll, "Some New Ideas on the Development of *sunna* as a Technical Term in Early Islam, *Jerusalem Studies in Arabic and Islam* 10 (1987), 97–118; Patricia Crone and Martin Hinds, *God's Caliph: Religious Authority in the First Centuries of Islam* (Cambridge, 1986), 58–96.

[5] Dārimī, I, 57–62.

[6] Bukhārī, *Ṣaḥīḥ*, IX, 112–39.

[7] Abū Dāwūd, *Kitāb* no. 39 (II, 504–46).

[8] Ibn Abī Zayd, 105–26.

[9] Ibn Ḥibbān, *Ṣaḥīḥ*, I, 176–215. The *Ṣaḥīḥ* of Ibn Ḥibbān was rearranged by 'Alā' al-Dīn al-Fārisī (d. AH 739). See the introduction of the editor (al-Arna'ūṭ) in the first volume of the book.

[10] E.g. Baghawī, *Maṣābīḥ*, I, 150.

[11] For a study of the development of Muḥammad's image as head of state and as law-giver during the first centuries of Islam, see Crone and Hinds, *God's Caliph*.

"The Adjudications (*aqḍiya*) of the Messenger of God".[12] The traditions assembled in this section delineate the various legal cases in which the Prophet is presented as a judge.

II

The traditions about the Prophet were designed to provide the Islamic community not only with the legal basis for everyday life, but also with the historical dimension of the Islamic collective self-image. According to the prevailing historical outlook of the Muslims, the emergence of Muḥammad as the last of all prophets marked the goal towards which the world's sacred history was moving.[13] Therefore, traditions about Muḥammad's prophetic mission were sometimes recorded in the section devoted to the world's history, in Arabic, *tārīkh*. Thus, in the rearranged compilation of Ibn Ḥibbān, the section named *Tārīkh* begins with the creation of the world, then proceeds to traditions in which central events in the Prophet's life are dealt with, such as the confrontation with the polytheists, the *hijra* ("emigration") from Mecca to Medina, and his death. There are also traditions about his virtues, his external appearance, his miracles, etc. All this is followed by traditions in which the Prophet foretells the future history of the Muslim community which is to unfold after his own death.[14]

For the Shīʿis too, Islamic history rests on a universal basis. World history revolves round the lives of the twelve *imāms*. The section *Tārīkh* in the Shīʿī compilation of al-Kulīnī (d. AH 329) is, indeed, devoted to the biographies of these persons. The chapter about Muḥammad, who is the prototype of all imams, contains traditions about the chronology of his life, his status as the best of all prophets, his pre-existence, his birth and early years as an orphan, the virtues of his grandfather ʿAbd al-Muṭṭalib and of his uncle Abū Ṭālib, who brought him up, his death, etc. This is followed by chapters about the imāms.[15]

Attention was paid in the *muṣannaf* compilations not only to the universal position of Islam in general, but also to its status in relation to particular non-Islamic communities, especially the Jews and the Christians. These are considered in Islam as the "People of the Book" (*ahl al-kitāb*), which means that like the Muslims, they too belong to a monotheistic religion with a revealed scripture. The traditions about the *ahl al-kitāb* deal with the legal relations between

[12] Ibn Abī Shayba, X, 155–84.
[13] This concept of history as progress is also known in Judaism and Christianity. And cf. Carr, *What is History*, 110.
[14] Ibn Ḥibbān, *Ṣaḥīḥ*, XIV, 5–602; XV, 5–268.
[15] Kulīnī, I, 439–554.

them and the Muslims, and in the *Muṣannaf* of 'Abd al-Razzāq (d. AH 211) these traditions are already assembled in special sections called *Ahl al-kitāb*.[16] But the main interest was focussed on the historical relations between the Muslims and the People of the Book. According to the Islamic historical outlook, the previous prophets of the People of the Book were just a prelude to the emergence of Muḥammad. In order to illustrate the course of this universal history, special "books" were dedicated by some compilers to the "stories" (*aḥādīth, tawārīkh*) of the various prophets, beginning with Adam. Such sections are to be found in the *Ṣaḥīḥ* of al-Bukhārī[17] and the *Mustadrak* of al-Ḥākim al-Naysābūrī (d. AH 404),[18] as well as in some later compilations.[19] The same material sometimes occurs under the heading of *Qiṣaṣ* ("Stories"), which indicates a somewhat more popular level of the material.[20] The stories about the prophets may recur in sections labelled *Faḍā'il* or *Manāqib*, "Virtues". A book named *Faḍā'il* is included in the compilation of Ibn Abī Shayba,[21] and contains chapters which add up to a systematic survey of the virtues of each and every prophet, beginning with Muḥammad himself, then returning to previous prophets. The *Faḍā'il* section in the *Ṣaḥīḥ* of Muslim (d. AH 261) has a similar structure.[22] In the much later compilation of al-Muttaqī al-Hindī (d. AH 975), entitled *Kanz al-'ummāl fī sunan al-aqwāl wa-l-af'āl*, the "book" of *Faḍā'il* also begins with Muḥammad, and then proceeds to the previous prophets.[23]

It is noteworthy that the traditions enumerating the virtues of Muḥammad considerably outnumber those dealing with each of the other prophets; not surprisingly, the compilers of the *ḥadīth* collections took greater interest in Muḥammad than in any other prophet. The traditions about him deal with his perfect character, his prophetic qualities, his noble descent, his names, his external appearance, his miracles, etc. A prominent place is assigned to these very issues in the Introduction of al-Dārimī (d. AH 255) to his *Sunan*. In fact, the *faḍā'il* sections are sometimes devoted exclusively to Muḥammad, as well as to other members of the Muslim community, thus placing the rest of the prophets outside the scope of the *faḍā'il*. This is the case in the sections named *Manāqib*

---

16 'Abd al-Razzāq, *Muṣannaf*, VI, 3–132; X, 311–78.
17 Bukhārī, *Ṣaḥīḥ*, IV, 159–216 (*Kitāb* no. 60).
18 *Mustadrak*, II, 542–600.
19 Ibn Ḥajar, *Maṭālib*, III, 269–99.
20 *Kanz*, XV, 150–74.
21 Ibn Abī Shayba, XI, 430–567.
22 Muslim, VII, 58–108 (*Kitāb* no. 43).
23 *Kanz*, XI, 366–524.

in the compilations of al-Bukhārī[24] and al-Tirmidhī,[25] as well as in the same sections of some later compilations.[26]

In some later compilations the "book" about Muḥammad's virtues, miraculous powers, and eminence among the other prophets, is called *'Alāmāt al-nubuwwa*, "Signs of Prophethood".[27] Another title is *Shamā'il*, "Good Qualities".[28] Special sections without specific names were dedicated by some compilers to traditions praising the respect and love of the Muslims for their prophet, and urging them to respect him and pray for him.[29]

Occasionally, *faḍā'il* sections like that in Muslim, for example, may include more strictly biographical details, such as the chronology of the Prophet's career.[30] Sometimes, specific events in his prophetic life were singled out and given a section of their own. For example, in the rearranged *Ṣaḥīḥ* of Ibn Ḥibbān, the third "book" is named *Isrā'*,[31] and the traditions recorded under this heading relate the Prophet's nocturnal journey from Mecca to Jerusalem and his ascension to heaven. In the *Musnad* of Abū 'Awāna (d. AH 316), special chapters are devoted to the first stages of Muḥammad's prophetic career, from the first revelation to the ascension to heaven.[32]

The miraculous ascension to heaven may occur in the sections named *Īmān*, "Faith". For the Muslims, *īmān* does not only mean belief in Allāh as the only God, but also in Muḥammad as His messenger. The ascension is regarded as one of the most notable reasons for believing in Muḥammad's prophethood, and has an important bearing on theological issues, as the Prophet is said to have met in heaven not only the other prophets, but also Allāh Himself. This event was therefore recorded in sections discussing dogmatic aspects of faith; it occurs in the sections named *Īmān* in the compilations of Muslim[33] and al-Haythamī.[34] Ibn Ḥazm (d. AH 456) deals with this event in his *Muḥallā* in the section entitled *Tawḥīd*, "Unity [of God]".[35]

---

[24] Bukhārī, *Ṣaḥīḥ*, IV, 225–53 (*Kitāb* no. 61).

[25] Tirmidhī/*Tuḥfa*, X, 74–457 (*Kitāb* no. 46).

[26] E.g. Baghawī, *Maṣābīḥ*, IV, 31–233 (*Kitāb* nos. 27–28); Ibn Ḥajar, *Maṭālib*, IV, 3–166 (*Kitāb* no. 39).

[27] *Majma' al-zawā'id*, VIII, 217–317.

[28] *Kanz*, VII, 31–274.

[29] Bayhaqī, *Shu'ab*, II, 129–34, 193–219.

[30] Muslim, VII, 89 (43, *Bāb kam aqāma l-nabiyyu bi-Makka wa-l-Madīna*, "On How Long the Prophet Stayed in Mecca and Medina").

[31] Ibn Ḥibbān, *Ṣaḥīḥ*, I, 233–60.

[32] Abū 'Awāna, I, 109–31.

[33] Muslim, I, 99–107.

[34] *Majma' al-zawā'id*, I, 69–83.

[35] Ibn Ḥazm, *Muḥallā*, I, 36.

But the main proofs that Muḥammad is indeed God's messenger, in whom every one must believe, are the very prophetic revelations he received. This is the reason why Muslim included the traditions about Muḥammad's first Quranic revelation in the *Kitāb al-īmān* in his compilation.[36] In al-Bukhārī's *Ṣaḥīḥ* the very first section of the entire compilation is dedicated to the beginning of Muḥammad's Quranic revelations (*Bad' al-waḥy*). This theme was given a special section in the compilation of Ibn Ḥibbān.[37]

The elevated status of the Quran as the main manifestation of prophethood is reflected in the fact that in numerous *muṣannaf* compilations there are "books" named *Faḍā'il al-Qur'ān*, "Virtues of the Quran". The traditions assembled under this heading deal with various practical aspects of the public recitation of the Quranic text, and praise the reading and learning of the Quran and devotion to its rulings. The history of the Quranic text is treated in traditions discussing the origins of the vocabulary of the Quranic language, its variant readings, and the chronology of its revelation. The collection of the various written revelations after the death of the Prophet is also described. The modes of interpretation of the Quran are scrutinized in traditions trying to establish legitimate ways of exegesis, and special traditions are designed to guide the believers in handling their individual Quran copies. The relation between the Quran and the scriptures of the Jews and the Christians is the subject of traditions trying to disclose parallelism between specific *sūra*s and certain books of the Bible. Specific chapters and portions of the Quran are praised as the most elevated parts of the scripture.[38] Shīʿī collections also have chapters named *Faḍā'il al-Qur'ān*;[39] in addition to the above issues, the traditions assembled in these works put forward the contention that only the Shīʿīs adhere to the true message of the Book of God.

III

Apart from trying to put Muḥammad on the universal map of the successive prophetic revelations, the Muslims were no less eager to highlight the local achievements of Muḥammad as a fighting prophet who succeeded in defeating

---

[36] Muslim, I, 97–99.

[37] Ibn Ḥibbān, *Ṣaḥīḥ*, I, 216–32.

[38] ʿAbd al-Razzāq, *Muṣannaf*, III, 335–84; Ibn Abī Shayba, X, 456–565; Dārimī, II, 521–66 (*Kitāb* no. 23); Bukhārī, *Ṣaḥīḥ*, VI, 223–45 (*Kitāb* no. 66); Muslim, II, 190–208 (*Kitāb* no. 6); Tirmidhī/*Tuḥfa*, VIII, 178–276 (*Kitāb* nos. 42–43); Nasā'ī, *Kubrā*, V, 3–34 (*Kitāb* no. 75); *Mustadrak*, I, 550–75; Bayhaqī, *Shuʿab*, II, 319–557; Baghawī, *Maṣābīḥ*, II, 107–35; Ibn Ḥajar, *Maṭālib*, III, 282–99; *Kanz*, I, 510–624.

[39] Kulīnī, II, 596–634.

polytheism in Arabia. The documentation of Muḥammad's battles against the Arabian infidels (mainly Quraysh), which were undertaken after his *hijra* (emigration) from Mecca to Medina, served legal needs as well. The Prophet's campaigns constituted a precedent for the various rules of warfare with infidels.

The compilers of *ḥadīth* recorded the traditions about Muḥammad's military activities in Medina under various headings. To begin with, various data about Muḥammad the warrior may be found in the sections about the holy war against non-Muslims. These sections are entitled *Jihād*. For example, ʻAbd al-Razzāq (d. AH 211) recorded in the *Kitāb al-jihād* of his compilation traditions containing such biographical details as Muḥammad's banners, swords, armour, riding beasts, etc. Most notable here are the traditions trying to determine the exact number of raids undertaken by Muḥammad.[40] The section on *jihād* in the *Sunan* of Saʻīd ibn Manṣūr (d. AH 227)[41] contains the texts of some letters the Prophet wrote to certain non-Muslim leaders urging them to embrace Islam, and the same kind of information may be found in the *jihād* section of al-Bukhārī.[42] Al-Ḥākim (d. AH 404) recorded in the *Kitāb al-jihād* of his *Mustadrak* traditions about Muḥammad's raids on such places as Mecca and Ṭā'if.[43] The *Muḥallā* of Ibn Ḥazm (d. AH 456) is not an ordinary *ḥadīth* compilation, but rather a legal compendium; nevertheless, the *Kitāb al-jihād* in this book has some traditions on the affair of Ḥudaybiyya, adduced to illustrate a legal dilemma.[44]

Traditions about Muḥammad's battles were also recorded under the heading of *Maghāzī*.[45] This term denotes “the virtues of the warriors”,[46] which seems to suggest pre-Islamic Arabian types of epic. In the earliest comprehensive *ḥadīth* compilations, the term *maghāzī* covers the entire life of Muḥammad, including his pre-*hijra* days in Mecca. This means that the early Muslims treated the Meccan period of Muḥammad as a prelude to his warlike period in Medina. Thus, the *Muṣannaf* of ʻAbd al-Razzāq (d. AH 211) has a *kitāb* named *Maghāzī*[47] which begins with a comprehensive report of Ibn Shihāb al-Zuhrī (Medinan d. AH 124). The report begins with some episodes from the life of Muḥammad's grandfather (ʻAbd al-Muṭṭalib), and goes on to tell about Muḥammad's early years in Mecca, his first prophetic revelation, his public

40 ʻAbd al-Razzāq, *Muṣannaf*, V, 287–89, 294–98.
41 Saʻīd ibn Manṣūr, II, 187–91.
42 Bukhārī, *Ṣaḥīḥ*, IV, 38, 39, 49, 54–58, 64–65 (56:60, 62, 89, 102, 121).
43 *Mustadrak*, II, 120–22.
44 Ibn Ḥazm, *Muḥallā*, VII, 307–308.
45 On this term, see Martin Hinds, s.v. “Maghāzī”, *EI*².
46 See *Lisān*, s.v. *gh.z.w.*: *wa-l-maghāzī, manāqib al-ghuzāt.*
47 ʻAbd al-Razzāq, *Muṣannaf*, V, 313–492.

preaching in Mecca, the conversion of ʻUmar, and the *isrā'*. This is followed by more reports of al-Zuhrī as well as other traditionists about some campaigns which took place after Muḥammad's *hijra* to Medina, including the story of the *hijra* itself. There are also reports about Muḥammad's last illness and death, as well as accounts about the first caliphs who succeeded Muḥammad. The compilation of Ibn Abī Shayba (d. AH 235) also has a section named *Maghāzī*,[48] which covers the same span of time as does the *Maghāzī* section of ʻAbd al-Razzāq, i.e. from the Year of the Elephant, in which the Prophet was said to have been born, till the death of the Prophet and the reign of the first four caliphs. The history of the latter appears to represent in the perception of the Muslim scholars and believers the same sacred history as represented by the emergence of the Prophet himself. Therefore, the lives and career of the Rāshidūn are recorded as a natural sequence to that of the prophet.

But in later compilations a distinction is made between the various periods of Muḥammad's life, the term *maghāzī* being narrowed down to the more specific sense of "military campaigns". This is the case in the *Ṣaḥīḥ* of al-Bukhārī (d. AH 256), where the *Kitāb al-maghāzī* (no. 64) only includes the actual campaigns of the Prophet in Medina. His earlier years are included in the previous section, which is dedicated to the virtues of the first Muslims, including those of the Prophet himself. In the *Jāmiʻ* of Ibn Abī Zayd (d. AH 386) as well, the term *maghāzī* has a similarly restricted meaning. The title of the section about the Prophet's life is *al-Hijra wa-l-maghāzī wa-l-tārīkh*.[49] The term *maghāzī* again only stands for the actual campaigns, whereas *hijra* stands for the arrival of Muḥammad in Medina, and *tārīkh* signifies the reports about the caliphs who succeeded Muḥammad. In a separate chapter of the *Jāmiʻ* the general chronology of Muḥammad's life is given.[50] In the *Mustadrak* of al-Ḥākim (d. AH 404) the reports about the Prophet's life are divided into subsections among which *maghāzī* again stands only for the Medinan period and the actual campaigns.[51] For the earlier periods such headings as *Baʻth* ("Prophetic Mission") and *Dalā'il al-nubuwwa* ("Proofs of Prophethood") are used.[52] The same narrow meaning of the term *maghāzī* is discernible in other compilations of a later date.[53]

---

48 Ibn Abī Shayba, XIV, 283–601.

49 See Ibn Abī Zayd, 265.

50 *Ibid.*, 126–38.

51 *Mustadrak*, III, 19–61.

52 *Ibid.*, II, 613.

53 *Kashf al-astār*, II, 297–358 (*Kitāb al-hijra wa-l-maghāzī*). In *Kanz*, X, 375–636, the campaigns are grouped under the heading of *Ghazawāt*. Thus there is not much ground for the

Yet another heading for the reports about the battles of Muḥammad is *Siyar*, i.e. "Campaigns" (the verb *sāra* means to set out to, to journey).[54] Unlike *maghāzī*, however, *siyar* does not stand for just the actual story of Muḥammad's campaigns, but rather for the practical precedents, inherent in the reports, which should be followed during any other military combat with infidels. In this sense the term often occurs in the singular form *sīra* which denotes the same as *sunna*, i.e. way of conduct.[55] In some compilations, like that of al-Tirmidhī (d. AH 279), a "book" named *al-Siyar* (no. 19)[56] is wholly dedicated to traditions about Muḥammad's conduct during various campaigns, as well as to his statements on how to treat the enemies of the Muslims. This is followed by two other sections (20–21) entitled *Jihād*, which deal with the idea of holy war as a noble and praiseworthy act, as well as with more practical aspects of holy war. The compilation of al-Dārimī contains a similar "book" named *Siyar* (no. 17) which is separate from the "book" named *Jihād* (no. 16). Again, the latter deals mainly with the virtues of the idea of the holy war, whereas the former is about its practical aspects, including occasional allusions to Muḥammad's own campaigns. The same applies to Nasā'ī's *al-Sunan al-kubrā*, where the section *Siyar* (no. 78), dealing with practical aspects of war, including allusions to the Prophet's campaigns, is separate from the "book" of *Jihād* (no. 29), in which the virtues of the idea of holy war are enumerated.

But the heading *Siyar* is not always separate from that of *Jihād*. Thus, Muslim (d. AH 261) has in his *Ṣaḥīḥ* a "book" named *al-Jihād wa-l-siyar*,[57] in which are included traditions about the *jihād* in general, as well as chronologically arranged reports about the campaigns of the Prophet. In fact, the titles *Siyar* and *Jihād*, are sometimes interchangeable. Many compilations lack a section named *Jihād*, having only one named *Siyar* which covers all the issues treated elsewhere under *Jihād*. This applies to the compilation of Zayd ibn 'Alī (d. AH 122), the *Masā'il* of Aḥmad ibn Ḥanbal, Ṭaḥāwī's *Sharḥ ma'ānī al-āthār*, the *Ṣaḥīḥ* of Ibn Ḥibbān, and the *Mabsūṭ* of Sarakhsī.[58]

---

observation of Hinds (s.v. "Maghāzī", EI^2) about the "declining interest in *maghāzī* as such" among the compilers after the third century AH.

[54] On *siyar*, cf. Hinds, s.v. "Maghāzī", EI^2. Cf. also Michael Bonner, "Some Observations Concerning the Early Development of *Jihād* on the Arab–Byzantine Frontier", *Studia Islamica* 75 (1992), 5–31.

[55] *Lisān*, s.v. *s.y.r.*

[56] Tirmidhī/*Tuḥfa*, V, 152–246.

[57] Muslim, V, 139–201 (*Kitāb* no. 32).

[58] Zayd ibn 'Alī, *Musnad*, 313–23; Aḥmad ibn Ḥanbal, *Masā'il* ('Abdallāh), 246–61; Ṭaḥāwī, *Sharḥ ma'ānī*, III, 206–75; Ibn Ḥibbān, *Ṣaḥīḥ*, X, 331–556; Sarakhsī, X, 2–144.

Since Muḥammad's life as a whole (i.e. not just his military deeds) was regarded as a source of moral guidance, the term *siyar* eventually came to cover the entire biography of Muḥammad. The "book" named *Siyar* in the *Sunan* of al-Bayhaqī (d. AH 458)[59] begins with the creation of the world and the history of the prophets, as if to suggest that the life of Muḥammad runs in a universal course. This is followed by traditions about his first prophetic revelations and other events in Mecca, and the *hijra* to Medina. Then come traditions about the permission given to the Muslims to fight their enemies, and about the obligation of *jihād*. The compilation of Nūr al-Dīn al-Haythamī (d. AH 807) includes a "book" named *al-Maghāzī wa-l-siyar*[60] covering Muḥammad's actual campaigns, as well as his pre-*hijra* struggle against the non-Muslims in Mecca, his preliminary contacts with the people of Medina, and his subsequent *hijra* to that place.

But when dealing with the large scale of Muḥammad's life, the singular form *sīra* was usually preferred to *siyar*. In one of the *ḥadīth* collections of Ibn Ḥajar (d. AH 852), the section of Muḥammad's life is accordingly named *Kitāb al-sīra wa-l-maghāzī*.[61] It opens with the birth of the Prophet and ends with his death.

IV

The *ḥadīth* compilations arranged as *muṣannaf* were meant for practical usage, or rather, for the purpose of *fiqh*, i.e. the legal study of the various topics of the *sunan*. Most of the *muṣannaf* compilations only contain traditions which met certain critical standards. Al-Bukhārī, Muslim, and others only accepted those traditions which they considered *ṣaḥīḥ*, i.e. "sound". Compilers like al-Ḥākim added many traditions which had been rejected by al-Bukhārī and Muslim, but they too confined their selection to what they believed to be equally sound. Thus many traditions were left out of the *muṣannaf* compilations. These traditions are no less important for our study, because they illuminate additional angles of the Islamic outlook, often less conservative and hence rejected, but still significant. Comparing them with the traditions of the *muṣannaf* compilations may reveal basic stages in the literary development of the stories about the life of the Prophet. On the whole, it will become clear that in many rejected traditions, the contents lack some essential dogmatic features, a

[59] Bayhaqī, *Sunan*, IX, 2–182.
[60] *Majma' al-zawā'id*, VI, 17–227.
[61] Ibn Ḥajar, *Maṭālib*, IV, 167–263.

deficiency which caused the compilers to ignore them. Many of these traditions seem to be earlier than the more conventional traditions which gained admission into the *muṣannaf* compilations.

In our quest of the traditions rejected by the *muṣannaf* compilers, several sources—all of them biographical collections—are at our disposal. Unlike the *muṣannaf* compilations, these sources were not intended for practical guidance. Their objective was more comprehensive: documenting the various available versions of the story of the Prophet's life, including such as were not generally recognised as sound. For this reason the scope of the traditions preserved in the biographical sources is often wider than that of the traditions of the *muṣannaf* compilations.

The first biographical source to be mentioned is Muḥammad's biography compiled by Ibn Isḥāq (d. AH 150). Unfortunately, this work is not available in its original form, but only in some later abridged recensions. Best known is the recension of Ibn Hishām (d. AH 218), who, in calling it "The *Sīra* of the Messenger of Allāh", is one of the earliest authors to use the term *sīra* in its biographical sense. The original compilation of Ibn Isḥāq was probably known as *Maghāzī*.[62] An earlier recension of Ibn Isḥāq is that of Yūnus ibn Bukayr (d. AH 199),[63] which contains valuable details omitted from the recension of Ibn Hishām.

On the whole, the original collection of Ibn Isḥāq is arranged as one coherent story covering the entire life of Muḥammad, introduced by the pre-Islamic sacred history of the world. The story was built up from separate traditions which Ibn Isḥāq himself collected and arranged according to his own judgement. In fact, different versions of one and the same scene were combined by Ibn Isḥāq into a series of sequential events. For example, in Ibn Hishām there is a tradition of Muḥammad ibn Ka'b al-Quraẓī about a meeting of a Meccan leader ('Utba ibn Rabī'a) with the Prophet.[64] The tradition is immediately followed by the tradition of Ibn 'Abbās about the meeting of an entire group of leaders, including 'Utba, with Muḥammad.[65] It is clear that we are confronted with two versions of the same episode, because both meetings take place when Quraysh are alarmed by the increasing number of the Muslims, and each time the same proposals are made to Muḥammad. The only difference is that each version uses

---

[62] See Hinds, s.v. "Maghāzī", *EI*^{2}.

[63] See Alfred Guillaume, "New Light on the Life of Muhammad", *Journal of Semitic Studies*, Monograph no. 1 (Manchester, n.d.); Miklos Muranyi, "Ibn Isḥāq's *Kitāb al-Maġāzī* in der *riwāya* von Yūnus b. Bukayr, *Jerusalem Studies in Arabic and Islam* 14 (1991), 214–75.

[64] Ibn Hishām, I, 313.

[65] *Ibid.*, I, 315–19.

different extracts from the Quran. Nevertheless, Ibn Isḥāq treats the two traditions as accounts of two successive meetings. His introduction to the second tradition opens with the typical *thumma*, "afterwards", "and then".[66]

The author following Ibn Isḥāq in antiquity whose work has been preserved is al-Wāqidī (d. AH 207). His book is entitled *Kitāb al-maghāzī*, and only covers the Medinan period. Al-Wāqidī, like Ibn Isḥāq, combined different traditions into one sequence of events. The third author to be mentioned is al-Wāqidī's secretary, Ibn Sa'd (d. AH 230), whose *Ṭabaqāt* is dedicated to the biographies of the Companions of the Prophet and their Successors. The first volume contains the biography of the Prophet himself, and largely draws on al-Wāqidī. The importance of this volume is tremendous, preserving as it does accounts about the Meccan period of the Prophet which are not included in the available edition of al-Wāqidī's *Maghāzī*. Al-Balādhurī (d. AH 279) is the author of the *Ansāb al-ashrāf*, a colossal collection of the biographies of the people of Quraysh in which the first volume is about Muḥammad. Many traditions have been recorded in this volume which are not to be found in any of the earlier biographical sources. The well-known *Annals* of Muḥammad ibn Jarīr al-Ṭabarī (d. AH 310) contain a biography of Muḥammad, which is recorded as part of the world's history. Apart from extracts from Ibn Isḥāq, it records many other early traditions which are not to be found in any other earlier source. Of the later sources, special note should be made of al-Bayhaqī's (d. AH 458) *Dalā'il al-nubuwwa*. This is a seven-volume compilation which encompasses a great mass of traditions extracted from earlier biographical and other *ḥadīth* collections, including some which have been lost. As the name of the book indicates, it contains traditions illuminating the miraculous aspects of Muḥammad's prophetic persona.

Apart from the biographical collections, there are compendia of *ḥadīth* proper which are arranged according to a biographical criterion. They document the traditions each Companion transmitted about the Prophet, and are arranged according to the names of the Companions. They are often called *Musnad*. Here traditions may also be found which were left outside the *muṣannaf* compilations. Most outstanding in this field is the *Musnad* of Aḥmad ibn Ḥanbal (d. AH 241). Other similarly arranged and very useful compilations are the *Musnad* of Abū Ya'lā (d. AH 307), and especially Ṭabarānī's (d. AH 360) *al-Mu'jam al-kabīr*.

---

[66] On the use of transitional formulae like *thumma* in Islamic historical writing, see also Albrecht Noth and Lawrence I. Conrad, *The Early Islamic Historical Tradition: a Source Critical Study* (Princeton, 1994), 57–58.

Finally, the corpus of exegesis (*tafsīr*) of the Quran should be mentioned. The *muṣannaf* collections themselves most often have a "book" named *Kitāb al-tafsīr* containing traditions alluding to specific Quranic verses. They are usually arranged according to the Quranic sequence of the *sūra*s and verses. The presence of such "books" in the *muṣannaf* compilations (in addition to the books of *Faḍā'il al-Qur'ān*) indicates the conviction of the compilers that the Book of God should be taken as a source of moral and practical guidance. For this reason believers must be aware not only of its virtues, but of its actual interpretation.

Traditions were collected for the purpose of *tafsīr* not only in the *muṣannaf* works, but also in separate individual compilations, some of them very early. One of the earliest compilers of *tafsīr* traditions whose work has come down to us is Muqātil ibn Sulaymān (d. AH 150). Other notable compilers of traditions for the purpose of *tafsīr* are the above-mentioned 'Abd al-Razzāq (d. AH 211) who also composed a voluminous *muṣannaf*, and especially al-Ṭabarī (d. AH 310).

In the field of *tafsīr*, the biography of the Prophet and the Book of God emerge linked to each other. In the course of the ensuing study it will become clear that this link was originally created outside the realm of *tafsīr*. It came into being within the *sīra* of Muḥammad, out of which the compilers of the *tafsīr* works eventually gleaned most of their material, which came to be technically known as *asbāb al-nuzūl*, "occasions of revelation".

PART I

ATTESTATION

1

The Biblical Annunciation

THE EMERGENCE OF THE PROPHET of Islam as perceived by the Muslim believers is the focus and culmination of the world's sacred history (*tārīkh*). This history proceeds through a continuous series of divine revelations delivered by successive prophets of whom Muḥammad is the last. Each prophet is elected to his mission in accordance with a predestined divine scheme. Glimpses of this historical outlook, already found in the earliest biographies of Muḥammad, are marked by a clear apologetic trend. From the very beginning of their contacts with the *ahl al-kitāb*, the Muslims had to sustain the dogma that Muḥammad did indeed belong to the same exclusive predestined chain of prophets in whom the Jews and the Christians believed. In order to do so, the Muslims had to establish the story of Muḥammad's life on the same literary patterns as were used in the *vitae* of the other prophets. Since all of those prophets were biblical figures, Muḥammad's biography had to be shaped according to biblical models. This was supposed to convince the People of the Book who refused to recognize Muḥammad as a prophet like their own.[1]

The shaping of the image of the prophet of Islam along biblical lines is typically exemplified in the theme of annunciation. Being regarded as a prophet whose election is predestined, Muḥammad's actual emergence in Arabia is annunciated by the previous prophets to whom the aim of God's historical scheme is revealed in advance, and whose task it is to pave the way for the emergence of Muḥammad. In their quest for literary evidence of the annunciation of their prophet, the Muslims used the same device as that used by the Christians for Jesus; they looked for attestation in previous sacred scriptures, and identified their own prophet with the messianic saviour whose emergence was believed to have been foretold in numerous biblical passages. These passages are quoted verbatim in Arabic translation in many polemical treatises by Muslim writers surveyed already by Goldziher and others.[2] One of the earliest writers of these

[1] The function of Jewish, Christian, and other materials in the *sīra* was noticed long ago. See e.g. Horovitz, "Zur Muḥammadlegende", 41–53; *idem*, "Biblische Nachwirkungen in der Sira", *Der Islam* 12 (1922), 184–89; Sellheim, "Prophet, Chalif und Geschichte", 53–71.

[2] Ignaz Goldziher, "Ueber muhammadanische Polemik gegen Ahl al-kitāb", *Zeitschrift der Deutschen Morgenländischen Gesellschaft* 32 (1878), 341–87; reprinted in his *Gesammelte Schriften*, II (Hildesheim, 1968), 1–47. There is also a study in Hebrew by Eliyahu Straus [Ashtor], in *Sefer ha-zikkaron le-beit ha-midrash le-rabbanim be-vina*

monographs was ʻAlī ibn Rabban al-Ṭabarī (d. *ca.* AH 250[3]), who devoted the bulk of his book *al-Dīn wa-l-dawla fī ithbāt nubuwwat al-nabī Muḥammad* to the biblical quotations which were believed to refer to the prophet of Islam. Later writers not discussed by Goldziher and the others adduced similar quotations,[4] and even contemporary Muslims keep repeating them for the same apologetic purposes.[5]

In the present investigation, however, our attention will focus not so much on polemical writings of late Muslim theologians as on the early biographical sources and *ḥadīth* compilations. These sources seem to indicate that Muslim reliance on the Bible began much earlier than is usually assumed by Islamicists.[6]

I

The Quran already contains some explicit manifestations of the contention that the emergence of the prophet of Islam was prognosticated in the sacred scriptures of the Jews and the Christians. In 61:6 the Quran states that Jesus brought to his people the good tidings about a prophet who would come after him, whose name is "Aḥmad". It has already been noticed by Islamicists that "Aḥmad" could be related to the statements in the New Testament about the coming of the Paraclete, the "Comforter" (John 14:16 and 26; 15:26). It has been noted that "Aḥmad" reflects the perception of Paraclete in the sense of the Greek *periklutos*, "celebrated", hence "Aḥmad". Scholars are not convinced, however, whether the Quranic Aḥmad itself already draws on the New Testament.[7]

Whatever the case may be, the early biographies of Muḥammad do identify the Prophet with the Paraclete of the New Testament. Ibn Isḥāq (d. AH 150)

(Jerusalem, 1946), 182–97. And see also M.J. Kister, "*Ḥaddithū ʻan banī isrāʼīla wa-lā ḥaraja*", *Israel Oriental Studies* 2 (1972), 222–25; John Wansbrough, *Quranic Studies* (Oxford, 1977), 63–65; also the recent study of Camilla Adang, *Muslim Writers on Judaism and the Hebrew Bible from Ibn Rabban to Ibn Hazm*, Ph.D. thesis (Nijmegen, 1993).

[3] See on him, Fuat Sezgin, *Geschichte des arabischen Schrifttums* (Leiden, 1967–proceeding), III, 236–40.

[4] E.g. Ibn al-Jawzī, *Wafā*, I, 61–73 (quoting Ibn Qutayba); Ibn Kathīr, *Bidāya*, VI, 178–81.

[5] See e.g. editor's note in Qiwām al-Sunna, *Dalāʼil*, I, 336–39 (relying on Ibn Taymiyya's *al-Jawāb al-ṣaḥīḥ*).

[6] E.g. Adang, *Muslim Writers*, 101.

[7] See A. Guthrie and E.F.F. Bishop, "The Paraclete, Almunhamanna and Aḥmad", *The Muslim World* 41 (1951), 251–56; W. Montgomery Watt, "His Name is Aḥmad", *The Muslim World* 43 (1953), 110–17; Joseph Schacht, s.v. "Aḥmad", *EI*[2]; Geoffrey Parrinder, *Jesus in the Qurʼān* (London, 1977), 96–100.

records in his *Sīra*[8] a verbatim quotation from the Gospel of John, and renders the Paraclete as *al-Munḥamannā* (cf. the Hebrew *menaḥem*, "comforter"); he says that *al-Munḥamannā* in Syriac is "Muḥammad", and that in Greek it is *al-Baraqlīṭis* (Paraclete).[9]

The same identification of the Paraclete with the Prophet recurs in the earliest extant commentaries on Quran 61:6. Already Muqātil ibn Sulaymān (d. AH 150) says that "Aḥmad" in Syriac is *fāraqlīṭā*.[10] This indicates that the identification of the Quranic "Aḥmad" with the Paraclete of the New Testament is much earlier than is usually assumed by modern scholars. Later commentators like al-Rāzī (d. AH 607) adduced from the New Testament the verbatim quotations of the Paraclete passages in their commentary on the Quranic verse about Aḥmad.[11]

But the Paraclete is not the only instance of biblical annunciation of the Islamic prophet. The Quran itself already utilises further biblical references for the same purpose. In Quran 7:156–58 God says to Moses that He will extend His compassion to those who will follow "the messenger, the prophet, the *ummī*, whom they find written with them, in the Torah and the Gospel...." This passage implies that Muḥammad is described in the scriptures of the Jews and the Christians as "the prophet, the *ummī*".

The significance of *ummī* has been much discussed in modern scholarship, and cannot be easily translated.[12] Some hitherto unnoticed aspects of its significance will, nevertheless, be revealed through the ensuing examination of the literary employment of the *ummī* idea in the early biographical traditions. This will bring to light other biblical passages which nourished the earliest traditions about the annunciation of Muḥammad.

The title *ummī* turns up in the early biographical traditions in the context of attestation, and is often produced as an epithet given to the prophet of Islam already in the Bible. Some such traditions were recorded by Ibn Sa'd (d. AH 230). According to one of them, the Prophet was called *ummī* already in the "book of Abraham" (i.e. Genesis). This tradition, transmitted by the Kūfan

---

[8] Ibn Hishām, I, 248.

[9] See further Alfred Guillaume, *The Life of Muhammad*: a *Translation of Ibn Isḥāq's Sīrat Rasūl Allāh* (Oxford, 1974), 104 n. 1.

[10] Muqātil, II, fol. 195a.

[11] Rāzī, XXIX, 313. For the identification of the Quranic "Aḥmad" with the Paraclete, see also Ibn Kathīr, *Bidāya*, VI, 181.

[12] Recent studies on *ummī* are Isaiah Goldfeld, "The Illiterate Prophet (*nabī ummī*): an Inquiry into the Development of a Dogma in Islamic Tradition, *Der Islam* 57 (1980), 58–67; Norman Calder, "The *Ummī* in Early Islamic Juridic Literature", *Der Islam* 67 (1990), 111–23; Khalil 'Athamina, "*Al-Nabiyy al-Umiyy* [sic.]...", *Der Islam* 69 (1992), 61–81.

Successor (*tābi'ī*) al-Sha'bī (d. AH 103), says that in the codex (*majalla*) of Abraham the following is written:

> Many peoples shall come out of your son, till the *ummī* prophet comes, who will be the seal of the prophets.[13]

The passage employed here is, to all appearances, Genesis 17:20. There God promises Abraham to multiply his son Ishmael exceedingly, to bless him with twelve princes, and to turn him into a great nation. This is a key biblical prophecy in favour of the children of Ishmael, of which the Muslims seem to have made the utmost use. In the tradition of al-Sha'bī the twelve princes of Genesis 17:20 became the one Islamic prophet, with the biblical "nation" (in Hebrew, *goy*), becoming *ummī*, i.e. one of the *umma*, or "nation".

The parallelism between *goy* and *ummī* is indeed striking. In the Talmud the Hebrew *goy* means "gentile", i.e. not belonging to the Jewish people. *Ummī* seems to denote exactly the same, i.e. one who belongs to a non-Jewish *umma* (= one of *ummot ha-'olam*, the "nations of the world"). In its metaphorical sense, *goy* in Hebrew is also a Jew who is ignorant concerning the Torah and religious duties. This connotation also seems to have been condensed into the Arabic *ummī* (pl. *ummiyyūn*).[14] Thus the biblical promise to make Ishmael into a great *goy* became in the tradition of al-Sha'bī a promise to transform Ishmael's seed into an *ummī* prophet. It may well be that already the *ummī* passage of Quran 7:156–58 alludes to this very biblical *goy* verse.

Genesis 17:20 was further exploited by later Muslim theologians who discovered that the numeric values of the letters of the Hebrew *bi-me'od me'od* ("exceedingly") add up to those of the Hebrew letters forming the name Muḥammad (92), and stated that Muḥammad's name in the "books of Abraham" was *Mūd Mūd*, or *Mād Mād*, etc.[15]

But let us return to Ibn Sa'd, who has yet another tradition about Abraham and the *ummī* prophet. This one has a Companion *isnād*, i.e. a list of successive transmitters concluding in a Companion of the Prophet, in this case, Ibn 'Abbās; he is quoted by the Meccan Successor 'Aṭā' ibn Abī Rabāḥ (d. AH

---

[13] Ibn Sa'd, I, 163.

[14] Nöldeke, in the original edition of his *Geschichte des Qorāns* (10 n. 3), already suggested the Hebrew *goyim* as the origin of the Quranic *ummiyyūn*. However, this has been left out in the Nöldeke–Schwally edition where *'am ha-areṣ* is preferred (I, 14 n. 1). Most Islamicists since Horovitz have preferred the Hebrew *ummot ha-'olām*.

[15] Khargūshī (MS Br. Lib.), fol. 74a. For other variations and interpretations see Khafājī, *Nasīm*, II, 406; Ibn Kathīr, *Bidāya*, VI, 178–79; Ṭabarsī, *A'lām al-warā*, 16, 21 (the entire biblical verse in Hebrew vocalization!); Ibn Shahrāshūb, I, 131, 246. Cf. Wansbrough, *Quranic Studies*, 64.

114).[16] But the text is slightly distorted; its correct form has been preserved by al-Suyūṭī, who quotes Ibn Sa'd.[17] It relates that when Abraham was ordered to expel Hagar, he set out with her to the wilderness, mounted on al-Burāq, the wonderful riding beast. When they reached Mecca, the angel Gabriel ordered him to dismount, because this was the place where *al-nabī al-ummī*[18] was destined to come out of the seed of his son (i.e. Ishmael).

In yet another tradition of the Medinan Successor Muḥammad ibn Ka'b al-Quraẓī, who was of Jewish descent (d. AH 117), the prediction about the *ummī* prophet is delivered directly to Hagar.[19] When Hagar set out with her son, Ishmael, an unseen voice said to her:

> ...your son will be the father of many peoples, and out of his people will come the *ummī* prophet who will reside in the *ḥaram* [of Mecca].

This no doubt reflects Genesis 21:18, which, again, is a *goy* passage. It forms part of the address of the angel to Hagar when she and her son ran out of water in the wilderness of Beer-sheba:

> ...for I will make him a great nation (*...le-goy gadol*).

The Hebrew *goy* in this passage seems to have prompted the allusion to the *ummī* prophet of the Arabs.

Ibn Sa'd has one more tradition of Muḥammad ibn Ka'b al-Quraẓī, containing God's revelation to Jacob:

> I shall send out of your loins kings and prophets till I send the prophet, the *ḥaramī*, whose nation shall build the Temple, and he will be the seal of the prophets, and his name is Aḥmad.[20]

Here Muḥammad is nicknamed not *ummī*, but rather *ḥaramī*, i.e. of the sacred territory of Mecca. Nevertheless, this passage is also based on a biblical *goy* clause, Genesis 35:11, where God addresses Jacob in Beth-el with the following promise:

> ...a nation (*goy*) and a company of nations shall be of thee, and kings shall come out of thy loins.

---

[16] Ibn Sa'd, I, 163–64.
[17] Suyūṭī, *Khaṣā'iṣ*, I, 24.
[18] Ibn Sa'd has *al-nabiyy alladhī*, instead of the correct reading.
[19] Ibn Sa'd , I, 164.
[20] *Ibid*., I, 163. See also Suyūṭī, *Khaṣā'iṣ*, I, 25.

In another tradition recorded by Ibn Sa'd, the locution *nabī ummī* is mentioned in a prophecy to an unnamed prophet of the Children of Israel. This is a Baṣran tradition traced back to Ibn 'Abbās in which God says:[21]

> My anger at you has become great, for you did not keep My word. Therefore I have sworn, the wind of holiness shall not come to you till I send the *ummī* prophet from the land of the Arabs; the wind of holiness shall come upon him.

The biblical passage which seems to be echoed here is Jeremiah 5:12–15, where the people of Israel is thus reproached:

> 12. They have belied the Lord.... 13. And the prophets shall become wind, and the word is not in them.... 15. Lo, I will bring a nation (*goy*) upon you from afar, O house of Israel, saith the Lord: it is a mighty nation, it is an ancient nation....

This very passage of Jeremiah was interpreted by the theologian Ibn Rabban as foretelling the emergence of the Muslims. The word *goy* was conceived in his translation in its strict collective biblical sense, and was rendered as *umma*, "nation".[22] In the tradition of Ibn 'Abbās, however, *goy* is perceived as "gentile", and has accordingly become the *ummī* prophet. The phrase "from afar" is rephrased in the tradition as "from the land of the Arabs".

Later sources abound in further traditions in which God foretells the *ummī* prophet to various biblical prophets. These accounts also seem to draw on biblical *goy* passages. In one of them, Exodus 32:10–14, Moses hears God's scheme to destroy the sinful children of Israel, and to make Moses into a great *goy* instead of the Israelites. Moses, however, prays for mercy on their behalf. In Muslim tradition a similar situation seems to have been duplicated in a prophetic tradition (i.e. one uttered by the Prophet himself) circulated by the Syrian Companion Abū Umāma al-Bāhilī (d. *ca.* AH 81). The children of Israel are slain in the wilderness by an ancient Arab tribe (Ma'add), and Moses prays for God's help against the Arabs. God tells Moses not to pray, because *al-nabī al-ummī* is destined to emerge from them.[23]

Prophecies about the *ummī* prophet were not only searched for in biblical *goy* passages, but also read into other apocalyptic visions of the Bible. Daniel's apocalypse about "a kingdom which shall never be destroyed" (Daniel 2:44)

---

[21] The *isnād*: Maslama ibn 'Alqama (Baṣran)←Dāwūd ibn Abī Hind (Baṣran d. AH 139)←Ibn 'Abbās. See Ibn Sa'd, I, 166.

[22] Ibn Rabban, *al-Dīn wa-l-dawla*, 174. Cf. Goldziher, "Polemik", 379 (no. 50).

[23] Ṭabarānī, *Kabīr*, VIII, no. 7629; Suyūṭī, *Khaṣā'iṣ*, I, 25. The *isnād*: Shaddād ibn 'Abdallāh (Abū 'Ammār, Syrian)←Abū Umāma←Muḥammad.

was interpreted in a tradition of Ka'b al-Aḥbār (d. AH 32), a Jewish convert to Islam, as foretelling the emergence of the *ummī* prophet.[24]

Statements about the biblical origin of the epithet *ummī* are also included in traditions without specific references to the biblical text. A tradition of the Yemeni Successor Wahb ibn Munabbih (d. AH 110) merely mentions the Prophet's epithet *ummī* as a part of what is said to be his biblical description.[25] In a tradition of Muqātil ibn Ḥayyān (d. *ca.* AH 150), Jesus is said to have been told by God about the need to believe in the *ummī* prophet.[26]

That *ummī* is a biblical epithet of Muḥammad is also stated in the realm of Quranic exegesis, relating to 29:48. This verse reads:

> You could neither read a book before this one [was revealed], nor write it with your right hand; had you done so, the unbelievers would have doubted [you].

This verse was believed to convey the idea that Muḥammad was illiterate, and therefore unaware of previous scriptures, which proved the authenticity of his own revelation. The idea that the sincerity of any prophet is proven through his illiteracy is, indeed, very early, and it emerges already in the earliest Christian sources.[27] The verse just quoted indicates that Islam has applied it to its own prophet since the Quran itself. In Quranic exegesis (*tafsīr*), the illiteracy of the Prophet was made part of the theme of annunciation. Muḥammad's biblical descriptions were said to have included illiteracy; this is already stated in a tradition of Mujāhid (Meccan d. AH 104),[28] and other early exegetes say the same.[29]

The concept of Muḥammad's illiteracy as part of his biblical description was actually combined with his biblical description as *ummī*. In this context, *ummī* means illiterate, again in accordance with the Hebrew *goy*. Already Muqātil ibn Sulaymān (d. AH 150) states that Quran 29:48 refers to the Jews. If the Prophet could read and write, they would have said: "The one whose description we

---

[24] Abū Nu'aym, *Dalā'il*, no. 44. For the Islamic interpretation of this passage in Daniel, see also Ibn Rabban, *al-Dīn wa-l-dawla*, 181; Goldziher, "Polemik", 379 (no. 46).

[25] Abū Nu'aym, *Dalā'il*, no. 33. See also Suyūṭī, *Khaṣā'iṣ*, I, 33–36; Ibn Kathīr, *Tafsīr*, III, 496–97. For further prophecies attributed to Wahb about *al-nabī al-ummī*, see Khargūshī (MS Tübingen), fol 69b–70a; Zurqānī, VI, 204.

[26] Bayhaqī, *Dalā'il*, I, 378. See also Ṭabarsī, *A'lām al-warā*, 21–22; Ibn 'Asākir, II, 45-46.

[27] A.J. Wensinck, "Muhammed und die Propheten", *Acta Orientalia* 2 (1924), 192; Wansbrough, *Quranic Studies*, 63.

[28] The *isnād*: Abū Usāma (Kūfan d. AH 201)←Idrīs ibn Yazīd al-Awdī←al-Ḥakam←Mujāhid. See Ṭabarī, *Tafsīr*, XXI, 4–5. See also Ibn 'Aṭiyya, XII, 231; Qurṭubī, XIII, 351; Suyūṭī, *Durr*, V, 147–48.

[29] Farrā', II, 317; Zajjāj, IV, 171; Wāḥidī, *Wasīṭ*, fol. 141b.

find in the Torah is *ummī*, being able neither to read a book nor to write it with his right hand."[30] Al-Ṭabarī has recorded similar traditions which are of still earlier authorities: Ḍaḥḥāk ibn Muzāḥim (Khurāsānī d. AH 102) is said to have stated that the prophet of God could neither read nor write, and God described him thus in the Torah and the Gospel, namely, that he is *nabī ummī*, who neither reads nor writes.[31] The same is repeated in other *tafsīrs*.[32] It follows that the term *ummī* acquired the meaning of illiteracy considerably earlier than some Islamicists have assumed.[33]

The annunciation of the *ummī* prophet as treated by Muslim tradition is not always confined to textual reports about the Bible. In other traditions, the anticipation of the emergence of the *ummī* prophet is conveyed through stories about conditions in Arabia on the eve of Islam. The idea of the *ummī* prophet is made part of the messianic hopes of the Jews of Arabia (most of them living in Medina). These are polemical stories aimed at showing that the Jews should have recognized the Prophet, and that their failure to do so contradicted the prescriptions of their own scriptures. This forms part of the accusation against the Jews of concealing (*kitmān*), or deleting the textual evidence of the Bible, or denying the identification of Muḥammad with the prophet of their books.[34] The word *ummī*, like Aḥmad, became a label denoting the Prophet whom the Jews originally expected, but later denied.

The stories about the Jews utilize some Quranic verses. The early biography of Ibn Isḥāq (d. AH 150), as preserved in the recension of Yūnus ibn Bukayr (d. AH 199),[35] contains a chapter describing conditions in Arabia on the eve of Islam. Ibn Isḥāq says that Jewish and Christian scholars knew better than the

---

[30] Muqātil, printed edition, III, 386: *inna llādhī najidu fī l-Tawrāt na'tuhu huwa ummī lā yaqra'u l-kitāba wa-lā yakhuṭṭuhu bi-yadihi*. This statement is quoted verbatim from Muqātil in Baghawī, *Ma'ālim*, IV, 381. And see also the same formulation in Zamakhsharī, III, 208; Qurṭubī, XIII, 351 (without naming Muqātil). But cf. Muqātil, MS II, fol. 73b–74a: *inna llādhī najidu fī l-Tawrāt ba'athahu llāhu 'azza wa-jalla lā yaqra'u l-kitāba wa-lā yakhuṭṭuhu* (*ummī* does not occur).

[31] The *isnād*: Abū Mu'ādh (al-Faḍl ibn Khālid, of Marw d. AH 211)←'Ubayd ibn Sulaymān (of Marw)←Ḍaḥḥāk. See Ṭabarī, *Tafsīr*, XXI, 5. Cf. Māwardī, *Nukat*, IV, 287; Suyūṭī, *Durr*, V, 148; Ṭabarsī, *Majma'*, XX, 370.

[32] Ibn Qutayba, *Gharīb al-Qur'ān*, 338: *hum yajidūnaka ummiyyan fī kutubihim, fa-law kunta taktubu la-rtābū*. See also Ibn al-Jawzī, *Zād al-masīr*, VI, 277, 278; Ibn Kathīr, *Tafsīr*, III, 417.

[33] Goldfeld, "The Illiterate Prophet", 67: "...the noun acquired this sense during the third century of the *Hijra*." See also Calder, "The *Ummī*", 116.

[34] Cf. Wansbrough, *Quranic Studies*, 189–90.

[35] Ibn Bukayr, 83. See also Bayhaqī, *Dalā'il*, II, 74–75. The parallel passage in Ibn Hishām (I, 217) is abridged.

Arabs about the imminent emergence of Muḥammad, because they had found his description in their scriptures. They used to pray in his name for victory over the Arab idolaters, and told them that a prophet holding the religion of Abraham, whose name was Aḥmad, was about to come. This was the description which they had found in their books. Then Ibn Isḥāq adduces the Quranic *ummī* passage (7:157), which is followed by 61:6 (Aḥmad). He also cites Quran 2:89, where it is stated that the People of the Book used to pray for victory (*yastaftiḥūna*) over the infidels.

The latter Quranic verse (2:89) is alluded to in other traditions about the Jews' anticipation of a messianic saviour. In these traditions they warn their Arab neighbours in Medina of the coming prophet, telling them that under his leadership they would defeat them (i.e. the Arabs). But when he appears as the Arabian Muḥammad, the frustrated Jews do not believe in him, whereas the Arabs are those who make haste to follow him. Quran 2:89 is said to refer to this, and a tradition to that effect is quoted by Ibn Isḥāq from ʻĀṣim ibn ʻUmar ibn Qatāda (Medinan d. AH 120).[36] Ibn Isḥāq has one more tradition (of Ibn ʻAbbās) in which, after the appearance of Muḥammad, the Arab Muslims of Medina urge the Jews to embrace Islam, reminding them that Muḥammad is the very prophet in whose name the Jews used to pray for victory. But a Jew from the tribe of Banū l-Naḍīr (Salām ibn Mishkam) replies that Muḥammad is not the prophet whom they anticipated. Thereupon God reveals Quran 2:89.[37]

In other traditions of the same setting, the *ummī* notion is added to the presentation. The anticipated prophet is designated as *al-nabī al-ummī*, the gentile messianic saviour awaited by the Jews. For example, a tradition of Saʻīd ibn Jubayr (Kūfan d. AH 95) from Ibn ʻAbbās relates that the Jews of Khaybar used to fight against the Arabs of Ghaṭafān. Whenever the Jews were defeated, they asked God to give them victory in the name of *al-nabī al-ummī*, whom God had promised to send to them at the end of days. When they uttered this prayer, the Arabs of Ghaṭafān were defeated. However, when Muḥammad appeared, the Jews did not believe in him.[38] This tradition was also recorded in the *tafsīr* of 2:89.[39] Indeed, many other stories of the same kind may be found in the *tafsīr* compilations, on the same Quranic verse.[40] This implies that *sīra*

---

36 Ibn Hishām, I, 225. See also Ibn Bukayr, 84; Bayhaqī, *Dalāʼil*, II, 75–76.

37 Ibn Hishām, II, 196. The *isnād*: ʻIkrima (Medinan d. AH 105), or Saʻīd ibn Jubayr (Kūfan d. AH 95)←Ibn ʻAbbās.

38 Bayhaqī, *Dalāʼil*, II, 76–77.

39 *Mustadrak*, II, 263 (*Tafsīr*); Suyūṭī, *Durr*, I, 88.

40 For example, Mujāhid, I, 83; Muqātil, I, fol. 16b–17a; ʻAbd al-Razzāq, *Tafsīr*, I, 52; Huwwārī, I, 125; Ṭabarī, *Tafsīr*, I, 325–27; Samarqandī, *Tafsīr*, I, 136; Māwardī, *Nukat*, I, 158; Wāḥidī, *Asbāb*, 15; Ibn Kathīr, *Tafsīr*, II, 124–25; Suyūṭī, *Durr*, I, 87–88.

traditions alluding to Quranic verses eventually became appropriate exegetic material which was gladly taken up by the compilers of the books of *tafsīr* for the interpretation of the relevant Quranic passages.

II

Apart from the Paraclete and the *goy* passages already employed in the Quran, there are further biblical references which can be traced in Muslim tradition, where they fulfil the requirements of attestation.

In the biography of Ibn Isḥāq (in the recension of Yūnus ibn Bukayr) there is a tradition attributed to Ka'b al-Aḥbār alluding to a passage in the Old Testament.[41] It is related that Ka'b was once asked by Umm al-Dardā' in what manner the messenger of God was described in the Bible (*Tawrāt*). Ka'b said: "We find his description as follows:"

> Muḥammad the apostle of God, his name is al-Mutawakkil; he is not crude nor coarse, and he does not raise his voice in the streets (*aswāq*). He has been entrusted with the keys, that by him God may make blind eyes see, and deaf ears hear, and stammering tongues speak rightly, that they may testify that there is no God but Allāh....[42]

As already observed by Guillaume,[43] Ka'b's description is an elaboration on Isaiah 42:2, which forms part of the description of God's servant:

> He shall not cry, nor lift up, nor cause his voice to be heard in the street....

The Muslims were attracted to this passage, due to the fact that in the previous verse (42:1) Isaiah mentions the gentile nations (*goyim*) among which the servant of God will spread his justice.

Various versions which elaborate on the same passage of Isaiah, identifying the biblical servant of God as Muḥammad, are available in other traditions which are likewise traced back to Ka'b al-Aḥbār. All of them contain the "streets" (*aswāq*) clause, and were recorded by Ibn Sa'd. In one, which has a Syrian *isnād*, Ka'b communicates the "biblical" description of the Prophet to the Companion Ibn 'Abbās. It contains not only Muḥammad's description, but also the name of his birthplace (Mecca), and the destination of his *hijra*

[41] The *isnād*: Ibn Isḥāq←Muḥammad ibn Thābit ibn Shuraḥbīl (Ḥijāzī)←Umm al-Dardā' (Syrian)←Ka'b al-Aḥbār.

[42] Ibn Bukayr, 141–42. See also Bayhaqī, *Dalā'il*, I, 376–77; Dhahabī, *Sīra*, 50; Ibn Kathīr, *Bidāya*, VI, 61.

[43] Guillaume, "New Light", 32.

(Medina).[44] Two Iraqi (Kūfan) traditions have a similar description by Ka'b; one of them mentions Muḥammad's kingdom (*mulk*) in Syria.[45] Sometimes Ka'b's statement opens with the words *qāla llāhu* ("God said"), which is another way of indicating that the ensuing text is an extract from a holy scripture.[46] Another well-known authority on the scriptures of the People of the Book, namely, the Successor Wahb ibn Munabbih (Yemenī d. AH 110), appears as "quoting" a similar description of Muḥammad from Isaiah.[47] There is also a tradition of the Baṣran Successor Qatāda (d. AH 117) which is not traced back to any earlier authority.[48]

But the "streets" passage of the Bible was circulated under the names of other Islamic figures who were neither Jewish nor associated with Jewish scriptures, but rather were trustworthy Companions, and hence, more authoritative sources. One of them is Muḥammad's wife, 'Ā'isha. In a Kūfan tradition recorded by Ibn Sa'd she says that Muḥammad is described in the *Injīl* (!), i.e. the New Testament, as follows:

> He is not crude nor coarse, and he does not raise his voice in the streets....[49]

Moreover, the same description was circulated as an utterance of the Prophet himself, related on the authority of the Medinan/Kūfan Companion 'Abdallāh ibn Mas'ūd (d. AH 32). The Prophet reportedly stated: "My description is: 'Aḥmad, al-Mutawakkil, neither crude nor coarse....'"[50] It should be noted that in this particular version there is no indication of the biblical origin of the description.

---

[44] The *isnād*: Mu'āwiya ibn Ṣāliḥ ibn Ḥudayr (Ḥimṣī d. AH 158)←Abū Farwa←Ibn 'Abbās←Ka'b. See Ibn Sa'd, I, 360. Cf. Qiwām al-Sunna, *Dalā'il*, IV, 1335–36 (no. 220); Dhahabī, *Sīra*, 50. Cf. Adang, *Muslim Writers*, 11.

[45] Ibn Sa'd, I, 360. One has the *isnād*: 'Āṣim ibn Bahdala (Kūfan d. AH 128)←Abū l-Ḍuḥā (Muslim ibn Ṣubayḥ, Kūfan d. AH 100)←Abū 'Abdallāh al-Jadalī (Kūfan)←Ka'b. Another has the *isnād*: 'Āṣim ibn Bahdala←Abū Ṣāliḥ al-Sammān (Dhakwān, Medinan d. AH 101)←Ka'b. For the latter tradition, see also Ibn Shabba, II, 635.

[46] See Ibn Shabba, II, 634–35; Abū Nu'aym, *Ḥilya*, V, 387; Bayhaqī, *Dalā'il*, I, 377, 160. The *isnād*: al-'Alā' ibn al-Musayyab and Ibrāhīm ibn Maymūn←al-Musayyab ibn Rāfi' (Kūfan d. AH 105)←Ka'b.

[47] Abū Nu'aym, *Dalā'il*, no. 33. See also Suyūṭī, *Khaṣā'iṣ*, I, 34–36.

[48] See Ibn Sa'd, I, 362.

[49] *Ibid.*, I, 363. The *isnād*: Yūnus ibn Abī Isḥāq (Kūfan d. AH 152)←'Ayzār ibn Ḥurayth (Kūfan)←'Ā'isha. See also Ibn Bukayr, 142; Ibn Shabba, II, 632–33; Bayhaqī, *Dalā'il*, I, 377–78; Ibn Kathīr, *Bidāya*, VI, 61.

[50] The *isnād*: Ibrāhīm ibn Yazīd al-Nakha'ī (Kūfan d. AH 96)←'Alqama ibn Qays (Kūfan d. AH 62)←'Abdallāh ibn Mas'ūd. See Ṭabarānī, *Kabīr*, X, no. 10046. See also Suyūṭī, *Khaṣā'iṣ*, I, 29.

During the third century AH, the most important *muṣannaf* compilations came into being. Out of the early biographical material, their authors selected traditions which conformed to their own ideas of what Muslims should know and believe about the life and person of their Prophet. It is most significant that in the authoritative *muṣannaf* compilations, such as those of al-Bukhārī (d. AH 256) and Muslim (d. AH 261), not even one of the above traditions may be found. A few of them were only recorded in the more peripheral collections of al-Dārimī (d. AH 255) and al-Ḥākim (d. AH 404). The former selected one of the above Syrian traditions of Ka'b al-Aḥbār, in which the latter transmits his information to the Companion Ibn 'Abbās, and included it in the Introduction of his compilation.[51] Al-Ḥākim recorded the above tradition of 'Ā'isha.[52] This means that the representatives of the mainstream of Islamic thinking were reluctant to acknowledge the merit of the scriptures of the People of the Book as sources of attestation, and were therefore inclined to dismiss traditions in which total reliance on those scriptures was implied, even though some of the *isnād*s could be regarded as "sound" (*ṣaḥīḥ*).

The compilers rather preferred traditions in which the attestation of the Prophet was based on more specifically Islamic documents, namely, the Quran itself. Such traditions were indeed available to them in the pool of early biographical material. To begin with, there is a tradition in Ibn Sa'd in which the source of information about Muḥammad's biblical description is not Ka'b al-Aḥbār, but rather the Medinan 'Abdallāh ibn Salām (d. AH 43). Although a Jew by birth, he enjoys a more authoritative position in Islam than that of Ka'b al-Aḥbār; he was a Companion of Muḥammad who acknowledged his message from the very outset. Ibn Salām's own report about Muḥammad's biblical description is similar to the above description of Ka'b, but it opens with a new element, an extract from the Quran. According to the tradition of Ibn Sa'd, the Medinan Zayd ibn Aslam (d. AH 136) reported that Ibn Salām used to say: "The description of the apostle of God in the *Tawrāt* is as follows:"

> *Yā ayyuhā l-nabiyyu innā arsalnāka shāhidan wa-mubashshiran wa-nadhīran wa-ḥirzan li-l-ummiyyīna....*: "Oh prophet, We have sent you to bear witness and good tidings, and to warn, and to safeguard the people...."

This is followed by the familiar statement that the apostle is neither crude nor coarse, and does not raise his voice in the streets. The tradition goes on to say

[51] Dārimī, I, 17 (*Muqaddima*, 2). Dārimī (I, 16, 17) also has two additional versions where Ka'b is quoted by Abū Ṣāliḥ (Dhakwān, Medinan d. AH 101). See also Abū Nu'aym, *Ḥilya*, V, 387; Qiwām al-Sunna, *Dalā'il*, IV, 1332–33 (no. 219).

[52] *Mustadrak*, II, 614.

that when Ka'b heard the words of Ibn Salām, he asserted that they were true,[53] thus reducing Ka'b's role to a confirmatory one. The description itself opens with a verbatim quotation of Quran 33:45 (cf. 48:8), which was interpolated into the biblical framework, thus becoming supposedly a part of the Bible.[54] Another tradition of this kind, with a Medinan *isnād* likewise concluding with 'Abdallāh ibn Salām, was recorded by al-Dārimī.[55]

But for the authors of the more authoritative *muṣannaf* compilations this was still not good enough: the authority of the tradition was still a Jew. The version which they preferred was traced back neither to Ka'b nor to Ibn Salām, but rather to an indigenous Arab Muslim, 'Abdallāh ibn 'Amr ibn al-'Āṣ (d. AH 63), a Qurashī Companion of the Prophet who is said to have been well versed in the Quran as well as in the Bible.[56] His version too was recorded by Ibn Sa'd. 'Abdallāh ibn 'Amr is asked by the Medinan story-teller 'Aṭā' ibn Yasār (d. AH 103) about Muḥammad's description in the Bible, and the latter responds: "Indeed, he is described in the *Tawrāt* by some of his descriptions in the Quran." Then he recites Quran 33:45, followed by the familiar elaboration on Isaiah, in which the Prophet is one who does not raise his voice in the streets, etc. Afterwards Aṭā' asks Ka'b al-Aḥbār about it, and the latter corroborates the words of 'Abdallāh ibn 'Amr.[57] This is the version which al-Bukhārī selected for his *Ṣaḥīḥ*; but in his version the corroboration of Ka'b has been omitted, leaving 'Abdallāh ibn 'Amr ibn al-'Āṣ as the sole authority. Al-Bukhārī recorded it in *Kitāb al-buyū'* (34:50), under the heading: "The Interdiction to Raise One's Voice in the Market".[58] The word *aswāq* ("streets"), of the biblical description of the Prophet was obviously taken by him in its literary sense ("markets").

The interpolation of a Quranic extract into the above traditions reveals an aspect of the literary role of the Quranic text in Muslim *ḥadīth*. In this specific case, the Quranic passage was added to the traditions in order to lend the bibli-

53 Ibn Sa'd, I, 360–61. See also Qiwām al-Sunna, *Dalā'il*, III, 835 (no. 128).

54 For more examples of Quranic passages regarded as part of the Torah, see Kister, "*Ḥaddithū*", 226.

55 Dārimī, I, 16 (*Muqaddima*, 2). The *isnād*: Sa'īd ibn Abī Hilāl (Egyptian d. AH 135)←Hilāl ibn Usāma (Medinan)←'Aṭā' ibn Yasār (Medinan story-teller, d. AH 103)←'Abdallāh ibn Salām. See also Bayhaqī, *Dalā'il*, I, 376; Qiwām al-Sunna, *Dalā'il*, IV, 1337–38 (no. 221); Ibn Kathīr, *Bidāya*, VI, 60–61.

56 Aḥmad, *Musnad*, II, 222. See also Kister, "*Ḥaddithū*", 231.

57 Ibn Sa'd, I, 362. The *isnād*: Hilāl ibn Abī Hilāl (Medinan)←'Aṭā' ibn Yasār←'Abdallāh ibn 'Amr ibn al-'Āṣ. See also Ibn Shabba, II, 633–34; Bukhārī, *Adab mufrad*, I, no. 246; Aḥmad, *Musnad*, II, 174; Bayhaqī, *Dalā'il*, I, 374, 375; *idem*, *Shu'ab*, II, 147 (no. 1410); Dhahabī, *Sīra*, 49; Ibn Kathīr, *Bidāya*, VI, 60.

58 Bukhārī, *Ṣaḥīḥ*, III, 87.

cal description some of the authority of the Islamic scripture. No exegetic consideration was involved in this process. However, as soon as Quranic extracts became part of a tradition, the tradition itself became exegesis, for the simple reason that it contained reference to a Quranic verse. The exegetes of the Quran composed the *tafsīr* of the canon by assembling any available traditions they could lay hands on, provided they contained Quranic excerpts. The above traditions formed no exception: the authors spotted some of them and made them part of the *tafsīr* of the relevant Quranic passages. Thus the tradition of ʻAbdallāh ibn ʻAmr ibn al-ʻĀṣ was picked up and recorded by al-Bukhārī in the exegesis of 48:8, in the *Kitāb al-tafsīr* (65) of his *Ṣaḥīḥ*.[59] The same tradition was recorded by Ibn Kathīr in the *tafsīr* of 33:45.[60] But the majority of the commentators recorded this tradition in the *tafsīr* of the Quranic *ummī* passage (7:156–58), to illustrate Muḥammad's biblical description.[61]

The process of Islamisation of the biblical description of Muḥammad did not cease with the interpolation of a Quranic extract into it. The downgrading of the Bible as a document of attestation is indicated in other versions, where the Prophet's description has been entirely detached from the biblical sphere, being incorporated instead into existing literary portraits displaying Muḥammad's outer appearance and morals. Such "historical" descriptions of Muḥammad's moral conduct, which, of course, the believers are supposed to adopt as their model, are widely current. The most prevailing one is again that of the Companion ʻAbdallāh ibn ʻAmr ibn al-ʻĀṣ, who is made to state that Muḥammad never behaved indecently (*lam yakun fāḥishan....*). His statement has a Kūfan *isnād*[62] and is recorded in the biographical sources,[63] as well as in several *muṣannaf* compilations, including al-Bukhārī and Muslim.[64] A similar statement is attributed to the Companion Anas ibn Mālik. who reportedly said that the Prophet was neither in the habit of abusing (*sabbāb*), nor of offending (*faḥḥāsh*), or cursing (*laʻʻān*). His statement was circulated with a Medinan

---

[59] *Ibid.*, VI, 169–70.

[60] Ibn Kathīr, *Tafsīr*, III, 496. Ibn Kathīr (*ibid.*, III, 496–97) has also recorded another similar tradition on the authority of Wahb ibn Munabbih (Yemenī d. AH 110).

[61] Ṭabarī, *Tafsīr*, IX, 57; Baghawī, *Maʻālim*, II, 553; Ibn al-ʻArabī, *Aḥkām*, II, 794; Ibn ʻAṭiyya, VII, 178–79; Qurṭubī, VII, 299; Ibn Kathīr, *Tafsīr*, II, 253; Suyūṭī, *Durr*, III, 131. The version of Kaʻb al-Aḥbār was recorded in Baghawī, *Maʻālim*, II, 553–54; Suyūṭī, *Durr*, III, 132.

[62] Aʻmash (Kūfan d. AH 148)←Shaqīq ibn Salama (Abū Wāʼil, Kūfan d. AH 82)←Masrūq ibn al-Ajdaʻ (Kūfan d. AH 63)←ʻAbdallāh ibn ʻAmr.

[63] Ibn Saʻd, I, 377; Aḥmad, *Musnad*, II, 161, 189, 193; Baghawī, *Shamāʼil*, I, no. 204; Ibn Kathīr, *Bidāya*, VI, 36.

[64] Ibn Abī Shayba, VIII, no. 5369 (*Adab*); Bukhārī, *Ṣaḥīḥ*, IV, 230 (61:23); V, 34 (62:27); VIII, 15, 16 (78:38, 39); Muslim, VII, 78 (43:68); Tirmidhī/*Tuḥfa*, VI, no. 2041 (25:47).

isnād[65] and was recorded in biographical sources,[66] as well as in al-Bukhārī's *Ṣaḥīḥ*.[67]

The statement that the Prophet did not let his voice be heard in the streets (*aswāq*) was incorporated into this portrait of his, and was thus transformed from a biblical prophecy about him into an historical account of his actual conduct. This appears in its "historical" form in the description attributed to 'Ā'isha, where she is being made to say that Muḥammad's morals were the best of all people. He was neither crude, nor did he raise his voice in the streets. He was never vindictive, but always forgiving. Her statement was also circulated with a Kūfan *isnād*[68] and was recorded in biographical sources,[69] as well as in some *muṣannaf* compilations, like that of al-Tirmidhī.[70] A similar "historical" description, including the "streets" clause, was transmitted on the authority of the Companion Abū Hurayra; it includes a depiction of Muḥammad's external appearance.[71]

III

To lend the biblical attestation more genuinely Islamic authority, some quotations were cast in the form of a prophetic *ḥadīth*.[72] In these *ḥadīth*s the Prophet himself gives in the first person his own biblical description. The utterances represent what we may call the "self-attestation" of the prophet, and they are part of his self-portrait. In these *ḥadīth*s Muḥammad identifies himself in various biblical prophecies.

One biblical quotation which was to become prophetic *ḥadīth* appears in its assumed biblical form in Muḥammad's early biographies, where it is said to have been current among the Jews of Banū l-Naḍīr.[73] It runs as follows:

---

65 Fulayḥ ibn Sulaymān (Medinan d. AH 168)←Hilāl ibn Abī Maymūna (Medinan)←Anas.

66 Ibn Sa'd, I, 369; Ibn Shabba, II, 636; Aḥmad, *Musnad*, III, 126, 144, 158; Baghawī, *Shamā'il*, I, no. 206; Ibn Kathīr, *Bidāya*, VI, 36–37.

67 Bukhārī, *Ṣaḥīḥ*, VIII, 15 (78:38).

68 Abū Isḥāq al-Sabī'ī (Kūfan Shī'ī d. AH 126–29)← Abū 'Abdallāh al-Jadalī (Kūfan)←'Ā'isha.

69 Ibn Sa'd, I, 365; Ibn Shabba, II, 637; Tirmidhī, *Shamā'il*, 200; Aḥmad, *Musnad*, VI, 174, 236, 246; Ṭayālisī, *Musnad*, no. 1520; Bayhaqī, *Dalā'il*, I, 315; Baghawī, *Shamā'il*, I, no. 205; Ibn Kathīr, *Bidāya*, VI, 36.

70 Ibn Abī Shayba, VIII, no. 5382 (*Adab*); Tirmidhī/*Tuḥfa*, VI, no. 2085 (25:69); Ibn Ḥibbān, *Ṣaḥīḥ*, XIV, no. 6443.

71 The *isnād*: Ibn Abī Dhi'b (Medinan d. AH 159)←Abū Ṣāliḥ *mawlā* of al-Taw'ama (Medinan)←Abū Hurayra. See Ibn Shabba, II, 607; Aḥmad, *Musnad*, II, 328, 448; Bayhaqī, *Dalā'il*, I, 316; Ibn Kathīr, *Bidāya*, VI, 36.

72 See also Goldziher, *Muslim Studies*, II, 148–49.

73 Wāqidī, I, 367. See also Khargūshī (MS Tübingen), fol. 65a.

> Al-Ḍaḥūk (the Laughing), al-Qattāl (the Slaying), Red Eyed, Arriving from the South, Riding a Camel, Wearing a Cloak, Partaking of a Slice, Carrying his Sword upon his Shoulder....

Some biblical extracts are indeed embedded in this description, occurring also in later polemical sources. As observed by Goldziher,[74] "Riding a Camel" is derived from Isaiah 21:7, where "riding an ass ['a chariot of asses']" and "riding a camel ['a chariot of camels']" were taken by Muslim writers to represent Jesus and Muḥammad respectively.[75] (But sometimes, Muḥammad was rather presented as Riding an Ass[76]). As for Carrying his Sword upon his Shoulder, this is probably a reflection of Isaiah 9:5 ("and the government shall be upon his shoulder").[77]

These biblical depictions later assumed the form of a prophetic *ḥadīth*, circulated on the authority of a Companion. Ibn 'Abbās is said to have heard the Prophet say:

> My name in the Torah is Aḥmad, al-Ḍaḥūk, al-Qattāl, Riding a Camel, Wearing a Cloak, Partaking of a Slice, Carrying his Sword upon his Shoulder.[78]

But the process of Islamisation through self-attestation affected not only the form of the biblical quotations, but their contents as well. Genuine Quranic material was incorporated into them. One prophetic statement of this kind combines the Bible and the Quran as equal sources of certification. Muḥammad states:

> My name in the Torah is Aḥīd, because I divert (*aḥīdu*) my community from Hell. My name in the *Zabūr* (Psalms) is al-Māḥī; God wipes off idolatry through me. My name in the Gospels is Aḥmad, and my name in the Quran is Muḥammad, because I am praised among the inhabitants of heaven and earth.

---

[74] Goldziher, "Polemik", 377 (no. 25).

[75] See e.g. Ibn Rabban, 149–50; Khafājī, *Nasīm*, II, 404. And cf. the epithet Rider of the Camel also in Khargūshī (MS Br. Lib.), fol. 75a; Kulīnī, VIII, 43, 139; Ibn Shahrāshūb, I, 134; Ibn Kathīr, *Bidāya*, VI, 62.

[76] Abū Nu'aym, *Dalā'il*, no. 40. Cf. Khargūshī (MS Br. Lib.), fol. 58a. On the tension between the camel and the ass as Muḥammad's riding beasts see Suliman Bashear, "Riding Beasts on Divine Missions: an Examination of the Ass and Camel Traditions", *Journal of Semitic Studies* 36 (1991), 37–75. Unfortunately, Goldziher's findings are not duly acknowledged in this study.

[77] For the messianic significance of Isaiah 9:5 in Muslim context, see Ibn Rabban, 146–47. Cf. also Goldziher, "Polemik", 378 (no. 35).

[78] Suyūṭī, *Khaṣā'iṣ*, I, 192–93 (from Ibn Fāris).

The tradition appears in some *tafsīrs* on Quran 61:6,[79] and recurs in some later sources.[80] The form Aḥīd (or Aḥyad) is probably derived from Hebrew *(yaḥīd* = one and only), and seems to have already been known to Muqātil ibn Sulaymān (d. AH 150).[81]

The content of other prophetic utterances of self-attestation is purely Quranic, lacking any biblical allusions. All of them open with the declaration: *anā...*, "I am...." One of them consists of Quran 2:129, where Abraham prays:

> Our Lord, send among them a messenger from amongst them, that he may recite to them Your signs, and teach them the book and the wisdom....

A prophetic statement using this verse for self-attestation was recorded by Ibn Sa'd. It has a Kūfan *isnād*, lacking a Companion (*mursal*).[82] The Prophet states: "I am the [subject of] the prayer of my father Abraham." This is followed by a verbatim quotation of Quran 2:129. This tradition implies, of course, that the Quranic prayer of Abraham is a prophecy about Muḥammad. An extended statement of the Prophet, referring also to the good tidings of Jesus about Aḥmad (Quran 61:6), is included in a Medinan tradition quoted by Ibn Sa'd from al-Wāqidī. This is related on the authority of some Medinan Successors, and in it the Prophet says: "I am the prayer of my father Abraham, and Jesus Son of Mary announced the good tidings about me."[83]

There are more versions, all of Syrian provenance, of the same statement of Muḥammad. In all of them an additional prediction is included which is derived not from the Quran, but rather from an episode of the Prophet's infancy legends. The episode takes place during the pregnancy of his mother, Āmina. Ibn Isḥāq relates that while pregnant with Muḥammad, she had a vision in which she saw light spreading out of her, reaching as far as the forts of Buṣrā in Syria.[84] Light (*nūr*) is a prevalent symbol of Muḥammad's prophethood,[85] and the glorious role of Syria as the future abode of Islam is forecast here by mak-

---

79 Māwardī, *Nukat*, V, 529; Qurṭubī, XVIII, 84.

80 Khafājī, *Nasīm*, II, 408; Suyūṭī, *Khaṣā'iṣ*, I, 192 (on the authority of Ibn 'Abbās).

81 Muqātil, I, fol. 22a (in *tafsīr* of 2:130, 'Abdallāh ibn Salām): ...*yuqālu lahu Aḥyad* [MS: *Aḥmad*] *yaḥīdu ummatahu 'ani l-nār* (in prophecy to Moses).

82 Ibn Sa'd, I, 149. The *isnād*: Juwaybir ibn Sa'īd al-Balkhī (Kūfan d. AH 140–50)←Ḍaḥḥāk ibn Muzāḥim (Khurāsānī. d. AH 102)←Muḥammad.

83 Ibn Sa'd, I, 149 (Wāqidī). The Successors are 'Umar ibn Abī Anas and 'Abdallāh ibn 'Abd al-Raḥmān ibn Ma'mar (Abū Ṭuwāla, Medinan d. AH 134).

84 Ibn Hishām, I, 166; Ibn Bukayr, 45.

85 See Uri Rubin, "Pre-Existence and Light: Aspects of the Concept of Nūr Muḥammad", *Israel Oriental Studies* 5 (1975), 62–119.

ing it the final destination of that light. Syrian traditionists incorporated Āmina's vision into the above self-portrait of Muḥammad. The vision is included, to begin with, in a tradition of the Syrian Companion Abū Umāma al-Bāhilī (d. *ca.* AH 81), who is said to have asked the Prophet: "What marked the beginning of your affair?" Muḥammad replied: "The prayer of my father Abraham, the good tidings of Jesus, and my mother saw light come out of her, which illuminated the forts of Syria."[86] In another Syrian tradition one more element is included, which reflects the concept of Muḥammad's pre-existence.[87] This is by the Syrian Companion ʻIrbāḍ ibn Sāriya (Ḥimṣī d. AH 75), and in it Muḥammad provides his eternal prophetic profile:

> I already was the servant of God and the seal of prophets when Adam was still rolling in his clay. I shall tell you more about it: the prayer of my father Abraham, the announcement of Jesus about me, and the vision my mother saw....

This was a widely current tradition,[88] which was also accepted into a few *muṣannaf* compilations, where it was recorded to illustrate various aspects of Muḥammad's prophetic status.[89]

As seen above, traditions with Quranic verses embedded in them were readily taken up by the commentators of the Quran, who were always looking for relevant material for their *tafsīr* compilations. Indeed, some of the traditions about the prayer of Abraham and the announcement of Jesus were recorded by the exegetes in the *tafsīr* of the respective Quranic verses. The tradition of ʻIrbāḍ ibn Sāriya was recorded by al-Ṭabarī in the *tafsīr* of 2:129,[90] as well as in that of 61:6.[91] Moreover, in spite of its non-biblical character, the same tradition was included by some in the *tafsīr* of 33:45, which, as seen above, was believed to be a replica of a biblical profile of Muḥammad.[92]

---

[86] Aḥmad, *Musnad*, V, 262. The *isnād*: Faraj ibn Fuḍāla (Ḥimṣī d. AH 177)←Luqmān ibn ʻĀmir (Ḥimṣī)←Abū Umāma. Cf. Ibn Saʻd, I, 102, 149. And see Ṭayālisī, *Musnad*, no. 1140; Bayhaqī, *Dalāʼil*, I, 84; Ṭabarānī, *Kabīr*, VIII, no. 7729; Qiwām al-Sunna, *Dalāʼil*, I, 239 (no. 1).

[87] For which see Rubin, "Pre-Existence", 67–71.

[88] Ibn Saʻd, I, 149. The *isnād*: Saʻīd ibn Suwayd (Syrian)←ʻAbd al-ʻAʻlā ibn Hilāl al-Sulamī←ʻIrbāḍ ibn Sāriya. See also Ibn Shabba, II, 636; Bukhārī, *Tārīkh kabīr*, VI, 68–69; *idem*, *Tārīkh ṣaghīr*, I, 39; Aḥmad, *Musnad*, IV, 127, 128; Bayhaqī, *Dalāʼil*, I, 80, 83; II, 130; Abū Nuʻaym, *Ḥilya*, VI, 89–90; Ṭabarānī, *Kabīr*, XVIII, nos. 629–631; Baghawī, *Shamāʼil*, I, 6 (no. 4).

[89] Ibn Ḥibbān, *Ṣaḥīḥ*, XIV, no. 6404; *Mustadrak*, II, 600.

[90] Ṭabarī, *Tafsīr*, I, 435.

[91] Ṭabarī, *Tafsīr*, XXVIII, 57. See also Suyūṭī, *Durr*, VI, 213–14; Ibn Kathīr, *Tafsīr*, IV, 360 (including the tradition of Abū Umāma).

[92] *Mustadrak*, II, 418 (*Tafsīr*); Suyūṭī, *Durr*, V, 207.

In other prophetic statements opening with *anā*, "I am", no historical reference is made. Self-attestation is achieved by simply recounting lists of the various Arab names of the prophet. Most of them do not occur in the Quran in their actual form, but they nevertheless rest on Quranic vocabulary and imagery, each of the names attesting to a different aspect of his prophetic role. One of these traditions is Syrian, and is circulated on the authority of the Companion 'Awf ibn Mālik al-Ashja'ī (d. AH 73).[93] Muḥammad's statement is as follows: "I am al-Ḥāshir, and I am al-'Āqib, and I am al-Muqaffī (var. al-Muṣṭafā)." These names signify his position as the ultimate prophet before the day of resurrection (Ḥāshir), being the last of all prophets, who was sent in their footsteps ('Āqib, Muqaffī). This specific list is recorded as part of a story about the refusal of the Jews of Medina to recognize Muḥammad as their messianic deliverer. The Prophet makes this statement in their synagogue, where he is said to have come on a Jewish holiday and asked the Jews to produce twelve people who would testify that he is God's messenger, so that He would forgive them their sins. When they refuse, Muḥammad announces his four names. As he is about to leave the synagogue, one of the Jews calls him back. This Jew, who proves to be 'Abdallāh ibn Salām, swears by God that Muḥammad is indeed the prophet whose description the Jews have found in the Torah. His fellow Jews call him a liar, so he joins Muḥammad, and they both leave the synagogue together. Thereupon God reveals Quran 46:10 ("... and a witness from among the children of Israel bears witness to its like, and believes...."). The tradition was recorded by Aḥmad ibn Ḥanbal and al-Ṭabarānī,[94] and it recurs in some *muṣannaf* compilations in the chapter about the virtues of 'Abdallāh ibn Salām.[95]

More such *anā* statements of Muḥammad were recorded by Ibn Sa'd in his chapter about the names of the Prophet. All of them open with the two best-known Quranic names, Muḥammad (e.g. 48:29) and Aḥmad, followed by other names which signify his eschatological role. One of the traditions is of the Meccan Mujāhid (d. AH 104), who does not mention a Companion as his source.[96] Apart from Aḥmad and Muḥammad, the Prophet is here named Messenger of Mercy, Messenger of War, Muqaffī, and Ḥāshir. A similar prophetic statement recorded by Ibn Sa'd was circulated on the authority of the Companion

---

93 The *isnād*: Ṣafwān ibn 'Amr (Ḥimṣī d. AH 100)←'Abd al-Raḥmān ibn Jubayr ibn Nufayr←Jubayr ibn Nufayr (Ḥimṣī d. AH 75)←'Awf ibn Mālik.

94 Aḥmad, *Musnad*, VI, 25; Ṭabarānī, *Kabīr*, XVIII, no. 83. And see also Suyūṭī, *Durr*, VI, 39 (on Quran 46:10).

95 Ibn Ḥibbān, *Ṣaḥīḥ*, XVI, no. 7162; *Mustadrak*, III, 415.

96 The *isnād*: Mālik ibn Mighwal (Kūfan d. AH 159)←Abū Ḥuṣayn ('Uthmān ibn 'Āṣim, Kūfan d. AH 128)←Mujāhid. See Ibn Sa'd, I, 105. Cf. Ibn Shabba, II, 632 (+ Nabī al-Tawba).

Ḥudhayfa ibn al-Yamān (d. AH 36).[97] Ibn Sa'd has another tradition of the Companion Jubayr ibn Muṭ'im (Medinan d. AH 58), quoted by his son Nāfi' ibn Jubayr (Medinan d. AH 99);[98] it was also recorded by al-Ḥākim.[99] The tradition of the same Companion was circulated by another son of his as well, namely, Muḥammad ibn Jubayr. This Muḥammad was quoted by al-Zuhrī (Medinan d. AH 124), and the tradition recurs in many sources other than Ibn Sa'd,[100] as well as in the *muṣannaf* compilations,[101] where it was recorded in special chapters dedicated to lists of Muḥammad's names and appellations. It was also included in the *tafsīr* of 61:6, to illustrate the function of the name Aḥmad.[102]

As for Ibn Sa'd, he recorded a similar prophetic statement on the authority of the Companion Abū Mūsā al-Ash'arī (d. *ca.* AH 42–53).[103] This was accepted into several *muṣannaf* compilations[104] and *tafsīr* books.[105] More prophetic statements containing similar lists of names are found in sources other than Ibn

[97] The *isnād*: 'Āṣim ibn Bahdala (Kūfan d. AH 128)←Zirr ibn Ḥubaysh (Kūfan d. AH 83)←Ḥudhayfa. See Ibn Sa'd, I, 104; Tirmidhī, *Shamā'il*, 212; Bukhārī, *Tārīkh ṣaghīr*, I, 36; Aḥmad, *Musnad*, V, 405; Dhahabī, *Sīra*, 10–11. See also *Kashf al-astār*, III, no. 2379. Another *isnād*: Abū Bakr ibn 'Ayyāsh←'Āṣim←Abū Wā'il←Ḥudhayfa. See Tirmidhī, *Shamā'il*, 211; Baghawī, *Shamā'il*, I, no. 151. See also *Kashf al-astār*, III, no. 2378. And see also Ibn Abī Shayba, XI, no. 11738.

[98] The *isnād*: Ja'far ibn Abī Waḥshiyya (= ibn Iyās, Baṣran d. AH 125)←Nāfi'←Jubayr. See Ibn Sa'd, I, 104; Bayhaqī, *Dalā'l*, I, 155; Aḥmad, *Musnad*, IV, 81, 83–84; Ṭabarānī, *Kabīr*, II, no. 1563; Dhahabī, *Sīra*, 9. See also Ṭayālisī, *Musnad*, no. 942. Another *isnād*: Ṣafwān ibn Sulaym (Medinan d. AH 132)←Abū l-Ḥuwayrith ('Abd al-Raḥmān ibn Mu'āwiya, Medinan d. AH 128)←Nāfi' ibn Jubayr←Jubayr ibn Muṭ'im. See Ṭabarānī, *Kabīr*, II, no. 1564.

[99] *Mustadrak*, II, 604.

[100] See Ibn Shabba, II, 631; Tirmidhī, *Shamā'il*, 210–11; Ṭabarī, *Tārīkh*, I, 1788 (III, 178–79); Ḥumaydī, I, no. 555; Bukhārī, *Tārīkh ṣaghīr*, I, 35; Aḥmad, *Musnad*, IV, 80, 84; Abū Ya'lā, XIII, no. 7395; Bayhaqī, *Dalā'il*, I, 152–54; Abū Nu'aym, *Dalā'il*, no. 19; Ṭabarānī, *Kabīr*, II, nos. 1520, 1522–28; Baghawī, *Shamā'il*, I, no. 150; Dhahabī, *Sīra*, 8.

[101] See 'Abd al-Razzāq, *Muṣannaf*, X, no. 19657; Muslim, VII, 89 (43:124–25); Tirmidhī/*Tuḥfa*, VIII, no. 2996; Ibn Abī Shayba, XI, no. 11737; Dārimī, II, no. 2775; Ibn Ḥibbān, *Ṣaḥīḥ*, XIV, no. 6313.

[102] Bukhārī, *Ṣaḥīḥ*, VI, 188 (65, Sūra 61); Wāḥidī, *Wasīṭ*, fol. 278b; Ibn Kathīr, *Tafsīr*, IV, 359–60; Ṭabarsī, *Majma'*, XXVIII, 61.

[103] The *isnād*: 'Amr ibn Murra ibn 'Abdallāh (Kūfan d. AH 118)←Abū 'Ubayda ibn 'Abdallāh ibn Mas'ūd (Kūfan)←Abū Mūsā. See Ibn Sa'd, I, 104–105. See also Ibn Bukayr, 142; Ṭabarī, *Tārīkh*, I, 1788 (III, 178); Aḥmad, *Musnad*, IV, 404; Ibn Shabba, II, 632; Bukhārī, *Tārīkh ṣaghīr*, I, 36; Bayhaqī, *Dalā'il*, I, 156–57; Ṭaḥāwī, *Mushkil*, II, 51; Daylamī, *Firdaws*, I, no. 96; Ṭabarānī, *Ṣaghīr*, I, 80; Dhahabī, *Sīra*, 9.

[104] Ibn Abī Shayba, XI, no. 11739; Muslim, VII, 90 (43, *Bāb fī asmā'ihi*); *Mustadrak*, II, 604; Bayhaqī, *Shu'ab*, II, no. 1400.

[105] In *tafsīr* of 61:6: Ibn Kathīr, *Tafsīr*, IV, 360. In *tafsīr* of 33:45: Qurṭubī, XIV, 200.

Sa'd, and are traced back to the Companions Jābir ibn 'Abdallāh (Medinan d. AH 77),[106] Ibn 'Umar,[107] and Ibn 'Abbās.[108]

Such wide circulation of prophetic self-attestation points to the extent of interest the Muslims took in the subject. In fact, their preoccupation with the names and epithets of their Prophet[109] was as compelling as their preoccupation with the names and epithets of God. In both cases they circulated traditions containing lists of those names, discussed the significance of each of them, and tried to systematize this field of knowledge by fixing the exact number of names. In one more version, a number is appended to the list. This is a tradition of the Meccan Companion Abū l-Ṭufayl 'Āmir ibn Wāthila (d. AH 110)[110] in which Muḥammad states: "I have with God ten names: Muḥammad, Aḥmad, Abū l-Qāsim, al-Fātiḥ, al-Khātam, al-'Āqib, al-Ḥāshir, al-Māḥī." Abū l-Ṭufayl could only remember eight out of the ten. Another version of Abū l-Ṭufayl contains the total ten, including Yāsīn and Ṭāhā.[111]

The idea of awarding prophets a fixed number of names is very early, and is already known in Jewish *midrash*, where it is stated that a prophet is called by ten names. The variety of names adduced (Emissary, Trustee, Servant, Messenger, Seer, Scout, Beholder, Angel, Prophet, Man of God), reflects the various aspects of the prophet's person and mission.[112]

But the number which the early Muslims seem to have preferred for their own prophet was five. This number appears in the *Sīra* of Ibn Isḥāq in one more version of the above tradition of Zuhrī←Muḥammad ibn Jubayr←Jubayr ibn Muṭ'im. In the present version Muḥammad states: "I have five names: I am Muḥammad, Aḥmad, al-Māḥī—by whom God wipes off disbelief, al-'Āqib, al-Ḥāshir—in whose footsteps people will be resurrected."[113] In one of the versions with the same *isnād*, the Prophet is said to have uttered this statement as a kind of battle cry against the polytheists of Quraysh.[114] The tradition recurs in

[106] Ṭabarānī, *Kabīr*, II, no. 1750. The *isnād*: 'Ubaydallāh ibn 'Amr (Jazīran d. AH 180)←'Abdallāh ibn Muḥammad ibn 'Aqīl (Medinan d. AH 142)←Jābir.

[107] Huwwārī, IV, 347 (in *tafsīr* of 61:6).

[108] The *isnād*: Salama ibn Nubayṭ (Kūfan)←al-Ḍaḥḥāk ibn Muzāḥim (Khurāsānī. d. AH 102)←Ibn 'Abbās. See Ṭabarānī, *Ṣaghīr*, I, 58–59; *idem*, *Awsaṭ*, III, no. 2301.

[109] For which see already Andræ, *Person*, 272–76.

[110] The *isnād*: Ismā'īl ibn Ibrāhīm al-Taymī (Kūfan)←Sayf ibn Wahb (Baṣran)←Abū l-Ṭufayl. See Abū Nu'aym, *Dalā'il*, no. 20.

[111] See Daylamī, *Firdaws*, I, no. 97; Mālik/Zurqānī, V, 515; Suyūṭī, *Durr*, IV, 289; *idem*, *Khaṣā'iṣ*, I, 191–92.

[112] *Bereshit Rabba*, XLIV; *Avot de-Rabbi Natan*, XXXIV.

[113] Ibn Bukayr, 142. Cf. Ibn Sa'd, I, 105; Bayhaqī, *Dalā'il*, I, 154; Ṭaḥāwī, *Mushkil*, II, 50; Ṭabarānī, *Kabīr*, II, nos. 1521, 1529–30.

[114] Ṭabarānī, *Kabīr*, II, no. 1532.

some *muṣannaf* compilations,[115] as well as in *tafsīr* books.[116] It was reportedly discussed in the court of the Umayyad caliph ʻAbd al-Malik, who asked Jubayr's son, Nāfiʻ, what was the number of names included in his father's tradition. Nāfiʻ claimed that they were six (including Khātam).[117]

However, the above versions of Jubayr's tradition where the list of names is unnumbered gained much wider circulation, which indicates that the Muslims chose not to limit the names of Muḥammad to any specific small number. In fact, they preferred to point to the largest number possible. Some of them stated that Muḥammad's names were 99, like those of God, while others maintained that they amounted to 300.[118] Some Ṣūfis stated that God and Muḥammad had 1000 names each.[119]

Later sources reveal an increased interest in gleaning from the Quran names and epithets of the Prophet for the purpose of attestation. Forms which were extracted verbatim from the scripture were systematically arranged in long lists.[120] Scholarly discussions were devoted to the significance of Muḥammad's Quranic names, and it was observed that some of them were derived from the names of God (Muḥammad and Aḥmad from Ḥamīd, etc.).[121] The idea of such divine derivation (Muḥammad from Maḥmūd) already appears in a poetic verse attributed to Muḥammad's poet, Ḥassān ibn Thābit.[122] The same verse is ascribed to Abū Ṭālib as well.[123]

The issue of the number of Muḥammad's Quranic names was also tackled, and even assumed the form of a prophetic statement. The prophet is said to have declared: "I have seven names in the Quran: Muḥammad, Aḥmad, Yāsīn, Ṭāhā,

---

115 Mālik/Zurqānī, V, 510; Bukhārī, *Ṣaḥīḥ*, IV, 225 (61:17); Nasāʼī, *Kubrā*, VI, 489 (no. 11590 [82, Sūra 61:6]); Bayhaqī, *Shuʻab*, II, no. 1397.

116 In *tafsīr* of 61:6: Suyūṭī, *Durr*, VI, 214. In *tafsīr* of 33:45: Qurṭubī, XIV, 200.

117 See Ibn Saʻd, I, 105; Bukhārī, *Tārīkh ṣaghīr*, I, 36; Bayhaqī, *Dalāʼil*, I, 156; Ṭaḥāwī, *Mushkil*, II, 50; Dhahabī, *Sīra*, 9. See also *Mustadrak*, IV, 273–74; Bayhaqī, *Shuʻab*, II, no. 1398. This report was circulated with the *isnād*: Saʻīd ibn Abī Hilāl (Egyptian d. AH 135)←ʻUtba ibn Muslim (Medinan)←Nāfiʻ ibn Jubayr.

118 *Fatḥ al-bārī*, VI, 406.

119 Ibn al-ʻArabī, *Aḥkām*, III, 1546 (on Quran 33:45); *Fatḥ al-bārī*, VI, 407.

120 E.g. Khargūshī (MS Br. Lib.), fol. 73a–b; Bayhaqī, *Dalāʼil*, I, 159; Ṭabarsī, *Aʻlām al-warā*, 15. And see on the role of these names in everyday Muslim life and in mystical thought, Annemarie Schimmel, *And Muhammad is His Messenger: the Veneration of the Prophet in Islamic Piety* (Chapel Hill, 1985), 105–22, 257–59.

121 Khafājī, *Nasīm*, II, 413–14.

122 Ḥassān, *Dīwān*, 306 (no. 152). See also Māwardī, *Nukat*, V, 529. And see Andræ, *Person*, 274.

123 Bukhārī, *Tārīkh ṣaghīr*, I, 38; Bayhaqī, *Dalāʼil*, I, 161; *Fatḥ al-bārī*, VI, 404; Mālik/Zurqānī, V, 512.

Muddaththir, Muzzammil, 'Abdallāh."[124] Some writers maintained that the Quranic names were only five (Muḥammad, Aḥmad, 'Abdallāh, Ṭāhā, Yāsīn),[125] while others were able to transmit no less than 400 such names.[126]

With Muḥammad's own self-attestation, which draws heavily on the Quran, the process of the Islamisation of his originally biblical attestation was completed.

---

[124] Khafājī, *Nasīm*, II, 392 (from al-Naqqāsh).
[125] Abū Zakariyyā, in Bayhaqī, *Dalā'il*, I, 159. See also Dhahabī, *Sīra*, 9–10.
[126] Ibn Shahrāshūb, I, 130–31.

2

The Arabian Annunciation

I

THE THEME OF ANNUNCIATION is demonstrated further in stories which anchor the idea of attestation in the local Arabian background of the Prophet's life. These are not only polemical stories about the Arabian Jews who await the Prophet's appearance, only to reject him later on, but also anecdotes about Arabs who never cease to believe in him, once they become aware of his expected emergence. Muḥammad features in these traditions not as a Quranic prophet deriving his attestation from that scripture, but first and foremost as an Arab whose attestation is rooted in local Arabian history. Although the stories are constructed as if to assert Muḥammad's genuine message, they are actually designed to promote the interests, claims, and status of certain Arab groups vying for recognition in medieval Islamic society. The stories thus demonstrate the political function of the theme of annunciation.

Some traditions revolve round south Arabian ancestors. The traditions about them seem to have been circulated by Muslims belonging to the Anṣār, i.e. the Aws and the Khazraj, who were of south Arabian descent and dwelt in Medina. The struggle of the Anṣār for recognition in Islam as reflected in traditions glorifying their past has already been noticed by Goldziher.[1]

One specific tradition, attributed to the Companion Ibn 'Abbās,[2] revolves round the king of Yemen, Sayf ibn Dhī Yazan, who is said to have obtained his knowledge about Muḥammad from a secret book he inherited from his forefathers. He communicates his knowledge to 'Abd al-Muṭṭalib (Muḥammad's grandfather), who has come to Yemen to congratulate the king on his recent ascension to the throne. Sayf is able to tell 'Abd al-Muṭṭalib the name of the Prophet and describe his external appearance. The king stresses, obviously, that the new religion of the Prophet will establish itself in Yathrib (= Medina), where Muḥammad will enjoy the support of the Anṣār. He also alludes to the

[1] *Muslim Studies*, I, 90–95. For traditions relating the virtues of the Yemeni forefathers, see also Rubin, "Pre-Existence", 79–80.

[2] The *isnād*: Muḥammad ibn al-Sā'ib al-Kalbī (Kūfan d. AH 146)←Abū Ṣāliḥ (Bādhām, *mawlā* of Umm Hāni')←Ibn 'Abbās.

persecution about to be perpetrated by Quraysh on Muḥammad.[3] The political slant of the story is evident enough.

Other traditions about south Arabian history reintroduce the Jews as the source of the textual attestation of Muḥammad. They disclose the information to a south Arabian mythological forefather, namely, the *tubba'* (i.e. a Yemeni ruler) Tubān As'ad Abū Karib. Ibn Isḥāq relates that this *tubba'* raided the Ḥijāz, but was prevented from attacking Medina by a pair of Medinan rabbis of Qurayẓa who were able to tell him about the future emigration of Muḥammad to that town.[4] In a tradition of the Medinan Companion Ubayy ibn Ka'b recorded by Ibn Sa'd,[5] the Jews provide a full description of Muḥammad in which he is depicted as Riding a Camel, etc. This is the very description which, as seen above, was circulated as a prophetic *ḥadīth*. There is also a story about a *tubba'* who, a thousand years before the birth of Muḥammad, came to the Ḥijāz, was told by Jewish scholars about the Prophet, believed in him, and left a letter for him in Medina. In due course, this document was handed over to Muḥammad by the Medinan Companion Abū Ayyūb. The Jewish scholars of the time of this *tubba'* had settled in Medina in anticipation of the Prophet, and the Anṣār are said to have been descendants of those Jewish rabbis.[6]

Other tribal units managed to circulate the same kind of stories about people living among them in pre-Islamic times who foretold the emergence of the Prophet. One of these clans is Iyād (of the northern tribal group of Ma'add). In the stories circulated about their pre-Islamic heroes, the orator Quss ibn Sā'ida is mentioned.[7] He is said to have been a god-fearing ascetic who believed in the Last Judgement. The traditions attribute to him a prophecy about the advent of a new and better religion, and about the emergence of a righteous prophet. There are traditions in which the Prophet himself is said to have heard him preach in

---

[3] See Kharā'iṭī, *Hawātif*, 188–93 (no. 20); Azraqī, 99–102; Abū Nu'aym, *Dalā'il*, no. 50; *Aghānī*, XVI, 75–77; Ibn Kathīr, *Bidāya*, II, 328–30; Ibn Shahrāshūb, I, 20–21. The same story is also circulated with a family *isnād* of Sayf ibn Dhī Yazan himself. See Bayhaqī, *Dalā'il*, II, 9–14; Suyūṭī, *Khaṣā'iṣ*, I, 202–204. And see also Ya'qūbī, II, 12; Mas'ūdī, *Murūj*, II, 83–84.

[4] Ibn Hishām, I, 21–22.

[5] Ibn Sa'd, I, 158–59. The *isnād*: Dāwūd ibn al-Ḥuṣayn (Medinan d. AH 135)←'Ikrima (Medinan d. AH 105)←Ibn 'Abbās←Ubayy ibn Ka'b.

[6] Khargūshī (MS Tübingen), fol. 93b–95b; al-Ṣafūrī, *Nuzhat al-majālis*, II, 92 (from al-Khargūshī); Ibn Shahrāshūb, I, 17–18; *Biḥār al-anwār*, XV, 222–24; Kister, "*Ḥaddithū*", 232–33.

[7] See several traditions about Quss in Ibn Sa'd, I, 315; Bayhaqī, *Dalā'il*, II, 101–13; Abū Nu'aym, *Dalā'il*, no. 55; Suyūṭī, *Khaṣā'iṣ*, I, 70; Zurqānī, I, 182–83; Ibn Shahrāshūb, I, 246–47; *Biḥār al-anwār*, XV, 183–86, 227–29, 234–35, 241–48.

'Ukāẓ in pre-Islamic times, and to have repeated his pious address later on to his own Companions.

In the traditions of Arabian annunciation a special role is assigned to the ancestors of Quraysh, Muḥammad's own tribe. Although they all died as infidels before Islam, Muslim tradition attributes religious and moral integrity to them, and describes them as belonging to a chosen race selected by God to provide Muḥammad with the most noble pedigree.[8]

To establish their religious virtues, traditions were circulated in which these Qurashī ancestors know in advance about the coming prophet. A tradition of the Medinan Successor Abū Salama (d. AH 94), son of the celebrated Qurashī Companion 'Abd al-Raḥmān ibn 'Awf, glorifies the Meccan ancestor Ka'b ibn Lu'ayy, who is said to have preached to the Meccans each Friday. The text of his preaching is composed in rhymed prose, or *saj'*, like the utterances of soothsayers. In it he foresees the future appearance in Mecca of a prophet whose name will be Muḥammad. Ka'b ibn Lu'ayy is said to have died 560 years before Muḥammad's emergence.[9]

In other traditions about the forefathers of Quraysh, their knowledge about the Prophet comes to them through dreams.[10] The ancestor al-Naḍr ibn Kināna is said to have seen in his dream a green tree with golden boughs, which grew out of his back and reached the sky. He told experts in the Ka'ba about his dream, and they interpreted it as signifying future honour and power.[11] In a tradition of the Qurashī Companion Abū l-Jahm ibn Ḥudhayfa ibn Ghānim, a similar dream is seen by Muḥammad's grandfather, 'Abd al-Muṭṭalib.[12] Al-'Abbās, ancestor of the 'Abbāsid dynasty, was also credited with a dream of annunciation in which the emergence of the Prophet is symbolized as a bird coming out of the nostril of Muḥammad's father, 'Abdallāh.[13]

---

[8] Cf. Rubin, "Pre-Existence", 71–79.

[9] Abū Nu'aym, *Dalā'il*, no. 46.

[10] On dreams in Islamic literature, see M.J. Kister, "The Interpretation of Dreams", *Israel Oriental Studies* 4 (1974), 67–103; Leah Kinberg, *Morality in the Guise of Dreams* (Leiden, 1994), 16–48.

[11] Mas'ūdī, *Ithbāt al-waṣiyya*, 98; Rubin, "Pre-Existence", 64.

[12] Abū Nu'aym, *Dalā'il*, no. 51. The higher part of the *isnād* is "pre-Islamic": Abū Bakr ibn 'Abdallāh ibn Abī l-Jahm←'Abdallāh ibn Abī l-Jahm←Abū l-Jahm ibn Ḥudhayfa ibn Ghānim←Abū Ṭālib←'Abd al-Muṭṭalib.

[13] Suyūṭī, *Khaṣā'iṣ*, I, 121 (Abū Nu'aym). See also Rubin, "Pre-Existence", 64–65.

II

In the stories about pre-Islamic Arabian figures involved in the annunciation of the Prophet, a special role is assigned to individual persons who eventually became Muḥammad's Companions. Many of them are said to have known about his future emergence already in pre-Islamic times. Their knowledge comes from the holy scriptures of the Jews and the Christians, and it brings about their eventual conversion. Such traditions are designed to assert the ancient link between them and the Prophet, and the stories are usually circulated by the descendants of these Companions.

One of these Companions is al-Jārūd ibn al-Mu'allā of the tribe of 'Abd al-Qays. He is said to have been a Christian originally, and to have come to the Prophet with a delegation of his tribe. In the story about him (related on the authority of Ibn 'Abbās), he tells Muḥammad that he has read about him in the *Injīl* (i.e. the gospels). He also tells him about Quss ibn Sā'ida.[14]

Other Companions of Muḥammad who were neither Christians nor Jews appear in similar stories of annunciation designed to attest to their own virtues. The stories take place in pre-Islamic times, and in them these Companions obtain their knowledge about Muḥammad's looming emergence not directly from the scriptures, but through monotheistic scholars who are well versed in them. The latter are sometimes described as *ḥanīf*s, who are the representatives of the local pre-Islamic Arabian monotheism usually associated with the figures of Abraham and Ishmael. In the stories about these Abrahamic believers the attestation of the Prophet is provided through the assertion that he is the one destined to restore the true religion of Abraham in Arabia.

A most illustrious *ḥanīf* is Zayd ibn 'Amr ibn Nufayl, a member of the Qurashī clan of 'Adī ibn Ka'b, to which 'Umar ibn al-Khaṭṭāb also belongs. The Companion who obtains knowledge from Zayd about the impending emergence of Muḥammad is 'Āmir ibn Rabī'a, a confederate of the Khaṭṭāb family. Zayd's source of information is not stated explicitly, but the assumption seems to be that it has been derived from sacred scriptures possessed by Jews and Christians, with whom Arabian *ḥanīf*s are usually said to have been in contact. The story, which is related by the Companion 'Āmir ibn Rabī'a himself, was circulated by his son.[15] In it, Zayd ibn 'Amr decides to abandon the idols of the Meccans and to follow the religion of Abraham instead. He leaves Mecca, and

---

[14] E.g. Bayhaqī, *Dalā'il*, II, 105–106. Cf. Ibn Ḥajar, *Iṣāba*, I, 441–43.

[15] The *isnād*: Zuhrī←'Abdallāh ibn 'Āmir ibn Rabī'a←'Āmir ibn Rabī'a. See Fākihī, IV, no. 2419; Abū Nu'aym, *Dalā'il*, no. 52. A shortened version is recorded in Ibn Sa'd, I, 161–62; Ṭabarī, *Tārīkh*, I, 1143–44 (II, 295); Ibn Kathīr, *Bidāya*, VI, 64.

on his way out of town he meets 'Āmir. Zayd tells 'Āmir about his strife with the Meccans, adding that he awaits the emergence of a prophet from the seed of Ishmael, from the clan of 'Abd al-Muṭṭalib. Saying that he is not sure whether he will live to see him, he then offers to give 'Āmir the full description of that prophet, so that 'Āmir can recognize him, should he meet him. He describes the future prophet as a person of medium height, whose hair is of medium length, whose eyes are somewhat reddish, who has the seal of prophethood between his shoulders, whose name is Aḥmad, and whose birthplace is Mecca. His fellow tribesmen will force him out of his birthplace and will reject his message, till he emigrates to Yathrib, where his enterprise will be crowned with success. Then Zayd tells 'Āmir that he has toured many regions in quest of the religion of Abraham, and has met with Jews and Christians, all of whom told him that the religion of Abraham was the religion of the prophet who was due to appear in Mecca; all of them described him to Zayd in the same way.

There are many more traditions about Companions in pre-Islamic times meeting with Christian scholars and hermits who derive their information from their sacred scriptures. One such Companion is the Qurashī Ṭalḥa ibn 'Ubaydallāh (d. AH 36), who relates the story himself. He says that he was in the Syrian market of Buṣrā, where a hermit was inquiring whether any Meccan was present. When Ṭalḥa presented himself to him, the hermit asked whether "Aḥmad" had appeared yet. Ṭalḥa asked who Aḥmad was, and the hermit said that he was the son of 'Abdallāh and was due to appear as a prophet in Mecca in that very month. He urged Ṭalḥa to be the first to join that prophet. Ṭalḥa hurried back to Mecca and found out that a prophet named Muḥammad had just appeared, and that Abū Bakr, a member of Ṭalḥa's own clan (Taym), had already joined him. Ṭalḥa came to Abū Bakr and told him about the hermit's words, and Abū Bakr introduced Ṭalḥa to Muḥammad. The tradition appears in Ibn Sa'd,[16] and was also recorded by al-Ḥākim.[17]

The Syrian Sulamī Companion 'Amr ibn 'Abasa, who claimed to be one of the very first Muslims,[18] hears in advance some details about the Prophet from a member of the People of the Book. He relates that he became bored with idolatry, and in his search for a better faith, met the scholar who told him that a

[16] Ibn Sa'd, III, 214–15. The *isnād*: Makhrama ibn Sulaymān al-Wālibī (Medinan d. AH 130)←Ibrāhīm ibn Muḥammad ibn Ṭalḥa (Medinan/Kūfan d. AH 110)←Ṭalḥa. See also Bayhaqī, *Dalā'il*, II, 166; Qiwām al-Sunna, *Dalā'il*, II, 437–39 (no. 38).

[17] *Mustadrak*, III, 369.

[18] Cf. Michael Lecker, *The Banū Sulaym* (Jerusalem, 1989), 74, 94–95.

prophet was about to appear in Mecca who would reject the idols of his people.[19]

Companions of Muḥammad received not only verbal information from Christian scholars about the coming prophet, but visual presentation as well. Jubayr ibn Muṭ'im, whom we already met as an authority on prophetic self-attestation, is not an early Muslim. Nevertheless, he too is said to have been in Syria (Buṣrā) very shortly after Muḥammad emerged in Mecca, and to have learnt about him from the local Christians. They showed him Muḥammad's portrait, and he confirmed that it was indeed the new Meccan prophet.[20] Thus it is implied that Muḥammad's attestation was asserted to this Companion at a very early stage.

However, the attestation of Muḥammad is not only made in advance. In some cases, monotheists carry it out retrospectively, for Companions who are Muslims already. 'Alī ibn Abī Ṭālib, for instance, is known in Muslim tradition as an intimate Companion of Muḥammad, and the Prophet's description is transmitted on 'Alī's authority in many traditions. In one of them, transmitted by some of his descendants, 'Alī relates that he was once dispatched to Yemen by Muḥammad. A Jewish rabbi met him there and asked him to describe the Prophet to him. The Jew was consulting a book he had brought with him. 'Alī gave a detailed description of the Prophet, and the rabbi verified it according to his own book, and even completed details which had slipped 'Alī's memory.[21] In a Companion tradition of Abū Hurayra, a similar scene takes place even later, after the the death of Muḥammad. 'Alī describes the Prophet to a Jewish rabbi from Jerusalem, and the latter affirms that 'Alī's description concurs with the one given in the Torah.[22]

In some cases, the Prophet himself is present in the meeting between the attesting scholar and the Companion. The scholar not only knows about the Prophet from his scriptures, but performs on Muḥammad himself a physiognomic

---

[19] One version of the story was recorded in Ibn Sa'd, IV, 217–18, with the *isnād*: Shahr ibn Ḥawshab (Syrian d. AH 100)←'Amr ibn 'Abasa. Another one is recorded in Abū Nu'aym, *Dalā'il*, no. 198, where the story is quoted from 'Amr by Abū Umāma al-Bāhilī (Syrian Companion d. AH 81–86).

[20] The *isnād*: Sa'īd ibn Muḥammad ibn Jubayr←his father←his grandfather Jubayr ibn Muṭ'im. See Bukhārī, *Tārīkh kabīr*, I, no. 545; Bayhaqī, *Dalā'il*, I, 384–85; Abū Nu'aym, *Dalā'il*, no. 12; Ṭabarānī, *Kabīr*, II, no. 1537; Ibn Kathīr, *Bidāya*, VI, 63; *idem*, *Tafsīr*, II, 253. Another *isnād*: 'Alī ibn Rabāḥ (Egyptian d. AH 117)←Jubayr. See Ṭabarānī, *Kabīr*, II, no. 1609.

[21] Ibn Sa'd, I, 412–13; Ibn 'Asākir (*Mukhtaṣar*), II, 65-66; Suyūṭī, *Khaṣā'iṣ*, I, 185–86 (from Ibn Sa'd and Ibn 'Asākir).

[22] Ibn 'Asākir (*Mukhtaṣar*), II, 42-43; Suyūṭī, *Khaṣā'iṣ*, I, 187 (Ibn 'Asākir).

examination, and discloses his attesting conclusions to the Companion. The scholar in one particular story is the well-known hermit Baḥīrā,[23] and the story about him forms part of Muḥammad's infancy legends. The person who receives the information is Muḥammad's paternal uncle, Abū Ṭālib, whose role is significant in view of the fact that he is ʻAlī's father. Although Abū Ṭālib is usually said to have died an infidel, his participation in this scene of attestation makes him a devotee of Muḥammad, if not a proper Companion.

The earliest extant version of the story is that of Ibn Isḥāq. The Prophet, still a boy, joins his uncle Abū Ṭālib on a trade journey to Syria. The caravan camps near Buṣrā, where Baḥīrā observes them from his cell. He notices that a tiny cloud is hovering over Muḥammad's head, protecting him from the sun, while the boughs of a tree under which the boy is sitting bend so as to cover him from the sun. Baḥīrā invites them all to supper, but Muḥammad, being the youngest, stays behind to guard the goods. Baḥīrā encourages the people to bring the boy along, interrogates him, finds the seal of prophethood on his back, and discloses to Abū Ṭālib the great future in store for his young nephew. He urges him to protect the boy from the Jews, who will be his cruellest foes. Ibn Isḥāq adds that some of them even intended to assassinate the boy while he was still in Buṣrā, but the hermit prevented them from doing so.[24] A similar story was recorded by Ibn Saʻd on the authority of al-Wāqidī.[25] There are, in fact, further traditions about similar meetings of Abū Ṭālib and Muḥammad with several other hermits who, likewise, reveal to Abū Ṭālib his nephew's destiny.[26] These recur in Shīʻī sources.[27]

In other versions, however, another Companion takes part in the meeting with the hermit, beside Abū Ṭālib. This is none other than Abū Bakr. Abū Bakr was to become a prominent Companion and the first caliph, but his right to rule was denied by ʻAlī's supporters. Thus the interpolation of Abū Bakr's name into the Baḥīrā story reveals the non-Shīʻī side of the impact of political tensions on the story of Muḥammad's life. Abū Bakr's name appears, to begin with, in a tradition of the Companion Abū Mūsā al-Ashʻarī (d. AH 42–53).[28] Muḥammad is again in the caravan of Abū Ṭālib, but in this version the meeting with the hermit (whose name is not stated), takes place not during Muḥammad's child-

---

23 About him, see A. Abel, s.v. "Baḥīrā", *EI*².

24 Ibn Hishām, I, 191–94. See also Ibn Bukayr, 73–78; Ṭabarī, *Tārīkh*, I, 1123–24 (II, 277–78). See also Abū Nuʻaym, *Dalāʼil*, 169 (no. 108); Bayhaqī, *Dalāʼil*, II, 28.

25 See Ibn Saʻd, I, 153–55.

26 See *ibid.*, I, 153.

27 Ibn Shahrāshūb, I, 36–38; *Biḥār al-anwār*, XV, 193–201.

28 The *isnād*: Yūnus ibn Abī Isḥāq (Kūfan d. AH 152)←Abū Bakr ibn Abī Mūsā←Abū Mūsā.

hood, but in the very month of his prophetic emergence. This is indicated in the words of seven Byzantine soldiers who were sent in search of the Prophet, about whom they knew from their scriptures, and whom they were ordered to kill. They say: "We have come because this prophet is about to appear (*khārij*) this month." The hermit protects Muḥammad from them, and they are persuaded to believe in the Prophet. Only towards the end of the tradition does Abū Bakr's name suddenly emerge. It is stated that Abū Ṭālib sent Muḥammad back (to Mecca), and that Abū Bakr (!) sent his client Bilāl with him. This tradition was recorded in biographical sources,[29] as well as in some *muṣannaf* compilations.[30] The clause about Abū Bakr is apparently a remainder of an originally separate tradition which only survived in this interpolated extract. At any rate, Abū Bakr's presence on the scene is designed to allude to the early date of his own Islamic persuasion.

A whole comprehensive tradition in which Abū Bakr is actually the only Companion attending the scene of the meeting with Baḥīrā was circulated on the authority of Ibn 'Abbās.[31] Upon hearing the prognosis of the hermit about Muḥammad, Abū Bakr's heart is filled with "persuasion and belief"; when Muḥammad becomes a prophet, he follows him. Here too it is implied that Abū Bakr's Islamic persuasion is of a very early date, which supports his claim to be the first male Muslim.

Yet another Companion whose name was associated with the story of the hermit is Khadīja, Muḥammad's wife. In fact, she is considered the first female Companion. Her presence on the scene of attestation with the hermit is achieved through her agent, Maysara. In a tradition recorded by Ibn Isḥāq, Maysara and Muḥammad go to Syria with Khadīja's commodities. The hermit, whose name is not mentioned, notices Muḥammad and tells Maysara about him. Maysara communicates the details to his mistress Khadīja, who thus becomes aware of Muḥammad's prophetic mission and remarkable destiny, and thereupon decides to marry him.[32] In al-Wāqidī's version (related by Khadīja's maid, the Com-

---

[29] Ṭabarī, *Tārīkh*, I, 1125–26 (II, 278–79); Kharā'iṭī, *Hawātif*, 194–96 (no. 22); Qiwām al-Sunna, *Dalā'il*, I, 381–83 (no. 26); Bayhaqī, *Dalā'il*, II, 24–25; Abū Nu'aym, *Dalā'il*, 170–72 (no. 109); *idem*, *Ṣaḥāba*, III, 188–89 (no. 1259). Cf. Ibn Ḥajar, *Iṣāba*, I, 353.

[30] Tirmidhī/*Tuḥfa*, X, 90–92 (*Faḍā'il*); Ibn Abī Shayba, XI, 479 (no. 11782, *Faḍā'il*); *Mustadrak*, II, 615–16 (*Dalā'il al-nubuwwa*).

[31] The *isnād*: Ibn Jurayj (Meccan d. AH 150)←'Aṭā' ibn Abī Rabāḥ (Meccan d. AH 114)←Ibn 'Abbās. See Abū Nu'aym, *Ṣaḥāba*, III, 188 (no. 1258); Qiwām al-Sunna, *Dalā'il*, I, 389–91 (no. 28). See also Wāḥidī, *Asbāb*, 216 (on 46:15).

[32] Ibn Hishām, I, 199–200. See also Ibn Bukayr, 81; Ṭabarī, *Tārīkh*, I, 1127–28 (II, 280–81); Bayhaqī, *Dalā'il*, II, 66–67.

panion Nafīsa bint Munya [= bint Umayya]),[33] the name of the hermit who speaks to Maysara is Nasṭūr, whereas in other versions he is again Baḥīrā.[34]

Ibn Isḥāq and other biographers of Muḥammad arranged the various traditions according to their implicit chronology, and placed Muḥammad's journey to Syria with Abū Ṭālib before the journey with Maysara. This was in accordance with their typical harmonizing historically oriented outlook, which implied that there were at least two different journeys of Muḥammad to Syria, during different stages of his life. The truth is, however, that the traditions actually reflect several versions of one and the same scene of attestation, each designed to magnify a different Companion of Muḥammad by making him (or her) a party to it.

The Companions of Muḥammad learn about him not only in meetings with believing wise scholars; like some Qurashī ancestors, they too become aware of the approaching emergence of the Prophet through dreams. Their dreams cause them to embrace Islam, and their conversion is thus elevated to the rank of a divinely inspired act.

Some of the traditions pertain to persons from among the Anṣār (the Aws and the Khazraj). One such tradition is about the Companion Abū Umāma As'ad ibn Zurāra of the Khazraj, who professed monotheism in Medina long before the arrival of Muḥammad.[35] It is related in a tradition of Ḥarām ibn 'Uthmān al-Anṣārī (d. AH 150) that one day, as he was returning from Syria with forty other Medinan traders, Abū Umāma had a dream in which he was told that a prophet was about to appear in Mecca, and that he should follow him. The sign confirming the truth of the dream would be that all the traders would die during the journey, except for himself, and another person whose eye will be injured. When they camped in their next station, all of them were inflicted with the plague (*ṭā'ūn*); the only survivors were As'ad and another person whose eye was infected (*ṭu'ina*).[36]

Other traditions are about people of the Muhājirūn (Quraysh). One of them is Abū Bakr, whom we have already met as witness to the attestation of Baḥīrā. Another story about him and Baḥīrā was circulated on the authority of Ka'b al-Aḥbār. In it, Abū Bakr is credited with a dream of his own, which Baḥīrā only interprets for him. The hermit says that the dream means that a prophet will appear in Mecca and that Abū Bakr will be his successor. The tradition goes on to

[33] Ibn Sa'd, I, 156.

[34] Khargūshī (MS Br. Lib.), fol. 22a. Quoted from al-Khargūshī in Zurqānī, I, 198–99; Ḥalabī, I, 133. See also Ibn Ḥajar, *Iṣāba*, I, 177.

[35] Ibn Sa'd, I, 218.

[36] *Ibid.*, I, 165–66.

say that when Muḥammad announced his mission, Abū Bakr came to him, and the Prophet knew at once what dream he had experienced, and thereupon Abū Bakr joined him.[37]

Another Companion is Khālid ibn Sa'īd, one of the first Muslims, whose conversion is said to have been caused by a dream. In a tradition of the Medinan Successor Ṣāliḥ ibn Kaysān, Khālid relates that he saw darkness blanketing Mecca, then light emerged from the well of Zamzam, which first illuminated the Ka'ba, then the entire area of Mecca, then the palm trees of Yathrib. A voice from within the light was heard reciting a cryptic text about the end of the power of the demons and about the emergence of the Prophet, as well as about some events which were to unfold later on in Mecca. Khālid tells his dream to his brother 'Amr, and the latter interprets it as indicating an event among the clan of 'Abd al-Muṭṭalib.[38]

Another celebrated member of the acclaimed group of first Muslims is 'Amr ibn Murra al-Juhanī, who is known as a traditionist. The conversion of this Companion to Islam was also caused by a dream. He relates that he had his dream while making his way to Mecca on a pilgrimage; he saw light coming out of the Ka'ba, and a voice from within that light announced the approaching emergence of Muḥammad.[39]

III

The attestation of Muḥammad in its Arabian context is not only of monotheistic provenance. In other traditions the source of attestation is pagan, and it is communicated through representatives of local pre-Islamic Arabian culture, i.e. mantic soothsayers. Unlike the stories of monotheistic attestation, which were prompted by polemical needs, the stories of pagan attestation are designed to bring out the local achievement of Islam in eliminating Arabian polytheism.

Soothsayers meet Muḥammad in person, and by his physiognomy recognize him as the future prophet. Their reaction to their own discovery is usually hostile (like that of the Jews). For example, in a tradition of a Successor (Abū Ḥāzim al-A'raj) recorded by Ibn Sa'd, it is related that when Muḥammad was five years old, a *kāhin* (soothsayer) came to Mecca and saw the boy in the company of his wet-nurse and his grandfather 'Abd al-Muṭṭalib. The *kāhin* exclaimed: "People of Quraysh, kill this boy, because he is about to slay you and

---

[37] Ibn 'Asākir (*Mukhtaṣar*), XIII, 39; Suyūṭī, *Khaṣā'iṣ*, I, 72 (from Ibn 'Asākir).

[38] Ibn Sa'd, I, 166. For another dream of his, see Bayhaqī, *Dalā'il*, II, 172–73. See also Rubin, "Pre-Existence", 65.

[39] Suyūṭī, *Khaṣā'iṣ*, I, 264–65; Rubin, "Pre-Existence", 65.

divide you." 'Abd al-Muṭṭalib ran away with the child, and henceforth Quraysh were afraid of him.[40] In another Successor tradition (of Zayd ibn Aslam) recorded by Ibn Sa'd, Muḥammad's wet-nurse (Ḥalīma) takes him to an Arab physiognomist in 'Ukāẓ. The expert is terrified to discover that the boy will kill the Arabs and destroy their idols. The wet-nurse hurries away with the boy, and from then on she never exposed the boy again to such examinations.[41]

Apart from stories about direct meetings between *kāhins* and the Prophet, there are cases in which the knowledge of the soothsayers is communicated as an apocalyptic vision revealed long before the actual emergence of the Prophet. This is the case in a story about two pre-Islamic southern oracles, Saṭīḥ and Shiqq. They foretell about Muḥammad to a pre-Islamic south Arabian king, Rabī'a ibn Naṣr, who is said to have had an apocalyptic dream which frightened him. The tradition about it draws on the story of Daniel, and is recorded in the *Sīra* of Ibn Isḥāq. The king requests his advisers to guess what his dream was, as well as to interpret it. They are unable to tell him his dream, and suggest that two seers be summoned—Saṭīḥ and Shiqq. Saṭīḥ is the first to arrive, and tells the king his dream. The king saw, so Saṭīḥ tells him, fire bursting out of the darkness and spreading to the shore of his own land. The king confirms the details and Saṭīḥ proceeds to interpret the vision. The black people of Abyssinia are about to invade Yemen. So much for the dream. Now the king poses some questions to Saṭīḥ about the aftermath of the Abyssinian invasion. Saṭīḥ says that the Abyssinians will rule the country, till another Yemeni leader—of the Dhū Yazan family—drives them out, then his own reign will come to an end with the advent of a prophet whose rule will prevail till the Last Judgement. Then Shiqq arrives and communicates to the king almost the same prophecy.[42]

In another tradition on the authority of Ibn 'Abbās, Saṭīḥ predicts the advent of Islam to the frightened pagan leaders of Mecca. His statement constitutes an entire apocalyptic vision in which he alludes not only to the Prophet and to the end of paganism, but to the succeeding rulers and their history. His source of information is elevated here to the level of *ilhām* ("inspiration") from God.[43]

---

[40] Ibn Sa'd, I, 166–67. The *isnād*: Muḥammad ibn al-Faḍl ibn 'Aṭiyya (Kūfan d. AH 180)←Abū Ḥāzim al-A'raj (Salama ibn Dīnār, Medinan d. AH 140).

[41] *Ibid.*, I, 151–52. The *isnād*: 'Abdallāh ibn Zayd ibn Aslam←Zayd ibn Aslam (Medinan d. AH 136).

[42] Ibn Hishām, I, 15–19; cf. 70, 72–73. See also Ṭabarī, *Tārīkh*, I, 910–14 (II, 112–14); Abū Nu'aym, *Dalā'il*, no. 70; Marzūqī, *Azmina*, II, 263–65; Qazwīnī, *'Ajā'ib al-makhlūqāt*, 204; Dhahabī, *Sīra*, 14–15; Damīrī, *Ḥayawān*, I, 602–603; *Biḥār al-anwār*, XV, 232–34.

[43] Abū Nu'aym, *Dalā'il*, no. 69; Khargūshī (MS Tübingen), fol. 1a–2b; Suyūṭī, *Khaṣā'iṣ*, I, 83–87. See also *Biḥār al-anwār*, XV, 217–18, 299–324 (a prolonged version quoted from Abū l-Ḥasan al-Bakrī).

The emergence of Muḥammad was also announced by the demons (*jinn*), who were regarded as the main source of information for the *kāhins*. The voices (*hawātif*) of the *jinn* were heard coming out of various haunted places and objects. Their address is usually composed in rhymed prose (*saj'*) and verses, and contains declarations about the emergence of the Prophet and the end of paganism. A typical case is that of the soothsayer Sawād ibn Qārib, who heard his *jinnī* companion announce in some poetic verses that a righteous prophet had just appeared in Mecca. Sawād joined the Prophet and became a Muslim.[44] A collection of the stories of this kind is included in the recently published *Kitāb al-hawātif* of al-Kharā'iṭī (d. AH 327). In these traditions the idea of the submission of Arabian paganism to Islam is brought to its fullest manifestation.

---

[44] E.g. Kharā'iṭī, *Hawātif*, no. 3. Cf. Ibn Hishām, I, 223–24; Ṭabarī, *Tārīkh*, I, 1144–45 (II, 296–97); Bayhaqī, *Dalā'il*, II, 243–54; Kulīnī, VIII, no. 375.

PART II

PREPARATION

3

Initiation

The Opening of Muḥammad's Breast

ATTESTATION IS ONLY ONE THEME reflecting the idea of the predestined election of Muḥammad to the prophetic office. Another theme that serves to promote the idea of election is that of preparation. Like many prophets, Muḥammad too is said to have been prepared for his future assignment at a very early stage of his life, already before he actually started his prophetic mission.

One of the crucial preparatory acts which he experiences is a ceremony of initiation, consisting of the opening of his breast and the purification and adaptation of his heart to the prophetic disposition. Important observations concerning the traditions about this ceremony have already been made by Harris Birkeland.[1] Some scholars before him suggested Christian and other non-Arab legends as the original models of the story.[2] As for Birkeland, he dedicated his own study to laborious attempts at reconstructing the history of the various Islamic versions, as if each of them represented a certain stage in a hypothetical process of dogmatic development. He also addressed himself to the question of the "authentic experience" of the Prophet that comprises the background of the story.[3] In his efforts to isolate the "earliest" versions of the story, he seems to have overlooked some basic points important to the understanding of the traditions within the general context of the story of Muḥammad's life. For this reason, a reconsideration of the entire corpus of traditions about the opening of Muḥammad's breast is called for. Our attention will be focussed on the process by which the universal theme of physical purification was adapted to Islamic models.

I

The theme of purification emerges in Muḥammad's earliest biographies. It is included in a peculiar story of attestation recorded by Ibn Isḥāq, in which an Arab *kāhin* announces to his audience:

---

[1] *The Legend of the Opening of Muhammed's Breast* (Oslo, 1955).
[2] E.g. Josef Horovitz, "Muhammeds Himmelfahrt", *Der Islam* 9 (1918), 170.
[3] Birkeland, *Opening*, 57.

Oh people, God honoured Muḥammad and elected him;
He purified his heart and loaded it;
His stay among you, Oh people, is a short one.[4]

The actual act of purification as related in the earliest sources forms part of Muḥammad's infancy legends, which means that the event takes place long before his actual prophetic emergence. In this setting it is not only a story of preparation, but of annunciation as well. The event takes place in the desert, where the young Muḥammad lives after having been sent away from Mecca and entrusted to a bedouin wet-nurse, Ḥalīma, from the tribe of Banū Sa'd.

One of the earliest versions of the story is that of Ibn Shihāb al-Zuhrī (Medinan d. AH 124), as preserved by 'Abd al-Razzāq, whose compilation is arranged according to the *muṣannaf* system. Zuhrī's story, which actually surveys the entire life of the Prophet, was recorded by 'Abd al-Razzāq in the "book" of *Maghāzī*. Unfortunately, Zuhrī's sources are not stated. Concerning the opening of the breast, Zuhrī relates that one day, as the boy was with his wet-nurse's daughter, some people came and cut his belly open (*fa-shaqqaw baṭnahu*). The daughter ran home and told her mother about it. The wet-nurse hurried out and found the boy standing, his face white with terror. She did not see anyone around. Fearing that some harm had been done to the boy, she decided to return him to his mother in Mecca; but when she came to Mecca with him, the mother told her that the boy was in no danger. She also said that she knew that no harm could befall her son because, when she had been pregnant with him, she had seen light come out of her which illuminated the forts of Syria.[5] The light in this tradition predicts the future territorial dimension of Muḥammad's mission. The fact that the story of the opening is related in juxtaposition with the mother's vision of light indicates that it is not only a story of initiation, but also one of annunciation. But in Zuhrī's version nothing is said about the event apart from the actual opening of the body; the immediate purpose of the act is not indicated. This may be due to the abridged form of Zuhrī's entire account of Muḥammad's life.

A more detailed story is related on the authority of Ḥalīma herself, and quoted by 'Abdallāh ibn Ja'far ibn Abī Ṭālib (d. AH 80).[6] This version of her tale was recorded in Ibn Isḥāq's (d. AH 150) biography of the Prophet as pre-

---

[4] Ibn Hishām, I, 222.

[5] 'Abd al-Razzāq, *Muṣannaf*, V, 317–18. The *isnād*: Ma'mar ibn Rāshid (Baṣran d. AH 154)←Zuhrī. Cf. Bayhaqī, *Dalā'il*, I, 88.

[6] The *isnād*: Jahm ibn Abī Jahm, *mawlā* of al-Ḥārith ibn Ḥāṭib←'Abdallāh ibn Ja'far ibn Abī Ṭālib (d. AH 80)←Ḥalīma. Cf. Birkeland, *Opening*, 9.

served in the recension of Ibn Bukayr.[7] Ḥalīma relates that Muḥammad was playing one day with his foster brothers behind their tents, when suddenly one of the children went running home and told the wet-nurse that two people dressed in white had come and laid Muḥammad on the ground and cut his belly open (*fa-shaqqā baṭnahu*). Upon hearing this, Ḥalīma and her husband rushed out and found Muḥammad standing, his face white with terror. He told them that the two people who had cut his belly open had taken out of it "something which they threw away", and then restored his body to its normal state. In this version the procedure explicitly includes purification. The two men in white remove from his body some unspecified evil element, thus preparing him for his future prophetic mission. In the ensuing part of the story, details similar to those given by al-Zuhrī are repeated, i.e. the return of the boy to Mecca and the discourse between the alarmed wet-nurse and the confident mother. The latter stresses that Satan has no hold on the boy, a statement exhibiting an early manifestation of the concept of the *'iṣma*, i.e. Muḥammad's immunity against evil powers due to God's protection.[8]

In another more elaborate version of Ḥalīma's story, three men open his body and remove from it a black spot (*nukta sawdā'*), which they tell him has been the share of Satan (*ḥaẓẓ al-shayṭān*) in him. They wash his internal parts with snow, using vessels of silver and emerald, fill his open heart with something unspecified, and seal his body with a seal (*khātam*) of light. Finally, they weigh him against the rest of his people, and he outweighs them.[9] Then they fly away into the sky. This encounter is only one event in the prolonged story of the wet-nurse as recorded in Bayhaqī's *Dalā'il*, where Ḥalīma is quoted by Ibn 'Abbās.[10] Some new noteworthy details appear in this version. The purification leads to the actual establishment of the *'iṣma*, as Satan's share (which is present in every human being[11]) is removed from Muḥammad's soul. The basins out of which the water for his purification is poured are described in typical gnostic symbols (diamonds, gold, silver, etc.); like the light itself, they signify pure holiness. The seal with which his body is sealed is a typical emblem of

[7] Ibn Bukayr, 50–51. See also Bayhaqī, *Dalā'il*, I, 135.

[8] On the *'iṣma*, see e.g. Andræ, *Person*, 124–74; Harris Birkeland, *The Lord Guideth* (Uppsala, 1956), 29–32.

[9] For the act of weighing, see also Noth/Conrad, 170 (in connection with the Persian idea of the "thousandman").

[10] The *isnād*: 'Alī ibn 'Abdallāh ibn 'Abbās←'Abdallāh ibn 'Abbās←Ḥalīma. See Bayhaqī, *Dalā'il*, I, 140–41.

[11] Only Jesus and his mother are said to have been immune against Satan's touch since their birth. See the tradition of Abū Hurayra in Bukhārī, *Ṣaḥīḥ*, IV, 151 (59:11), 199 (60:44); *Mustadrak*, II, 594. Muḥammad's own demonic associate became a Muslim. See Ibn Ḥibbān, *Ṣaḥīḥ*, XIV, nos. 6416–17; *Majma' al-zawā'id*, VIII, 228.

prophethood, which in numerous other traditions appears as an organic part of his body. Thus the initiation includes not only purification, but loading of prophetic utilities.

There are other similar versions of the story of the opening which are not transmitted directly from Ḥalīma. In Ibn Sa'd there is one such tradition on the authority of al-Wāqidī (d. AH 207) in which Muḥammad is said to have been four years old.[12] A similar tradition was recorded by Abū Nu'aym on the authority of some members of the tribe of Ḥalīma, Sa'd.[13]

The early biographies contain further versions of the same scene in which it is set in a clear context of annunciation. These have the form of prophetic *ḥadīth* in which Muḥammad himself tells the story of the opening of his breast. In these versions, the scene forms part of the prophetic self-attestation seen in Chapter 1, based on the prediction of the emergence of Muḥammad in the prayer of Abraham (Quran 2:129), and in the announcement of Jesus (Quran 61:6). The scene of the opening of the breast was incorporated into Syrian versions of those traditions which include the vision of light seen by Muḥammad's mother. When added to the above annunciations, the scene of the opening becomes one of a series of indications attesting to the authenticity of Muḥammad's prophethood. This new setting of the scene reveals a process of adaptation to more specific Islamic models designed to turn the story into a legitimate component of the life of the prophet. After all, in the above infancy versions of the scene Muḥammad is no different from any other prophet who is elected, purified, and initiated into his future prophetic office.

A Syrian tradition with this setting of prophetic utterance already appears in Ibn Isḥāq's biography, transmitted by the Successor Khālid ibn Ma'dān (Ḥimṣī d. AH 103).[14] The Prophet is asked by some of his followers to tell them about himself, and in response he states that he is Abraham's prayer, the good tidings of Jesus about him, and the light which his mother saw in her dream. These manifestations are followed by the story of the opening of his breast when he was in the tribe of his wet-nurse. The scene includes cleansing, removing of a black spot, and weighing.[15] In yet another version of Khālid ibn Ma'dān with a

[12] Ibn Sa'd, I, 112.

[13] Abū Nu'aym, *Dalā'il*, 161 (no. 197). The *isnād*: 'Abd al-Ṣamad ibn Muḥammad al-Sa'dī←his father←his grandfather.

[14] The *isnād*: Thawr ibn Yazīd (Ḥimṣī d. AH 153)←Khālid ibn Ma'dān←unnamed group of Muḥammad's Companions.

[15] Ibn Hishām, I, 175–76; Ibn Bukayr, 51; Ibn Sa'd, I, 150; Ṭabarī, *Tārīkh*, I, 979 (II, 165); Bayhaqī, *Dalā'il*, I, 83–84, 145–46; Ibn Sayyid al-Nās, *'Uyūn al-athar*, I, 35; Ibn Kathīr, *Bidāya*, II, 275. Cf. Andræ, *Person*, 52–53; Rubin, "Pre-Existence", 87–88.

prophetic *isnād* in which the Prophet is quoted by the Companion 'Utba ibn 'Abd, the beginning of Muḥammad's "affair" (*amr*) is only illustrated by the opening and by the mother's vision of light. In this tradition the opening of the breast is aimed not merely at purification, but at the installation of actual inspiration. The opening is carried out by two birds that look like eagles, and includes the removal of two black blood clots, washing, filling with *sakīna*, sealing with "the seal of prophethood" (*khātam al-nubuwwa*), and weighing.[16] The *sakīna*, according to its Hebrew signification, is the spirit of God, which means that its installation in Muḥammad's breast signals the beginning of his potential prophetic inspiration.

Another tradition, recorded by al-Ṭabarī, is of the Medinan Companion Shaddād ibn Aws (d. AH 58). In it, the opening is again adduced by the Prophet as an illustration of the beginning of his "affair" (*amr*). Muḥammad refers to the prayer of Abraham and to the good tidings of Jesus, as well as to his mother's vision of light. The scene of the opening which follows, is focussed on the motif of light (*nūr*) which symbolizes his prophetic mission. During the opening, his heart is sealed with a seal of light and filled with the "light of prophethood and wisdom".[17]

There are more prophetic traditions of the opening in which it is entirely isolated, i.e. not coupled with any other sign. But the event itself still has a function of annunciation, forecasting Muḥammad's prophetic future. One of these "isolated" versions is that of 'Urwa ibn al-Zubayr (Medinan d. AH 94), as recorded by al-Ṭabarī.[18] The Prophet is asked by the Companion Abū Dharr what the first sign was that made him absolutely sure that he was going to become a prophet. In response, the Prophet tells him the story of the opening of his breast. The event takes place in Mecca, not in the desert. It includes weighing, opening of belly and heart, removal of Satan's share from his heart, washing, filling of his heart with *sakīna*, and sealing of his body with a *khātam*. In another tradition, the Prophet relates the story in response to the inquiry of the Companion Abū Hurayra, who wishes to know when Muḥam-

---

[16] The *isnād*: Khālid ibn Ma'dān←'Abd al-Raḥmān ibn 'Amr ibn 'Abasa al-Sulamī (Syrian d. AH 110)←'Utba ibn 'Abd. See Aḥmad, *Musnad*, IV, 184–85; Bayhaqī, *Dalā'il*, II, 7–8; Ibn Kathīr, *Bidāya*, II, 275–76; *Fatḥ al-bārī*, VI, 409; Suyūṭī, *Khaṣā'iṣ*, I, 159–60; Zurqānī, I, 159. Cf. Ṭabarānī, *Kabīr*, XVII, no. 323 (*isnād* only); also Birkeland, *Opening*, 55–56.

[17] The *isnād*: Thawr ibn Yazīd al-Shāmī (Ḥimṣī d. AH 153)←Makḥūl (Syrian d. AH 112)←Shaddād ibn Aws. See Ṭabarī, *Tārīkh*, I, 974–76 (II, 160–63). Cf. *Fatḥ al-bārī*, VI, 409.

[18] Ṭabarī, *Tārīkh*, I, 1154–55 (II, 304–305). The *isnād*: 'Urwa←Abū Dharr←Prophet. See also Abū Nu'aym, *Dalā'il*, no. 167; Qiwām al-Sunna, *Dalā'il*, I, 248–50 (no. 2); Ibn 'Asākir (*Mukhtaṣar*), II, 89; Ibn Kathīr, *Bidāya*, II, 276; also Birkeland, *Opening*, 15–16.

mad's prophetic "affair" (*amr*) began.[19] The event takes place in the desert, when he is ten or twenty years old. The opening is performed by the angels Gabriel and Michael, who wash his body and remove from his heart hatred and envy, loading it with compassion and mercy instead.

II

In all the versions surveyed thus far, the act of initiation through opening and purification is an element of annunciation which reflects the idea of predestined election. But the same story appears not only in the context of annunciation, but also in that of revelation. In the traditions of this kind, the initiation through opening of the breast is not merely a sign of a relatively remote prophetic future, but rather a prelude to the actual onset of prophetic inspiration. As a preamble of revelation, the opening is an intimate experience of Muḥammad, which, like his prophetic visions, is not witnessed by anyone else. From the chronological point of view, the event is now much later, occurring during the actual beginning of Muḥammad's prophetic mission. The story of the opening has indeed much in common with the theme of revelation. Like the first revelation, the opening revolves round a dramatic, if not traumatic, appearance of angels, so that both events could unite within one narrative sequence.

The traditions with this setting of the opening are equipped with prophetic *isnāds*. A prophetic tradition recorded by al-Ṭayālisī (d. AH 204) sets the opening in the very location of Muḥammad's first Quranic revelation. The tradition has a Baṣran *isnād*, with 'Ā'isha being the Companion,[20] and Muḥammad relates the event in the first person. He and his wife Khadīja are spending the month of Ramaḍān in seclusion on the mountain of Ḥirā'. One day Gabriel and Michael appear, and the latter performs the opening on Muḥammad. This includes cutting of his belly, removing of something unspecified, washing, and sealing with *khātam*. Then Gabriel tells him to recite the opening passage of Sūrat al-'Alaq (96), which is considered the first Quranic passage to be revealed to Muḥammad (*iqra' bi-smi rabbika....*, "Recite in the name of your Lord...."). This is followed by weighing. There is also a tradition of the *sīra* expert 'Abdallāh ibn Abī Bakr (Medinan d. AH 135), whose source is not

---

[19] Abū Nu'aym, *Dalā'il*, no. 166. The *isnād*: Mu'ādh ibn Muḥammad ibn Mu'ādh ibn Muḥammad ibn Ubayy ibn Ka'b←his father←his grandfather←Ubayy ibn Ka'b←Abū Hurayra←Prophet; also Birkeland, *Opening*, 16–17.

[20] The *isnād*: Abū 'Imrān al-Jawnī (Baṣran d. AH 128)←*rajul* (Yazīd ibn Bābanūs [Baṣran])←'Ā'isha. See Ṭayālisī, *Musnad*, no. 1539; also Abū Nu'aym, *Dalā'il*, 215–16 (no. 163); *Fatḥ al-bārī*, VI, 409; Birkeland, *Opening*, 21–23.

stated. In it Muḥammad dreams about the opening, and tells his dream to his wife Khadīja.[21]

A dramatic appearance of an angel, followed by an extraordinary vision, is the subject of another well-known story in Muḥammad's biography which takes place when he is already an active prophet. This is the story of his ascension to heaven. The event is known as the *isrā'*, or "nocturnal journey". This term is based on Quran 17:1, where reference is made to such a journey by the Quranic prophet from "al-Masjid al-Ḥarām" to "al-Masjid al-Aqṣā". The latter location is identified with the well-known mosque in Jerusalem bearing that name. "Al-Masjid al-Ḥarām" is the mosque encompassing the Ka'ba and other nearby sacred sites. Muslim tradition relates that the Prophet was taken in the night from Mecca to Jerusalem and thereafter ascended to heaven, accompanied by Gabriel. His actual ascension is known as the *mi'rāj*. Although the early biographical sources contain traditions in which the *isrā'* is said to have started not in al-Masjid al-Ḥarām, but elsewhere in Mecca,[22] the most prevalent view has become the Quranic one, namely, that when the journey started, the Prophet was in the vicinity of the Ka'ba, i.e. within al-Masjid al-Ḥarām.

The *isrā'–mi'rāj* is in itself not only a magnificent event of revelation, but also one of confirmation. During his journey through the seven heavens, Muḥammad meets the prophets one by one. They all know that he was due to be sent as a prophet, and all of them bless him, thus confirming his prophetic assignment. The ascension is therefore an event in which the initiation of the Prophet is completed. Hence, it is quite easy to see how the story of the opening—itself an act of initiation—could become a part of the story of confirmation, being made a prelude to the *isrā'–mi'rāj*. But it is equally clear that the combination between the opening and this particular story is secondary.[23] The earliest versions of the story of the *isrā'*, as recorded by Ibn Isḥāq, for example, are not yet connected in any way to the opening.[24] The link between the opening and the *isrā'–mi'rāj* forms another step towards adapting the former scene to genuine Islamic models having firm Quranic links, and thus turning it into an acceptable component of the story of Muḥammad's life.

One of the traditions in which the opening already appears as a prelude to the ascension was recorded by al-Ṭabarī. It is of the Baṣran Companion Anas ibn

---

[21] See Ibn Sayyid al-Nās, *'Uyūn al-athar*, I, 82–83. See also *Fatḥ al-bārī*, XIII, 400 (from Abū Bishr al-Dawlābī). Cf. Birkeland, *Opening*, 23.

[22] From the house of Umm Hāni', daughter of Abū Ṭālib: Ibn Hishām, II, 43; Bayhaqī, *Dalā'il*, II, 373–74. From the Shi'b of Abū Ṭālib: Ibn Sa'd, I, 214.

[23] Thus also Birkeland, *Opening*, 13–15, 26 (against Bevan, Schrieke, and Horovitz).

[24] See Ibn Hishām, II, 36–50.

Mālik (d. AH 91–95), who is quoted by the Baṣran Successor Maymūn ibn Siyāh.[25] Anas tells the story in the third person, not as a verbatim first-person quotation of the Prophet:

> When Muḥammad was sent as a prophet, the angels Gabriel and Michael came to him while he was asleep near the Ka'ba. It was the custom of Quraysh to sleep there (in order to have true dreams—U.R.). Then they went away, and soon three angels returned and cut his belly open. They fetched water from the well of Zamzam and washed his inner parts and cleansed him thereby of whatever was there of doubt (*shakk*), or idolatry (*shirk*), or ignorance (*jāhiliyya*), or error (*ḍalāla*). Then they filled his belly with faith and wisdom (*īmānan wa-ḥikmatan*), and then ascended to heaven with him....

In this tradition the process of the opening is described in most specific terms, which turns the initiation into an act of dogmatic guidance. This accords with the particular context of the story—the beginning of actual preaching. At this advanced stage, Muḥammad is in need of the specific contents of his prophetic message, which cannot be delivered to him without shifting his heart from idolatry to monotheism. As for the physical setting, the most noteworthy specific new detail is the mention of the well of Zamzam as the specific source of the water with which he is cleansed. Zamzam is a sacred well within al-Masjid al-Ḥarām in Mecca, located a few meters away from the Ka'ba. Its appearance in the story provides the necessary link to the location of the ascension.[26] It should be added that the history of Zamzam is associated in the Islamic tradition with the image of Gabriel, who is said to have originated the well for Hagar and her son Ishmael when they were wandering in the wilderness of Mecca.[27] It is therefore only natural that the water Gabriel uses to cleanse Muḥammad should come from that very well. This is a development in the inner contents of the story of the opening, which in turn facilitated its linking to the story of the ascension.

[25] The *isnād*: 'Anbasa ibn Sa'īd ibn al-Ḍurays al-Asadī←Abū Hāshim al-Wāsiṭī←Maymūn ibn Siyāh←Anas. See Ṭabarī, *Tārīkh*, I, 1158–59 (II, 307–308). See also *idem*, *Tahdhīb* (Ibn 'Abbās), I, no. 720. Cf. Birkeland, *Opening*, 14. His claim that this was originally a tradition about Muḥammad's first revelation is not convincing.

[26] See also Birkeland, *Opening*, 34.

[27] E.g. Ibn Hishām, I, 116; Fākihī, II, 5–11. And see G.R. Hawting, "The Disappearance and Rediscovery of Zamzam and the 'Well of the Ka'ba' ", *Bulletin of the School of Oriental and African Studies* 43 (1980), 44–54.

III

None of the hitherto mentioned versions of the opening of Muḥammad's breast gained wide circulation in the *muṣannaf* compilations; in the Six Books they are not quoted at all. Only some of them appear in the less authoritative compilations. One of the above Syrian prophetic versions was recorded by al-Dārimī and by al-Ḥākim.[28] The latter states that the *isnād* of the tradition is "sound". Al-Dārimī too recorded the prophetic tradition of 'Urwa, but he only adduced the first part (weighing), discarding the actual opening and purification.[29]

The rearranged compilation of Ibn Ḥibbān is the only *muṣannaf* book to contain the story of Ḥalīma as transmitted by Ibn Isḥāq. But in his version, unlike the above-mentioned one of Ibn Bukayr, the removal of the evil spot from Muḥammad's body is not mentioned. Instead, the boy tells his worried wet-nurse that he does not know what the two people in white have done to him (*lā adrī mā ṣana'ā*).[30] This alteration seems significant, for it reflects a progressive change in the perception of the *'iṣma* of the Prophet. Whereas in the early traditions seen above the *'iṣma* is established by the removal of Satan's share from his soul, now there is nothing to remove, because the *'iṣma* is total and absolute: Muḥammad's soul never contained any evil parts.

In fact, the version of Ibn Ḥibbān is not the only one in which the removal of the evil spot was suppressed. The same took place in some of the biographical sources themselves. In the recension of Ibn Hishām of the *Sīra* of Ibn Isḥāq, Ḥalīma's version has nothing concerning an evil spot: Muḥammad only says that the men searched his internal parts, and that he did not know what they were looking for.[31]

But other versions of the story do appear in the *muṣannaf* compilations, even in the most authoritative ones. In all of them the opening is a prelude to the *isrā'–mi'rāj*. They were selected by the *muṣannaf* authors, who had a special interest not so much in the opening itself as in the ascension. This event was considered by them as tremendously important, because during the ascension the most basic religious duty—daily prayer—was prescribed. The compilers

---

[28] The tradition is of Khālid ibn Ma'dān←'Abd al-Raḥmān ibn 'Amr ibn 'Abasa al-Sulamī←'Utba ibn 'Abd. See Dārimī, I, 20 (no. 13); *Mustadrak*, II, 616–17 (*Tārīkh*).

[29] Dārimī, I, 21 (no. 14). Full version in other *muṣannaf* compilations: *Kashf al-astār*, III, no. 2371; *Majma' al-zawā'id*, VIII, 258–59.

[30] Ibn Ḥibbān, *Ṣaḥīḥ*, XIV, no. 6335. See also Abū Ya'lā, XIII, no. 7163; Abū Nu'aym, *Dalā'il*, no. 94; Ṭabarānī, *Kabīr*, XXIV, no. 545.

[31] Ibn Hishām, I, 173–74. See also Ṭabarī, *Tārīkh*, I, 972 (II, 160); Ibn Kathīr, *Bidāya*, II, 275; Ibn Sayyid al-Nās, *'Uyūn al-athar*, I, 34. Birkeland (*Opening*, 6–8), not being aware of Ibn Bukayr, takes Ibn Hishām's version to be the earliest. He defines it as a version of "investigation".

recorded the traditions in which the opening precedes the ascension, alongside traditions without the opening. Hardly any versions with the opening allude to an act of removing something evil from Muḥammad's body or heart, thus leaving unblemished the concept of total *'iṣma*. They only retain the loading of the actual components of monotheistic creed (*īmān*) and wisdom (*ḥikma*). Like the above tradition of al-Ṭabarī, all the traditions are traced back to the Companion Anas ibn Mālik. In most of them, Anas tells the tale about the Prophet indirectly, i.e. in the third person.

To begin with, al-Bukhārī recorded a tradition which has the *isnād*: Sharīk ibn 'Abdallāh ibn Abī Namir (Medinan d. AH 144)←Anas. Al-Bukhārī included it in the "book" of *Tawḥīd* ("[God's] Unity"),[32] with an abridged version recurring in a chapter about the nature of Muḥammad's sleep.[33] The tradition says that three people had come to Muḥammad before he began receiving revelations (*qabla an yūḥā ilayhi*); he was sleeping in the Masjid. They went away and reappeared another night, when he was sleeping there as before. Only his eyes were asleep, but his heart was awake; this was the way prophets used to sleep. They carried him to the well of Zamzam, where they handed him over to Gabriel. The latter cut his body open and washed his inner parts, filled his breast with faith and wisdom (*īmānan wa-ḥikmatan*), and ascended to heaven with him.

The clause *qabla an yūḥā ilayhi* preserves traces of the story of the opening as a prelude to the first revelation. However, since the ascension itself is usually dated to the time when Muḥammad was already acting as a prophet, Muslim scholars could not but treat this clause as an error of one of the transmitters.[34] In all other versions, such dating of the story is no longer repeated.

The chapter about the *isrā'* in the *Ṣaḥīḥ* of Muslim contains several traditions with the opening. One of them, however, has no direct allusion to the *isrā'*. It has the Baṣran *isnād*: Thābit al-Bunānī (d. AH 123)←Anas, with Thābit being quoted by Ḥammād ibn Salama (Baṣran d. AH 167). The tradition relates that Gabriel came to Muḥammad when he was playing with the other boys. The angel cut his heart open, removed a black spot, and said: "This is Satan's part in you." Then he washed him with water from the well of Zamzam and replaced his heart in his breast. The other boys who witnessed the event hurried to his

[32] Bukhārī, *Ṣaḥīḥ*, IX, 182 (97:37). See also Abū 'Awāna, I, 125–26. Cf. Muslim, I, 102.

[33] Bukhārī, *Ṣaḥīḥ*, IV, 232 (61:24).

[34] E.g. *Fatḥ al-bārī*, XIII, 399. For this reason the clause *qabla an yūḥā ilayhi* was omitted from the text of the same tradition of Sharīk←Anas as recorded in Fākihī, II, 26–27 (no. 1075). It is preserved, however, in Ṭabarī, *Tahdhīb* (Ibn 'Abbās), I, no. 719. And cf. Birkeland, *Opening*, 18–21. His assumption (p. 20) that the clause is a secondary addition (!) is inconceivable.

mother—that is, to his wet-nurse—and told her about it. She and her husband came to the boy and found him standing, his face white with terror.[35] It is quite surprising to find such a tradition in the compilation of Muslim. Here, the event is still dated to Muḥammad's childhood, long before the ascension, and something evil is still being removed from his body. Muslim seems to have included it in the chapter about the *isrāʾ* only because of the reference to Zamzam, which provides the link to the ascension, and also because other versions with the same *isnād* do allude to the *isrāʾ*. (This very tradition may be found in some other less authoritative *muṣannaf* compilations,[36] as well as in biographical sources.[37])

Indeed, Muslim himself recorded another version of the Bunānī←Anas group, where the event is no longer dated to Muḥammad's childhood. It was circulated on the authority of al-Bunānī by Sulaymān ibn al-Mughīra (Baṣran d. AH 165), and is a proper prophetic *ḥadīth* in which the Prophet tells his own tale in the first person. Unfortunately, however, only the beginning of the tradition appears in the available text of Muslim.[38] Explicit allusion to Muḥammad's ascension is only made in the complete text of the same version as recorded by al-Bayhaqī.[39] The Prophet is taken away from his family and is brought to the well of Zamzam, where he is washed with its water. Then a golden basin is being brought to him,[40] and his heart is filled with faith and wisdom (*īmān wa-ḥikma*), then he is taken up to the first heaven.

It is noteworthy that the verb indicating the opening is not *shaqqa*, as is the case in the former versions, but rather *sharaḥa*; the object of the opening is not the "belly" or the "heart", but rather the "breast" (*fa-shuriḥa ṣadrī*). This particular version was evidently subjected to Quranic models. Quran 94:1 speaks about an act of *sharḥ ṣadr* experienced by the Quranic prophet, and the application of this verse to the story of the opening of the breast illustrates the tendency

[35] Muslim, I, 101–102 (1, *Bāb al-isrāʾ*).

[36] Abū ʿAwāna, I, 125 (*Mabʿath*); Ibn Abī Shayba, XIV, no. 18406 (*Maghāzī*); Ibn Ḥibbān, *Ṣaḥīḥ*, XIV, nos. 6334, 6336.

[37] Ibn Saʿd, I, 150–51; Fākihī, II, 25–26 (no. 1073); Bayhaqī, *Dalāʾil*, I, 146–47; II, 5; Abū Nuʿaym, *Dalāʾil*, no. 168. See also Abū Yaʿlā, VI, nos. 3374, 3507; Aḥmad, *Musnad*, III, 121, 149, 288; Qiwām al-Sunna, *Dalāʾil*, I, 251–53 (no. 3); Ibn Kathīr, *Bidāya*, II, 276.

[38] Muslim, I, 101.

[39] Bayhaqī, *Dalāʾil*, I, 147. See also Dhahabī, *Sīra*, 22.

[40] *thumma utītu bi-ṭastin min dhahab*. Muslim's version is corrupt and incomplete. Instead of the correct *utītu*, it has: *unziltu*, with which this version concludes. This has led Birkeland (*Opening*, 24–25), who was unaware of the complete and correct version, to the wrong assumption that the tradition refers to the first revelation.

of Muslim tradition to dress the life of the Prophet in Quranic cloths, thus conferring more authoritative status on it.[41]

Yet another version of the Bunānī←Anas group was circulated by 'Abd Rabbihi ibn Sa'īd (Medinan d. AH 139). It is recorded in al-Nasā'ī's *Sunan*, and is related in the third person.[42] Two angels, so it says, came to Muḥammad and took him to Zamzam, cut his belly open, cleansed his inner parts with its water, then filled him with wisdom and knowledge (*ḥikmatan wa-'ilman*). No explicit mention of the ascension is made, but the story is preceded by the statement that prayer was prescribed in Mecca. This is an allusion to the ensuing events of the ascension.

A tradition with similar details (opening—washing with water of Zamzam—filling with wisdom and faith—ascension) appears in al-Bukhārī's *Ṣaḥīḥ* in the chapter dealing with the prescription of prayer. The tradition has the *isnād*: al-Zuhrī (Medinan d. AH 124)←Anas←Abū Dharr, and is a prophetic *ḥadīth* related by Muḥammad in the first person. Al-Bukhārī also recorded it in the chapter about Zamzam in the "book" of Pilgrimage (*Ḥajj*), and in the "book" about the previous prophets. It reappears in Muslim and in Abū 'Awāna.[43] The act of opening is indicated here with the verb *faraja*. The tradition recurs outside the *muṣannaf* compilations,[44] and is also available with a slightly shortened *isnād*, without Abū Dharr.[45] In another variant, Abū Dharr is replaced by the Medinan Companion Ubayy ibn Ka'b.[46]

The most prevalent group of traditions in the *muṣannaf* compilations has the *isnād*: Qatāda (Baṣran d. AH 117)←Anas←Mālik ibn Ṣa'ṣa'a. The tale is a prophetic *ḥadīth* related in the first person. The version circulated on the authority of Qatāda by Hishām al-Dustuwā'ī (Baṣran d. AH 152) has the following familiar sequence of events: opening, washing with Zamzam water, filling with wisdom and persuasion, and ascension.[47] In another version with the same

---

41 And see Birkeland, *Opening*, 40–47.

42 Nasā'ī, *Kubrā*, I, 141 (no. 316 [2:2]). Cf. Ṭabarānī, *Kabīr*, I, no. 744; Ibn 'Asākir (*Mukhtaṣar*), II, 83; Ibn Kathīr, *Bidāya*, II, 276 (Ibn 'Asākir).

43 Bukhārī, *Ṣaḥīḥ*, I, 97 (8:1); II, 191 (25:76); IV, 164–65 (60:5); Muslim, I, 102; Abū 'Awāna, I, 133, 135. See also Birkeland, *Opening*, 18.

44 Abū Ya'lā, VI, no. 3616; Fākihī, II, 24 (no. 1071); Bayhaqī, *Dalā'il*, II, 379.

45 The *isnād*: Yūnus ibn Yazīd (Egyptian d. AH 159)←Zuhrī←Anas. See Fākihī, II, 26 (no. 1074).

46 The *isnād*: Yūnus ibn Yazīd←Zuhrī←Anas←Ubayy. See Abū Ya'lā, VI, no. 3614; Aḥmad, *Musnad*, V, 122, 143. In the two latter versions the ascension is not included, just the opening. For the complete version see Ibn Kathīr, *Tafsīr*, III, 10.

47 Bukhārī, *Ṣaḥīḥ*, IV, 133 (59:6); Nasā'ī, *Kubrā*, I, 138 (no. 313 [2:1]); Abū 'Awāna, I, 120–121. Cf. Muslim, I, 105. Outside the *muṣannaf* compilations this version is recorded in Ṭabarī, *Tahdhīb* (Ibn 'Abbās), I, no. 721; Aḥmad, *Musnad*, IV, 207; Ṭabarānī, *Kabīr*, XIX, no. 599.

Qatāda *isnād*, circulated by Hammām ibn Yaḥyā (Baṣran d. AH 163), the name of Zamzam does not occur, for some obscure reason.[48] More significant, however, is another version of the Qatāda group which was circulated on his authority by Sa'īd ibn Abī 'Arūba (Baṣran d. AH 156).[49] Here the well of Zamzam reappears, and the wording of Quran 94:1 is again employed. The act of opening is referred to as *sharḥ ṣadr*.

There are other traditions where the act of opening, signified again as *sharḥ*, occurs in contexts other than that of the ascension. Yūnus ibn Bukayr has a Kūfan prophetic tradition with such usage, which is recorded in the chapter about Muḥammad's childhood. In it two angels looking like cranes perform on him an act of *sharḥ ṣadr*. The *isnād* is *mursal*, lacking a Companion, and the Prophet is quoted by the Successor Yaḥyā ibn Ja'da al-Qurashī.[50] The vocabulary of 94:1, as well as 94:2, was also incorporated into a tradition preserved in the *Sīra* of Sulaymān al-Taymī (d. AH 143), in which the opening takes place during the first revelation of Muḥammad. Before posing to him the demand to recite (*iqra'*), Gabriel says: *allāhumma, uḥṭuṭ wizrahu wa-shraḥ ṣadrahu wa-ṭahhir qalbahu....*, "Oh God, remove his burden and expand his breast and purify his heart...."[51]

IV

We have just seen how the vocabulary of Quran 94:1 was used in some versions of the story of the opening. Once linked to this event, the Quranic verse acquired a specific interpretation (not necessarily the original) which was preserved and later used by the Quran exegetes when they began to assemble the "occasions of revelation" (*asbāb al-nuzūl*) of the various Quranic verses. Thus a textual link which originated in a literary process within the realm of *sīra* became *tafsīr*. Indeed, several of the above versions of the opening—even those without direct allusion to 94:1—reappear in the exegesis of this verse in various

[48] Bukhārī, *Ṣaḥīḥ*, V, 66–67 (63:42); Ibn Ḥibbān, *Ṣaḥīḥ*, I, no. 48. See also Aḥmad, *Musnad*, IV, 208; Bayhaqī, *Dalā'il*, II, 377–78.

[49] See Muslim, I, 103–104; Ibn Khuzayma, I, 153 (no. 301); Abū 'Awāna, I, 116–17. See also Fākihī, II, 25 (no. 1072); Bayhaqī, *Dalā'il*, II, 373–74; Qiwām al-Sunna, *Dalā'il*, I, 257, no. 5.

[50] The *isnād*: Abū Sinān al-Shaybānī (Kūfan)←Ḥabīb ibn Abī Thābit (Kūfan d. AH 119)←Yaḥyā ibn Ja'da←Prophet. See Ibn Bukayr, 51; also Bayhaqī, *Dalā'il*, I, 146; Suhaylī, *Rawḍ*, I, 188 (*shaqq*).

[51] See Ibn 'Asākir (*Mukhtaṣar*), XXVI, 278; Ibn Kathīr, *Bidāya*, III, 14 (from Ibn 'Asākir, who quotes Sulaymān al-Taymī).

tafsīr compilations, beginning with Huwwārī (third century AH).[52] Since, in some of these versions, the opening precedes the *isrā'*, it is not surprising to find the same versions recorded in the *tafsīr* of the Quranic *isrā'* verse (17:1).[53] Here[54] there is one more Baṣran version in which the act of opening (performed by Michael and Gabriel using Zamzam water) is again referred to as *sharḥ ṣadr*. Unlike all previous versions where the ascension is preceded by the opening, this one is not attributed to Anas, but rather to the Companion Abū Hurayra.[55]

V

Finally, it is noteworthy that a scene of breast opening, although an abortive one, is included in the story of the life of another Arab hero, namely, Umayya ibn Abī l-Ṣalt, an eminent poet from the tribe of Thaqīf. The traditions about him also revolve round the idea of election. He is presented as a god-fearing monotheist, a *ḥanīf* who adhered to the religion of Abraham. He knew from the holy scriptures he had read that a prophet was about to be sent among the Arabs. He wished to be elected as that prophet, and almost was, but Muḥammad finally became the Arabian prophet instead of him. He therefore envied Muḥammad for the rest of his life, and never embraced Islam.[56] The explicit aim of the traditions is to relate the virtues of this person through the story about how he was almost elected as the Arabian prophet. Implicit in the tale is the unique virtue of Muḥammad, the only Arab to be initiated into the prophetic office.

Like Muḥammad whom, when still a boy, wise men examine and recognize as the future prophet, Umayya is also put to the test by Christian hermits who anticipate the emergence of the Arabian prophet. In one of the stories,[57] Umayya sets out on a journey and comes across a church, where he meets an

---

[52] See Huwwārī, IV, 515. And see also Naḥḥās, *I'rāb*, V, 251; Ibn 'Aṭiyya, XVI, 325; Rāzī, XXXII, 2; Qurṭubī, XX, 104–105; Ibn Kathīr, *Tafsīr*, IV, 524; Suyūṭī, *Durr*, VI, 363. See also the sections of *Tafsīr* in Tirmidhī/*Tuḥfa*, IX, 273–75 (no. 3404); *Mustadrak*, II, 528.

[53] See e.g. Huwwārī, II, 397, 400; Ṭabarī, *Tafsīr*, XV, 3–6.

[54] Ṭabarī, *Tafsīr*, XV, 6 (nos. 8, 9. The numbering of the traditions is my own); Ibn Kathīr, *Tafsīr*, III, 17.

[55] The *isnād*: al-Rabī' ibn Anas al-Bakrī (Baṣran d. AH 139)←Abū l-'Āliya al-Riyāḥī (Baṣran d. AH 90)←Abū Hurayra.

[56] See e.g. *Aghānī*, III, 187–88; Bayhaqī, *Dalā'il*, II, 116–17. See also Uri Rubin, "*Ḥanīfiyya* and Ka'ba: An Inquiry into the Arabian Pre-Islamic Background of *Dīn Ibrāhīm*", *Jerusalem Studies in Arabic and Islam* 13 (1990), 94–96.

[57] *Aghānī*, III, 188.

old man who says to him: "Surely you are accompanied [by a hidden companion]." Umayya confirms the observation, and then the hermit asks about the companion and about his own habits. Upon hearing the details, he tells Umayya that he might be the future prophet of the Arabs, but the signs indicate that he is not. His companion is a demon and not an angel, and the rest of his behaviour is also different from that of the real prophet.

The stories about Umayya form an entire mythology culminating in the opening of his breast, which is supposed to signify his election and initiation. But the opening must of course fail, because it is Muḥammad who was elected as the prophet of the Arabs. The traditions about the opening of Umayya's breast have already been touched upon by some Islamicists, but they seem to have misunderstood them, taking the opening as an efficacious operation during which the poetic inspiration was installed in his heart.[58] Such interpretation of the story is not borne out by the actual texts. When the event takes place, Umayya is already a poet. The event is borrowed from the life of Muḥammad and functions as an attempted initiation into something greater then poetry, i.e. prophethood.

In all versions of the story, the opening of Umayya's breast is performed by two birds. This does not seem to be an archaic element, as held by some,[59] but rather a deliberate device intended to diminish the degree of sacredness of the event as compared with that of Muḥammad, where genuine angels are usually involved.

One of the versions was transmitted by al-Zuhrī (Medinan d. AH 124), himself an expert on Muḥammad's biography. In his story, the opening takes place at the house of Umayya's sister, who is also the one who tells the story. Umayya visited her one day, and fell asleep on a bed in her house. Suddenly the roof was split open, and two birds appeared. One descended on Umayya's breast, the other remained hovering above. The former cut his breast open, pulled out his heart, and cut it. The bird hovering above said to the other: "Has he perceived (*a-wa'ā*)?" The other answered: "Yes." Then the first one said: "Has he accepted (*a-qabila*)?" The other answered: "He refused." Then the lower bird put the heart back into its place and ascended. Umayya followed the two departing birds with his eyes and called them back, uttering some verses in which he stated his obedience to them (*Labbaykumā! Labbaykumā*!....[60]). So they returned, and the opening was performed once more. But again Umayya

[58] See Andræ, *Person*, 53; Horovitz, "Himmelfahrt", 171–73; Birkeland, *Opening*, 8.

[59] E.g. Birkeland, *Opening*, 8, 57.

[60] The same verses recur in the story of his last illness. See *Aghānī*, III, 191–92; Mas'ūdī, *Murūj*, I, 71.

"perceived" but failed to "accept", therefore the birds turned away and the poet called them back once more with the same verses. The opening was performed for the third time, but again, to no avail, because Umayya kept on refusing to "accept". He called them back again, but the birds disappeared and the roof was closed. Umayya woke up stroking his chest. His sister asked if he was in any pain, and he said that he only felt some warmth across his breast.[61]

The scene of the opening of Umayya's breast was also related by al-Zubayr ibn Bakkār (Medinan d. AH 256):[62] Umayya is asleep, two birds arrive, one remains at the door, and the other cuts his heart open, but immediately returns it to its place. The bird at the door asks: "Has he perceived?" The other bird answers: "Yes." The bird at the door: "Has he become righteous (*zakā*[63])?" The other bird: "No."[64]

The same story is related in other versions to Muḥammad himself. This is done by Umayya's sister, Fāri'a, an eyewitness to the event. In a tradition of Ibn Isḥāq from al-Zuhrī, Fāri'a comes to Muḥammad after the conquest of Mecca. The Prophet, attracted by her beauty and wits, asks her to recite some of her late brother's verses, but she offers to tell him something more wonderful. Then she relates the story of the opening of Umayya's breast. An additional significant detail appears at the end of her story. As Umayya wakes up, he sees his sister in a terrified disposition. He asks her what the matter is, and she tells him what has just been done to him by the two birds. Umayya himself feels no pain, and soothes his alarmed sister, saying: "Something good was intended for me, but then was diverted from me." Then follows the story of Umayya's last illness and death. Upon hearing the story of Fāri'a, Muḥammad says to her: "Your brother is like him to whom God brought His signs, but then he cast them off."[65] In this version allusion is made to Quran 7:175. Already 'Abd al-Razzāq (d. AH 211) has included in his commentary on this verse the story of

[61] The *isnād*: 'Abd al-'Azīz ibn 'Imrān (Medinan d. AH 197)←'Abd al-Raḥmān ibn 'Abdallāh ibn 'Āmir ibn Mas'ūd←al-Zuhrī. See *Aghānī*, III, 189–90; also Ibn Ḥajar, *Iṣāba*, I, 252 (Ibn Shabba).

[62] The *isnād*: al- Zubayr←'Amr ibn Abī Bakr al-Mawṣilī←an anonymous Kūfan.

[63] The verb *zakā*, "to be righteous", occurs in the Quran (24:21), where it is interpreted as denoting acceptance of Islam. See e.g. Ṭabarī, *Tafsīr*, XVIII, 80–81.

[64] *Aghānī*, III, 188–89.

[65] Ibn Kathīr, *Bidāya*, II, 224–26. The *isnād*: Ibn Isḥāq←Zuhrī←Sa'īd ibn al-Musayyab (Medinan d. AH 94). See also Ibn 'Abd al-Barr, *Istī'āb*, IV, 1889–90 (abridged). Cf. Baghawī, *Ma'ālim*, II, 571, where the scene takes place during Umayya's last illness. Short references to the sister's story may also be found in Ibn Ḥajar, *Iṣāba*, VIII, 51.

the opening of Umayya's breast. The tradition he selected is of al-Kalbī (Muḥammad ibn al-Sā'ib, Kūfan d. AH 146).[66]

In conclusion, the stories about Umayya demonstrate the universality of some hagiographic models of election and initiation which may wander from the biography of one hero to that of another. But in the case of Umayya, the events are bound to result in failure, because it is Muḥammad who was elected for the divine prophetic office.

[66] See 'Abd al-Razzāq, *Tafsīr*, I, 243. See also Ibn Kathīr, *Bidāya*, II, 224. For the tradition of al-Kalbī, see also Fākihī, III, nos. 1970–71.

4

Guidance

From Polytheism to Monotheism

THE PREPARATION OF THE PROPHET is not confined to initiation through physical purification. It also consists of spiritual purification through religious guidance. This issue has already been encountered in some stories of his physical purification, and in the present chapter further traditions about his dogmatic guidance will be reviewed. In all of them this is an independent subject, not just an ingredient in another story. These traditions deal with the pre-prophetic period of the life of the Prophet, when he is presented as still adhering to the religion (*dīn*) of his own tribe. The traditions are aimed at showing how during this stage of his life, he was already led away from the local pagan practices which he used to observe.

Some aspects of these traditions have already been treated by various Islamicists. They have noticed in particular that Muḥammad is said to have been a pagan once, and have concluded that here an "historical" kernel has been preserved. Tor Andræ, for example,[1] concluded from these traditions that early Islam preserved the Quranic "human" image of the Prophet, which means that for Andræ these traditions are untouched by any tendentious elaboration. It seems, however, that all the available traditions in which allusion is made to Muḥammad's pre-prophetic paganism are in themselves "tendentious". All of them tell the story of guidance, a theme preserving an early form of the concept of the Prophet's *'iṣma*, i.e. his protection from sin and error. In themselves these stories bear nothing unique compared to other prophets who are said to have been guided to the right path. The Muslims spread them in accordance with their wish to provide Muḥammad with an appropriate sacred biography, like that of other prophets. The following observations will reveal, however, some problems within the inner Islamic context which denied most of these stories wide circulation. This was due to the fact that the outlook of Muḥammad's *'iṣma,* which established itself in the mainstream of Islamic thinking, was focussed not on the theme of guidance, but rather on that of total

[1] Andræ, *Person*, 132.

immunity to sin and error, lasting since the first moment of his existence and pre-existence till the Day of Resurrection.[2]

I

The universal theme of guidance was adapted in Muslim tradition to the local Arabian pre-Islamic surroundings in which the Meccan prophet spent his early years. In some of these traditions, religious guidance is administered to the Prophet through human agents. In one case it is the same person whom we have already met as a source of annunciation for one of the would-be Companions. This is the *ḥanīf* Zayd ibn ʻAmr ibn Nufayl, who in the present context meets Muḥammad in person and communicates his knowledge directly to him, and whose role of annunciation is thus broadened to include guidance as well. He is said to have taught the young Muḥammad that sacrificing to idols was wrong, and that these idols were impotent.

The traditions about Zayd's meeting with Muḥammad have already attracted the attention of quite a few Islamicists, but all of them have been concerned with its supposed historical aspects, concentrating on the pagan state of mind which these traditions attributed to Muḥammad.[3] Arthur Jeffery, for example, maintains that these traditions, as well as others of a similar gist which he mentions, are the ones farthest removed from the "idealizing tendency", and therefore are "*a priori* the most likely to be genuine".[4] Guillaume and Kister speak about the "original form" of the story, which seems to imply that they too consider it as altogether free of any tendentious elaboration.[5] But the traditions about Zayd ibn ʻAmr do have a certain "tendency" in them, in that they all relate the story of guidance.

The story of Zayd in his capacity as Muḥammad's religious mentor is extant in several versions. In all of them his meeting with Muḥammad is attended by a third party, Muḥammad's adopted son, Zayd ibn Ḥāritha. Let us begin with the versions of the *muṣannaf* compilations. The most significant is the one recorded by al-Ḥākim in the section devoted to the Companions, in the chapter about the virtues (*manāqib*) of Zayd ibn Ḥāritha. The same tradition, related by

---

[2] For the eternal dimensions of Muḥammad's *ʻiṣma*, see Rubin, "Pre-Existence", 74–79, 103–104.

[3] See e.g. Arthur Jeffery, "Was Muhammad a Prophet from his Infancy?", *The Muslim World* 20 (1930), 232–33; Guillaume, "New Light", 27–28. A detailed survey of the various versions may be found in M.J. Kister, "A Bag of Meat", *Bulletin of the School of Oriental and African Studies* 33 (1970), 267–75.

[4] Jeffery, "Was Muhammad", 228.

[5] Guillaume, "New Light", 7; Kister, "A Bag of Meat", 275.

Zayd ibn Ḥāritha in the first person, reappears in sources outside the *muṣannaf* compilations, some of which are earlier than al-Ḥākim's *Mustadrak.*[6] According to the attached *isnād*, his story was transmitted from him by Medinan authorities, beginning with Zayd's own son, Usāma.[7] Zayd relates that he and Muḥammad sacrificed an animal on one of the sacred stones (*nuṣub*, pl. *anṣāb*) in Mecca. They roasted it and then put it in their bag and took it along with them. On their way they met Zayd ibn ʻAmr. They saluted each other with the traditional pre-Islamic greeting. The Prophet asked the *ḥanīf* why Quraysh held grudges against him, and Zayd replied that this was because he desecrated their religion. He added that he had set out in quest of the true religion, and visited various places in Arabia and Syria. An old wise man in the Jazīra had told him that the true religion he sought was about to emerge in Arabia, and that its prophet was bound to appear soon. Following the advice of the old man, Zayd returned to Arabia expecting to meet the prophet when he appeared, but as yet nothing had happened. After hearing Zayd's story, the Prophet summoned him to partake of the meat he had with him. Zayd asked what it was, and Muḥammad said: "It is an ewe which we have sacrificed on one of the sacred stones." Zayd said that he did not eat of meat sacrificed to a deity other than God. After the encounter with Zayd ibn ʻAmr, Muḥammad and Zayd ibn Ḥāritha came to the statues of the idols Isāf and Nā'ila (near the Kaʻba). The people used to stroke them during circumambulation (*ṭawāf*) around the Kaʻba, but Muḥammad forbade Zayd to touch them. From then on, so Zayd relates, he never touched them again till the beginning of Muḥammad's prophethood.

In this story, the usual theme of annunciation is combined with that of guidance. The former has no particular results, but the latter does, in that it causes the Companion Zayd ibn Ḥāritha to abandon paganism. The effect on Muḥammad, although not stated explicitly, is the same.

It seems that al-Ḥākim was unaware of the purport of the story he recorded. The tradition is followed in his *Mustadrak* by a remark to the effect that it is "sound" according to the principles of Muslim; but neither he nor al-Bukhārī recorded it. Al-Ḥākim also says that the virtue of Zayd ibn Ḥāritha is clear in this tradition, because it is stated that he abandoned idolatry already before the beginning of Muḥammad's prophethood. Al-Ḥākim says nothing about Muḥammad's own guidance, which is the main topic of the story. Perhaps he ignored it intentionally because like any other Muslim scholar of his time he be-

---

[6] See Abū Yaʻlā, XIII, no. 7212; Ṭabarānī, *Kabīr*, V, no. 4663; *Kashf al-astār*, III, no. 2755; Bayhaqī, *Dalā'il*, II, 124–26; Khargūshī (MS Br. Lib.), fol. 27b–28a.

[7] The *isnād*: Muḥammad ibn ʻAmr ibn ʻAlqama (Medinan d. AH 144)←Abū Salama ibn ʻAbd al-Raḥmān ibn ʻAwf (Medinan d. AH 94) and Yaḥyā ibn ʻAbd al-Raḥmān ibn Ḥāṭib (Medinan d. AH 104)←Usāma ibn Zayd←Zayd ibn Ḥāritha.

lieved that Muḥammad needed no guidance, being immune from sin and error from the first moment of his existence. This outlook represents, in fact, the dogma of the *'iṣma* in its most rigid manifestation, when no longer standing for guidance, but rather for total immunity. This is the reason why other compilers of *muṣannaf* collections ignored it altogether.

The descendants of the *ḥanīf* Zayd ibn 'Amr took much pride in the story about their monotheistic ancestor, notwithstanding the role of the Prophet in it. They, and especially his son Sa'īd, became notable Muslims, Sa'īd being one of the first Meccans to embrace Islam. It is therefore only natural to find that Zayd's descendants appear in the *isnād* of another similar tradition about his guidance of the young Muḥammad. This tradition appears in various sources outside the *muṣannaf* compilations, but in none of the latter.[8]

But the story was most popular among the Muslims when the dogma of the *'iṣma* was not yet so rigid. At that stage no fault could yet be found with a story telling how Muḥammad stopped sacrificing to the idols. Such a story conveyed the idea of the Prophet's *'iṣma* in its milder manifestation, when still focussed on guidance, not on total immunity. The original popularity of the tradition is indicated by the fact that it was recorded by Muḥammad's earliest biographers. All the versions recorded by them are prophetic, i.e. quoted from the Prophet himself; this indicates that the story was given the most authoritative tool of circulation, an *isnād* reaching back to the Prophet himself. The *Sīra* of Ibn Isḥāq (d. AH 150) has it in the recension of Yūnus ibn Bukayr, where the Prophet tells the story in the first person. Unfortunately, the full *isnād* is not given.[9] Mūsā ibn 'Uqba (d. AH 141), another of the Medinan *sīra* authors, transmitted the story with the *isnād*: Sālim ibn 'Abdallāh ibn 'Umar (Medinan d. AH 105)←Ibn 'Umar←Prophet. The story is quoted from the Prophet in the third person.[10] There is also a version of 'Urwa ibn al-Zubayr (Medinan d. AH 94), on the authority of 'Ā'isha. Here again the Prophet speaks in the first person.[11]

---

[8] The *isnād*: Nufayl ibn Hishām←Hishām ibn Sa'īd←Sa'īd ibn Zayd ibn 'Amr ibn Nufayl. See Aḥmad, *Musnad*, I, 189; Ṭayālisī, *Musnad*, 32 (no. 234); Ṭabarānī, *Kabīr*, I, no. 350; also Ibn Bukayr, 118; *Kashf al-astār*, III, no. 2754. The tradition recurs in the *tarjama* of Sa'īd ibn Zayd in Ibn 'Abd al-Barr's *Istī'āb* (II, 616–17).

[9] Ibn Bukayr, 118. See Guillaume, "New Light", 27.

[10] See Ibn Sa'd, III, 380 (*tarjama* of Sa'īd ibn Zayd); Ibn 'Abd al-Barr, *Istī'āb*, II, 617 (*tarjama* of Sa'īd ibn Zayd); Aḥmad, *Musnad*, II, 68–69, 127; Fākihī, IV, 126–27 (no. 2455); *Aghānī*, III, 16.

[11] The *isnād*: Hishām ibn 'Urwa←'Urwa←'Ā'isha. See Abū Nu'aym, *Dalā'il*, 188 (no. 131); also Khargūshī (MS Br. Lib.), fol. 27b; Suyūṭī, *Khaṣā'iṣ*, I, 220–21 (from Abū Nu'aym); *Kanz*, XII, no. 34080 (*Faḍā'il*). And see another tradition of 'Urwa, Khargūshī (MS Br. Lib.), fol. 28a–b.

However, within the realm of the *muṣannaf* compilations none of the versions of the story of Muḥammad's meeting with Zayd is widely current. Apart from al-Ḥākim, who ignored its basic import, later authors who have it include Ibn Ḥajar (d. AH 852), who recorded it in a chapter about the virtues of Zayd ibn 'Amr.[12] Of the authors of the more authoritative Six Books, only al-Bukhārī has cited it. The version he chose is the one of Mūsā ibn 'Uqba, which bears an interesting variant reading. While the version outside the *muṣannaf* compilations explicitly states that Muḥammad was the one to offer the sacrificial meat to Zayd (*...fa-qaddama ilayhi rasūlu llāhi sufratan....*), in the variant reading in al-Bukhārī it is stated that the meat was offered to Muḥammad, and that it was he who refused to eat of it (*...fa-quddimat ilā l-nabī sufratun fa-abā an ya'kula minhā....*). The tradition in this form was recorded by al-Bukhārī in the chapters about Muḥammad's early years.[13]

The variant reading in the tradition of Mūsā ibn 'Uqba reflects a change in the attitude of Muslim scholars towards the early traditions about Muḥammad's life. While the story was originally intended to describe the transition from idolatry to monotheism that Muḥammad experienced with Zayd's guidance, Muslim scholars eventually became sensitive to all kinds of unflattering dogmatic implications which could be deduced from the innocent stories. Above all, one could note the fact that before the transition to monotheism took place, Muḥammad was an idolater like everyone else in Mecca. This idea could not be tolerated by Muslim scholars for whom the *'iṣma* of the Prophet should mean total and eternal immunity from paganism, preventing him from committing sins during every moment of his life, even before he became a prophet. Thus the variant reading shifts the sinful sacrificial act from Muḥammad to an unspecified person, leaving the Prophet immune from idolatry, and the story clear of its initial point. It is no longer a preparation story, and Zayd's role has become devoid of significance. The art of story-telling has thus given way to the art of academic manipulations. The earlier version of the story was only preserved in another section of al-Bukhārī's *Ṣaḥīḥ*, but here too only in a few particular recensions of this compilation.[14]

Supporters of the *'iṣma* in its total sense were also to be found beyond the ranks of the authors of the *muṣannaf* compilations. In the realm of the biographical compilations, Ibn Hishām is a no less zealous follower of the same dogma in its most advanced stage of development, which made him reject all

---

[12] Ibn Ḥajar, *Maṭālib*, IV, no. 4057.

[13] Bukhārī, *Ṣaḥīḥ*, V, 50 (63:24).

[14] *Ibid.*, VII, 118 (72:16). On the margin it is indicated that other recensions have: *fa-quddima ilā rasūli llāh sufratun*, "the Apostle of God was offered some sacrificial meat."

references to the idea of guidance. Accordingly, he simply omitted the entire story from his recension of Ibn Isḥāq, thus evading any possible hint of Muḥammad's pre-prophetic paganism.

II

The traditions about Zayd ibn ʻAmr represent only one type of the story of guidance, in which it is put into effect through external human instruction. In another type of story, which is also set in local Meccan ritual surroundings, guidance to monotheism is administered to Muḥammad by external non-human agents, i.e. angels. This elevates the event to the level of what we may call a "pre-prophetic revelation". None of these traditions gained admission into any of the *muṣannaf* compilations. Unlike the traditions about Zayd, the traditions about the angels were not subjected to textual manipulation, because, being focussed on angels, not on human beings, they were of no use for the purpose of *faḍāʼil*. Therefore, they only survived in the biographical sources, where the selection of material was less rigid.

In Ibn Saʻd we find a Medinan tradition circulated on the authority of Ibn ʻAbbās, who transmits to ʻIkrima (Medinan d. AH 105) the story of Umm Ayman, Muḥammad's nurse. She says that one day Muḥammad's uncle Abū Ṭālib, as well as his aunts, were angry with the Prophet because he had refused to take part in the public veneration of the Meccan idols. Thereafter, Muḥammad disappeared for a while, and soon returned, overcome with horror, to tell his aunts that he feared for his mental fitness. They reassured him, saying that as long as he retained his good moral traits, God would never surrender him to Satan's grip. He also told them that whenever he approached an idol, a tall person in white would appear, calling: "Hold back, Muḥammad, do not touch it!" From then on, so Umm Ayman relates, Muḥammad never participated in their rituals, till he became a prophet.[15] The same model recurs in the story of Muḥammad's first revelation, where he again experiences an alarming encounter with the angel and is then encouraged by his wife Khadīja (Chapter 5). In the present context, the encounter with the angel figures as a preparatory address designed to establish Muḥammad's monotheistic frame of mind.

A short similar tradition was circulated with a Meccan *isnād*; the Companion is again Ibn ʻAbbās, who is quoted by ʻAṭāʼ ibn Abī Rabāḥ (Meccan d. AH 114). Muḥammad attends a ritual in front of the idol Isāf, during which he is

[15] Ibn Saʻd, I, 158. See also Abū Nuʻaym, *Dalāʼil*, 186–87 (no. 129). Cf. Andræ, *Person*, 129. The *isnād*: Ḥusayn ibn ʻAbdallāh ibn ʻUbaydallāh ibn al-ʻAbbās (Medinan d. AH 141)←ʻIkrima←Ibn ʻAbbās←Umm Ayman.

seen gazing at the roof of the Ka'ba. To his worried relatives he says that he has just been prohibited from approaching that idol.[16]

In another Medinan tradition of the Companion Jābir ibn 'Abdallāh (d. AH 77), Muḥammad is not addressed by the angel, and rather only hears him speak to another angel: these two say to each other that they cannot take their place behind him, because he has just stroked an idol. Upon hearing this, Muḥammad decides never to participate again in the festivals of the idolaters.[17] There is also a similar story of 'Ā'isha in which the Prophet relates the event in the first person. He hears the angels Gabriel and Michael talk regretfully about his pagan conduct, and their words make him refrain from ever stroking the idols again.[18]

In another set of traditions in which he expresses his aversion to idolatry in the first person, Muḥammad's decision to abandon the worship of the idols of Quraysh is the result of his own insight. In a Medinan tradition of 'Urwa ibn al-Zubayr (d. AH 94) his statement of self-guidance is addressed to his wife Khadīja. Muḥammad is heard by one of his neighbours telling Khadīja that he will never worship Allāt and al-'Uzzā again. Khadīja says: "Leave Allāt, and leave al-'Uzzā." The neighbour adds that these were the idols they used to worship daily before bedtime.[19] This story likewise appears in none of the *muṣannaf* compilations. But the fact that the story has the Prophet himself utter his own self-guidance indicates again that the idea was once considered perfectly legitimate. However, it also shows that the attachment of a prophetic *isnād* to an account was not always sufficient to guarantee its admission into the canonical *ḥadīth* compilations.

Finally, there is another statement of Muḥammad in the first person about the idol al-'Uzzā. Ibn al-Kalbī (d. AH 204) relates that the Prophet said: "I sacrificed a reddish white ewe to al-'Uzzā when I was following the religion of my people."[20] This statement has attracted the attention of several Islamicists since

---

16 The *isnād*: Ṭalḥa ibn 'Amr (Meccan d. AH 152)←'Aṭā' ibn Abī Rabāḥ←Ibn 'Abbās. See Abū Nu'aym, *Dalā'il*, 187–88 (no. 130).

17 The *isnād*: Jarīr ibn 'Abd al-Ḥamīd al-Ḍabbī (Kūfan d. AH 188)←Sufyān al-Thawrī (Kūfan d. AH 161)←'Abdallāh ibn Muḥammad ibn 'Aqīl (Medinan d. AH 142)←Jābir ibn 'Abdallāh. See Abū Ya'lā, III, nos. 1877–78; Bayhaqī, *Dalā'il*, II, 35. See also Andræ, *Person*, 128; M.J. Kister, "The Sons of Khadīja", *Jerusalem Studies in Arabic and Islam* 16 (1993), 77.

18 See Suyūṭī, *Khaṣā'iṣ*, I, 222 (from Abū Nu'aym).

19 Aḥmad, *Musnad*, IV, 222; V, 362. See also Jeffery, "Was Muhammad", 231. The *isnād*: Hishām ibn 'Urwa (Meccan d. AH 146)←'Urwa ibn al-Zubayr←anonymous neighbour of Khadīja.

20 Ibn al-Kalbī, *Aṣnām*, 19.

Wellhausen first quoted it from Ibn al-Kalbī.[21] All of them have observed that it implies that Muḥammad was an idolater before he became a prophet,[22] but this observation misses the initial gist of the statement. The context in which it should be understood is guidance, i.e. God's deliverance of Muḥammad from polytheism. The statement alludes to the dramatic change which Muḥammad, with God's guidance and *'iṣma*, underwent since the days he was following the religion of his people till he became a prophet of God. It is significant that immediately following the above statement of Muḥammad, Ibn al-Kalbī records the verses from Quran 53:19–23 in which the three goddesses are declared impotent.

As stated above, none of these traditions was accepted into the *muṣannaf* compilations, where they were all ignored because Muslim scholars drew from them the irrelevant, although unavoidable, "historical" conclusion that the Prophet had once been an idolater. This did not fit into the concept of the total *'iṣma* which was supposed to make Muḥammad a monotheist from the very first moment of his life. This advanced concept established itself quite early, and it is manifest in the earliest extant biographies of Muḥammad. He is said to have stated his aversion to idols during negotiations with a Jewish trader whom he met in Syria while acting as Khadīja's agent.[23] He makes the same statement when he is still a young boy, during his meeting with the hermit Baḥīrā.[24] Therefore, stories indicating that he still needed guidance before he became a prophet had to remain peripheral.

III

The theme of the preliminary instruction of Muḥammad before he assumed the prophetic office is not confined to his transition from polytheism to monotheism. There are also traditions about his moral training . When he is still an ordinary young man, an external force prevents him from exposing himself in the nude, as was the routine among the idolaters. Again, most versions of the story about this remained outside the authoritative *muṣannaf* compilations, but let us begin with those which did gain entrance into them.

---

[21] Julius Wellhausen, *Reste arabischen Heidentums*, 3rd ed. (Berlin, 1961), 34.

[22] See e.g. Andræ, *Person,* 128; Jeffery, "Was Muhammad", 233–34; Kister, "A Bag of Meat", 275.

[23] Ibn Sa'd, I, 156.

[24] See the story of Ibn Isḥāq in Ibn Hishām, I, 193; Ibn Bukayr, 75. See also Abū Nu'aym, *Dalā'il*, 169 (no. 108); Bayhaqī, *Dalā'il*, II, 28. See also the tradition of al-Wāqidī to the same effect in Ibn Sa'd, I, 154.

Al-Bukhārī and Muslim recorded a version of this story which has the Ḥijāzī *isnād*: 'Amr ibn Dīnār (Meccan d. AH 126)←Jābir ibn 'Abdallāh (Medinan Companion d. AH 77), and was circulated by Zakariyyā ibn Isḥāq (Meccan). Both al-Bukhārī and Muslim recorded it as an illustration of the legal interdiction to bare one's body in public,[25] and it recurs outside the *muṣannaf* compilations.[26] The young Muḥammad, so the tradition goes, participated with Quraysh in the rebuilding of the Ka'ba. He carried stones with the others, and his uncle al-'Abbās suggested that he take off his loincloth and put it on his shoulder, so as not to be bruised by the stones he carried. Muḥammad followed his uncle's advice, but as soon as he took off his cloth, he lost consciousness and collapsed. After that day he was never seen naked again. Another version with the same *isnād* was circulated by Ibn Jurayj (Meccan d. AH 150) with slight changes in wording. When Muḥammad falls to the ground, his eyes are fixed to the sky. This version too was recorded by Muslim in the chapter about the need to maintain one's modesty in public. Al-Bukhārī recorded it in the section entitled *Ḥajj*, in the chapter dealing with the *faḍā'il* of Mecca, as well as in the chapters dealing with Muḥammad's early years.[27] It also appears outside the *muṣannaf* compilations.[28] There is yet another version outside the *muṣannaf* books which is likewise circulated under the name of Jābir ibn 'Abdallāh, quoted by Abū l-Zubayr (Muḥammad ibn Muslim ibn Tadrus, Meccan d. AH 126). Jābir states that he heard it directly from the Prophet (*akhbaranī l-nabiyyu*).[29] In it Muḥammad loses his dress unintentionally when he stumbles while carrying the stones; al-'Abbās plays only a quite neutral role: Muḥammad asks him to hand him his loincloth, and then covers himself.

In all other versions, which neither al-Bukhārī nor Muslim could accept, Muḥammad exposes himself of his own volition. One such version was recorded by 'Abd al-Razzāq and al-Ḥākim. The former included it in the "book" of pilgrimage, because it forms part of a detailed report about the rebuilding of the Ka'ba. The latter recorded it in the section of *Libās* ("clothing").[30] Both classifications distract the audience from the initial drift of the story. The tradi-

---

[25] Bukhārī, *Ṣaḥīḥ*, I, 102 (8:8); Muslim, I, 184 (3, *Bāb ḥifẓ al-'awra*).

[26] See Abū Ya'lā, IV, no. 2243; Aḥmad, *Musnad*, III, 310, 333; Bayhaqī, *Dalā'il*, II, 31; Abū Nu'aym, *Dalā'il*, 188–89 (no. 132); Dhahabī, *Sīra*, 35.

[27] Bukhārī, *Ṣaḥīḥ*, II, 179 (25:42); V, 51 (63:25).

[28] See Aḥmad, *Musnad*, III, 380; Bayhaqī, *Dalā'il*, II, 32; Abū Nu'aym, *Dalā'il*, 189 (no. 133); Ibn Kathīr, *Bidāya*, II, 287.

[29] The *isnād*: Ibn Lahī'a (Egyptian d. AH 174)←Abū l-Zubayr (Muḥammad ibn Muslim ibn Tadrus, Meccan d. AH 126)←Jābir ibn 'Abdallāh←Prophet. See *Fatḥ al-bārī*, III, 350 (from Ṭabarānī, Abū Nu'aym).

[30] 'Abd al-Razzāq, *Muṣannaf*, V, 103 (no. 9106); *Mustadrak*, IV, 179. See also Aḥmad, *Musnad*, V, 454, 455.

tion is of Ma'mar ibn Rāshid (Baṣran, d. AH 154), and has the Meccan *isnād* of 'Abdallāh ibn 'Uthmān ibn Khuthaym (d. AH 132)←the Companion Abū l-Ṭufayl ('Āmir ibn Wāthila, d. AH 110). Here the Prophet not only faints, but actually experiences a vision. As soon as he decides to put his loincloth upon his shoulder, he hears a voice saying: "Cover your nakedness!" He covers himself, and is never seen naked again. According to al-Ḥākim, the *isnād* of this tradition is "sound".

Al-Ḥākim has another tradition with the *isnād*: 'Ikrima (Medinan d. AH 105)←Ibn 'Abbās, as quoted by al-Naḍr Abū 'Umar ibn 'Abd al-Raḥmān al-Khazzāz (Kūfan).[31] In this tradition the time of the event is slightly different. The young Muḥammad is helping his uncle Abū Ṭālib in some repair works at the well of Zamzam. He takes off his loincloth to protect his shoulder, collapses to the ground, regains consciousness after a short while, and tells his anxious uncle that a person in white came to him, saying: "Cover yourself!" Ibn 'Abbās says that this was his first prophetic vision (*awwal mā ra'āhu l-nabiyyu* [ṣ] *mina l-nubuwwa*). His nakedness was never seen again after that day. This tradition too may be found outside the *muṣannaf* compilations, including an *awā'il* book.[32]

Another version of the 'Ikrima←Ibn 'Abbās tradition was circulated by Simāk ibn Ḥarb (Kūfan d. AH 123). In it Ibn 'Abbās hears the story directly from his father al-'Abbās, who acts as an eyewitness. Al-'Abbās speaks in the first person, telling how he and his nephew Muḥammad carried stones with the rest of Quraysh when the Ka'ba was renovated. They all took off their loincloths and put them on their shoulders. Suddenly he saw Muḥammad fall to the ground, gazing at the sky. Soon the Prophet got up, put his cloth on, and told al-'Abbās that he had just been forbidden to walk naked. Al-'Abbās decided not to talk about this incident, lest people should think that Muḥammad had gone mad (*majnūn*).[33]

The biographical sources have further versions in which Muḥammad takes off his loincloth of his own accord. One such version appears already in Ibn Isḥāq,[34] where the event is related in the first person as a story of the Prophet himself. Ibn Isḥāq recorded it as an illustration of how God protected

---

[31] *Mustadrak*, IV, 179. Cf. *Fatḥ al-bārī*, III, 350.

[32] See Ibn Abī 'Āṣim, *Awā'il*, no. 139 (under the heading of Muḥammad's first prophetic sign). See also Abū Nu'aym, *Dalā'il*, 190 (no. 135). Cf. Ibn Sa'd, I, 157 (without the part about Abū Ṭālib and Zamzam).

[33] See *Kashf al-astār*, II, no. 1158; Ibn Bukayr, 79; Bayhaqī, *Dalā'il*, II, 32–33; Abū Nu'aym, *Dalā'il*, 189–90 (no. 134); Ibn Kathīr, *Bidāya*, II, 287; *Fatḥ al-bārī*, III, 350.

[34] Ibn Hishām, I, 194–95; Ibn Bukayr, 79. See also Bayhaqī, *Dalā'il*, II, 31–32; Ibn Kathīr, *Bidāya*, II, 287.

Muḥammad during his early years, when he was still in the state of *jāhiliyya*. The situation in this particular story is not building, but rather playing. Muḥammad plays with other boys and carries stones with them for the game. When he takes off his loincloth, an unseen person strikes him and says: "Put on your loincloth!" He puts it on, thus being the only boy dressed. In the version of al-Wāqidī, the scene is again set in the rebuilding of the Ka'ba, and related in the third person. Having taken off his cloth, Muḥammad is thrown to the ground and hears a voice say: "Cover your nakedness" (*'awrataka*). This is the first time he was addressed [by an angel].[35] Then Abū Ṭālib suggests that he put his loincloth on his head, but Muḥammad refuses, saying that he was only thrown to the ground because he had taken it off.[36]

All these traditions comprise elements of a typical guidance story. God's preliminary protection of Muḥammad against the sins of the *jāhiliyya* is so intense that it even assumes the form of an actual vision involving fainting. Nevertheless, none of these traditions was accepted into the more authoritative *muṣannaf* compilations, because the concept of the *'iṣma* is still too flimsy in them. It is only focussed on guidance, not on total immunity. The advanced view of Muḥammad's total *'iṣma* could not tolerate the idea that he could ever have been seen naked in public. As seen above, the only version which al-Bukhārī and Muslim could accept was the one in which the idea of taking off his loincloth is not his own, but that of an elderly uncle, namely, al-'Abbās.

IV

There is one more guidance scene with the primitive form of *'iṣma* which only gained entrance to Ibn Ḥibbān's *Ṣaḥīḥ* and al-Ḥākim's *Mustadrak*. Muḥammad again contemplates something which he does not know is wrong, and only gives up his intention after being externally prevented from carrying it out. The topic here is the seeking of unlawful sexual pleasure.

Ibn Ḥibbān and al-Ḥākim record a tradition to this effect which they quote from Ibn Isḥāq and trace back to 'Alī ibn Abī Ṭālib.[37] The story takes place when Muḥammad is a shepherd (an essential theme in the early years of many prophets). He speaks in the first person, saying that he had only twice thought of resorting to the women whom the idolaters used to visit, but each time God

---

35 *fa-kāna dhālika awwala mā nūdiya*.

36 Ibn Sa'd, I, 145 (Wāqidī).

37 The *isnād*: Muḥammad ibn 'Abdallāh ibn Qays ibn Makhrama←al-Ḥasan ibn Muḥammad ibn 'Alī←his father←his grandfather, 'Alī. See *Mustadrak*, IV, 245 (*Tawba wa-ināba*); Ibn Ḥibbān, *Ṣaḥīḥ*, XIV, no. 6272.

protected him from it. One night he asked his friend to look after his flock, while he went to Mecca for his pleasures. As he entered Mecca he heard sounds of music coming from a house where a wedding party was taking place. He stopped to listen, but God made him deaf to the music, and he fell asleep till the sun rose. The same events took place on another night, when he went to Mecca for the same purpose. From then on he never thought of seeking such *jāhilī* nightly enjoyments again. The tradition is recorded in the biographical sources as well, and may be found in Ibn Bukayr's recension of the *Sīra* of Ibn Isḥāq.[38] Ibn Hishām, however, expunged it from his own version of Ibn Isḥāq. The authoritative *muṣannaf* compilations also ignored it, which again accords with their general tendency to adapt the early years of Muḥammad to the more advanced dogma of his total *'iṣma*.

V

Apart from traditions relating the actual shift of Muḥammad from *jāhiliyya* to Islam, there are further indications of the idea of guidance which were likewise denied wide circulation. These are traditions about Muḥammad's pre-prophetic period which focus on the contrast which already existed between the divinely protected youth and his fellow tribesmen. The underlying idea of these traditions is that even while Muḥammad was still following the religion of his people, he was already distinct from them in his morals and ritual conduct.

The following passage is recorded in Yūnus ibn Bukayr's recension of Ibn Isḥāq's biography of the Prophet, and is also cited by al-Wāqidī on the authority of the Medinan Dāwūd ibn al-Ḥuṣayn (d. AH 135).[39] The passage summarises Muḥammad's early years with his uncle Abū Ṭālib:

> The messenger of God grew up, God protecting him and keeping him away from the filth of the *jāhiliyya* and from its vices, for the sake of the honour and the mission which He had in store for him, while he was still following the religion of his people (*wa-huwa 'alā dīni qawmihi*). Consequently, he became the most perfect young man in Quraysh—in manhood, in outer appearance, in noble manners, in granting protection, in character...—to the extent that he was only known among his fellow tribesmen as *al-amīn* ("trustworthy").[40]

---

[38] Ibn Bukayr, 79. See also Suhaylī, *Rawḍ*, I, 19; Ṭabarī, *Tārīkh*, I, 1126–27 (II, 279); Bayhaqī, *Dalā'il*, II, 33–34; Abū Nu'aym, *Dalā'il*, 186 (no. 128); Suyūṭī, *Khaṣā'iṣ*, I, 219; Ibn Kathīr, *Bidāya*, II, 287–88; *Kashf al-astār*, III, no. 2403; *Majma' al-zawā'id*, VIII, 229.

[39] Ibn Sa'd, I, 121.

[40] Ibn Bukayr, 78. Cf. Guillaume, "New Light", 20. See also Bayhaqī, *Dalā'il*, II, 30. Cf. the discussion of this statement in Ibn Kathīr, *Bidāya*, II, 289.

The early biographies have more specific illustrations of the singular position of Muḥammad among his fellow tribesmen. The most typical example is Muḥammad's participation in the rites of the pilgrimage at 'Arafa, a place outside the sacred territory of Mecca. This site was only frequented by the non-Meccan Arabs; the Meccans (Quraysh) confined themselves to the sacred places inside the territory of Mecca and regarded themselves as *ḥums*, those whose devotional practices during the *ḥajj* were only focussed on Mecca and the Ka'ba.[41] There were, however, some exceptions. It is related that the Qurashī Shayba ibn Rabī'a did take part in the rites at 'Arafa.[42] In Islam, participation in the ceremony (usually called *wuqūf*, "standing [before God]") at 'Arafa is considered a most pious act, one of the relics of the ancient monotheistic heritage of Abraham. Accordingly, the well-known *ḥanīf* Zayd ibn 'Amr ibn Nufayl is said not to have only abandoned the worship of the idols and other pagan customs, but also to have taken part in the *wuqūf* at 'Arafa.[43]

As for Muḥammad, the story about his own participation in the *wuqūf* there is usually circulated on the authority of the Medinan Companion Jubayr ibn Muṭ'im (d. AH 58), who speaks in the first person as an eyewitness. The earliest version of Jubayr's story was recorded by Ibn Isḥāq, but it only survives in the recension of Ibn Bukayr;[44] Ibn Hishām chose to avoid it for reasons which will soon become clear. Jubayr relates that he saw Muḥammad perform the *wuqūf* in 'Arafa when the latter was still following the religion of his people (*wa-huwa 'alā dīni qawmihi*). Jubayr adds that Muḥammad was the only member of his tribe to take part in the rite; this was due to God's guidance, which had led him to do the right thing. This story illustrates the unique position of Muḥammad among his people, even while he still shared their religion. Already at that early stage, God inspired him towards the right way of conduct.

This setting of the story did not gain wide circulation: its intrinsic concept of *'iṣma* was too primitive, being focussed just on guidance, not on total immunity, and thus not eliminating a phase of paganism in Muḥammad's life. The clause "while he was still following the religion of his people" (*wa-huwa 'alā*

[41] See e.g. M.J. Kister, "Mecca and Tamīm", *Journal of the Economic and Social History of the Orient* 8 (1965), 138; Uri Rubin, "The Ka'ba: Aspects of its Ritual Functions", *Jerusalem Studies in Arabic and Islam* 8 (1986), 127.

[42] See Wāqidī, III, 1102, a tradition with the *isnād*: Mūsā ibn Ya'qūb (Medinan)←his paternal uncle←'Abdallāh ibn al-Walīd ibn 'Uthmān ibn 'Affān←Asmā' bint Abī Bakr.

[43] See Ibn Sa'd, III, 380 (from al-Wāqidī). The *isnād*: Mūsā ibn Maysara al-Dīlī (Medinan)←Abū Bakr ibn 'Ubaydallāh ibn Abī Mulayka (Meccan)←Ḥujayr ibn Abī Ihāb (Meccan Companion).

[44] See Ibn Bukayr, 98. See also Bayhaqī, *Dalā'il*, II, 37. The *isnād*: 'Abdallāh ibn Abī Bakr ibn Muḥammad ibn 'Amr ibn Ḥazm (Medinan d. AH 135)←'Uthmān ibn Abī Sulaymān (Meccan)←Nāfi' ibn Jubayr (Medinan d. AH 99)←Jubayr ibn Muṭ'im.

dīni qawmihi) could not be repeated by traditionists who in the meantime had become aware of the advanced form of the concept of Muḥammad's total *'iṣma* from idolatry. For them, no tradition about the Prophet could contain such a clause, whatever the context. Consequently, in some sources in which the same tradition is quoted from Ibn Isḥāq, the clause *wa-huwa 'alā dīni qawmihi* is entirely missing.[45] In the recension of Ibn Hishām the whole story of Jubayr was avoided, and in the above passage about the Prophet's early years with Abū Ṭālib, the crucial clause *wa-huwa 'alā dīni qawmihi* was cut out, surviving only in the recension of Yūnus ibn Bukayr.[46]

Moreover, sometimes the problematic clause of Ibn Isḥāq's version of Jubayr's story was replaced by a different indication of the time which was less offensive to the dogma of the total *'iṣma*. This emendation even made this tradition acceptable to some authors of the *muṣannaf* compilations. Thus, in the section dealing with the rites of the pilgrimage to Mecca (*Manāsik*) in the *Ṣaḥīḥ* of Ibn Khuzyama, Ibn Isḥāq's tradition only has the neutral chronological indication: "during the Jāhiliyya" (*fī l-jāhiliyya*), which says nothing of Muḥammad's own religion at that time.[47] In the version of Ibn Isḥāq's tradition recorded by Aḥmad ibn Ḥanbal, Jubayr sees Muḥammad perform the *wuqūf* in 'Arafa "before he began to receive prophetic revelations" (*qabla an yunzala ilayhi*), which is also vague enough.[48] This particular version was accepted by al-Ḥākim into the section of the pilgrimage rites of his *Mustadrak*.[49]

Apart from that of Ibn Isḥāq, there are other traditions with the story of Jubayr, all of them harmless enough to be admitted into the sections on the *ḥajj* in several *muṣannaf* compilations. None of them says that the event took place before Muḥammad became a prophet, thus excluding any doubts as to his religious state of mind at that time. In the *Mustadrak* of al-Ḥākim the above tradition of Ibn Isḥāq is followed by a tradition with the Meccan *isnād*: Ibn Jurayj ('Abd al-Malik ibn 'Abd al-'Azīz, d. AH 150)←his father←Jubayr ibn Muṭ'im.[50] Jubayr says that he saw Muḥammad at 'Arafa, "after (!) he began receiving revelations" (*ba'da mā unzila ilayhi*). The idea of guidance disappeared from this version without trace.

The same applies to the most prevalent tradition recorded in the *muṣannaf* compilations. It has the Meccan *isnād*: Sufyān ibn 'Uyayna (d. AH 196)←'Amr ibn Dīnār (d. AH 126)←Muḥammad ibn Jubayr ibn Muṭ'im (Medinan)←Jubayr

[45] E.g. Fākihī, V, 35 (no. 2788); Ṭabarānī, *Kabīr*, II, nos. 1577, 1578.
[46] Ibn Hishām, I, 194.
[47] Ibn Khuzayma, *Ṣaḥīḥ*, IV, 257–58 (no. 2823).
[48] Aḥmad, *Musnad*, IV, 82. Cf. Wāqidī, III, 1102.
[49] *Mustadrak*, I, 482.
[50] *Ibid.* See also Aḥmad, *Musnad*, IV, 84; Ṭabarānī, *Kabīr*, II, no. 1598.

ibn Muṭʻim, and bears no indication of time. Jubayr sees Muḥammad at ʻArafa, and merely wonders what brings him there, as he was a member of the *ḥums*, for whom ʻArafa was not one of the stations of the *ḥajj*.[51]

The long-developing sensitivity to Muḥammad's integrity, as the model of the perfect Muslim, has thus caused the rejection of the innocent early story about God's guidance of the pagan Muḥammad, in which only a simple concept of *ʻiṣma* is already embedded.

VI

The idea of God's guidance, with which Muḥammad was blessed while still adhering to "the religion of his people" (*dīn qawmihi*), was also read into some passages of the Quran. But the Quranic link which was supposed to provide more authority for the notion did not help much either. The Muslims soon deployed the tool of exegesis (*tafsīr*) to suppress the notion of guidance, in favour of that of the total immunity.

The idea of *dīn qawmihi* was read into Quran 93:7. This verse reads:

> *wa-wajadaka ḍāllan fa-hadā*: "He found you erring and guided [you]."

For the interpretation of the "error" in which the Quranic prophet was found, and of the guidance which redeemed him of that error, the early exegetes imported from Muḥammad's biographies the idea of *dīn qawmihi*. The interpretation of the Kūfan al-Suddī (d. AH 128) reads:

> *wa-wajadaka ḍāllan—kāna ʻalā amri qawmihi arbaʻīna ʻāman*: "He found you erring—he (i.e. Muḥammad) adhered to the affair of his people for 40 years."[52]

This interpretation restricts the verse to the 40 years of the pre-prophetic period of Muḥammad's life. Al-Suddī seems to maintain that the guidance of God referred to in the verb *fa-hadā* stands for God's guidance which He bestowed

---

[51] See Dārimī, II, no 1878 (5:49); Bukhārī, *Ṣaḥīḥ*, II, 199 (25:91); Muslim, IV, 44 (15: *Bāb fī l-wuqūf....*); Nasāʼī, *Kubrā*, II, 424 (no. 4009 [28:201]); Ibn Ḥibbān, *Ṣaḥīḥ*, IX, no. 3849; Bayhaqī, *Sunan*, V, 113. Outside the *muṣannaf* compilations the tradition may be found in Fākihī, V, 35–36 (no. 2789); Ḥumaydī, *Musnad*, I, no. 559; Aḥmad, *Musnad*, IV, 80; Ṭabarānī, *Kabīr*, II, no. 1556; Ibn Kathīr, *Bidāya*, II, 289.

[52] Ṭabarī, *Tafsīr*, XXX, 149. See also Zajjāj, V, 340; Ibn ʻAṭiyya, XVI, 322; Rāzī, XXXI, 215 (al-Suddī); Qurṭubī, XX, 99 (Kalbī, Suddī). Some modern scholars have already discussed this statement of al-Suddī, without, however, being aware of its significance. See e.g. Andræ, *Person*, 127–28; Birkeland, *Lord*, 28–29.

upon Muḥammad when He found him "erring", i.e. adhering to the *dīn* of his tribe. According to al-Suddī, then, the Quranic verse may be rendered: "God found you a pagan, and guided you [while still a pagan]." This is the exact reflection of the idea of the above traditions of Ibn Isḥāq.

But the interpretation of al-Suddī could not prevail. Like the above traditions, it could not be harmonized with the dogma of the total *'iṣma* which eventually established itself. The implication that Muḥammad once adhered to the religion of his people was suppressed in later versions of Ibn Isḥāq's traditions, and the same had to be done concerning the interpretation of al-Suddī. The "pagan" insinuation inherent in this interpretation had to be eliminated; so for this purpose, the interpretation of al-Suddī was reinterpreted. Al-Zamakhsharī (d. AH 538) says that the Prophet only adhered to the "affair" (*amr*) of his people in the sense that he shared their ignorance of the "revealed sciences" (*'ulūm sam'iyya*), i.e. the practical laws, not in the sense that he shared their disbelief in God. The latter denotation, he adds, is incredible because prophets are supposed to be immune to disbelief, before their first revelation as well as after it.[53]

Already before al-Zamakhsharī another way of reinterpretation was pursued, one in which the "error" was shifted from Muḥammad to his contemporary polytheists. Commenting on the *ḍāll* passage, al-Māwardī (d. AH 450) says: "He found your people in error and directed you towards guiding them." Al-Māwardī goes on to observe that "this is the sense of the words of al-Suddī" (*wa-hādhā ma'nā qawli l-Suddī*).[54] For al-Māwardī, then, *ḍāll* does not mean "erring", but rather "dwelling among erring people". He reads this meaning into the interpretation of al-Suddī, thus making the Prophet innocent of error. Other commentators interpreted the words of al-Suddī in the same manner.[55] This way of looking at the Quranic *ḍāll* passage also exists as an independent interpretation already known to al-Farrā' (d. AH 207) and al-Ṭabarī (*wajadaka fī qawmin ḍullālin fa-hadāka*, "found you among erring people and guided you").[56] This view is attributed to (Ibn al-Sā'ib) al-Kalbī (d. AH 146),[57] and recurs in Shī'ī commentaries.[58]

---

[53] Cf. Zamakhsharī, IV, 264–65; Qurṭubī, XVI, 59 (on 42:52).

[54] Māwardī, *Nukat*, VI, 294 (no. 3).

[55] See e.g. Qurṭubī, XX, 97.

[56] Farrā', III, 274; Ṭabarī, *Tafsīr*, XXX, 149. See also Samarqandī, *Tafsīr*, III, 487. The same idea was also traced back to Ibn 'Abbās. See Suyūṭī, *Durr*, VI, 362 (from Ibn Mardawayhi): *wajadaka bayna ḍāllīna fa-stanqadhaka min ḍalālatihim.*

[57] See Ibn 'Aṭiyya, XVI, 322; Ibn al-Jawzī, *Zād al-masīr*, IX, 159; Rāzī, XXXI, 215.

[58] Ṭūsī, *Tabyān*, X, 369 (3); Ṭabarsī, *Majma'*, XXX, 137 (3).

Nevertheless, in this kind of interpretation the Quranic *fa-hadā* ("guided") is still understood in the sense of *fa-hadāka* ("guided you"), which could imply that the Prophet himself needed guidance, just like the other "erring people" (*ḍullāl*).[59] This was soon straightened out. In another version of the same interpretation, recorded by al-Samarqandī (d. AH 375), *fa-hadā* is interpreted as *fa-hadāhum bika*, "He (i.e. God) guided them through you."[60]

A new variant reading (*qirā'a*) of the Quranic *ḍāll* verse was eventually circulated which reflected precisely this idea:

> *wa-wajadaka ḍāllun fa-hudiya*: "an erring person found you and was guided [by you]."[61]

The same line of thought is preserved in another interpretation in which the Quranic *ḍāll* is shifted from the active to the passive sense, being said to indicate *madlūl 'anka*, "missed [by others]", i.e. he was unknown (*khāmil al-dhikr*).[62] *Ḍāll* was also explained as denoting *ḍālla*, i.e. a "solitary tree" (*shajara farīda*) in the desert by which people find their way, or a lost sheep searched for by the people.[63]

Apart from recasting the interpretation of al-Suddī, the exegetes had recourse to other interpretations which provided the Quranic *ḍāll* with an inoffensive non-pagan sense. Many of these interpretations were based on the evidence of the Quran itself. Verse 42:52 states that before the "Spirit" (*al-rūḥ*) was revealed to him, the Prophet lacked knowledge (*mā kunta tadrī*) of the "book" (*kitāb*) and of the "creed" (*īmān*). This statement was ideal for the desired non-pagan interpretation of the Quranic *ḍāll*: before he became a prophet, Muḥammad naturally was aware neither of the contents of the Quran (*kitāb*), nor of the components of the Islamic creed (*īmān*). Thus he was ignorant, but not pagan. Most exegetes, beginning with Yaḥyā ibn Sallām (d. AH 200), refer to this verse in their

---

59 See Rāzī, XXXI, 215: *wajadaka ḍāllan, ya'nī kāfiran fī qawmin ḍullāl.* See also Ibn 'Aṭiyya, XVI, 322; Ṭūsī, *Tabyān*, X, 369 (3): *wajadaka fī qawmin ḍullāl, ay, fa-ka-annaka wāḥidun minhum.*

60 Samarqandī, *Tafsīr*, III, 487. See also Rāzī, XXXI, 216 (10); Qurṭubī, XX, 97.

61 Māwardī, *Nukat*, VI, 294; Qurṭubī, XX, 99; Birkeland, *Lord*, 31.

62 See Ibn 'Aṭiyya, XVI, 322; Ibn al-Jawzī, *Zād al-masīr*, IX, 159; Tha'ālibī, IV, 423 (from Muḥammad ibn 'Alī al-Tirmidhī and 'Abd al-'Azīz ibn Yaḥyā). See also the Shī'ī *tafsīrs* of Ṭūsī, *Tabyān*, X, 369 (4); Ṭabarsī, *Majma'*, XXX, 138 (7). And cf. *Lisān*, s.v. *ḍ.l.l.* (V, 2603): *wa-aṣlu l-ḍalāl al-ghaybūba.*

63 See Rāzī, XXXI, 216 (6). See also Qurṭubī, XX, 98–99; Tha'ālibī, IV, 423 (from al-Tha'labī). And see Ṭabarsī, *Majma'*, XXX, 138 (from al-'Ayyāshī); Qummī, *Tafsīr*, II, 426, 426–27. Cf. *Lisān*, s.v. *ḍ.l.l.* (IV, 2602): *al-kalima al-ḥakīma ḍāllatu l-mu'min.*

interpretation of the *ḍāll* passage. They explain that Muḥammad was *ḍāll* in the sense that he was ignorant of the contents of the Quran, or the laws, or of the nature of his prophetic office, etc.[64]

Later commentators added other Quranic verses serving the same aim. They adduced Quran 16:78, which states that "God brought you knowing nothing out of your mothers' wombs",[65] and Quran 12:3, which states that before the revelation of the Quran, the Prophet was "one of the heedless" (*min al-ghāfilīn*). The latter verse was the basis of the interpretation of *ḍāll* as *ghāfil*, i.e. "not being ambitious", "not aspiring [to become a prophet]".[66] The word *ḍalālika* of Quran 12:95, perceived as "your love", was adduced for the interpretation that *ḍāll* means "loving", i.e. Muḥammad was in a state of love for God, and of yearning for His guidance, and God guided him to serve his beloved God by teaching him the law (*sharī'a*).[67] Or, that Muḥammad's love was originally for his uncle Abū Ṭālib, i.e. for a human object, till God diverted it towards Himself.[68] The word *ḍalalnā* of Quran 32:10, taken to mean "we lost our way" was used for *ḍāll* in the sense of "lost" (among the *kuffār* of Mecca), so that *fa-hadā* implies that God supported Muḥammad in his struggle against them, or distinguished him from them.[69]

Some verses, however, were adduced for the interpretation of *ḍāll* as referring to situations of Muḥammad's prophetic period, not the pre-prophetic one. Quran 2:144 ("We have seen you turning your face about in the heaven....") was adduced for the explanation of *ḍāll* in the sense of searching for the right direction of prayer (*qibla*).[70] Quran 16:44, where the Prophet is requested to explain to the people what has been sent down to them, was the origin of the interpretation that *ḍāll* denoted Muḥammad's embarrassment concerning the correct understanding of the Quranic revelations.[71]

---

64 See Yaḥyā ibn Sallām, fol. 395; Huwwārī, IV, 513–14; Zajjāj, V, 339–40; Māwardī, *Nukat*, VI, 294 (nos. 1–2); Wāḥidī, *Wasīṭ*, fol. 336a; Samarqandī, *Tafsīr*, III, 487; Baghawī, *Ma'ālim*, V, 589; Zamakhsharī, IV, 264; Ibn 'Aṭiyya, XVI, 322; Ibn al-Jawzī, *Zād al-masīr*, IX, 158; Rāzī, XXXI, 215–16 (1); Qurṭubī, XX, 96–97; Tha'ālibī, IV, 423; Ibn Kathīr, *Tafsīr*, IV, 523.

65 Rāzī, XXXI, 216 (7).

66 *Ibid.*, XXXI, 216 (8); Qurṭubī, XX, 96 (refers also to 20:52).

67 Māwardī, *Nukat*, VI, 294 (no. 9); Rāzī, XXXI, 217 (14); Qurṭubī, XX, 97; Tha'ālibī, IV, 423 (from Ibn 'Aṭā').

68 Qurṭubī, XX, 98 (from Abū Bakr al-Warrāq).

69 Rāzī, XXXI, 216 (5); Qurṭubī, XX, 99. Close to this meaning is the interpretation of *ḍāll* in the sense of *ḍā'i'*, i.e. lost within his people and rejected as a leader. See Māwardī, *Nukat*, VI, 294 (no. 8); Rāzī, XXXI, 217 (16); Qurṭubī, XX, 97.

70 Māwardī, *Nukat*, VI, 294 (no. 6); Rāzī, XXXI, 216 (12). See also Qurṭubī, XX, 97.

71 Māwardī, *Nukat*, VI, 294 (no. 7); Qurṭubī, XX, 98; Tha'ālibī, IV, 423 ('Iyāḍ from al-Junayd, d. AH 298).

The term *ḍāll* was further explained in the sense of "forgetful". This was based on Quran 2:282: ...*an taḍilla iḥdāhumā fa-tudhakkira iḥdāhumā l-ukhrā*...., "if one of the two women forgets, let the other one remind her."[72] Certain *sīra* episodes were sometimes imported for the illustration of this meaning. It was related by some that the *ḍāll* verse referred to his ascension to heaven (the *mi'rāj*), during which Muḥammad forgot the words he should have used for praising God.[73] Others suggested that the Quran refers to his forgetfulness concerning the *istithnā'* (saying *in shā'a llāh*, "God willing") when he promised to answer "tomorrow" some questions posed to him.[74]

Apart from verses of the Quran, the exegetes used various scenes from the *sīra* to provide the Quranic *ḍāll* with an inoffensive non-pagan sense. In Ibn Isḥāq there is a story to the effect that after Muḥammad had spent some time with his wet-nurse, Ḥalīma, in the tribe of Sa'd, she brought him back to Mecca, and the boy lost her (*aḍallahā*) in the crowd. People initiated a search, till finally he was retrieved by Waraqa ibn Nawfal and "another man" (identified in other traditions as Abū Jahl), who brought him to his grandfather, 'Abd al-Muṭṭalib.[75] The exegetes did not fail to import this story, in which the word *aḍallahā* could so readily become a linking word to the Quranic *ḍāll* verse. This episode first occurs in the exegesis of the *ḍāll* verse in a tradition of al-Kalbī (d. AH 146), Ibn Isḥāq's contemporary. It is traced back either to Abū Ṣāliḥ (Bādhām, a *mawlā*, or "client", of Umm Hāni'), or to 'Ikrima (d. AH 105). The story of the wet-nurse and the lost Muḥammad is glossed here by the statement: "And this is [the meaning of] the verse: *wa-wajadaka ḍāllan fa-hadā*.[76] The same episode recurs in the interpretation of the *ḍāll* verse in later *tafsīrs*,[77] including Shī'ī ones.[78] The application of this particular story to the Quranic *ḍāll* verse made it mean: "He found you losing your way" (*ḍāll 'an al-ṭarīq*).

This concrete sense of the Quranic verse was anchored by the exegetes in some other pre-prophetic episodes which they imported from Muḥammad's bi-

---

[72] Māwardī, *Nukat*, VI, 294 (no. 5); Ibn al-Jawzī, *Zād al-masīr*, IX, 159 (quoting Tha'lab).

[73] Rāzī, XXXI, 217 (18).

[74] Qurṭubī, XX, 97.

[75] Ibn Hishām, I, 176. See also Ibn Kathīr, *Bidāya*, II, 277 (Ibn Isḥāq); Andræ, *Person*, 34. In other versions the boy is found by Abū Mas'ūd al-Thaqafī. See Khargūshī (MS Br. Lib.), fol. 39b.

[76] Balādhurī, *Ansāb*, I, 95. Birkeland (*Lord*, 32) claims wrongly that this interpretation represents "opinions which had originated in the time after aṭ-Ṭabarī".

[77] See Baghawī, *Ma'ālim*, V, 589; Zamakhsharī, IV, 264–65; Ibn 'Aṭiyya, XVI, 322; Rāzī, XXXI, 216 (2, 3); Qurṭubī, XX, 97, 97–98; Ibn al-Jawzī, *Zād al-masīr*, IX, 158. Cf. Ibn Qutayba, *Mushkil*, 457.

[78] Ṭabarsī, *Majma'*, XXX, 137–38 (4, 5).

ography. One of them is the journey to Syria which Muḥammad made with Maysara, Khadīja's agent.[79] The imported version of the story of this journey is recorded on the authority of Sa'īd ibn al-Musayyab (d. AH 100), and first appears in the exegesis of the *ḍāll* verse in the *Tafsīr* of al-Baghawī (d. AH 516). Iblīs leads Muḥammad's camel astray, and Gabriel blows the devil off to a distant place (India; other versions say Abyssinia), and restores Muḥammad to the caravan.[80] The expulsion of Iblīs by Gabriel whenever the former tries to harm Muḥammad is an independent motif, figuring in other contexts as well.[81]

Later exegetes, like al-Rāzī (d. AH 607), imported from Muḥammad's early years further situations by which they provided the Quranic *ḍāll* with other non-religious meanings. One such meaning was *ḍāllan 'an umūr al-dunyā*, "detached from worldly matters". This was based by the exegetes on those chapters in the biography of Muḥammad where he becomes Khadīja's employee and starts conducting her commercial affairs.[82] It was explained that the Quranic *ḍāll* signifies his withdrawn state of mind before Khadīja hired him.[83]

Another sense attached to the Quranic *ḍāll* was supported by the reports about the marriage bond which had existed among Muḥammad's daughters and pagan men from the tribe of Quraysh. According to the early biographical traditions, the Prophet married off his daughters Ruqayya and Umm Kulthūm to the sons of Abū Lahab.[84] This situation of legal ties with *mushrikūn* ("polytheists") was incorporated into the exegesis of the Quranic *ḍāll* verse by Tha'lab (d. AH 291).[85]

Apart from episodes from the pre-prophetic period, the exegetes used *sīra* chapters from the prophetic period as well. Al-Rāzī and others imported the stories of Muḥammad's first prophetic visions. It was explained that the Quranic *ḍāll* verse referred to Muḥammad's fear of the angel, and to his eventual soothing by God (*fa-hadā*, "and guided [you]", obviously being interpreted here in the sense of *fa-hadda'a*, "and calmed [you]").[86]

---

79 E.g. Ibn Hishām, I, 199–201; Ibn Bukayr, 81, 114; Ibn Sa'd, I, 129–31, 156–57.

80 Baghawī, *Ma'ālim*, V, 589; Zamakhsharī, IV, 265; Ibn al-Jawzī, *Zād al-masīr*, IX, 159 (3); Rāzī, XXXI, 216 (4); Qurṭubī, XX, 97 (Sa'īd ibn Jubayr); Ibn Kathīr, *Tafsīr*, IV, 523. The same is recorded in Shī'ī compilations. See Ṭabarsī, *Majma'*, XXX, 138 (6).

81 Abū Nu'aym, *Dalā'il*, no. 136; *Majma' al-zawā'id*, VIII, 232 (thrown to the river Jordan); Khargūshī (MS Tübingen), fol. 68a (to India).

82 For which see, for example, Ibn Hishām, I, 198–201.

83 Rāzī, XXXI, 217 (15). And cf. Birkeland, *Lord*, 32–33.

84 See Ibn Hishām, II, 306–307; Ibn Sa'd, VIII, 36–37; Balādhurī, *Ansāb*, I, 401; Ibn Qutayba, *Ma'ārif*, 62. See also Kister, "The Sons of Khadīja", 72, 74.

85 Tha'lab, *Majālis*, 398. See also Ibn 'Aṭiyya, XVI, 322 (from Tha'lab).

86 Rāzī, XXXI, 217 (13).

The *mi'rāj*, i.e. Muḥammad's nocturnal ascent to heaven, was again made a *sabab* of our verse. It was said that the verse referred to his inability to find his way to heaven, till God guided him to heaven on the night of the *mi'rāj*.[87]

Muḥammad's *hijra* from Mecca to Medina was imported too; this, of course, changed the chronology of revelations.[88] In the imported version, which is only found in one Shī'ī compilation, a linking word of the root *ḍ.l.l.* seems to have been installed: "When Muḥammad made the *hijra* to Medina, he and his guide lost their way" (*...ḍalla fī l-ṭarīq, wa-ḍalla dalīluhu*).[89] In another interpretation, the *ḍāll* verse is said to refer to Muḥammad's inability to perform the *hijra* because he had been captured by Quraysh, which caused him distress and perplexity till, finally, God gave him permission to depart from Mecca and made him succeed in all his enterprises.[90] In the original narrative of the *hijra* as recorded in the early *sīra*s, God's permission is indeed mentioned,[91] but Muḥammad's perplexity was something that was only added to the story for obvious exegetic aims.

Finally, al-Rāzī records an interpretation based not on the *sīra* but on the (Shī'ī) dogma of *taqiyya* ("dissimulation"), which restores the Quranic *ḍāll* to its older sense of pre-prophetic religious erring, but maintains that the Prophet only pretended to be a pagan, so as to avoid open conflict with his fellow tribesmen.[92]

All these interpretations are the result of the effort of the exegetes to adapt the Quranic *ḍāll* to the dogma of Muḥammad's total *'iṣma*. This they tried to achieve by offering various kinds of interpretations designed to replace the interpretation of al-Suddī, the only one to preserve the notion of *dīn qawmihi*. The result was suppression of the entire idea of guidance.

---

87 *Ibid.*, XXXI, 217 (17); Qurṭubī, XX, 98.

88 Sūrat al-Ḍuḥā is generally considered Meccan, but sometimes Medinan as well. See Ibn al-Ḍurays, *Faḍā'il*, 35 (from Ibn Jurayj).

89 Ṭūsī, *Tabyān*, X, 369 (5). Al-Ṭūsī notes that assuming Sūra 93 is Meccan, the verse is predicting future events.

90 Māwardī, *Nukat*, VI, 294 (no. 4); Rāzī, XXXI, 216 (11); Qurṭubī, XX, 97; Ṭūsī, *Tabyān*, X, 369 (5).

91 'Urwa ibn al-Zubayr, for example, relates that Muḥammad came to Abū Bakr asking him to accompany him, on the day Allāh "permitted" (*adhina*) him to make the *hijra*. See Ibn Hishām, II, 128–29.

92 Rāzī, XXXI, 217 (19).

VII

The *ḍāll* verse (93:7) is by no means the only Quranic passage into which the idea of guidance could be read. Another suitable verse occurs in 94:2:[93]

> ...*wa-waḍaʿnā ʿanka wizraka*: "and We have removed your burden from you."

Al-Ḍaḥḥāk ibn Muzāḥim (of Khurāsān, d. AH 102) explains that the "burden" (*wizr*) which was lifted from the Prophet was his "polytheism" (*al-shirk*).[94] This interpretation links the verse to the idea of guidance: Muḥammad was blessed by God, who redeemed him of idolatry. This is the very same idea reflected in the above *sīra* stories containing various instances in which this guidance is administered to Muḥammad through various agents.

But as in all the above cases, this interpretation did not gain wide circulation; Muslim scholars soon stripped the interpretation of its positive significance, focussing their attention on the bare allusion to the stage of paganism in the Prophet's life. As elsewhere, the insinuation that Muḥammad was once a polytheist could not last. Therefore, it is clear why the word *shirk*, "polytheism", is missing from all other interpretations of the same verse. This loaded word was replaced by several different, vaguer, phrases.

Already in the interpretations of some of al-Ḍaḥḥāk's contemporaries, the "burden" (*wizr*) with which Muḥammad was laden is only referred to as his "sin" or "sins" (*dhanb*, *dhunūb*) in the Jāhiliyya. This is how the interpretation of al-Ḥasan al-Baṣrī (d. AH 110) was formulated,[95] as well as that of Mujāhid (d. AH 104).[96] The latter interpretation is the one repeated by al-Bukhārī.[97] Al-Farrāʾ (d. AH 207) says that the "burden" which was taken off is the "fault" (*ithm*) of the Jāhiliyya.[98]

Others avoided even the word *jāhiliyya*. Thus Ibn Zayd (Medinan d. AH 182) says that the "burden" is the "sin" (*dhanb*) of Muḥammad "before he became a prophet".[99] In their effort to avoid allusion to polytheism others used the word "faults" (*adnās*), again without marking it as *jāhilī*, merely saying that

---

93 Cf. Andræ, *Person*, 132; Birkeland, *Lord*, 40–42, 45–49.

94 Ṭabarī, *Tafsīr*, XXX, 150 (no. 4). The *isnād*: Abū Muʿādh (al-Faḍl ibn Khālid, of Marw, d. AH 211)←ʿUbayd ibn Sulaymān←al-Ḍaḥḥāk ibn Muzāḥim (of Khurāsān. d. AH 102).

95 The interpretation of al-Ḥasan is quoted in Yaḥyā ibn Sallām, fol. 395 (*wa-hiya l-dhunūb allatī kānat ʿalayhi fī l-jāhiliyya*). See also Huwwārī, IV, 515 (from *Tafsīr al-Ḥasan*); Naḥḥās, *Iʿrāb*, V, 252.

96 Mujāhid, II, 767 (*dhanbaka fī l-jāhiliyya*).

97 Bukhārī, *Ṣaḥīḥ*, VI, 213 (65, Sūra 94).

98 Farrāʾ, II, 275.

99 See Ṭabarī, *Tafsīr*, XXX, 150 (no. 5, *dhanbuhu qabla an yunabbaʾ*).

they were "before the age of 40".[100] The clause "in the Jāhiliyya" was also omitted from the above interpretation of Mujāhid, as represented in Ṭabarī's *Tafsīr*, leaving only the word *dhanbaka,* "your sin".[101] The words "sin" (*dhanb*), or "sins" (*dhunūb*), also appear alone, without being marked as *jāhilī*, in the interpretations of Qatāda (Baṣran d. AH 117)[102] and Muqātil (d. AH 150).[103] Other such interpretations use another Arabic term signifying "fault" (*ithm*), sometimes with reference to Quran 48:2.[104] The words "error and forgetfulness" (*khaṭa' wa-sahw*) are employed as well.[105] Al-Zamakhsharī preferred the word *faraṭāt,* which likewise denotes "errors".[106] He also recorded an interpretation according to which the "burden" was no more than the Prophet's ignorance of the religious laws (of which he could not have been aware before he became a prophet). Al-Rāzī added some other suggestions in the same vein: Muḥammad's "burden" during his early years was his "perplexity" (*ḥayra*), due to his ignorance of the right way of expressing his gratitude to his Lord, or his grief due to the death of Khadīja and Abū Ṭālib.[107]

Moreover, there are interpretations, most of them relatively late, which explicitly date the "burden" to the time after the beginning of Muḥammad's prophethood. In this case, the "burden" can certainly no longer be connected to any kind of idolatry. In al-Zamakhsharī it is stated that the "burden" is the Prophet's exertion in his struggle to convert his people (*tahālukuhu 'alā islām qawmihi*).[108]

Al-Rāzī again proves to be the most fruitful supplier of such ideas. He takes the *wizr* to be either the "burden" of the prophetic activity itself (*a'bā' al-nubuwwa*),[109] or Muḥammad's suffering of the persecution of Quraysh,[110] or

---

[100] Māwardī, *Nukat*, VI, 297; Qurṭubī, XX, 106.

[101] Ṭabarī, *Tafsīr*, XXX, 150 (no. 1). See also Māwardī, *Nukat*, VI, 297.

[102] 'Abd al-Razzāq, *Tafsīr*, II, 380. The *isnād*: Ma'mar ibn Rāshid (Baṣran, d. AH 154)←Qatāda. See also Ṭabarī, *Tafsīr*, XXX, 150 (nos. 2–3); Māwardī, *Nukat*, VI, 297; Rāzī, XXXII, 4.

[103] Muqātil, II, fol. 243a (*dhanbaka*).

[104] Abū 'Ubayda, *Majāz*, II, 303; Zajjāj, V, 341; Baghawī, *Ma'ālim*, V, 592; Ibn Kathīr, *Tafsīr*, IV, 524.

[105] This is the interpretation of al-Ḥusayn ibn al-Faḍl ibn 'Umayr (Kūfan d. AH 282). See Baghawī, *Ma'ālim*, V, 592; Qurṭubī, XX, 106.

[106] Zamakhsharī, IV, 266.

[107] Rāzī, XXXII, 5.

[108] Zamakhsharī, IV, 296.

[109] Rāzī, XXXII, 4. See also Qurṭubī, XX, 106 (from 'Abd al-'Azīz ibn Yaḥyā); Ṭabarsī, *Majma'*, XXX, 142.

[110] Rāzī, XXXII, 5. See also Ṭūsī, *Tabyān*, X, 372; Ṭabarsī, *Majma'*, XXX, 142 (from Abū Muslim al-Iṣfahānī, d. AH 459).

more specifically, his fear of the angel when he first appeared to him.[111] All these suggestions anchor the *wizr* in the major themes of the Prophet's career.

In other interpretations the "burden" is said to have been caused by the sins of his fellow tribesmen, in which case it could regain its pagan connotation.[112] Special note should be taken of a peculiar Shīʿī interpretation according to which the *wizr* is the "burden" of war against Mecca which ended successfully, thanks to ʿAlī's support.[113] The linguistic structure of this interpretation echoes Quran 47:4: ...*ḥattā taḍaʿa l-ḥarbu awzārahā*...., "till war lays down its loads...."

Thus, the case of the *wizr* of Quran 94:2, as well as that of the *ḍāll* passage of 93:7, have demonstrated the decline of the idea of guidance. What began as innocent attempt to apply to the Islamic Prophet the universal idea of God's guidance, ended up with total rejection of this idea in the canonical *ḥadīth* and later *tafsīr*. The personality of the Prophet thus became devoid of drama, with no wonderful transformation from a human being into a prophet of God.

---

[111] Rāzī, XXXII, 5. See also Qurṭubī, XX, 106.
[112] Baghawī, *Maʿālim*, V, 592; Rāzī, XXXII, 4.
[113] Qummī, *Tafsīr*, II, 428.

PART III

REVELATION

5

The Khadīja–Waraqa Story

THE GOAL OF INITIATION and guidance is revelation. Already in the previous chapters reference has been made to traditions describing the actual beginning of Muḥammad's prophetic revelations. We have seen that in some versions the event is linked to the opening of Muḥammad's breast (Chapter 3). Some models of the same scene recur in the story of guidance (Chapter 4). The present chapter is dedicated to a more concentrated study of additional versions of the beginning of Muḥammad's prophetic revelations. This moment has drawn the attention of numerous Islamicists, but all have tried to unveil the factual background of the story, not the textual history of the story itself.[1]

I

The moment of first revelation, which is so crucial in stories about many prophets, is attached with no less importance when retold about Muḥammad. It contains the usual components, such as visions of voices and light, startling appearance of a supernatural figure (mostly an angel), the inexperienced prophet's fear, address of the angel, etc. These elements were built into the private case of Muḥammad, the prophet that emerged in Mecca. His story is set, of course, in a Meccan scene, and the plot revolves round two figures of his closest family—his first wife Khadīja, and her cousin Waraqa ibn Nawfal, an Arabian Christian scholar. The latter is mentioned in the sources alongside Zayd ibn ʿAmr and other *ḥanīf*s who abandoned Meccan polytheism and searched for the true religion of Abraham.[2] His role links the story to the theme of biblical attestation (Chapter 1); his knowledge of the sacred scriptures enables him to assert that the first vision experienced by Muḥammad is indeed a genuine prophetic one,

---

[1] See e.g. Nöldeke–Schwally, I, 74–89; Richard Bell, "Mohammed's Call", *The Muslim World* 24 (1934), 13–19; *idem*, "Muhammad's Visions", *The Muslim World* 24 (1934), 145–54; Frants Buhl, *Das Leben Muhammeds*, trans. Hans H. Schaeder (Heidelberg, 1961), 134–38; Rudi Paret, *Mohammed und der Koran* (Stuttgart, 1966), 46–48; Theodor Lohmann, "Sure 96 und die Berufung Muḥammeds", *Mitteilungen des Instituts für Orientforschung* 14 (1968), 249–302, 416–69; Watt, *M/Mecca*, 39–52; Rudolf Sellheim, "Muḥammeds erste Offenbarungserlebnis", *Jerusalem Studies in Arabic and Islam* 10 (1987), 1–16.

[2] E.g. Ibn Hishām, I, 237–38.

and that Muḥammad is indeed the prophet referred to in the biblical annunciations. In fact, Waraqa plays the same role of attestation on an earlier occasion as well, just before Khadīja decides to marry Muḥammad. On that instance he recites some poetic verses in which he states his belief in the Prophet.[3] Khadīja's role in the story of revelation is to give the startled Muḥammad moral assistance and provide the link between him and Waraqa, thus making it possible for the attestation to take place. Indeed, the meeting between the Prophet and Waraqa marks the culmination of the events described in the story.

The theme of revelation was adapted not only to local Arabian surroundings, but also to Quranic models. The belief that the Quranic scripture contains Muḥammad's prophetic revelations made this document the most apt material for the literary shaping of the scene of his first prophetic visions. Various Quranic passages and ideas were used for the cultivation of the story, thus crediting it with Quranic authority. The actual Quranic process of revelation through an angel named Gabriel (Quran 2:97) was also fitted into the stories.

Let us begin with those traditions in which the process of "Quranisation" is already completed, then go back to those traditions in which the scene of revelation is still devoid of Quranic materials.

For the study of the "Quranised" versions we have to begin with the *muṣannaf* compilations. The story of the first revelation usually occurs in them under the heading of "The Beginning of Revelation". The story itself is available in various versions. In some of them the passage which the angel brings to Muḥammad first is the entire Sūrat al-Fātiḥa (1). This *sūra* was chosen to represent Gabriel's first Quranic revelation for the simple reason that it is placed at the very beginning of the canon.[4]

The tradition about the revelation of Sūrat al-Fātiḥa was transmitted on the authority of the Kūfan Companion Abū Maysara ʻAmr ibn Shuraḥbīl (d. AH 63). It has been recorded by Ibn Abī Shayba in the *Maghāzī* section of his compilation,[5] and appears in the biographical sources as well.[6] The story is that whenever Muḥammad went out he would hear a call (*nidā'*) addressing him: "Oh Muḥammad!" This frightened him, and when he returned home he told Khadīja that he feared he was losing his mind. She said: "Nay, God will never do this to you. I know you as an honest person; you deliver whatever is put in

---

[3] *Ibid.*, I, 203–204. See also *Mustadrak*, II, 609–10.

[4] There were other Quranic passages which were made part of Muḥammad's first prophetic vision, but no detailed narratives are available: *al-Tīn* (95): Ḥalabī, I, 261 (from "one of the exegetes"); *al-Qalam* (68): *Fatḥ al-bārī*, VIII, 521 (Mujāhid); Zurqānī, I, 222; Ḥalabī, I, 244.

[5] Ibn Abī Shayba, XIV, no. 18404. The *isnād*: Isrā'īl ibn Yūnus ibn Abī Isḥāq al-Sabīʻī (Kūfan d. AH 160)←Abū Isḥāq al-Sabīʻī (Kūfan Shīʻī d. AH 126–29)←Abū Maysara.

[6] Ibn Bukayr, 132–33. See also Balādhurī, *Ansāb*, I, 105–106; Bayhaqī, *Dalā'il*, II, 158.

your safekeeping, and you do good unto the kindred." Khadīja disclosed the Prophet's secret to Abū Bakr, who was Muḥammad's drinking companion (*nadīm*) in the Jāhiliyya. Abū Bakr brought Muḥammad to Waraqa ibn Nawfal, who advised Muḥammad to go out again and not to run away, should he hear the voice call him. Muḥammad followed his advice, and when he went out, he was indeed addressed once more. He answered the call, and the voice commanded him to recite the entire text of the *Fātiḥa*. Afterwards Muḥammad returned to Waraqa and told him what had befallen him. Waraqa said: "Rejoice, rejoice, I hereby declare that you are the messenger about whom Jesus said he would succeed him, and whose name is Aḥmad. I confess that you are Aḥmad and that you are Muḥammad. In a short while you will be summoned to wage war, and if am still alive, I will join in with you ...."

Apart from Khadīja and Waraqa, who belong to the basic narrative framework, the event is also attended in this version by Abū Bakr. As is the case in so many traditions about the attestation in its Arabian sphere (Chapter 2), here again a Companion has been interpolated into the story for the purpose of promoting his own virtues (*faḍā'il*). Abū Bakr's name was added to the story of Muḥammad's meeting with Waraqa, just as his name was linked to the meeting of the Prophet with Baḥīrā.

Another element which does not form part of the basic narrative is the Quranic passage. The *Fātiḥa* was only secondarily built into the basic tale, and in fact, there are other versions of the same Khadīja–Waraqa narrative framework in which the angel brings to Muḥammad an altogether different Quranic passage, the first verses of Sūrat al-'Alaq (96).

The opening passage of this *sūra* reads:

> *iqra' bi-smi rabbika....*: "recite in the name of your Lord...."[7]

This extract was chosen to represent the first Quranic revelation, because it is the only passage in the Quran where the imperative *iqra'*, "recite", opens an entire *sūra*. Therefore, the passage seemed applicable to the story of the first address of the angel, in which he commands the Prophet to start declaring the glory of his Lord.

The traditions in which the Khadīja–Waraqa narrative contains the *iqra'* passage gained wider circulation than those with the *Fātiḥa*. In the section assigned to the beginning of Muḥammad's prophethood in the *Ṣaḥīḥ* of al-

---

[7] On this passage, see e.g. Uri Rubin, "*Iqra' bi-smi rabbika*", *Israel Oriental Studies* 13 (1993), 213–30.

Bukhārī (no. 1),[8] there are traditions dealing with the ways in which revelations generally used to come to Muḥammad, as well as traditions about the very first Quranic revelation. The latter all bear the *iqra'* passage. The story with the same passage was recorded in the relevant section about Muḥammad's prophetic revelation in the rearranged compilation of Ibn Ḥibbān,[9] and was included in the *Musnad* of Abū 'Awāna in the section devoted to the first stages of the Prophet's career.[10] Even compilers who did not devote separate sections to the subject of the first revelation did not fail to record the story. It occurs in the section named *Maghāzī* in 'Abd al-Razzāq's compilation,[11] in the section named *Īmān* in Muslim's *Ṣaḥīḥ*,[12] in the section named *Siyar* in al-Bayhaqī's *Sunan*,[13] etc.

The tradition with the *iqra'* passage which al-Bukhārī and Muslim selected is the one with the notable Medinan *isnād* of al-Zuhrī (d. AH 124)←'Urwa ibn al-Zubayr (d. AH 94)←'Ā'isha. The assumption is, of course, that 'Ā'isha only heard the story when she came of age, i.e. long after the actual event. The specific version recorded by al-Bukhārī and Muslim was circulated by Zuhrī's disciple 'Uqayl ibn Khālid (d. AH 141), as well as by the Egyptian Yūnus ibn Yazīd (d. AH 159).[14] Rich in Quranic imagery, the tradition runs as follows:

> The first prophetic experience of the messenger of God was "a true dream in sleep" (*al-ru'yā al-ṣādiqa* [var. *al-ṣāliḥa*] *fī l-nawm*; cf. Quran 37:105, 48:27). Each time he dreamt, it would seem to him like the "light of dawn" (*falaq al-ṣubḥ*; cf. Quran 6:96). Then he began to find pleasure in solitude. He used to retire to a cave in the mountain Ḥirā', where he practiced *taḥannuth*....[15] When he was thus engaged in the cave of Ḥirā', the angel came to him, saying: "Recite!" (*iqra'*). Muḥammad said: "I am not reciting" (*mā anā bi-qāri'*). The [Prophet] said: "The angel seized me and gripped my body till I could bear it no longer. Then he released me and said: 'Recite'. I said: 'I am not reciting.' The angel seized me again and gripped my body till I could bear it no longer. Then he released me and said: 'Recite'. I said: 'I am not reciting.' The angel seized me for the third time and gripped my body till I could bear it no longer. Then he

[8] Bukhārī, *Ṣaḥīḥ*, I, 2–22.
[9] Ibn Ḥibbān, *Ṣaḥīḥ*, I, 216–19 (no. 33).
[10] Abū 'Awāna, I, 110–12.
[11] 'Abd al-Razzāq, *Muṣannaf*, V, no. 9719.
[12] Muslim, I, 97–98.
[13] Bayhaqī, *Sunan*, IX, 6.
[14] Bukhārī, *Ṣaḥīḥ*, I, 3–4 (*Bad' al-waḥy*, 1); Muslim, I, 97–98 (*Īmān, Bāb bad' al-waḥy*).
[15] For which see M.J. Kister, "'*Al-Taḥannuth*': an Inquiry into the Meaning of a Term", *Bulletin of the School of Oriental and African Studies* 31 (1968), 223–36; Norman Calder, "*Ḥinth, birr*....: an Inquiry into the Arabic Vocabulary of Vows", *Bulletin of the School of Oriental and African Studies* 51 (1988), 214–39.

> released me and said: 'Recite in the name of your Lord who created....'" The Prophet repeated it, his heart palpitating with terror. Then he returned home to Khadīja, saying: "Cover me [with cloths]" (*zammilūnī, zammilūnī*), so they covered him till he overcame his anxiety. He told Khadīja what had taken place, and said: "I fear for myself." Khadīja said: "God will never disgrace thee...."[16] Then Khadīja took him to her cousin Waraqa, who had become a Christian in the Jāhiliyya, wrote Hebrew, and used to copy passages from the Gospels (*Injīl*) in Hebrew.... The Prophet told him about the things he had seen, and Waraqa said to him: "This is the *nāmūs*[17] which God sent down unto Moses...."

In this tradition the *iqra'* passage has been fitted into the basic narrative by means of what we may call a "linking word". This is contained in Muḥammad's utterance: *mā aqra'*, which has been derived from the Quranic *iqra'*. This repetitive line of Muḥammad has converted the repetitive Quranic *iqra'* into a divine response to Muḥammad's indisposition to recite. An additional linking word is the request *zammilūnī* uttered by Muḥammad. This links the events to the opening passage of Sūrat al-Muzzammil (73), where the title *al-muzzammil* signifies the Quranic prophet. However, the actual revelation of this Quranic passage is not stated in the story, the *iqra'* passage remaining the only Quranic revelation.

A parallel version of the Zuhrī←'Urwa←'Ā'isha tradition appears in the biographical sources.[18] This version, transmitted from al-Zuhrī by the Jazīran al-Nu'mān ibn Rāshid, contains some additional details not included in the version of the *muṣannaf* compilations. Gabriel visits Muḥammad twice, the first interview ending with Muḥammad's flight to Khadīja. Only during the second encounter is the *iqra'* passage revealed. But before this takes place, Muḥammad is so frightened that he tries to take his own life by throwing himself off a cliff. The angel stops him, saying: "Oh Muḥammad, I am Gabriel and you are the messenger of God." The absence of the attempted suicide in the former version of the Zuhrī←'Urwa←'Ā'isha tradition seems to have made it more acceptable to the *muṣannaf* compilers.

Another tradition with an attempted suicide, which likewise remained outside the *muṣannaf* compilations, is that of the Meccan story-teller 'Ubayd ibn 'Umayr (d. AH 68), who relates his tale to 'Abdallāh ibn al-Zubayr (Meccan d. AH 72). The first part of the story is related in the third person. At the point

---

[16] On the significance of Khadīja's words in this story, see M.J. Kister, "'God Will Never Disgrace Thee'", *Journal of the Royal Asiatic Society*, 1965, 27–32.

[17] On the significance of this term, see Bell, "Mohammed's Call", 15–16.

[18] Ṭabarī, *Tārīkh*, I, 1147 (II, 298–99).

where the *iqra'* passage is revealed, the narration shifts to Muḥammad himself, who carries on the story in the first person and mentions the attempted suicide. The tradition abounds in Quranic material. Apart from the *iqra'* passage, it contains the idea that revelation of the Quran began in the month of Ramaḍān (Quran 2:185), as implied in the statement that our episode took place during the same month. Moreover, the appearance of Gabriel is said to have taken place at night (*laylan*), which echoes the Quranic verses about *laylat al-Qadr* (97:1) and "the blessed night" (44:2), both indicating the time when the scripture was first sent down to the Quranic prophet. The tradition was preserved by Ibn Isḥāq (d. AH 150), and is quoted from him in al-Ṭabarī's *Tārīkh*.[19] In the version of Ibn Hishām, Muḥammad's attempted suicide is expunged.[20]

The traditions with the *iqra'* passage were also picked up by the Quran exegetes in their quest for the "occasions of revelation" (*asbāb al-nuzūl*). Thus, in the *Tafsīr*s of 'Abd al-Razzāq (d. AH 211) and al-Ṭabarī (d. AH 310), some of the above traditions are recorded in the exegesis of the *iqra'* passage.[21] But already before them, exegetes like Muqātil ibn Sulaymān (d. AH 150) were aware of the same traditions, stating that the *iqra'* passage was Muḥammad's first revelation.[22]

II

There are other traditions with the Khadīja–Waraqa narrative framework which only survived in the biographical sources. All of them occur in Ibn Sa'd, and their *isnād*s indicate that they were first put into circulation in the Ḥijāz (Mecca and Medina). All of them delineate the chain of events which led to Muḥammad's interview with Waraqa ibn Nawfal, but none of them refer to any specific Quranic revelation. All the traditions mention only non-verbal visions of voices and light. The fact that these traditions lack the essential Quranic allusions seems to have made them of no interest to the compilers of the *muṣannaf* collections. In themselves these versions preserve the sheer universal elements of revelation adapted to Arabian surroundings, but not yet to Quranic models.

One of these traditions is of the Meccan 'Ammār ibn Abī 'Ammār (d. *ca.* AH 105), who quotes Ibn 'Abbās:[23]

---

[19] The *isnād*: Ibn Isḥāq←Wahb ibn Kaysān (Meccan d. AH 127)←'Abdallāh ibn al-Zubayr←'Ubayd ibn 'Umayr. See Ṭabarī, *Tārīkh*, I, 1150 (II, 300–301). Cf. Ibn Bukayr, 121; Fākihī, IV, 86–89 (no. 2420); Bayhaqī, *Dalā'il*, II, 148.

[20] Ibn Hishām, I, 253.

[21] 'Abd al-Razzāq, *Tafsīr*, II, 384–85; Ṭabarī, *Tafsīr*, XXX, 161.

[22] Muqātil, II, fol. 244b.

[23] Ibn Sa'd, I, 195. See also Aḥmad, *Musnad*, I, 312; Ṭabarānī, *Kabīr*, XII, no. 12839.

> The Prophet said: "Oh Khadīja, I hear a voice and see light, and I am afraid the demon has taken possession of me." She said: "God will not do such a thing to you, oh son of 'Abdallāh." Then she came to Waraqa ibn Nawfal and told him about this, and he said: "If he is telling the truth, then this is an angel (*nāmūs*) like the one of Moses. If I am still alive when he is sent as a prophet, I shall support him and help him and believe in him."

There is a similar tradition of Hishām ibn 'Urwa (d. AH 146) on the authority of his father 'Urwa ibn al-Zubayr (d. AH 94).[24] It too knows only of a non-verbal vision, and runs as follows:

> The Prophet said: "Oh Khadīja, I hear a voice and see light, and I am afraid I have become a *kāhin*." She said: "God will not do such a thing to you, Oh son of 'Abdallāh. You tell the truth, deliver whatever is entrusted with you, and support your needy kindred."

These versions, in which no verbatim extract from the Quran is used to describe Muḥammad's first revelation, seem to contain only the basic Khadīja–Waraqa narrative framework, with the universal elements of revelation; it is essentially independent of the Quranic concept of revelation, for the very notion that the Prophet saw light and heard voices is alien to the Quran. Nowhere in the scripture is there any reference to visions of light (*ḍaw'*), or to the hearing of a voice (*ṣawt*). Neither is there in the Quran any reference to a terrifying encounter with the angel which causes the Prophet a critical state of anxiety. The fear with which Muḥammad reacts to his first prophetic experience in the story seems to have its origin in biblical conventions of the terror and fright with which prophets and other human beings react to the appearance of God (e.g. Judges 6:22–23; 13:22; Isaiah 6:5). Only the actual words with which the Prophet expresses to his wife Khadīja his fear for himself reflect Quranic themes, and this indirectly. He fears for his mental integrity, or that he has become a *kāhin*, etc. The Quran itself (52:29, 68:2, 69:42, 81:22) states that the prophet is neither a sorcerer (*kāhin*) nor a madman (*majnūn*).

The basic tale of Muḥammad's first revelations therefore accords with biblical rather than Quranic conventions, and the story was initially designed to meet apologetic needs. The scene of the beginning of prophetic revelations was of vital importance to the *vita* with which Muḥammad had to be endowed in order to match the prophets of the "People of the Book". But Quranic elements had soon to be fitted into the basic narrative in order to provide it with a more au-

[24] See Ibn Sa'd, I, 195.

thoritative status. After all, the Quran itself was the main manifestation of Muḥammad's inspiration, therefore a proper story about his inspiration should have apt Quranic links. Such links are only noticeable in another tradition recorded by Ibn Sa'd. In this tradition the non-Quranic visions of voices and light are replaced by the appearance of the angel himself, whose Quranic name is mentioned explicitly. The tradition has the Medinan *isnād* of Dāwūd ibn al-Ḥuṣayn (d. AH 135)←'Ikrima (d. AH 105)←Ibn 'Abbās, and reads:[25]

> When the Messenger of God was staying like this on the mountain Ajyād, he saw an angel against the horizon, throwing one leg over the other. He heard him say: "Oh Muḥammad, I am Gabriel; oh Muḥammad, I am Gabriel!" This frightened Muḥammad, and whenever he looked up at the sky he saw him again. He returned hurriedly to Khadīja and told her what had befallen him, saying: "Oh Khadīja, there is nothing I hate more than these idols and the *kāhins*, and I am afraid I have become a *kāhin*." She said: "No, oh husband, do not say such things; God will never do such a thing to you. You support your needy kindred and tell the truth and deliver whatever is entrusted to you, and your morals are honourable." Then she went to Waraqa ibn Nawfal, this being her first visit to him, and told him what the messenger of God had told her. Waraqa said: "By God, your husband tells the truth; this is the beginning of prophethood. The great *nāmūs* has come to him. Tell him to think only good of himself."

The "horizon" (*ufuq*) against which the angel is seen is the very place where the Quran locates the angel (53:7, 81:23),[26] and Khadīja's statement that the morals (*khuluq*) of Muḥammad are honourable seems to echo Quran 68:4.

But in spite of the more massive presence of Quranic materials in this version, the vision itself still lacks a verbatim Quranic extract. Gabriel merely utters some words of introduction in which he presents himself to Muḥammad. Only the versions with the verbatim Quranic revelations—Sūrat al-Fātiḥa, and especially the *iqra'* passage—could gain access into the *muṣannaf* compilations. Of all the versions of the Khadīja–Waraqa story, only they could best serve the aim of illustrating the beginning of Muḥammad's prophetic revelations in its most authoritative setting.

---

[25] *Ibid.*, I, 194–95. See also Balādhurī, *Ansāb*, I, 104 (no. 190).
[26] See Bell, "Mohammed's Call", 15.

* * *

The motif of non-Quranic visions of voices and light is present not only in some versions of the Khadīja–Waraqa tale, but also in traditions designed to fix the chronology of Muḥammad's first years of prophethood. These are harmonising traditions which try to squeeze the non-Quranic visions and the proper Quranic revelations into one progressive sequence of events. One of the traditions of this kind is recorded in the *Ṣaḥīḥ* of Muslim.[27] Here it is said that the Prophet remained in Mecca fifteen years, during seven of which he used to hear voices and see light, and in the course of the other eight years he was receiving the *waḥy*, i.e. the proper revelation of the Quran. In Medina he spent ten years. This tradition was circulated with the *isnād* of the Meccan ʿAmmār ibn Abī ʿAmmār (d. *ca.* AH 105) from Ibn ʿAbbās.[28] Another tradition recorded by al-Balādhurī says that Gabriel appeared to Muḥammad on Monday, 17 Ramaḍān, on the mountain Ḥirāʾ, when the Prophet was 40 years old. The tradition adds that earlier on, the prophet already heard [voices] and saw [light].[29]

It is noteworthy that in yet another group of traditions, the visions which precede the revelations administered by Gabriel are also said to have been prompted by an angel, thus being elevated from simple voices and light to the rank of prophetic revelations. In one tradition the name of the angel is Michael, which is known from the Quran (2:98). The tradition has the Iraqi *isnād* of Dāwūd ibn Abī Hind (Baṣran d. AH 139)←ʿĀmir al-Shaʿbī (Kūfan d. AH 103). It says that Michael was put in charge of Muḥammad, and that for three years he initiated him to the "modalities" (*asbāb*) of prophethood. When the Prophet was 43, Gabriel took over the role of Michael: he brought him the Quranic revelations for ten years in Mecca, and for ten more years in Medina. The Prophet died at the age of 63. This tradition was recorded by ʿAbd al-Razzāq in his *Muṣannaf* in the section *Janāʾiz*, i.e. funeral rites.[30] This somewhat bizarre classification arises from the fact that Muḥammad's age at death is provided here. A similar tradition is found in Ibn Saʿd.[31] Its *isnād* is identical to the Iraqi *isnād* of the tradition of al-Shaʿbī about Michael, and the only difference is in the name of the angel who precedes Gabriel. This time he is Isrāfīl, not

---

[27] Muslim, VII, 89 (43, *Bāb kam aqāma l-nabiyy (ṣ) bi-Makka wa-l-Madīna*).

[28] See the same tradition also in Ibn Saʿd, I, 224; Aḥmad, *Musnad*, I, 266, 279, 294, 312; Ṭabarānī, *Kabīr*, XII, no. 12840; Bayhaqī, *Dalāʾil*, VII, 240.

[29] Balādhurī, *Ansāb*, I, 104 (no. 188). The *isnād*: Abū Bakr ibn ʿAbdallāh ibn Abī Sabra (d. AH 162)←Isḥāq ibn ʿAbdallāh ibn Abī Farwa (d. AH 144)←Abū Jaʿfar (the Imām Muḥammad ibn ʿAlī al-Bāqir, d. AH 114).

[30] ʿAbd al-Razzāq, *Muṣannaf*, III, no. 6785.

[31] Ibn Saʿd, I, 191. See also Ṭabarī, *Tārīkh*, I, 1249 (II, 387); Bayhaqī, *Dalāʾil*, II, 132; Ibn ʿAbd al-Barr, *Istīʿāb*, I, 36; Ibn Kathīr, *Bidāya*, III, 4. See also Yaʿqūbī, II, 23.

Michael. Isrāfīl is not mentioned in the Quran, for which reason the version with his name seems to have been left outside the *muṣannaf* compilations. The compilers (in this case, 'Abd al-Razzāq) preferred the version with the name of the Quranic Michael to that with the non-Quranic Isrāfīl.

In fact, the version with Isrāfīl provoked the objection of several scholars. Ibn Sa'd relates that he mentioned the tradition about Isrāfīl to his master al-Wāqidī, and the latter responded: "The scholars of our town (i.e. Medina) do not know that Isrāfīl attended the Prophet. The scholars and the *sīra* experts say that once the revelation had been sent down to Muḥammad, no angel associated with him till he died except Gabriel."[32] In al-Ṭabarī's *Tārīkh*,[33] where another version of the same Iraqi tradition about Isrāfīl is recorded, al-Wāqidī himself inquires of his own Medinan masters about this, and they reject it. Thus, for a tradition about the prophetic inspiration of Muḥammad to be accepted by all scholars, it had to fit Quranic modes of revelation. Since Michael is the only angel mentioned in the Quran besides Gabriel, only traditions with him were recognised as sound.

---

[32] Ibn Sa'd, I, 191.

[33] Ṭabarī, *Tārīkh*, I, 1249 (II, 386–87).

6

The Lapse of Revelation

(*Fatrat al-waḥy*)

I

THE LINK BETWEEN GOD AND MAN through prophetic revelation may sometimes be interrupted, which causes the recipient of revelation a serious crisis. The Bible has some examples of such crisis caused by the departure of the spirit of God (e.g. I Samuel 16:14). This traumatic aspect of revelation also emerges in the life of Muḥammad. In his case it was turned into the anti-climax of his meeting with Waraqa. But the lapse of revelation takes place only to end with the resumption of revelation, which reaffirms the God–prophet link. This event provides another angle of the trial which the Prophet had to endure before being fully initiated into the prophetic office.

The traditions refer to the lapse of revelation as *fatrat al-waḥy*, "the interval in the prophetic inspiration" (lit. "the cooling down of the prophetic inspiration"[1]). The story of the interval deserves examination, because here the process of adaptation was again not entirely successful, due to some dogmatic problems that it caused.

Let us again begin with the *muṣannaf* compilations. Here another version of the Zuhrī←'Urwa←'Ā'isha tradition of the Khadīja–Waraqa story is recorded, and relates an extended chain of events. This version was circulated by the Baṣran *sīra* expert Ma'mar ibn Rāshid (d. AH 154). The interview with Waraqa is followed by the *fatrat al-waḥy*, during which Muḥammad does not meet the angel. The absence of the angel gives Muḥammad a fresh cause for agony: this time he is not in a state of fear of the angel, but of yearning to meet him again. In the version of Ma'mar, when the *fatra* takes place Muḥammad is distressed and tries to end his life by throwing himself from a cliff. This is only prevented by the angel, who resumes his visits at the last moment, saying to the desperate Prophet: "Oh Muḥammad, you are truly the messenger of God." But the angel disappears again into another *fatra*, so Muḥammad repeats his attempt to take his own life, only to be saved once more by the reappearance of the angel with more encouraging words.

[1] There are various opinions concerning how long this *fatra* lasted. See Suhaylī, *Rawḍ*, I, 281; Shāmī, II, 363–64; Mughulṭāy, fol. 115b–116a.

Muḥammad's suicidal intentions put him in an unflattering situation of lack of self-confidence, which seems to be the reason why, in the former versions of the Zuhrī←'Urwa←'Ā'isha tradition, the whole story of the *fatra* was left out. Not many compilers recorded the complete version. Apart form al-Bukhārī, only 'Abd al-Razzāq, Abū 'Awāna and Ibn Ḥibbān have it.[2] Except for their compilations, the tradition only recurs outside the *muṣannaf* compilations.[3] Al-Bukhārī himself did not record it in the chapter about the first revelation, relegating it to a less conspicuous location in a chapter dealing with the interpretation of dreams.[4]

The *fatra* story, like the Khadīja–Waraqa one, consists of a basic narrative framework into which different Quranic passages were embedded. Ma'mar's version of the Zuhrī←'Urwa←'Ā'isha tradition consists of just this plain framework, with no Quranic connection. The same applies to another tradition preserved only by Ibn Sa'd, related on the authority of Ibn 'Abbās. The story is told in the third person, and here too Muḥammad tries to take his own life, because of the *fatra*, and is saved at the last moment by the angel Gabriel.[5]

In other versions, which we shall now see, certain extracts from the scripture have been incorporated into the episode of the *fatra*, thus confirming the link between the life of Muḥammad and the Quran.

One of the extracts used is 74:1–2:

(1) *Yā ayyuhā l-muddaththir* (2) *qum fa-andhir*: "Oh *Muddaththir*, rise and warn...."

This passage occurs in a tradition which was given a much more prominent place in the standard *ḥadīth* compilations. Nothing is said in it about Muḥammad's mental distress. This is a tradition of al-Zuhrī, who quotes the Medinan Abū Salama ibn 'Abd al-Raḥmān ibn 'Awf (d. AH 94)←the Companion Jābir ibn 'Abdallāh. The *muṣannaf* compilers included it quite readily in the chapters about the beginning of Muḥammad's prophethood,[6] and it is also

---

[2] 'Abd al-Razzāq, *Muṣannaf*, V, no. 9719; Abū 'Awāna, I, 110–12; Ibn Ḥibbān, *Ṣaḥīḥ*, I, no. 33.

[3] E.g. Aḥmad, *Musnad*, VI, 232–33; Bayhaqī, *Dalā'il*, II, 135–38; Abū Nu'aym, *Dalā'il*, no. 162; Dhahabī, *Sīra*, 64; Ibn Kathīr, *Bidāya*, III, 2–3. See also Fākihī, IV, 94–95 (no. 2430).

[4] Bukhārī, *Ṣaḥīḥ*, IX, 37–38 *(Ta'bīr*, 1).

[5] See Ibn Sa'd, I, 196. The *isnād*: Dāwūd ibn al-Ḥuṣayn (Medinan d. AH 135)←Abū Ghaṭafān ibn Ṭarīf (Medinan)←Ibn 'Abbās.

[6] See Bukhārī, *Ṣaḥīḥ*, I, 4 (*Bad' al-waḥy*); Muslim, I, 98–99 (*Īmān, Bāb bad' al-waḥy*); Tirmidhī/*Tuḥfa*, IX, 244–45; and see also 'Abd al-Razzāq, *Muṣannaf*, V, 323–24; Abū 'Awāna, I, 112–13.

found in the biographical sources.[7] Said to have formed part of a longer *ḥadīth* that Jābir transmitted about the lapse of revelation, the story describes how the *fatra* was brought to an end by the revelation of the *Muddaththir* passage, and is related in the first person as Muḥammad's own account:

> ...While I was walking I heard a voice from the sky. I looked up, and behold! There was the angel that had come to me in Ḥirā' sitting on a throne between heaven and earth. I was frightened by him, and returned [home], saying: "Cover me up! cover me up!" Thereupon God revealed: *Yā ayyuhā l-muddaththir, qum fa-andhir*. From then on the revelation amplified and continued uninterruptedly.

In this tradition Muḥammad acts with greater mental stability and self confidence. He is not grieved by the absence of the angel, nor does he try to kill himself; he is merely frightened by the renewed appearance of the angel. The *Muddaththir* passage which marks the end of the *fatra* figures as a divine response to the Prophet's hiding under his cloths in fear of the angel. The hiding prophet who is called *Muddaththir*, i.e. "the one wrapped up in cloths", is commanded to "rise and warn" (v. 2), which means that he should cast off the covers under which he hides and start acting with resolution.[8]

It should be noted, however, that the revelation of the *Muddaththir* passage is not always related in connection with the *fatra*. Ibn Hishām has a tradition which indicates a much later time for the revelation of the *Muddaththir* passage, already when open strife between Muḥammad and Quraysh had broken out. Muḥammad is said to have been deeply distressed because everyone in Mecca rejected his prophetic message; so he returned home, and in his agony he wrapped himself up in his cloths. Thereupon the *Muddaththir* passage was revealed.[9] This chronology never gained general support, the prevailing view remaining that the *Muddaththir* passage was revealed following the *fatra*, being the second Quranic revelation after the *iqra'* passage. Sometimes it was even said to be the first to be revealed.[10]

---

[7] Balādhurī, *Ansāb*, I, 109 (no. 201). See also Aḥmad, *Musnad*, III, 325, 377, 377–78; Bayhaqī, *Dalā'il*, II, 138, 140, 156–57; Ṭabarī, *Tārīkh*, I, 1155–56 (II, 306); Abū Nu'aym, *Dalā'il*, 215 (no. 162); Dhahabī, *Sīra*, 69; Ibn Kathīr, *Bidāya*, III, 3; Cf. also Balādhurī, *Ansāb*, I, 108 (no. 198); Ṭabarī, *Tārīkh*, I, 1155 (II, 305–306); Fākihī, IV, 93 (no. 2428).

[8] On the significance of the *Muddaththir* passage, see Uri Rubin, "The Shrouded Messenger: On the Interpretation of *al-Muzzammil* and *al-Muddaththi*r", *Jerusalem Studies in Arabic and Islam* 16 (1993), 96–107.

[9] Ibn Hishām, I, 310.

[10] See the statement attributed to Jābir ibn 'Abdallāh in Ibn al-Ḍurays, *Faḍā'il*, no. 25. See also Bukhārī, *Ṣaḥīḥ*, VI, 200–201 (65, Sūra 74); Muslim, I, 99 (1, *Bāb bad' al-waḥy*); and

II

Some versions preserved in the biographical sources reveal yet another Quranic passage which was incorporated into the story of the *fatra* instead of the *Muddaththir* passage. Most versions with this extract were never included in the standard *ḥadīth* compilations, which means that not all traditions in which a Quranic verse occurs were automatically accepted. The specific traditions to which we refer were rejected by the compilers of *ḥadīth* because they clashed too bluntly with the image of the Prophet as the compilers saw it.

The Quranic passage which appears in these traditions is the third verse of Sūrat al-Ḍuḥā (93):

> *mā wadda'aka rabbuka wa-mā qalā*: "Your Lord has not forsaken you, nor does He hate [you]."

This passage of Sūrat al-Ḍuḥā was imported from the scripture and fitted into the story of the *fatra* by means of linking words derived from the Quranic *wadda'aka*, "[has not] forsaken you", and *qalā*, "[does not] hate [you]". The words were turned from negative into affirmative mode, and incorporated into lines uttered by certain people during the *fatra*, so that the Quranic passage itself became a denial of these lines.

In the earliest extant biographical sources the lines negated by the Quranic revelation are uttered by the Prophet himself. The following passage appears in the *Sīra* of Ibn Isḥāq, but, as in several previous cases, it was only preserved in the recension of Yūnus ibn Bukayr (d. AH 199):[11]

> Then the revelation stopped coming to the apostle of God for a while, till he became distressed and grieved. He spoke to himself about the effect it had on him, saying: "I am afraid my associate (i.e. the angel) has become hateful of me (*qalānī*) and has deserted me (*wadda'anī*)." Then Gabriel brought him Sūrat al-Ḍuḥā....

Muḥammad's linking words *qalānī*, "[God's angel] has become hateful of me", and *wadda'anī*, "[God's angel] has deserted me", have turned the Quranic *mā wadda'aka* passage into an antiphony denying Muḥammad's apprehension that the Lord *did* desert him and *did* hate him. The *mā wadda'aka* passage thus seems to have been provided with a new context, on a different level from its original one. An unbiased reading of Sūrat al-Ḍuḥā as a whole leads to the con-

---

Balādhurī, *Ansāb*, I, 107–108 (no. 197), 109–10 (no. 203); Ṭabarī, *Tārīkh*, I, 1153–54 (II, 303–304); Aḥmad, *Musnad*, III, 392; Bayhaqī, *Dalā'il*, II, 155–56.

[11] Ibn Bukayr, 135; Guillaume, "New Light", 30.

clusion (reached already by Birkeland[12]) that originally it had nothing to do with the supposed interruption of the prophetic inspiration. The verses that follow the *mā wadda'aka* passage in the scripture do not contain a promise to resume the allegedly interrupted visions, but rather a promise to give the Quranic prophet satisfaction on the socio-economic level. This promise is inherent in the survey of the Quranic prophet's private history which is marked by the constant improvement of his socio-economic status (vv. 6–8). When fitted into the *fatra* episode, the *mā wadda'aka* passage was given the role of redeeming the Prophet from his temporary loss of confidence in his Lord.

The story of Ibn Isḥāq in which the *fatra* causes Muḥammad to utter explicit words of doubt concerning God's love for him could not, of course, enter the *muṣannaf* compilations. The compilers could not repeat a story in which the Prophet features in such a sceptical state of mind. Moreover, even within the realm of Muḥammad's biography the story underwent significant changes designed to attenuate its scepticism and render it less offensive to the dogma of Muḥammad's *'iṣma*. This dogma in its most rigid formulation would have it that he never doubted the presence of his Lord, hence he could never state that God has deserted him and hates him.[13]

To begin with, in the parallel version of Ibn Isḥāq's *fatra* tradition, as recorded in the recension of Ibn Hishām (d. AH 213), the lines of Muḥammad saying that his Lord has deserted him are omitted altogether.[14] The survival of the Prophet's unbecoming words in Yūnus ibn Bukayr indicates once again that his text preserves an earlier and more representative version of Ibn Isḥāq's biography of Muḥammad.

Apart from suppressing Muḥammad's words, other versions disclose a different means of modification, retaining the words but attributing them to people other than Muḥammad. Their survival secured the essential link with the *mā wadda'aka* passage. Such versions are found in the exegesis of this passage, where they provide the occasions of its revelation (*asbāb al-nuzūl*).

In the *Tafsīr* of al-Ṭabarī there are some such versions in which the linking words are uttered by the most likely person to know about Muḥammad's anxiety, namely, his wife Khadīja. A tradition of Hishām ibn 'Urwa (d. AH 146) from his father 'Urwa ibn al-Zubayr (d. AH 94) relates that when Gabriel stopped coming to Muḥammad for a while, he was grieved, and Khadīja said to him: "Surely, your Lord hates you (*qalāka*), if He causes you such sorrow."

---

[12] Birkeland, *Lord*, 16–17.

[13] See Rāzī, XXXI, 209, about the objection of the scholars to the idea that Muḥammad might have thought that God had deserted him; and Birkeland, *Lord*, 15.

[14] Ibn Hishām, I, 257–58.

Thereupon, the reassuring *mā wadda'aka* passage was revealed.[15] Apart from the authors of *tafsīr*, only two *ḥadīth* compilers included this version in their compilations. Ibn Abī Shayba (d. AH 235) has recorded it in the section named *Faḍā'il*.[16] For him the tradition represents an example of how the Quran praises the Prophet by stressing that the Lord has never abandoned him. Al-Ḥākim (d. AH 404) recorded the same tradition in the section labelled *Tārīkh*, in the chapter of the biography of Muḥammad.[17] But the majority of the *ḥadīth* compilers ignored the story because they were more aware of its less flattering aspects, namely, the doubts Khadīja was said to have cast on the Prophet. This woman was Muḥammad's first and most beloved wife, and the reputation she had among the Muslims as Muḥammad's most supportive spouse did not permit stories in which she passed such distrustful judgement on her husband's state of mind.[18] However, outside the *muṣannaf* compilations the story about Khadīja was circulated quite freely, and was gladly taken up by the authors of *tafsīr* in their ceaseless quest for *asbāb al-nuzūl*. One such tradition recorded in Ṭabarī's *Tafsīr* has the *isnād*: Abū Isḥāq al-Shaybānī (Sulaymān ibn Abī Sulaymān, Kūfan d. AH 129–42)←'Abdallāh ibn Shaddād (d. AH 81–82). This was circulated by 'Abd al-Wāḥid ibn Ziyād (Baṣran d. AH 176).[19] There is also a Shī'ī version on the authority of the Medinan imām Abū Ja'far Muḥammad al-Bāqir (d. AH 114), recorded in a Shī'ī Quran commentary.[20]

However, even within the realm of *tafsīr*, the concern for the reputation of Khadīja did eventually have its effect on the story of the *fatra*. In the majority of the traditions recorded by the authors of *tafsīr*, the improper words are uttered not by Khadīja, but rather by some of Muḥammad's renowned foes. One of them is Umm Jamīl, wife of Abū Lahab, who is said to have uttered the insulting linking text (*mā arā ṣāḥibaka illā qad qalāka*), after revelation stopped coming to Muḥammad for a few days. This is only said to have taken place after the revelation of Sūrat al-Masad (111), in which she and her husband are

---

[15] Ṭabarī, *Tafsīr*, XXX, 148 (no. 22). See also Ibn Bukayr, 135; Wāḥidī, *Asbāb*, 256; Ibn 'Aṭiyya, XVI, 321; Bayhaqī, *Dalā'il*, VII, 60; Suyūṭī, *Durr*, VI, 360. In Samarqandī, *Tafsīr*, III, 486, the same is recorded on the authority of the Kūfan al-Suddī (d. AH 128).

[16] Ibn Abī Shayba, XI, no. 11813.

[17] *Mustadrak*, II, 610–11.

[18] The idea that Khadīja might have scolded Muḥammad was refuted by several Muslim scholars. See *Fatḥ al-bārī*, III, 7. Some of them maintained that assuming the story was true, Khadīja uttered the words not with malice, but rather out of sincere concern. See Bayhaqī, *Dalā'il*, VII, 60.

[19] Ṭabarī, *Tafsīr*, XXX, 148 (no. 17), 162 (no. 3); *idem*, *Tārīkh*, I, 1148–49 (II, 299–300). See also Ibn al-'Arabī, *Aḥkām*, IV, 1948; Rāzī, XXXI, 209; Suyūṭī, *Durr*, VI, 360.

[20] Qummī, *Tafsīr*, II, 428. Cf. Ibn Shahrāshūb, I, 44.

cursed.[21] With the tradition about Umm Jamīl we move from the Ḥijāz to Iraq, where the tradition about her was circulated under the Kūfan (Shīʿī) *isnād* of Abū Isḥāq al-Sabīʿī (d. AH 126)←the Companion Zayd ibn Arqam (d. AH 66). In another Kūfan tradition the disparaging party is merely designated as "a woman". The tradition is of al-Aswad ibn Qays al-ʿAbdī, from the Companion Jundab ibn ʿAbdallāh al-Bajalī.[22] In another version of the same Aswad←Jundab tradition, the woman is "a member of his tribe" (*baʿḍ banāt ʿammihi*).[23] There is yet another version of the Aswad←Jundab tradition about the "woman" in which Muḥammad is said to have only suffered temporary illness (*ishtakā*), not lack of inspiration. This occurs in the biographical sources,[24] as well as in the *muṣannaf* compilations. Muḥammad is said to have been taken ill for a few days, which prevented him from performing night vigils. A "woman" mocked him, saying that his associate had deserted him, thereupon the *mā waddaʿaka* passage was revealed. This version of the Aswad←Jundab tradition was recorded by al-Bukhārī in the section of *Tafsīr*, in the commentary on the *mā waddaʿaka* passage.[25] He also recorded it under *Faḍāʾil al-Qurʾān*, in the chapter dealing with the different modes of revelation. In this context the tradition exemplifies interruption of revelations due to illness.[26] The tradition reappears in a chapter dealing with illness as a justified excuse for not praying during the night.[27] Other compilers recorded it in their chapters on the persecution suffered by the Prophet.[28]

Other Iraqi traditions have the linking words voiced by a collective group of enemies, the polytheists (*mushrikūn*) of Quraysh. This is the case in an additional version of the Aswad←Jundab tradition,[29] as well as in a tradition of the

---

[21] *Mustadrak*, II, 526–27 (*Tafsīr*); Suyūṭī, *Durr*, VI, 360; *Fatḥ al-bārī*, III, 7. See also Ibn ʿAṭiyya, XVI, 321; Ṭabarsī, *Majmaʿ*, XXX, 135–36; Baghawī, *Maʿālim*, V, 587; Zamakhsharī, IV, 263; Rāzī, XXXI, 209.

[22] Ṭabarī, *Tafsīr*, XXX, 148 (nos. 13, 15, 16); Wāḥidī, *Asbāb*, 256; *idem*, *Wasīṭ*, fol. 335a. See also Aḥmad, *Musnad*, IV, 312; Bayhaqī, *Dalāʾil*, VII, 58.

[23] Suyūṭī, *Durr*, VI, 360. See also Ṭabarānī, *Kabīr*, II, no. 1710.

[24] Aḥmad, *Musnad*, IV, 312, 313; Ṭabarānī, *Kabīr*, II, nos. 1709, 1711; Bayhaqī, *Dalāʾil*, VII, 59. See also Baghawī, *Maʿālim*, V, 587; Suyūṭī, *Durr*, VI, 360; and see also a version of the Aswad←Jundab tradition with *ishtakā*, where the scolding woman is Umm Jamīl, and the reason of Muḥammad's illness is poetry: Qurṭubī, XX, 93 (from al-Thaʿlabī); Ibn Kathīr, *Tafsīr*, IV, 522 (from Ibn Abī Ḥātim). See also Suyūṭī, *Durr*, VI, 360 ("a woman").

[25] See Bukhārī, *Ṣaḥīḥ*, VI, 213 (65, Sūra 93); and see also *ibid.*, II, 62 (19, *Bāb tark al-qiyām li-l-marīḍ*); Bayhaqī, *Sunan*, III, 14.

[26] Bukhārī, *Ṣaḥīḥ*, VI, 224 (66:1).

[27] *Ibid.*, II, 62 (19, *Bāb tark al-qiyām li-l-marīḍ*).

[28] Muslim, V, 182 (32, *Bāb mā laqiya min adhā l-mushrikīn*); Ibn Ḥibbān, XIV, no. 6566.

[29] ʿAbd al-Razzāq, *Tafsīr*, II, 379; Ṭabarī, *Tafsīr*, XXX, 148 (no. 14); Suyūṭī, *Durr*, VI, 360. See also Ṭabarānī, *Kabīr*, II, no. 1712.

Baṣran Ma'mar ibn Rāshid (d. AH 154).[30] Similarly, in a tradition quoted by the Baṣran al-Mu'tamir ibn Sulaymān (d. AH 187) from the *Sīra* of his father, Sulaymān al-Taymī (d. AH 143), the collective "Quraysh" is employed.[31] In a variant version of the above tradition about Khadīja, with the *isnād*: Abū Isḥāq al-Shaybānī←'Abdallāh ibn Shaddād, she is replaced by "unbelievers of Quraysh". This variant was circulated by Ḥafṣ ibn Ghiyāth (Kūfan d. AH 194).[32]

The traditions attributing the linking words of the *mā wadda'aka* passage to "the polytheists" (*al-mushrikūn*), or simply to "the people" (*al-nās*), were given predominance in the *asbāb al-nuzūl* of Sūrat al-Ḍuḥā, as recorded by such *tafsīr* authors as Yaḥyā ibn Sallām (d. AH 200), al-Farrā' (d. AH 207), and al-Zajjāj (d. AH 311). Similarly, the majority of the traditions recorded by al-Ṭabarī in his commentary on the *mā wadda'aka* passage have the *mushrikūn* or the *nās* utter the linking words. With these traditions, all of Iraqi provenance,[33] the time of the events has changed considerably. They are no longer anchored in the beginning of the prophetic visions of Muḥammad, but already in his open clash with the polytheists. Thus, the story of the *fatra* was transformed from one about personal prophetic agony into one of persecution.

The *fatra* traditions in which the linking words of the *mā wadda'aka* passage are uttered by Muḥammad's adversaries, and not by himself or by Khadīja, were the only ones which could be accepted into the more authoritative *ḥadīth* compilations. They conformed to the image of Muḥammad as a persecuted messenger who suffered the maltreatment and abuses of his fellow tribesmen. Thus, the version about the *mushrikūn* of the Aswad←Jundab tradition was recorded by Muslim and Ibn Ḥibbān. The former included it in the section entitled *al-Jihād wa-l-siyar*, in the chapter about the disparagements of the polytheists against Muḥammad.[34] In the rearranged compilation of Ibn Ḥibbān, the tradition is included in a similar chapter of the section of *Tārīkh*.[35]

---

[30] 'Abd al-Razzāq, *Tafsīr*, II, 379.

[31] Ibn 'Asākir (*Mukhtaṣar*), XXVI, 283; Ibn Kathīr, *Bidāya*, III, 14–15 (from Ibn 'Asākir, who quotes Sulaymān al-Taymī). Cf. *Fatḥ al-bārī*, VIII, 545.

[32] Balādhurī, *Ansāb*, I, 108–109 (no. 200).

[33] Yaḥyā ibn Sallām, fol. 395; Farrā', III, 273; Zajjāj, V, 339; Ṭabarī, *Tafsīr*, XXX, 148 (nos. 18–19, of the Baṣran Qatāda [d. AH 118]; no. 20, of al-Ḍaḥḥāk [d. AH 102]; no. 21, with the 'Awfī←Ibn 'Abbās Kūfan family *isnād*).

[34] Muslim, V, 182 (32, *Bāb mā laqiya min adhā l-mushrikīn*).

[35] Ibn Ḥibbān, *Ṣaḥīḥ*, XIV, no. 6565.

III

Finally, it should be noted that the episode of the *fatra* exists in further versions in which the withdrawal of prophetic inspiration comes as a punitive measure following a wrongdoing committed by either the Prophet himself or by the Muslims. That prophets may be deprived of inspiration due to unethical conduct is already known to Jewish *midrash*, where it is related that the holy spirit of God left King David for 22 years after his sin with Bath-Sheba.[36] In the Islamic traditions, the causes given for the departure of revelation vary. Each of the faults mentioned has been made a reason for the *fatra* for didactic purposes, by those who wished to warn the public against them.

In some traditions it is the recitation of poetry. That this caused the *fatra* is implied in a further version of the Aswad←Jundab tradition, recorded by al-Tirmidhī in the section of *Tafsīr*[37] and circulated by Sufyān ibn 'Uyayna (Meccan d. AH 196). The event is related in the first person by Jundab himself, who says that he was in a cave together with Muḥammad. The Prophet's finger began bleeding, and he recited the following *rajaz* verse:

hal anti illā iṣba'un damītī
wa-fī sabīli llāhi mā laqītī

You are just a bleeding finger;
What you suffer is for the cause of God.

Jundab goes on to say that subsequently Gabriel stopped coming to Muḥammad for a while, and the polytheists said that his Lord had forsaken him. Thereupon the *mā wadda'aka* passage was revealed. The episode of the poetic verse is also related as an independent event, without reference to the *fatra*, but still under the Aswad←Jundab *isnād*.[38] Only in the version recorded by al-Tirmidhī does the *fatra* occur as its result, thus implying that poetry and prophecy are

---

36 *Yalquṭ Shim'oni* on II Samuel 23.

37 Tirmidhī/*Tuḥfa*, IX, 272–73. Cf. Aḥmad, *Musnad*, IV, 312, 313; also Māwardī, *Nukat*, VI, 292; Ibn al-'Arabī, *Aḥkām*, IV, 1946; Rāzī, XXXI, 210. The same poetic verse is also attributed to al-Walīd ibn al-Walīd ibn al-Mughīra, one of Abū Baṣīr's men. See Wāqidī, II, 629; Balādhurī, *Ansāb*, I, 210. It is also attributed to 'Abdallāh ibn Rawāḥa. See Sa'īd ibn Manṣūr, II, no. 2835; *Fatḥ al-bārī*, X, 447, where there is also a discussion of the possibility that Muḥammad merely recited the verse, but did not compose it.

38 See Bukhārī, *Ṣaḥīḥ*, VIII, 43 (78:90, *Bāb mā yajūzu mina l-shi'ri wa-l-rajaz....*); IV, 22 (56:9). See also Muslim,V,181–82 (32:112, *Bāb mā laqiya min adhā l-mushrikīn*); Sa'īd ibn Manṣūr, II, nos. 2845–46; Abū Ya'lā, III, no. 1533; Ṭabarānī, *Kabīr*, II, nos. 1703–1708, 1719; and see Wakī', *Zuhd*, I, 325–26, with the notes of the editor.

mutually exclusive. This combination does not occur in any of the other *muṣannaf* compilations.

There are more traditions in which the *fatra* is caused by some other misdeeds of Muḥammad or his contemporaries. All of them remained outside the *muṣannaf* compilations, in spite of their innocent edifying purposes. They only appear in the biographical sources, as well as in the compilations of *tafsīr*, where they figure as *asbāb* of the *mā wadda'aka* passage.

According to some of them, the *fatra* happened because Muḥammad neglected to say *in shā'a llāh* ("God willing"). The story is that the Jews presented him with some questions which he promised to answer "tomorrow", but did not add *in shā'a llāh*. Therefore Gabriel stopped coming to him for some time.[39] This story seems to have been imported into the exegesis of the *mā wadda'aka* passage from Ibn Isḥāq, where the original story has nothing to do with this Quranic passage. The story as recorded by Ibn Isḥāq is that the polytheists tried to put Muḥammad's prophethood to the test by posing to him some questions which only a true prophet could answer. This in itself is a well-known motif in Muḥammad's biography. Well-versed scholars from among the People of the Book (including 'Abdallāh ibn Salām) are often said to have tested Muḥammad, and Gabriel always unravels the riddle for him.[40] In some cases the test draws on Quranic data. In our particular story, Muḥammad is asked about issues gleaned from Sūrat al-Kahf (18). In the story itself, the questions are formulated for the Meccans by the Jews of Medina. Muḥammad promises to answer the questions "tomorrow", but does not add *in shā'a llāh*. Therefore, Gabriel avoids him for fifteen days, the people of Mecca start to spread evil rumours about him, and Muḥammad is grieved and offended, till finally Gabriel brings him the entire Sūrat al-Kahf, which contains the required answers and includes a strict instruction as to saying *in shā'a llāh* (vv. 23–24).[41] At this point, Ibn Isḥāq adds that some say that when Gabriel resumed his sessions with the Prophet, the latter complained about Gabriel's absence, to which the

[39] Wāḥidī, *Wasīṭ*, fol. 335a–b; Baghawī, *Ma'ālim*, V, 587; Ṭabarsī, *Majma'*, XXX, 135; Ibn al-Jawzī, *Zād al-masīr*, IX, 154; Rāzī, XXXI, 210; Qurṭubī, XX, 93; Samarqandī, *Tafsīr*, III, 486; *Fatḥ al-bārī*, VIII, 545.

[40] For traditions with 'Abdallāh ibn Salām, see Bukhārī, *Ṣaḥīḥ*, IV, 160–61 (60:1); V, 88 (63:51); VI, 23 (65, Baqara); Aḥmad, *Musnad*, III, 108, etc.; Bayhaqī, *Dalā'il*, II, 528–29. Another tradition has a similar test to which Muḥammad is put by a group of Jews. See Aḥmad, *Musnad*, I, 278; Ṭabarānī, *Kabīr*, XII, no. 13012. For further traditions, see Suyūṭī, *Khaṣā'iṣ*, I, 473–81.

[41] Ibn Hishām, I, 322; Ibn Bukayr, 202; and see M.J. Kister, "Pare your Nails: a Study of an Early Tradition", *Near Eastern Studies in Memory of M.M. Bravmann, The Journal of The Ancient Near Eastern Society of Columbia University* 11 (1979), 67; Wansbrough, *Quranic Studies*, 122–25.

angel responded by reciting Quran 19:64 *(wa-mā natanazzalu illā bi-amri rabbika....,* "We only descend by the order of your Lord....").[42] This story was insinuated by Quran commentators into the exegesis of Sūrat al-Kahf,[43] of 19:64,[44] and, as we have just seen, also into that of the *mā wadda'aka* passage.

It may be noted in passing that exegetic traditions were also borrowed from the exegesis of the *mā wadda'ka* passage and fitted into that of 19:64, thus providing a good example of how Quranic verses may exchange *asbāb* with each other. Thus, al-Ṭabarī has recorded in his commentary on 19:64 some traditions which run along the same lines as those about the *fatra* of the *mā wadda'aka* passage. One of them speaks about Muḥammad's grief at Gabriel's absence (*iḥtibās*),[45] and another speaks about the allegations of the polytheists concerning his prophetic integrity.[46] As these traditions lack the linking words of 19:64, they only seem to be dim reflections of the *fatra* traditions of the *mā wadda'aka* passage. The *mā wadda'aka* passage itself is actually quoted verbatim by some exegetes commenting on 19:64.[47]

Another misdeed which is said to have caused the *fatra* is failure to observe the rules of personal hygiene, such as cleaning one's nails, teeth, etc. This is considered part of the ritual purity on which the primordial Abrahamic *fiṭra* ("natural religion") is based, and negligence of these rules was believed to obstruct divine inspiration. There are, for example, traditions stressing that dirty nails prevent true dreams.[48] This issue was insinuated into the *asbāb* of 19:64. A tradition of Mujāhid relates that Gabriel abandoned the Prophet because Muḥammad's companions had neither rubbed their teeth, nor clipped their nails, nor trimmed their moustaches, nor cleaned their finger joints. When Gabriel renewed his appearances, he brought this verse to Muḥammad.[49] Already in Muqātil's *Tafsīr* the same misbehaviour slid into the *asbāb* of the *mā wadda'aka* passage.[50]

The absence of Gabriel could also be the result of the presence of impure animals. Khawla, a servant at Muḥammad's household, relates that a dead

---

42 Ibn Hishām, I, 323.
43 Muqātil, I, fol. 222b (on 18:9).
44 Wāḥidī, *Asbāb*, 173 (19:64); Ibn al-Jawzī, *Zād al-masīr*, V, 249 (19:64).
45 Ṭabarī, *Tafsīr*, XVI, 78 (al-'Awfī←Ibn 'Abbās family *isnād*).
46 *Ibid.* (Mujāhid, al-Ḍaḥḥāk).
47 Muqātil, I, fol. 234a–b; Baghawī, *Ma'ālim*, III, 629–30; Zamakhsharī, II, 516.
48 See Kister, "Nails", *passim*. Traditions about *fatrat al-waḥy* are quoted on pp. 66–67.
49 Wāḥidī, *Asbāb*, 173; Ibn al-Jawzī, *Zād al-masīr*, V, 249.
50 Muqātil, II, fol. 242b. See also Ṭabarsī, *Majma'*, XXX, 135; Ibn al-Jawzī, *Zād al-masīr*, IX, 154; Rāzī, XXXI, 210; Qurṭubī, XX, 93–94.

whelp lay under Muḥammad's bed, due to which revelations did not occur till the *mā wadda'aka* passage was revealed.[51]

In conclusion, the *fatra* story was used as an instrument for promoting various didactic messages which originally had nothing to do with the basic structure of the *fatra* tale. This illustrates the modular nature of Muslim tradition, in which different stories and ideas could be assembled in ever-changing configurations, each serving its own particular purpose.[52]

---

[51] See Ṭabarānī, *Kabīr*, XXIV, 249 (no. 636); Wāḥidī, *Asbāb*, 256; *idem*, *Wasīṭ*, fol. 335b; Ibn Ḥajar, *Maṭālib*, III, 396–97 (no. 3806); *idem*, *Iṣāba*, VII, 628; Ibn al-Jawzī, *Zād al-masīr*, IX, 154; Suyūṭī, *Durr*, VI, 361; *Majma' al-zawā'id*, VII, 141. See another version (from Zayd ibn Aslam) in Baghawī, *Ma'ālim*, V, 587; Ibn 'Aṭiyya, XVI, 321; Rāzī, XXXI, 210; Qurṭubī, XX, 93, where Gabriel tells Muḥammad that the angels avoid houses in which dogs and pictures are present.

[52] This is also the case in *akhbār* historiography. Cf. Lawrence I. Conrad, "The Conquest of Arwād: a Source Critical Study in the Historiography of the Early Medieval Near East", in Averil Cameron and Lawrence I. Conrad , eds., *The Byzantine and Early Islamic Near East I: Problems in the Literary Source Material* (Princeton, 1992), 364–401, esp. 391–95 (nos. 2–3).

PART IV

PERSECUTION

7

Declaration

The *'Ashīra* Scene

THE STORIES OF PREPARATION and revelation proceed in the private sphere of Muḥammad's life. His public prophetic activity is the subject of the story of persecution. The latter is a well-known theme which already figures in the lives of quite a few biblical prophets, who are presented as suffering all kinds of torment for the noble cause of God. The story of persecution almost always presents the prophet as supported only by a small minority of devoted believers who are oppressed by a majority of non-believers. This applies especially to Jesus.[1]

In Islam the universal theme of persecution was made the leading theme of the story of Muḥammad's emergence in Mecca. The role of the tormenting foes, as well as of the few supporters, was assigned to members of the local Meccan tribe, Quraysh. The selection of the figures for the various roles at times reflects political tensions of medieval Islamic society which were read into the conditions of Muḥammad's Mecca. But the theme of persecution was adapted not only to Meccan surroundings, but also to Islamic textual models, i.e. to the Quran. This was quite an easy and successful task, because the Quran itself already contains detailed descriptions of persecution suffered by the Quranic prophet. The process of adaptation to this scripture can be followed from traditions in which the Quranic element is still absent, through traditions dominated by such models.

I

The first manifestation of persecution is embodied in the story of declaration. The Prophet is said to have appeared in public only after a period of hiding with his followers, for fear of Quraysh. In some traditions preserved by al-Balādhurī, an attempt is made to establish the chronology of Muḥammad's hiding period. One of the traditions is quoted from al-Wāqidī (d. AH 207), with the Medinan *isnād*: Zuhrī (d. AH 124)←'Urwa ibn al-Zubayr (d. AH 94)←'Ā'isha, and says that Muḥammad was preaching secretly for four years, then declared

[1] Cf. Sellheim, "Prophet, Chalif und Geschichte", 54–55.

his mission openly.[2] Another report of al-Wāqidī has an *isnād* reaching back to one of the Companions who embraced Islam during the hiding period. This is Saʿīd, son of the *ḥanīf* Zayd ibn ʿAmr ibn Nufayl, who belonged to ʿUmar's clan (ʿAdī ibn Kaʿb) and married ʿUmar's sister. Telling his own story in the first person to Ibn ʿAbbās, Saʿīd says that the Muslims concealed their new religion for one year, praying only in a closed house or an isolated ravine.[3] Another report of al-Wāqidī, as recorded by Ibn Saʿd, says that the hiding period lasted three years.[4]

In a special group of traditions the hiding stage is said to have been spent by Muḥammad in one specific place, a fortress called "Dār al-Arqam".[5] The *dār* was named after the Companion al-Arqam ibn Abī l-Arqam, who was a Qurashī of the clan of Makhzūm. The *dār* he owned in Mecca was situated at the hill of al-Ṣafā and is said to have been a sanctuary (*bayt*).[6] A comparison of the various versions of the story of Muḥammad's emergence from this place reveals the non-Quranic and Quranic levels of the narrative.

On the non-Quranic level, the story revolves round the figure of ʿUmar ibn al-Khaṭṭāb, who is said to have been the one whose early conversion to Islam added considerably to the power of the hiding Islamic party and enabled it to come out into the open. The pro-ʿUmar shaping of the story is self-evident. Al-Ḥākim has recorded two traditions about it in his *Mustadrak*. Both traditions appear in the section devoted to the biographies of the Prophet's Companions, in the chapter about our al-Arqam. These were circulated by the descendants of this Companion, and one of the traditions is related by his son ʿUthmān.[7] The tradition begins with the statement that al-Arqam was the seventh man to embrace Islam. The Prophet stayed at his *dār*, and many people joined him there as Muslims. When ʿUmar came to the *dār* and embraced Islam, the Muslims felt confident enough to come out of the shelter and perform the *ṭawāf* around the Kaʿba. The tradition goes on to survey the unfolding history of the *dār* in later generations. The second tradition recorded by al-Ḥākim is of al-Arqam's grandson, ʿUthmān ibn ʿAbdallāh, and also boasts of the role of their ancestor's *dār*.

---

[2] Balādhurī, *Ansāb*, I, 116 (no. 229).

[3] The *isnād*: Wāqidī←ʿAbdallāh ibn Muḥammad ibn Abī Yaḥyā (Medinan d. AH 174)←his father←Ibn ʿAbbās←Saʿīd ibn Zayd. See Balādhurī, *Ansāb*, I, 116 (no. 229).

[4] Ibn Saʿd, I, 216.

[5] For the traditions about Muḥammad's hiding in this place, cf. Miklos Muranyi, "Die ersten Muslime von Mekka—soziale Basis einer neuen Religion?", *Jerusalem Studies in Arabic and Islam* 8 (1986), 25–36.

[6] See Azraqī, 424. It is perhaps significant that in the traditions the house of Zayd ibn ʿAmr ibn Nufayl, Muḥammad's mentor, is also located near the Ṣafā. See Ibn Hishām, I, 246.

[7] *Mustadrak*, III, 502. The *isnād*: Yaḥyā ibn ʿImrān ibn ʿUthmān ibn al-Arqam←ʿUthmān ibn al-Arqam.

It states that the Prophet found shelter in that *dār* till he was joined by 40 people who embraced Islam. The last of them was ʻUmar. As soon as he arrived, the Muslims left the *dār* and confronted the polytheists (*mushrikūn*).[8] Of all the compilers of the *muṣannaf* collections, al-Ḥākim is perhaps the only one to have recorded these traditions, stressing that their *isnāds* are "sound". The same traditions survived only in the biographical sources, and appear in al-Arqam's biography as recorded in some books about the Companions,[9] and also in the earlier biography of Muḥammad by Ibn Saʻd.[10]

The biographical sources have other similar traditions in which the conversion of ʻUmar marks the crucial turning point in the transition from secret to public action. The focus of the story is shifted from al-Arqam, whose fortress is only mentioned vaguely as *al-dār*, without giving his name, to ʻUmar himself. One of these traditions is Baṣran, circulated under the name of the Companion Anas ibn Mālik, and contains the detailed story of the conversion of ʻUmar. In the part relevant to our immediate context of declaration, it is stated that as soon as ʻUmar embraced Islam, he induced Muḥammad to come out of his hiding place.[11] The story of ʻUmar's conversion was also recorded in the biography of Ibn Isḥāq. Here, Muḥammad's hiding place is vaguely referred to as a "sanctuary" (*bayt*) at al-Ṣafā. Ibn Isḥāq says that when ʻUmar embraced Islam, the Muslims left their hiding place and dispersed with increased self-confidence.[12]

In later sources which still preserve the non-Quranic layer of the story, there is a tradition of ʻĀʼisha in which the role of encouraging the Prophet to appear in public is assigned to Abū Bakr, her father.[13] Here the virtues of Abū Bakr are certainly promoted at the expense of those of ʻUmar.

The Quranic level of the same story of declaration is revealed in another group of traditions in which the hiding period of Muḥammad is ended neither

---

[8] *Ibid.*, III, 504. The *isnād*: ʻUthmān ibn ʻAbdallāh ibn al-Arqam←al-Arqam.

[9] See Ibn ʻAbd al-Barr, *Istīʻāb*, I, 132; Ibn Ḥajar, *Iṣāba*, I, 44.

[10] Ibn Saʻd, III, 242–43.

[11] *...fa-aslama wa-qāla: ukhruj yā rasūla llāh.* See Ibn Shabba, II, 659; Bayhaqī, *Dalāʼil*, II, 220. The *isnād*: Isḥāq ibn Yūsuf al-Azraq (Wāsiṭī, d. AH 195)←al-Qāsim ibn ʻUthmān al-Baṣrī←Anas ibn Mālik (d. AH 91–95).

[12] *fa-tafarraqa aṣḥāb rasūli llāh (ṣ) min makānihim wa-qad ʻazzaw fī anfusihim ḥīna aslama ʻUmaru maʻa islām Ḥamza.* See Ibn Hishām, I, 370–71. See also Balādhurī, *Shaykhān*, 139 (Wāqidī). In other traditions, Abū Bakr as well as ʻUmar urge Muḥammad to leave the *dār*. See Ibn Kathīr, *Bidāya*, III, 29–31 (quoted from Khaythama ibn Sulaymān). See also Shāmī, II, 428–29 (quoted here from "Sulaymān ibn Khaythama"). The tradition is of Muḥammad ibn ʻImrān←al-Qāsim ibn Muḥammad ibn Abī Bakr (Medinan d. AH 106)←ʻĀʼisha.

[13] Ibn ʻAsākir (*Mukhtaṣar*), XIII, 45.

by the instigation of 'Umar, nor by that of Abū Bakr, but rather by the command of God. This is the case in the following passage recorded by Ibn Isḥāq:

> Then people started to embrace Islam, men and women in groups, and Islam became renowned in Mecca, and people talked about it. Thereupon God commanded His messenger to declare openly (*an yaṣda'a*) what [came to him from God], and to disclose his affair (*amrahu*) to the people, and to call them to believe in Him. I have been informed that three years elapsed during which the apostle of God concealed (*akhfā*) his affair and hid it (*istatara bihi*) till God instructed him to reveal his religion. Then God said: *fa-'ṣda' bi-mā tu'maru....* And God said: *wa-andhir 'ashīrataka l-aqrabīn....*[14]

The two Quranic extracts embedded in this passage are 15:94, to which we shall refer as the *iṣda'* verse, and 26:214, which we may call the *'ashīra* verse.

As for the *iṣda'* verse, it reads:

> *fa-'ṣda' bi-mā tu'maru wa-a'riḍ 'ani l-mushrikīn*: "Declare[15] what you have been ordered to, and turn away from the polytheists."

This verse was employed not only in Ibn Isḥāq's *Sīra*, but also in a tradition preserved by Ibn Sa'd stating that after three years of hiding (*mustakhfiyan*), Muḥammad was commanded (by God) to declare (*...an yaṣda'a*) his mission openly.[16] The verse is not quoted verbatim, but the form *an yaṣda'a* clearly draws on it. Traditions with the *iṣda'* verse marking the end of the hiding stage were also used by the exegetes as material for the occasions of revelations (*asbāb al-nuzūl*) of this verse. Such traditions (mostly Iraqi) may be found in the *tafsīr* compilations.[17]

---

[14] Ibn Hishām, I, 280–81. See also Ibn Bukayr, 145; Ṭabarī, *Tārīkh*, I, 1169 (II, 318). See also Abū Nu'aym, *Dalā'il*, 265 ('Urwa, Zuhrī, Ibn Isḥāq).

[15] The root *ṣ.d.'.* basically means to break, or to cut open; figuratively, it means to cry out. Accordingly, the Quranic *iṣda'* was sometimes perceived in a liturgical sense, i.e. to recite the Quran loudly during prayer (*ijhar bi-l-Qur'ān fī l-ṣalāt*). See Mujāhid, I, 344. See also 'Abd al-Razzāq, *Tafsīr*, I, 351; Ṭabarī, *Tafsīr*, XIV, 47; Zajjāj, III, 186; Ibn 'Aṭiyya, X, 153; Ibn al-Jawzī, *Zād al-masīr*, IV, 420; Ibn Kathīr, *Tafsīr*, II, 559.

[16] Ibn Sa'd, I, 199. Cf. Balādhurī, *Ansāb*, I, 116 (no. 229); Ṭabarī, *Tārīkh*, I, 1174 (II, 322). The *isnād*: 'Abd al-Raḥmān ibn al-Qāsim ibn Muḥammad ibn Abī Bakr (Medinan d. AH 126)←his father.

[17] One with the *isnād*: Abū Usāma (Kūfan d. AH 201)←Mūsā ibn 'Ubayda (Medinan d. AH 152)←his brother 'Abdallāh ibn 'Ubayda. See Ṭabarī, *Tafsīr*, XIV, 47; also Baghawī, *Ma'ālim*, III, 413; Ibn al-Jawzī, *Zād al-masīr*, IV, 420. Another tradition is of al-Kalbī (Muḥammad ibn al-Sā'ib, Kūfan d. AH 146). See Huwwārī, II, 358; also Suyūṭī, *Durr*, IV, 106 (from Abū Nu'aym). There is also a tradition of Abū 'Ubayda from Ibn Mas'ūd (Medinan /Kūfan AH d. 32). See Ibn Kathīr, *Tafsīr*, II, 559; Suyūṭī, *Durr*, IV, 106; also Muqātil, I, fol. 199a.

The *'ashīra* verse is alluded to in a greater number of traditions, some of which appear in the *muṣannaf* compilations, as well as in the biographical sources. This verse reads:

wa-andhir 'ashīrataka l-aqrabīn...: "And warn your nearest relations...."

The *'ashīra* verse belongs to the Quranic eschatological stratum in which the Quranic prophet acts as *nadhīr*, "warner", i.e. about an imminent disaster awaiting those who cling to disbelief. The Quran labels this calamity as the "Hour" (*al-sā'a*); its portents are already manifest in this world.[18] In the *'ashīra* verse the Quranic prophet is ordered to warn only his nearest fellow tribesmen, for which reason this divine command was quite applicable to the story of the very first stages of Muḥammad's public preaching, when he was supposed to have been acting only among his own clan.

II

The traditions with the *'ashīra* verse marking the beginning of Muḥammad's public preaching are focussed on the contents of his actual address, as well as on the reaction of his audience to it. The theme of persecution is reflected in this reaction, and the various versions of the address itself shed light on the image of Muḥammad as a prophet making his first public attempts to draw attention to himself. But some of them also reflect various dogmatic as well as political notions which are not an intrinsic part of the topic of persecution. They rather illustrate the function of the story of Muḥammad's life as a medium for various kinds of propaganda. At this stage of our survey only the address will be discussed, saving the Qurashī reaction for the ensuing chapters.

In many of the versions of the *'ashīra* scene, the Prophet's address is dedicated to Doomsday. This accords with the immediate Quranic context of the *'ashīra* verse. Muḥammad makes a desperate attempt to alert his people to the Hour, which is described with battlefield imagery. Some of the traditions appear in the *muṣannaf* compilations. In Muslim and Abū 'Awāna they are recorded in the section on *īmān* (belief), which implies that only belief in God could save the people from their disastrous apocalyptic fate. One of the traditions is Baṣran, with the Companions Qabīṣa ibn al-Mukhāriq and Zuhayr ibn 'Amr al-Hilālī quoted by the Successor Abū 'Uthmān al-Nahdī (d. AH 100). They relate that following the revelation of the *'ashīra* verse, Muḥammad

---

[18] See Uri Rubin, s.v. "Sā'a" (part 3), *EI*[2].

climbed a mountain and addressed his own clan ('Abd Manāf) with the following warning:

> Alas for the sons of 'Abd Manāf! I am a warner. I am a man who has seen the enemy and hastens to warn his people, before the enemy gets ahead of him, and exclaims: "Alas, you are being attacked!"[19]

In this passage Doomsday is compared to a nearing enemy, and the Prophet is likened to a scout who tries to forewarn his own people of the looming danger. There is also a similar Baṣran tradition of the Companion Abū Mūsā al-Ash'arī (d. AH 42–53).[20]

Similar traditions about Muḥammad's warning following the revelation of the *'ashīra* verse are found in biographical sources. One was circulated under the name of the Companion al-Zubayr ibn 'Awwām (d. AH 36).[21] Another is again Baṣran, with an incomplete (*mursal*) chain of transmitters, i.e. an *isnād* lacking a Companion, and is of al-Ḥasan al-Baṣrī (d. AH 110).[22]

The same kind of traditions may be found in the exegesis of the *'ashīra* verse, where they function as *asbāb al-nuzūl* material. In some of them, the eschatological warning is reinforced by another extract from the Quran (34:46), which reads:

> *...in huwa illā nadhīrun lakum bayna yaday 'adhābin shadīd*: "...he is only a warner to you on the brink of a horrible disaster."

A part of this verse ("...a warner to you on the brink of a horrible disaster") was incorporated into Muḥammad's address in a tradition of the Companion 'Amr ibn Murra al-Juhanī.[23]

Muḥammad's role as *nadhīr*, "warner", is mentioned in the Quran time and again, not just in the *'ashīra* verse. In *ḥadīth* as well, his role as a warner is referred to in traditions not linked to the *'ashīra* scene, which add more angles to his function as *nadhīr*. In a tradition of Jābir ibn 'Abdallāh, for example, it is

---

[19] Muslim, I, 134 (1, *Bāb wa-andhir....*); Abū 'Awāna, I, 92–93.

[20] The *isnād*: 'Awf al-A'rābī (Baṣran d. AH 147)←Qasāma ibn Zuhayr (Baṣran)←Abū Mūsā. See Abū 'Awāna, I, 94; also Ibn Ḥibbān, XIV, no. 6551 (*Tārīkh*). These traditions also appear outside the *muṣannaf* collections. See Aḥmad, *Musnad*, III, 476; V, 60; Bayhaqī, *Dalā'il*, II, 178; Ṭabarānī, *Kabīr*, V, no. 5305; XVIII, no. 956.

[21] See Abū Ya'lā, II, no. 679. See also *Majma' al-zawā'id*, VII, 88.

[22] The *isnād*: 'Amr ibn 'Ubayd (Baṣran d. AH 142)←al-Ḥasan. See Ṭabarī, *Tārīkh*, I, 1173–74 (II, 322).

[23] Ṭabarī, *Tafsīr*, XIX, 74 (no. 19). The *isnād*: Jarīr ibn 'Abd al-Ḥamīd (Kūfan d. AH 188)←Mughīra ibn Miqsam (Kūfan d. AH 132)←'Amr ibn Murra al-Juhanī.

related that whenever Muḥammad mentioned in his *khuṭba* the impending Hour, his face became red with excitement, and his voice loud like that of *nadhīr jaysh* or *nadhīr qawm*, a scout shouting to his army or his people, warning them of the approaching enemy.[24] In a tradition of Abū Mūsā al-Ash'arī, Muḥammad states that he is like a man who shouts to his own people: "I have seen the enemy, I am the naked warner (*anā al-nadhīr al-'uryān*); save yourselves, save yourselves!"[25] The expression *al-nadhīr al-'uryān* is explained as signifying a scout who, having seen the approaching enemy, takes off his coat and waves it in order to warn his people that the enemy is nearby. This utterance is said to be pre-Islamic in origin, but Muslim writers disagree as to who used it first.[26]

The warning about the apocalyptic end forms the basic Quranic stratum of the *'ashīra* address upon which more specific ideas were built. In more elaborate versions Muḥammad is said not merely to have alerted his closest Qurashī relatives to the imminent calamity, but also to have warned them of the individual fates which awaited them in the Last Judgement. These versions of the *'ashīra* scene were designed to advertise the ethical dogma that each soul is responsible for its own deeds, and should be rewarded accordingly in the world to come. Muḥammad warns his nearest relations that his own intercession (*shafā'a*) will not save them, and tells them that they had better prepare their own good works for the Last Judgement. The idea is that kinship to the Prophet does not secure salvation. This seems to have some political anti-Shī'ī insinuations, because the Shī'īs used to boast of their kinship to Muḥammad (through his daughter Fāṭima), and hence of their right to Muḥammad's intercession.

Some traditions with this particular angle of the address are recorded in the *muṣannaf* compilations. The most current one has the *isnād* of Hishām ibn 'Urwa (Meccan d. AH 146)←'Urwa (Medinan d. AH 94)←'Ā'isha. Following the revelation of the *'ashīra* verse, Muḥammad declares:

> Oh Fāṭima, daughter of Muḥammad, oh Ṣafiyya, daughter of 'Abd al-Muṭṭalib, oh sons of 'Abd al-Muṭṭalib, I possess nothing to your credit with God, just ask me any share of my estate as you choose.

---

[24] Ibn al-Mubārak, *Musnad*, no. 87 (in section of *Qiyāma)*; Nasā'ī, *Kubrā*, I, 550 (no. 1786 [18:21]); Aḥmad, *Musnad*, III, 311, 319, 338, 371. And see also Aḥmad, *Musnad*, I, 167, where Muḥammad is said to have behaved like this when warning of the "days [= tribulations] of God" (*ayyām Allāh*).

[25] Bukhārī, *Ṣaḥīḥ*, VIII, 126 (81:26); IX, 115 (96:2); Muslim, VII, 63 (43, *Bāb shafaqatihi 'alā ummatihi*). And see also Ibn Abī l-Dunyā, *Ṣamt*, no. 622.

[26] *Fatḥ al-bārī*, XI, 270–71; *Tāj*, s.v. *n.dh.r.*; Suhaylī, *Rawḍ*, II, 48.

This tradition was recorded by the compilers under various headings. Muslim and Abū ʻAwāna recorded it in the section named *Īmān*, "Faith";[27] in the rearranged *Ṣaḥīḥ* of Ibn Ḥibbān it occurs in the section of *Tārīkh*, "History";[28] al-Tirmidhī included it in the section of *Zuhd*, "Asceticism".[29] Other compilers, however, added it to the section entitled *Waṣāyā*, "Testaments".[30] The latter classification was dictated by the reference to Muḥammad's estate. The tradition also occurs in sources other than the *muṣannaf* compilations.[31] Equally prevalent is a similar Kūfan tradition of Abū Hurayra quoted by Mūsā ibn Ṭalḥā (Medinan/Kūfan d. AH 103)[32]. It occurs under the same variety of headings: Muslim and Abū ʻAwāna included it in the section of *Īmān*,[33] Nasā'ī recorded it in the section of *Waṣāyā*,[34] and in the rearranged *Ṣaḥīḥ* of Ibn Ḥibbān it is under *Raqā'iq*, "Moral Exhortations".[35] The same tradition is available with another *isnād* leading up to Abū Hurayra. This is a tradition of al-Zuhrī in which Abū Hurayra is quoted by Sa'īd ibn al-Musayyab (Medinan d. AH 94) and Abū Salama ibn ʻAbd al-Raḥmān ibn ʻAwf (Medinan d. AH 94). This version too was included by some compilers in the section of *Īmān*,[36] whereas others added it to the section of *Waṣāyā*.[37]

The combination of the idea of individual reward and the story of the *'ashīra* verse changed its time of revelation from early Meccan to Medinan; persons like Fāṭima, to whom the statement is addressed, only came of age after the *hijra*. In fact, there is one more version of a Syrian provenance, of the Companion Abū Umāma al-Bāhilī (d. AH 81–86),[38] in which Muḥammad addresses all his

---

[27] Muslim, I, 133 (1, *Bāb wa-andhir....*, mentioning the Ṣafā); Abū ʻAwāna, I, 95.

[28] Ibn Ḥibbān, XIV, no. 6548.

[29] Tirmidhī/*Tuḥfa*, VI, no. 2412.

[30] Nasā'ī, *Kubrā*, IV, 108–109 (no. 6475 [55:6]); Bayhaqī, *Sunan*, VI, 280–81.

[31] Aḥmad, *Musnad*, VI, 187; Muḥibb al-Dīn al-Ṭabarī, *Dhakhā'ir*, 8; Ibn Kathīr, *Bidāya*, III, 39.

[32] The *isnād*: ʻAbd al-Malik ibn ʻUmayr (Kūfan d. AH 136)←Mūsā ibn Ṭalḥā←Abū Hurayra.

[33] Muslim, I, 133 (1, *Bāb wa-andhir....*); Abū ʻAwāna, I, 93–94.

[34] Nasā'ī, *Kubrā*, IV, 107–108 (no. 6471 [55:6]).

[35] Ibn Ḥibbān, II, no. 646. The tradition is also recorded in sources other than the *muṣannaf* compilations. See Aḥmad, *Musnad*, II, 333, 360, 361, 519; Bayhaqī, *Dalā'il*, II, 177–78; Muḥibb al-Dīn al-Ṭabarī, *Dhakhā'ir*, 8; Ibn Kathīr, *Bidāya*, III, 38.

[36] Muslim, I, 133 (1, *Bāb wa-andhir....*); Abū ʻAwāna, I, 94–95. And see also Ibn Ḥibbān, XIV, no. 6549 (*Tārīkh*); Bayhaqī, *Shu'ab*, V, no. 7021 (*Tawba*).

[37] Bukhārī, *Ṣaḥīḥ*, IV, 7–8 (55:11); Nasā'ī, *Kubrā*, IV, 108 (no. 6473 [55:6]); Bayhaqī, *Sunan*, VI, 280. Outside the *muṣannaf* compilations this tradition may be found in Bayhaqī, *Dalā'il*, II, 176.

[38] The *isnād*: ʻUthmān ibn Abī l-ʻĀtika (Syrian story-teller←ʻAlī ibn Yazīd al-Alhānī (Syrian d. *ca*. AH 120)←al-Qāsim ibn ʻAbd al-Raḥmān (Syrian d. AH 112)←Abū Umāma. See Ṭabarānī, *Kabīr*, VIII, no. 7890.

wives, including Ḥafṣa and Umm Salama; the latter two only married him after the *hijra*.

The statement of Muḥammad concerning free will was originally independent of the *'ashīra* address, as implied by the fact that there is another version of the above tradition of Abū Hurayra in which Muḥammad's statement is made independently of any Quranic revelation. This time Abū Hurayra is quoted by 'Abd al-Raḥmān ibn Hurmuz (or ibn Kaysān, al-A'raj, Medinan d. AH 117). The Prophet bids the family of 'Abd Manāf, as well as some Qurashī individuals, to "buy their souls" from God. Abū 'Awāna recorded this under *Īmān*;[39] al-Bukhārī, however, included it in the section named *Manāqib*, "Virtues",[40] due to the occurrence of the names of clans and individuals from Quraysh, which implies their honour.[41] Moreover, in the biographical sources, Muḥammad does not make the statement about individual responsibility until shortly before his death. On that occasion, he tells the people about the approaching *fitan* (apocalyptic tribulations), and entreats his daughter Fāṭima and his aunt Ṣafiyya to perform good deeds, because he has no right to intercede with God for them. The tradition with this setting is of the Meccan story-teller 'Ubayd ibn 'Umayr (d. AH 68).[42] A similar request is posed by the Prophet in a tradition of Ibn 'Abbās to the Prophet's uncle al-'Abbās, when the latter is already a very old man.[43] The same is told by Muḥammad to the entire clan of Hāshim in a tradition of the Meccan Companion 'Imrān ibn Ḥuṣayn (d. AH 52).[44] In a tradition of the Medinan Companion al-Ḥakam ibn Mīnā', Muḥammad addresses the entire tribe of Quraysh (whom he asks 'Umar to summon) with the demand to prepare their own good deeds for the next world, instead of indulging in worldly matters. Only if they do so, will he be able to help them.[45]

These versions remained outside the *muṣannaf* collections; in the latter, predominance was given to traditions in which Muḥammad's statement about the importance of one's own works appears in combination with the *'ashīra* verse.

---

[39] Abū 'Awāna, I, 95–96.

[40] Bukhārī, *Ṣaḥīḥ*, IV, 224–25 (61:13).

[41] The same tradition was also recorded in Aḥmad, *Musnad*, II, 350, 398–99, 448–49; Abū Ya'lā, XI, no. 6327.

[42] Ibn Sa'd, II, 215–16. The *isnād*: Abū Bakr [ibn 'Ubaydallāh] ibn Abī Mulayka (Meccan)←'Ubayd ibn 'Umayr.

[43] Aḥmad, *Musnad*, I, 206. The *isnād*: 'Alī ibn 'Abdallāh ibn 'Abbās (Medinan d. AH 118)←his father (Ibn 'Abbās)←his father (al-'Abbās).

[44] Ṭabarānī, *Kabīr*, XVIII, no. 354. The *isnād*: Abū Sahl←al-Ḥasan al-Baṣrī (d. AH 110)←'Imrān ibn Ḥuṣayn.

[45] Abū Ya'lā, III, no. 1579. The *isnād*: 'Abd al-Ḥamīd ibn Ja'far (Medinan d. AH 153)←Sa'īd al-Maqburī (Medinan d. AH 123)←Abū l-Ḥuwayrith (Medinan d. AH 128)←al-Ḥakam ibn Mīnā'. Cf. Ibn Ḥajar, *Iṣāba*, II, 110.

This combination seems to have been aimed at lending the idea of free will as much authority as possible by making it the outcome of a Quranic injunction.

Traditions with the combination of this idea and the *'ashīra* address recur in the exegesis of the *'ashīra* verse in many *tafsīr* collections, where they provide it with its *asbāb al-nuzūl*.[46] They are repeated in the sections labelled *Tafsīr* in some of the *muṣannaf* compilations.[47] Among these traditions there are some which were only preserved within the realm of *tafsīr*. One is a *mursal* tradition of al-Zuhrī (Medinan d. AH 124) in which all of the members of Quraysh are warned of their fate in the world to come.[48] Another *mursal* one is of the Baṣran Qatāda (d. AH 117), where the same warning is addressed to the clan of Hāshim.[49]

III

Apart from conveying seemingly anti-Shī'ī ideas, there are versions in which the *'ashīra* address advocates the opposite trend as well. In fact, these latter versions reflect the most essential Shī'ī tenet, namely, that 'Alī should have been Muḥammad's first successor (*waṣiyy*).[50] The interpolation of the topic of 'Alī's nomination into the *'ashīra* address is designed to imply that 'Alī's singular position was determined as early as the very beginning of Muḥammad's prophetic activity. The traditions of this sort contain descriptions of the reaction with which Muḥammad's address was met, which takes us back to the theme of persecution. The reaction of the audience puts 'Alī in the unique position of being the only one of Quraysh to offer his support to the Prophet, whereas all the others refrain from responding to Muḥammad's call. None of these traditions appears in the *muṣannaf* compilations; they are only recorded in the biographical sources.

---

[46] See e.g. 'Abd al-Razzāq, *Tafsīr*, II, 77; Ṭabarī, *Tafsīr*, XIX, 72–73, 75; Wāḥidī, *Wasīṭ*, fol. 109b; Baghawī, *Ma'ālim*, IV, 279–80; Suyūṭī, *Durr*, V, 96; Ibn Kathīr, *Tafsīr*, III, 349–50.

[47] See Bukhārī, *Ṣaḥīḥ*, VI, 140 (65, Sūra 26); Tirmidhī/*Tuḥfa*, IX, nos. 3236–37, 3239.

[48] The *isnād*: Salāma ibn Rawḥ ibn Khālid ibn 'Uqayl (Umayyad from Ayla, d. AH 197, transmitted Zuhrī's *kitāb* from 'Uqayl ibn Khālid)←'Uqayl ibn Khālid ibn 'Uqayl (*mawlā* of 'Uthmān from Ayla d. AH 141)←al-Zuhrī. See Ṭabarī, *Tafsīr*, XIX, 73 (no. 6).

[49] The *isnād*: 'Abd al-Razzāq←Ma'mar ibn Rāshid (Baṣran d. AH 154)←Qatāda (Baṣran d. AH 117). See 'Abd al-Razzāq, *Tafsīr*, II, 77; Ṭabarī, *Tafsīr*, XIX, 75 (no. 26). See also Suyūṭī, *Durr*, V, 96, where the same tradition is quoted from 'Abd ibn Ḥumayd, with Qatāda quoting al-Ḥasan al-Baṣrī (d. AH 110), and the story taking place before Muḥammad's death (*qabla mawtihi*). The tradition is also recorded on the authority of al-Ḥasan in Huwwārī, III, 243.

[50] Cf. Uri Rubin, "Prophets and Progenitors in the Early Shī'a Tradition", *Jerusalem Studies in Arabic and Islam* 1 (1979), 41–65.

Most such traditions are Iraqi. One of them, related on the authority of 'Alī himself, says that following the revelation of the *'ashīra* verse, Muḥammad summoned 30 people of his closest family, offered them food and drink, and asked: "Who of you is willing to act for my religion and for my prophecies, and in return will dwell in Paradise with me and become my successor (*khalīfatī*) in my family?" No one but 'Alī consented.[51] Muḥammad's reaction to 'Alī's willingness to support him is not related, but in other versions the Prophet explicitly accepts 'Alī as his supporter. One version is traced back to the Companion al-Barā' ibn 'Āzib,[52] and another to Ibn 'Abbās←'Alī. In the latter version, recorded by Ibn Isḥāq, 'Alī himself tells the tale in the first person. Muḥammad declares that 'Alī is to become his brother and heir (*waṣiyy*), as well as his successor (*khalīfa*).[53] Due to its clear Shī'ī colouring, this tradition was not included in Ibn Hishām's version of the *Sīra* of Ibn Isḥāq.[54] In the compilations of *tafsīr*, several of these versions recur in the commentaries on the *'ashīra* verse.[55] This was, of course, a story which the Shī'ī exegetes incorporated quite readily into their own exegesis of the Quranic *'ashīra* verse.[56]

The theme of 'Alī's nomination, like that of free will, is only a secondary accretion built upon the *'ashīra* scene for the purpose of providing it with authentication and Quranic authorisation. Traditions about the declaration of 'Alī as Muḥammad's successor are also available in their isolated form, lacking any reference to the *'ashīra* verse, or to any other Quranic revelation. In these plain versions, 'Alī assists Muḥammad in performing a miraculous spectacle designed to demonstrate Muḥammad's prophetic powers. Some of these traditions are Medinan. One such tradition, which is again traced back to 'Alī himself,

---

[51] Aḥmad, *Musnad*, I, 111. See also Suyūṭī, *Khaṣā'iṣ*, I, 308; Cf. Bazzār, III, no. 766. The *isnād*: al-A'mash (Kūfan d. AH 148)←al-Minhāl ibn 'Amr al-Asadī (Kūfan)←'Abbād ibn 'Abdallāh al-Asadī (Kūfan)←'Alī.

[52] Suyūṭī, *Khaṣā'iṣ*, I, 308–309 (from Abū Nu'aym, who quotes Ibn Isḥāq).

[53] The *isnād*: al-Minhāl ibn 'Amr (Kūfan)←'Abdallāh ibn al-Ḥārith ibn Nawfal ibn al-Ḥārith (Medinan d. AH 84)←Ibn 'Abbās←'Alī. The tradition is quoted from Ibn Isḥāq in Ṭabarī, *Tārīkh*, I, 1171–72 (II, 319–21). See also *Kashf al-astār*, III, no. 2417.

[54] The recension of Ibn Bukayr does have it, but only in a shortened version omitting 'Alī's nomination. See Ibn Bukayr, 145–46; also Bayhaqī, *Dalā'il*, II, 179–80; Abū Nu'aym, *Dalā'il*, 425 (no. 331); Suyūṭī, *Khaṣā'iṣ*, I, 306–307; Ibn Kathīr, *Bidāya*, III, 39–40.

[55] Ṭabarī, *Tafsīr*, XIX, 74–75 (no. 21); Baghawī, *Ma'ālim*, IV, 278–79; Ḥibarī, *Tafsīr*, 347–48; Ibn Kathīr, *Tafsīr*, III, 350–51; Ṭabarsī, *Majma'*, XIX, 187–88 (from al-Tha'labī). And see also Suyūṭī, *Durr*, V, 97 (from Ibn Mardawayhi).

[56] See Ḥibarī, *Tafsīr*, 347–48; Qummī, *Tafsīr*, II, 100; Ṭūsī, *Tabyān*, VIII, 67; Ṭabarsī, *Majma'*, XIX, 187–88. And see also the story in other Shī'ī compilations: Mas'ūdī, *Ithbāt al-waṣiyya*, 115–16; Ibn Shahrāshūb, I, 305–307.

was recorded by Ibn Sa'd.[57] Muḥammad asks Khadīja to cook supper for him, then tells 'Alī to summon the members of 'Abd al-Muṭṭalib's clan. When 40 of them show up, the Prophet orders 'Alī to feed the guests with the single meal, and all of them partake of it till they can eat and drink no more. But Muḥammad's uncle Abū Lahab dismisses the miracle as sheer *siḥr*, i.e. sorcery, thus frustrating Muḥammad's efforts to persuade the audience to believe in him. A few days later, the same people are invited to a similar banquet, the same miraculous multiplication of the food takes place, and this time Muḥammad addresses them. He asks who of them is willing to support him, and in return will become his "brother" and enter Paradise. 'Alī is the only one to consent. But as he is the youngest of them all and the smallest in structure, his father Abū Ṭālib says that he will be of no use to the Prophet. Similar events take place in a tradition recorded by Aḥmad ibn Ḥanbal, which is likewise attributed to 'Alī. The latter relates the story in the first person. He is again the only member of the family of 'Abd al-Muṭṭalib who is willing to pledge allegiance to Muḥammad, but Muḥammad is obliged to reject 'Alī due to his young age.[58]

'Alī's response to Muḥammad's call stands in clear contrast to the reaction of Quraysh, and especially to that of Abū Lahab. The reaction of the latter is embedded in further versions of the *'ashīra* scene itself. His reaction, which demonstrates the theme of persecution in its most vivid presentation, is the subject of the following chapter.

---

[57] Ibn Sa'd, I, 187. See also Suyūṭī, *Khaṣā'iṣ*, I, 307–308. The *isnād*: Nāfi' the *mawlā* of Ibn 'Umar (Medinan d. AH 117)←Sālim ibn 'Abdallāh ibn 'Umar (Medinan d. AH 105)←'Alī.

[58] The *isnād*: Abū 'Awāna al-Wāsiṭī (d. AH 176)←'Uthmān ibn al-Mughīra (Kūfan)←Abū Ṣādiq al-Azdī (Kūfan)←Rabī'a ibn Nājid (Kūfan)←'Alī. See Aḥmad, *Musnad*, I, 159.

8

The Reaction of Abū Lahab

THE REACTION OF THE MECCANS to Muḥammad's public appearance forms the core of the theme of persecution. Their first hostile reaction is described in the traditions of the *'ashīra* scene; many of its versions revolve round the Prophet's greatest enemy, his own paternal uncle, Abū Lahab.

I

The story of Abū Lahab's reaction demonstrates once again the Quranic role in the development of the story of Muḥammad's emergence, and illustrates various aspects of the process of adaptation of universal themes like persecution to Quranic models. The name of Abū Lahab is mentioned in Sūrat al-Masad (111), in which he and his wife are severely cursed and condemned to Hell.[1] This divine condemnation of a member of the Prophet's own clan (Hāshim) turned him in the eyes of later generations into a damned enemy of Islam, and made him the most suitable figure to represent the persecuting party in the story of persecution. His *sūra* was incorporated into various scenes of persecution together with an ever changing story about its revelation, which was made part of the scene itself. This applies first and foremost to the *'ashīra* scene. The actual wording of Sūrat al-Masad was made part of the lines uttered by Abū Lahab in reaction to Muḥammad's address, and the revelation of Sūrat al-Masad was actually made part of the story, functioning as a divine response to Abū Lahab's own hostile reaction.

The text uttered by Abū Lahab in the *'ashīra* scene consists of linking words derived from the first verse of Sūrat al-Masad. This verse reads:

> *tabbat yadā Abī Lahab...*: "perish the hands of Abū Lahab...."

The versions containing the reaction of Abū Lahab take the *'ashīra* address back to its basic apocalyptic level. The best-known tradition of this group is that of Sa'īd ibn Jubayr (Kūfan d. AH 95) from Ibn 'Abbās, and appears in the sec-

[1] On this *sūra* see Uri Rubin, "Abū Lahab and Sūra CXI", *Bulletin of the School of Oriental and African Studies* 42 (1979), 13–28.

tions of *Īmān* in Muslim and Abū 'Awāna.[2] God orders His Prophet to warn his nearest *'ashīra*, or "relations", so Muḥammad mounts the hill of the Ṣafā and warns the audience of the "attack" of the Last Judgement. His warning contains a part of Quran 34:46, in which, as already seen, he is "a warner on the brink of a horrible disaster". Abū Lahab says: *tabban laka*, "Damn you", and adds: "Is this what you called us for?" Then God reveals: *tabbat yadā Abī Lahab*.... In this sequence of events Sūrat al-Masad reciprocates the malicious utterance of Abū Lahab by wishing him the same kind of damnation. The tradition of Sa'īd ibn Jubayr←Ibn 'Abbās appears in the biographical sources as well.[3]

In fact, this setting of the *'ashīra* scene, including the revelation of Sūrat al-Masad, was known already to the earliest biographers of Muḥammad. The biographical sources have various additional versions of the same sort, the content of which is no different from that of the *muṣannaf* compilations. One is of the Kūfan al-Kalbī (d. AH 146). His version, also related on the authority of Ibn 'Abbās, was recorded by al-Balādhurī.[4] Other similar versions of al-Kalbī with the same Ibn 'Abbās *isnād* appear in Ibn Sa'd.[5] A tradition of 'Ikrima (Medinan d. AH 105) from Ibn 'Abbās is also recorded in these sources.[6]

The traditions with the revelation of Sūrat al-Masad were used by Quran exegetes as *asbāb* within the interpretation of this *sūra*. For this purpose they recorded the tradition of Sa'īd ibn Jubayr←Ibn 'Abbās.[7] Al-Bukhārī as well recorded the tradition in his section of *Tafsīr* for the same *sūra* .[8] This tradition, as well as the one of al-Kalbī, recurs in the exegesis of the *'ashīra* verse itself.[9]

---

[2] The *isnād*: al-A'mash (Kūfan d. AH 148)←'Amr ibn Murra ibn 'Abdallāh (Kūfan d. AH 118)←Sa'īd ibn Jubayr←Ibn 'Abbās. See Muslim, I, 134 (1, *Bāb wa-andhir*...., with the following clause added to the canonical *'ashīra* verse: ...*wa-rahṭaka minhum al-mukhliṣīn*); Abū 'Awāna, I, 92. See also Ibn Ḥibbān, *Ṣaḥīḥ*, XIV, no. 6550 (*Tārīkh*).

[3] Ṭabarī, *Tārīkh*, I, 1170 (II, 319); Aḥmad, *Musnad*, I, 307; Bayhaqī, *Dalā'il*, II, 181–82; Ibn Kathīr, *Bidāya*, III, 38. And cf. another version with the *isnād*: Sufyān al-Thawrī (Kūfan d. AH 161)←Ḥabīb ibn Abī Thābit (Kūfan d. AH 119)←Sa'īd ibn Jubayr←Ibn 'Abbās, in Ṭabarānī, *Kabīr*, XII, no. 12352. But here only the beginning of the scene is related.

[4] Balādhurī, *Ansāb*, I, 119–20 (no. 237). The *isnād*: al-Kalbī←Abū Ṣāliḥ (Bādhām, *mawlā* of Umm Hāni')←Ibn 'Abbās.

[5] See Ibn Sa'd, I, 74–75.

[6] *Ibid.*, I, 199–200; Balādhurī, *Ansāb*, I, 120 (no. 238). The *isnād*: Dāwūd ibn al-Ḥuṣayn (Medinan d. AH 135)←'Ikrima←Ibn 'Abbās.

[7] Ṭabarī, *Tafsīr*, XXX, 218 (nos. 6, 7, on Sūrat al-Masad).

[8] Bukhārī, *Ṣaḥīḥ*, VI, 221 (65, Sūrat al-Masad).

[9] The tradition of al-Kalbī: Huwwārī, III, 242–43 (on Quran 26:214). The tradition of Sa'īd ibn Jubayr: Bukhārī, *Ṣaḥīḥ*, VI, 140 (65, Sūra 26); Ṭabarī, *Tafsīr*, XIX, 73, 74 (nos. 14, 16, on 26:214); Baghawī, IV, 279 (on 26:214); Ibn Kathīr, *Tafsīr*, III, 349 (on 26:214).

It is noteworthy that Sūrat al-Masad sometimes overshadowed the *'ashīra* verse. There is an additional version of the tradition of Sa'īd ibn Jubayr←Ibn 'Abbās in which Sūrat al-Masad is the only Quranic revelation, the *'ashīra* verse being left out. This version was recorded by al-Bukhārī in his section of *Tafsīr*, in the chapter about Sūrat al-Masad.[10] This is reiterated in the biographical sources,[11] as well as in the commentaries on the *sūra*.[12]

II

In the Prophet's biography, his first public appearance is the most famous scene into which Abū Lahab was incorporated to play the role of the zealous persecuting foe. Within the inner context of this setting, the revelation of Sūrat al-Masad is prompted by the negative reaction of Abū Lahab to the Prophet's address. But there are several other scenes into which Abū Lahab's name was insinuated for the purpose of imparting the same theme of persecution, and the revelation of Sūrat al-Masad was made part of some of those episodes.

In some *muṣannaf* compilations there is a tradition of the Kūfan Companion Ṭāriq ibn 'Abdallāh al-Muḥāribī, speaking in the first person, which appears in the sections of *Maghāzī* or *Tārīkh*.[13] One day Ṭāriq sees the Prophet in the market of Dhū l-Majāz (near Mecca) calling the people to believe in God alone. Abū Lahab goes behind him and throws stones at Muḥammad's ankles, which start to bleed. This tradition, which is contained in the biographical sources,[14] was selected by the *muṣannaf* compilers as an illustration of the violent resistance Muḥammad encountered from some of his closest relations at the earliest stages of his public preaching.

Another tradition to the same effect appears only in the biographical sources, and is related on the authority of the Medinan Companion Rabī'a ibn 'Ibād. The location of the event varies from one version of his story to another: the market of 'Ukāẓ, or of Dhū l-Majāz, or of Minā. His story, also related in the first person, is available in several versions quoted from this Companion by various

---

[10] This is the version transmitted from al-A'mash by the Kūfan Abū Mu'āwiya al-Ḍarīr (d. AH 195). See Bukhārī, *Ṣaḥīḥ*, VI, 221–22 (65, Sūrat al-Masad).

[11] Balādhurī, *Ansāb*, I, 121 (no. 239); Ṭabarī, *Tārīkh*, I, 1170 (II, 318–19); Aḥmad, *Musnad*, I, 281; Bayhaqī, *Dalā'il*, II, 182.

[12] Ṭabarī, *Tafsīr*, XXX, 218 (no. 4). But in spite of the absence of the *'ashīra* verse, al-Ṭabarī also recorded it in his commentary of this verse as well (*Tafsīr*, XIX, 74).

[13] The *isnād*: Yazīd ibn Ziyād ibn Abī l-Ja'd (Kūfan)←Jāmi' ibn Shaddād al-Muḥāribī (Kūfan d. AH 118)←Ṭāriq. See Ibn Abī Shayba, XIV, no. 18414 (*Maghāzī*); *Mustadrak*, II, 611–12 (*Tārīkh*); Ibn Ḥibbān, *Ṣaḥīḥ*, XIV, no. 6562 (*Tārīkh*). See also Dāraquṭnī, *Sunan*, III, 44–45 (no. 186, *Buyū'*).

[14] See Ibn Bukayr, 232; Bayhaqī, *Dalā'il*, V, 380. See also Ibn Sa'd, I, 216.

Medinan Successors.[15] The event takes place when Rabī'a is still a boy. Abū Lahab's conduct is less violent, not involving physical assault; he only tells the audience to pay no heed to Muḥammad's call, and to adhere to their own idols. Thus, in the version that did gain access to the *muṣannaf* compilations, the persecution is more violent, which accords with the general trend to highlight the theme of persecution and make Muḥammad appear to be suffering all the more for the cause of his Lord.

In spite of the fact that the actual revelation of Sūrat al-Masad is not alluded to in either of the latter traditions, both of them were recorded by some exegetes in the interpretation of the *sūra*, thus making the scene a *sabab* of its revelation.[16] In fact, there is another version of a similar episode in which the *sūra* is made part of the actual event through the usual device of linking words, and reported from 'Abd al-Raḥmān ibn Hurmuz (or, ibn Kaysān, al-A'raj, Medinan d. AH 117). The place of the scene is not specified. Abū Lahab meets an Arab delegation that has come to Mecca to inquire about the new prophet. He tells them that Muḥammad is mentally ill, and adds: "Damn him...." (*fa-tabban lahu....*). The Prophet hears about this and becomes aggrieved; soon afterwards Sūrat al-Masad is revealed in response to this verbal offence of Abū Lahab. This tradition only appears in a few relatively late commentaries.[17]

The resistance of Abū Lahab as related in Muḥammad's biography is only the first link in a chain reaction. His response to Muḥammad's call causes the revelation of Sūrat al-Masad, which in turn prompts a no less hostile reaction from another person mentioned in the *sūra*, Abū Lahab's wife, known in the sources as Umm Jamīl. In some traditions found in the *muṣannaf* compilations she is offended by the *sūra,* which she perceives as a satirical attack (*hijā'*) on her husband and herself. In one of the traditions, she responds with a counter satirical verse of her own. The story about her rejoinder appears in a Ḥijāzī tradition of Asmā' bint Abī Bakr; of all the *muṣannaf* compilations, it has only been recorded in al-Ḥākim's *Mustadrak*, in the section of *Tafsīr*.[18] When

---

[15] They are: Sa'īd ibn Khālid al-Qāriẓī; Muḥammad ibn al-Munkadir (d. AH 130); Abū l-Zinād; Ḥusayn ibn 'Abdallāh ibn 'Ubaydallāh ibn al-'Abbās (d. AH 141); Zayd ibn Aslam (d. AH 136); Bukayr ibn 'Abdallāh ibn al-Ashajj (d. AH 117–27). See Ibn Hishām, II, 64–65; Ṭabarī, *Tārīkh*, I, 1204–1205 (II, 348–49); Aḥmad, *Musnad*, III, 492–93 (several traditions); IV, 341–42; Ṭabarānī, *Kabīr*, V, no. 4582–90.

[16] The tradition of Ṭāriq ibn 'Abdallāh al-Muḥāribī is recorded in Wāḥidī, *Wasīṭ*, fol. 350a; Qurṭubī, XX, 236. The tradition of Rabī'a ibn 'Ibād is found in Ibn Kathīr, *Tafsīr*, IV, 564.

[17] Māwardī, *Nukat*, VI, 364; Qurṭubī, XX, 235.

[18] *Mustadrak*, II, 361. The *isnād*: al-Walīd ibn Kathīr (Medinan/Kūfan d. AH 151)←Ibn Tadrus (Meccan)←Asmā'.

Umm Jamīl hears the text of Sūrat al-Masad, she comes wailing to the Prophet, a stone in her hand, and recites the following:

Mudhammaman abaynā
wa-dīnahu qalaynā
wa-amrahu ʿaṣaynā....

We reject Mudhammam
And loath his religion
And disobey his order....

Muḥammad retorts with the recitation of a Quranic verse (17:45) that says that whenever the Prophet recites the Quran, God draws a curtain between him and the unbelievers. This makes Muḥammad invisible to her, and she only sees Abū Bakr, who is with the Prophet. She protests to him that Muḥammad has recited *hijā'* (Sūrat al-Masad) against her. Abū Bakr denies this, and she goes away saying pathetically that everyone in Quraysh knows that she is of a most noble descent.

In the verse of Umm Jamīl the name of Muḥammad ("the praised one") is sarcastically changed into the opposite, Mudhammam ("the despicable one"). The tradition thus unveils the verbal aspect of the resistance that Muḥammad's sermons encountered.[19] But although the episode conforms to the general theme of persecution, it did not gain wide circulation in the *muṣannaf* compilations; al-Ḥākim remained the only one to record it. The insolent distortion of the Prophet's name within a satirical *hijā'* seems to have gone too far; the compilers could not reproduce such an insult to the Prophet's name, in spite of the sound *isnād* attesting to the transmission of the story. It only recurs in the biographical sources,[20] where the reaction of Umm Jamīl is said to have included the divorce of her sons from Muḥammad's daughters Ruqayya and Umm Kulthūm.[21] The story of her verses is repeated in Quran exegesis.[22]

---

[19] Muḥammad is also called "Mudhammam" in the utterance of Satan following the ʿAqaba meeting between the Prophet and the Anṣār. See Ibn Hishām, II, 90; Ṭabarī, *Tārīkh*, I, 1222 (II, 364); Bayhaqī, *Dalā'il*, II, 448.

[20] Ibn Isḥāq (Ibn Hishām, I, 381–82. Cf. Balādhurī, *Ansāb*, I, 122, [no. 245]) records the tradition without the *isnād*. The tradition with the *isnād* of Asmā' appears in Bayhaqī, *Dalā'il*, II, 195–96. See also Abū Yaʿlā, I, no. 53; Ḥumaydī, *Musnad*, I, no. 323.

[21] See Ibn Saʿd, VIII, 36, 37; Balādhurī, *Ansāb*, I, 122–23, 401; Bayhaqī, *Dalā'il*, II, 338–39. The story of the divorce is sometimes recounted without reference to Sūrat al-Masad. See Ibn Hishām, II, 306–307; Ibn Qutayba, *Maʿārif*, 62; *Aghānī*, XV, 2. And see Kister, "The Sons of Khadīja", 74, 75.

[22] Māwardī, *Nukat*, VI, 368.

As for the more authoritative *muṣannaf* compilations, they only have another tradition with the Muḥammad/Mudhammam device, which also appears in the early biographical sources.[23] Abū Lahab's wife and her verses are not mentioned in it. In this tradition of the Companion Abū Hurayra, the Prophet states that Quraysh ridicule him as "Mudhammam", but he remains "Muḥammad". Such a tradition, in which "Muḥammad" finally supersedes "Mudhammam", could easily be included in any of the *muṣannaf* compilations. Al-Bukhārī has recorded it in the book of *Manāqib*, in the chapter about the magnificence of Muḥammad's names.[24] In the rearranged *Ṣaḥīḥ* of Ibn Ḥibbān, the tradition is recorded in the section of the miracles of Muḥammad as an illustration of how God protects his Prophet and frustrates all the attempts of his adversaries to invoke a curse upon him (*'iṣma* against human foes).[25] Al-Nasā'ī put it in a more legal context, in the section named *Ṭalāq* (Divorce), in which various aspects of divorce proceedings are exemplified. The tradition at hand is recorded as an illustration of cases in which the mere utterance of certain words (like some formulae of divorce) is not always binding.[26]

The only version of the story of Umm Jamīl's reaction to Sūrat al-Masad which gained access into some of the *Faḍā'il* sections of the *muṣannaf* compilations is the one of Ibn 'Abbās.[27] Here her "Mudhammam" verses are entirely missing; she only protests to Abū Bakr that the Prophet has satirized her, while the Prophet himself is concealed from her eyes by an angel. This setting of the story, in which the insulting verses of the wife have been left out and the Prophet enjoys the active protection of an angel against her, renders the defeat of the woman complete. The compilers could therefore record it among other traditions about Muḥammad's virtues. Ibn Abī Shayba recorded it in the section of *Faḍā'il* which enumerates the virtues by which God blessed Muḥammad.[28] In the rearranged compilation of Ibn Ḥibbān it appears in the chapter about the Prophet's miracles, illustrating how God makes him invisible to his foes.[29] It

---

[23] Ibn Hishām, I, 382; also Ibn Sa'd, I, 106. And see Bukhārī, *Tārīkh ṣaghīr*, I, 36–37; Ḥumaydī, *Musnad*, II, no. 1136; Aḥmad, *Musnad*, II, 244, 340, 369.

[24] See Bukhārī, *Ṣaḥīḥ*, IV, 225 (61:17). The *isnād*: Ibn Abī l-Zinād (Medinan d. AH 174)←his father←al-A'raj (Medinan d. AH 117)←Abū Hurayra.

[25] The *isnād*: 'Aṭā' ibn Mīnā' (Medinan)←Abū Hurayra. Ibn Ḥibbān, *Ṣaḥīḥ*, XIV, no. 6503.

[26] Nasā'ī, *Kubrā*, III, 361 (no. 5631 [44:26]).

[27] The *isnād*: 'Aṭā' ibn al-Sā'ib (Kūfan d. AH 136)←Sa'īd ibn Jubayr (Kūfan d. AH 95)←Ibn 'Abbās.

[28] Ibn Abī Shayba, XI, no. 11817.

[29] Ibn Ḥibbān, *Ṣaḥīḥ*, XIV, no. 6511. See also *Kashf al-astār*, III, no. 2294; Bazzār, I, no. 15.

also appears outside the *muṣannaf* compilations,[30] including Quranic exegesis.[31]

Finally, the reaction of Umm Jamīl to the revelation of Sūrat al-Masad was linked to the affair of *fatrat al-waḥy* as well.[32] This is the case in traditions in which she not only protests against the Quranic *hijā'*, but also accuses the Prophet of having been forsaken by his Lord. This is followed by the revelation of the *mā wadda'aka* passage. A tradition with this sequence of events was included in the commentaries on the latter passage.[33] Thus another example of the sliding of *asbāb* from the exegesis of one Quranic passage into that of another is provided.

III

Further scenes into which Sūrat al-Masad was incorporated as a rejoinder to Abū Lahab's abusive words about the Prophet remained outside the *muṣannaf* compilations. They too tell the story of persecution, but the compilers ignored them because Abū Lahab's conduct as described in them did not sustain the image of the fanatic enemy of God and His Prophet. On the contrary, in these scenes Abū Lahab's resistance to Muḥammad only begins after helping and protecting the Prophet, and a specific reason is given for his regressing from protection to rejection. The theme of persecution in these versions is not yet fully developed to its well-established stereotypes. A closer look at the traditions with these scenes may clarify further why they were never taken up by the authors of the *muṣannaf* compilations.

In some of these stories, Abū Lahab is still the protecting uncle of Muḥammad who only becomes his enemy due to dogmatic differences. Ibn Sa'd recorded a tradition of al-Wāqidī relating that upon the death of Abū Ṭālib, Muḥammad's uncle and great defender, Muḥammad was afraid to leave his house lest the Meccans should harm him. Eventually Abū Lahab decided to grant him protection. He did indeed prevent Quraysh from troubling Muḥammad, but soon Quraysh incited Abū Lahab to ask the Prophet whether his grandfather 'Abd al-Muṭṭalib had been condemned to Hell. Muḥammad

[30] See Abū Ya'lā, I, no. 25; IV, no. 2358; Abū Nu'aym, *Dalā'il*, 193–94. Another *isnād*: Sa'īd ibn Kathīr ibn 'Ubayd the *mawlā* of Abū Bakr (Kūfan)←his father←Asmā'. Bayhaqī, *Dalā'il*, II, 196. And see also another version of Dāwūd ibn al-Ḥuṣayn (Medinan d. AH 135)←'Ikrima (Medinan d. AH 105)←Ibn 'Abbās (with Abū Bakr and 'Umar), in Balādhurī, *Ansāb*, I, 123 (no. 246).

[31] Muqātil, II, fol. 255a (in the *bayt* near the Ṣafā).

[32] See above, Chapter 6.

[33] The *isnād*: Abū Isḥāq al-Sabī'ī (Kūfan Shī'ī d. AH 126–29)←Zayd ibn Arqam (d. AH 65). See *Mustadrak*, II, 526–27 (*Tafsīr*, Sūra 93). And cf. Ṭabarī, *Tafsīr*, XXX, 220 (no. 13).

replied in the affirmative, whereupon Abū Lahab declared that from then on he would be Muḥammad's enemy forever.[34] The revelation of the *sūra* is added to the story in a second version recorded by al-Balādhurī. This relates that when Abū Lahab heard from Muḥammad that 'Abd al-Muṭṭalib had died as an infidel, he exclaimed: *tabban laka*! Thereupon, Sūrat al-Masad was sent down.[35] Such a story alluding to the protection granted by Abū Lahab to Muḥammad before he started to resist him, could not become a "sound" tradition acceptable to any of the *muṣannaf* compilers. The tradition in itself exhibits an early stratum of the persecution story, when fixed models for the absolutely negative presentation of his opponents were not yet fully developed. This paternal uncle of the Prophet is still fulfilling his natural role of protecting his nephew, and his Quranic demonic image has not yet taken full control of him. It is noteworthy that even the exegetes did not use this scene as a *sabab* for the interpretation of Sūrat al-Masad.

In other traditions, the dogmatic strife between Abū Lahab and Muḥammad is focussed on Abū Lahab's devotion to the goddess al-'Uzzā. These stories seem to consist of elaborations on Abū Lahab's personal name 'Abd al-'Uzzā, "Servant of al-'Uzzā".[36] In these versions he tries to protect al-'Uzzā from the Prophet. Ibn al-Kalbī (d. AH 204) relates that Abū Lahab once visited a notable Meccan leader (Abū Uḥayḥa) who was dying. The old man told his caller that he was afraid that Muḥammad would destroy the sanctuaries of al-'Uzzā, and Abū Lahab promised him to defend the cult of this deity.[37] The story of the revelation of Sūrat al-Masad was incorporated into this scene as well. In the version recorded by al-Wāqidī, Abū Lahab visits the dying custodian (*sādin*) of al-'Uzzā, Aflaḥ ibn Naḍr, who is worried because the worship of the goddess is under threat of extinction. Abū Lahab says to him: "Do not worry. I shall look after her when you are gone." Afterwards, he would say: "If al-'Uzzā prevails, I will have gained a 'hand' to my credit with her (*kuntu qad ittakhadhtu yadan 'indahā*), thanks to my attendance upon her. And if Muḥammad overcomes al-'Uzzā, which I do not believe will happen, well, he is my nephew."[38] Thereupon, God revealed: *tabbat yadā Abī Lahab*. The linking word included in Abū Lahab's utterance in this tradition is *yad*, derived from the Quranic *yadā*. In this tradition the word signifies *ni'ma*, i.e. "benefaction". Linked to

---

[34] Ibn Sa'd, I, 211.

[35] Balādhurī, *Ansāb*, I, 121 (no. 240).

[36] But his name is also said to have been 'Abd Manāf. See Qummī, *Tafsīr*, II, 450.

[37] Ibn al-Kalbī, *Aṣnām*, 23; Yāqūt, IV, 117. Cf. Balādhurī, *Ansāb*, IVb, 124 (with Abū Jahl as well). There are more traditions about the last illness of Abū Uḥayḥa describing his distress because of Muḥammad's deeds. See *Majma' al-zawā'id*, VI, 22.

[38] Wāqidī, III, 874. See also Balādhurī, *Ansāb*, I, 121 (no. 241); Azraqī, 81–82.

this specific episode, the *sūra* is revealed in order to deny the value of Abū Lahab's "two hands", which were extended in favour of al-'Uzzā, as well as in favour of his nephew Muḥammad. This tradition is found neither in the *muṣannaf* compilations nor in the *tafsīrs*. The reason for its rejection seems to be the reference to Abū Lahab as a source of protection and benefaction enjoyed by al-'Uzzā, as well as by his nephew Muḥammad. Such mild presentation of the theme of persecution was not good enough for the compilers, for whom Abū Lahab should have been the stereotyped foe whose evil conduct was his only trait. The explicit reference to al-'Uzzā increased the unpopularity of the tradition.

Another scene of the same type which is missing from the *muṣannaf* compilations, as well as from the commentaries, is the following: When Muḥammad and the clan of Hāshim were put by Quraysh under a boycott in the "ravine" (*shi'b*) of Abū Ṭālib, Abū Lahab abandoned Muḥammad, and as he was coming out of the *shi'b*, he declared his support for al-'Uzzā. Thereupon, the *sūra* about him was revealed. This version of the story was recorded in the recension of Ibn Bukayr of Ibn Isḥāq's *Sīra*.[39] In this case, however, no linking words are utilized. In Ibn Hishām's version of the same episode, linking words do occur, again derived from the Quranic "two hands" of Abū Lahab. This time they figure in their literary sense. He says: "Muḥammad promises me things I do not see, which he claims will come after I die. But what has he put in my hands except for these [promises]?" Then he blows at his two hands and says: "Damn you (*tabban lakumā*), I see in you nothing of what Muḥammad says." Therefore God sends down the *sūra* about him.[40] Such a story, in which Abū Lahab's abusive exclamation is addressed to his own hands, never gained the status of a "sound" tradition, endowed with a proper *isnād*, which the compilers could record. The latter preferred the fully developed story of persecution in which Abū Lahab curses the Prophet (the *'ashīra* scene), not his own hands, and in which he not only abuses him, but attacks him as well (the market scene).

In conclusion, the case of Abū Lahab illuminates the manner in which the *sīra* adapted the universal theme of persecution to Quranic models. A Quranic person damned by God was turned into a prototype of the Meccan polytheist who persecutes Muḥammad and whose clash with the Prophet is described with the

[39] Ibn Bukayr, 156.

[40] Ibn Hishām, I, 376. See also Balādhurī, *Ansāb*, I, 121 (no. 242). And see also another version of this episode where Sūrat al-Masad is not mentioned: Ibn Hishām, I, 376; Balādhurī, *Ansāb*, I, 122 (no. 243), 230 (no. 552).

vocabulary of his Quranic damnation. The implantation of the *sūra* cursing Abū Lahab in different scenes of persecution exemplifies the modular nature of the Quranic extracts which the biographers used simultaneously in numerous contexts.

9

The Reaction of Abū Ṭālib

I

IN THE STORY OF REACTION, as related about many prophets, rejection by opponents goes hand in hand with support from a chosen minority entourage. In the story of Muḥammad, support—like resistance—begins within his own clan. Whereas the source of resistance is his paternal uncle Abū Lahab, protection comes from another paternal uncle of his, Abū Ṭālib, who appears in the stories as Abū Lahab's direct opposite. Being ʻAlī's father, Abū Ṭālib's image was no doubt inspired by the political aims of the Shīʻīs, for whom the father of their great hero must have been as virtuous as his son. This is the reason why the traditions about Abū Ṭālib's heroic defence of the Prophet remained outside the Sunnī *muṣannaf* compilations. In the traditions that did gain access into them, the image of Abū Ṭālib changed considerably. This change will be elucidated in the following examination, beginning with the biographical sources.

Just as Abū Lahab's resistance to Muḥammad was first revealed through his reaction to Muḥammad's *ʻashīra* address, Abū Ṭālib's support for the Prophet is displayed during that very scene. A version preserving his supporting reaction to Muḥammad's address was recorded by al-Balādhurī, as related on the authority of the Companion Jaʻfar ibn ʻAbdallāh ibn Abī l-Ḥakam. When Muḥammad addresses the members of ʻAbd al-Muṭṭalib's family, in accordance with the *ʻashīra* verse, Abū Ṭālib offers Muḥammad his full support, but apologizes for not being able to abandon the religion of ʻAbd al-Muṭṭalib. Abū Lahab, on the other hand, demands that all activities of the Prophet be stopped. Abū Ṭālib retorts: "By God, we shall protect him as long as we live."[1]

Abū Ṭālib's support is related in further versions setting it in the stage of declaration, but not within the *ʻashīra* scene. Instead of delivering the intimate *ʻashīra* address, Muḥammad appears in these versions as already conducting a full-scale public campaign against the idols of Quraysh.

Such a setting of Abū Ṭālib's support for Muḥammad, within the context of the Prophet's religious confrontation with the Meccans, is contained in the report of Ibn Isḥāq. He relates that when Muḥammad disclosed his religion to his

---

[1] Balādhurī, *Ansāb*, I, 118–19 (no. 235). The *isnād*: Wāqidī←Abū Bakr ibn Abī Sabra (Medinan d. AH 162)←ʻUmar ibn ʻAbdallāh (Medinan?)←Jaʻfar ibn ʻAbdallāh.

fellow tribesmen and declared it openly (*ṣadaʿa*), Quraysh did not resist him, but when he started to disparage their idols, the Meccans united in opposing him, except for a few people whom God guided to Islam and who kept their religion secretly. Abū Ṭālib felt compassion for his nephew and protected him.[2] An abridged report to the same effect appears in al-Balādhurī, in a Syrian tradition related on the authority of the Baṣran Companion ʿIyāḍ ibn Ḥimār al-Mujāshiʿī.[3] The Shīʿī historian al-Yaʿqūbī has a similar report.[4] As for Ibn Isḥāq, he goes on to relate that when the leaders of Quraysh realized that Muḥammad reviled their idols and that Abū Ṭālib shielded him, they came to Abū Ṭālib and demanded that he either tell the Prophet to stop abusing their idols and their ancestors, or surrender him to them. Abū Ṭālib gently rejected their demands. Muḥammad resumed his campaign, till the leaders of Quraysh decided to pay a second visit to his sponsor. This time they not only complained to Abū Ṭālib, but threatened to wage war on him and his nephew. Abū Ṭālib did not dare break with Quraysh, but neither could he surrender the Prophet to them.

Ibn Isḥāq has another tradition of the same events, but with a more melodramatic atmosphere. It is of the Medinan Yaʿqūb ibn ʿUtba ibn al-Mughīra ibn al-Akhnas (d. AH 128), and relates that as soon as Abū Ṭālib heard the warning of Quraysh, he summoned Muḥammad and asked him not to burden him with more than he could bear. Muḥammad thought that Abū Ṭālib's resolution had withered away and that he was about to forsake him. He told his uncle that he would not give up his mission, even if the sun and the moon were put in his hands; then he burst into tears and turned away. Abū Ṭālib called him back and said: "Go, my nephew, and say whatever you think fit, and by God, I will never forsake you...."[5] A similar episode is described in another Medinan tradition, on the authority of a son of Abū Ṭālib, namely, the Companion ʿAqīl.[6] Ibn Isḥāq further relates that the leaders of Quraysh offered Abū Ṭālib a swapping deal. He would surrender Muḥammad to them, and in return they would deliver him a lad to foster, named ʿUmāra ibn al-Walīd, well known for his outstanding beauty and intelligence. As a result of Abū Ṭālib's refusal, a rift

---

[2] Ibn Hishām, I, 282–84; Ṭabarī, *Tārīkh*, I, 1174 (II, 322).

[3] Balādhurī, *Ansāb*, I, 117–18 (no. 234). The *isnād*: Makḥūl (Syrian d. AH 112)←ʿAbd al-Raḥmān ibn ʿĀʾidh (Syrian)←ʿIyāḍ ibn Ḥimār.

[4] Yaʿqūbī, II, 24.

[5] Ibn Hishām, I, 284–85; Ibn Bukayr, 154; Ṭabarī, *Tārīkh*, I, 1178 (II, 326).

[6] The *isnād*: Mūsā ibn Ṭalḥa (Medinan/Kūfan d. AH 103)←ʿAqīl ibn Abī Ṭālib. See Ibn Bukayr, 155; Bukhārī, *Tārīkh kabīr*, VII, 50–51 (no. 230); Ṭabarānī, *Kabīr*, XVII, no. 511.

was opened between him and Quraysh.[7] The latter story is also available in a tradition related by Mujāhid ibn Jabr (d. AH 104) on the authority of Ibn 'Abbās.[8]

The story of the visit of the leaders of Quraysh to Abū Ṭālib was, in fact, widely current among the earliest biographers of Muḥammad. One of them is 'Āṣim ibn 'Umar (Medinan d. AH 120), who adds that shortly after the meeting of the leaders with Abū Ṭālib, the entire clan of Hāshim (to which Muḥammad belonged) retreated to the *shi'b* ("ravine") of Abū Ṭālib, where they found refuge from the rest of the Quraysh, who had declared their determination to execute the Prophet.[9]

The occurrence of the name of Abū Ṭālib in the above traditions is especially significant in view of other versions of the same conflict between Muḥammad and Quraysh, from which Abū Ṭālib's name is absent. In these versions the leaders appeal directly to Muḥammad, who faces them alone, thus rendering their persecution all the more challenging. Two such versions[10] were recorded by Ibn Isḥāq. In these versions various extracts from the Quran are embedded, describing exchange of accusations between the Quranic prophet and his opponents (41:3–4, 13:31, 25:7–8, 17:90–93, 16:103). They accuse him of plagiarism, assert their refusal to accept his message, and challenge him to prove his case through miracles. In the *sīra*, these verses were turned into lines uttered by the Meccan leaders.[11]

II

Quranic links were added to other versions of confrontation in which the Prophet is not alone, but supported again by Abū Ṭālib. These also remained outside the *muṣannaf* compilations. The Quranic passage built into the narrative consists of the following passage from Sūrat Ṣād (38):

> (4)...the unbelievers said: "This is a conjurer, an impostor. (5) Has he turned the gods into one god? This is incredible."(6) Their gang departed, saying [to each other]: "Go and cling to your gods; this is something planned."

---

[7] Ibn Hishām, I, 285–87; Ibn Bukayr, 152–53 (with verses of Abū Ṭālib); Ṭabarī, *Tārīkh*, I, 1179 (II, 326–27).

[8] Balādhurī, *Ansāb*, I, 231–32 (no. 554, from Ibn Sa'd).

[9] *Ibid.*, I, 229–30 (no. 550, from al-Wāqidī).

[10] For which see also above, 15–16.

[11] Ibn Hishām, I, 313–19.

In the *sīra*, this documentation of a verbal conflict between the Quranic prophet and his fellow tribesmen was turned into lines uttered by the leaders of Mecca during their visit to Abū Ṭālib. In a tradition of the Kūfan al-Kalbī (d. AH 146), related on the authority of Ibn 'Abbās, the Meccan leaders, alarmed by the spread of Islam in their town, go to Abū Ṭālib and protest against Muḥammad's attacks on their idols. Abū Ṭālib summons the Prophet, and the leaders suggest that Muḥammad leave them and their idols alone, and in return they will leave him and his own god alone. Instead of accepting, Muḥammad suggests they profess the *shahāda*, i.e. that there is no God but Allāh and that Muḥammad is His prophet. The leaders get up in rage, saying to each other: "Go and cling to your gods; this is something planned...." (Quran 38:6–8).[12]

Considerable changes in the image of Abū Ṭālib are discernible in other versions of the visit of the leaders to him. These changes eventually made some of these versions acceptable to the Sunnī *muṣannaf* authors. To begin with, the time of the visit has changed; it no longer takes place during the stage of declaration, but much later, when Abū Ṭālib is already dying. Some versions with this dating of the meeting were circulated with the *isnād*: Sa'īd ibn Jubayr (Kūfan d. AH 95)←Ibn 'Abbās.[13] Abū Ṭālib's image has considerably changed too. This is clear in the tradition of Ibn 'Abbās recorded by Ibn Isḥāq.[14] Here the usual discourse takes place till the leaders refuse to profess the *shahāda* and leave, saying to one another the verses from Sūrat Ṣād (38). At this point the Prophet turns to the dying Abū Ṭālib and entreats him to utter the *shahāda* before he passes away, but Abū Ṭālib refuses. He says that he does not wish Quraysh to say that he only embraced Islam for fear of his looming death. However, while Abū Ṭālib dies, his brother al-'Abbās notices that he has moved his lips. Al-'Abbās puts his ear close to his mouth, and tells Muḥammad that Abū Ṭālib has just uttered the *shahāda*. The Prophet says: "I have not heard." But in another version of the same occurrence, in a tradition of al-Suddī (Kūfan d. AH 128), Abū Ṭālib's refusal is final. The leaders of Quraysh decide to ask Abū Ṭālib to tell his protégé to give up his attacks on their idols, fearing that when Abū Ṭālib is dead they would not be able to harm Muḥammad with-

---

[12] The *isnād*: al-Kalbī←Abū Ṣāliḥ (Bādhām, *mawlā* of Umm Hāni')←Ibn 'Abbās. See Balādhurī, *Ansāb*, I, 231 (no. 553).

[13] One of the versions is quoted from Ibn Jubayr by Yaḥyā ibn 'Umāra (or ibn 'Abbād, Kūfan). See Aḥmad, *Musnad*, I, 227. Another version is quoted from Ibn Jubayr by 'Abbād ibn Ja'far. See Ṭabarī, *Tārīkh*, I, 1177–78 (II, 325–26); Aḥmad, *Musnad*, I, 362. Both versions were circulated by al-A'mash (Kūfan d. AH 148).

[14] The *isnād*: al-'Abbās ibn 'Abdallāh ibn Ma'bad ibn 'Abbās (Medinan)←one of his family←Ibn 'Abbās. See Ibn Hishām, II, 58–60; also Ibn Bukayr, 236–37.

out being accused of taking advantage of Abū Ṭālib's demise. The usual discourse takes place till the leaders leave, saying to one another the verses from Sūrat Ṣād. At this point the Prophet turns to the dying Abū Ṭālib and entreats him to utter the *shahāda*, but the latter refuses, saying that he adheres to the religion of the old ancestors. Thereupon another Quranic verse is revealed, namely, 28:56, which says that the Quranic prophet cannot guide whom he likes.[15]

The new setting of the scene has shifted the focus from Abū Ṭālib's protection of Muḥammad to the issue of Abū Ṭālib's own persuasion, so that the story now culminates in the Prophet's unfulfilled request that his uncle profess the *shahāda*. The image of Abū Ṭālib has been reduced here from a heroic defender of Muḥammad to a cowardly old man who does not dare renounce the old religion of his fellow tribesmen. In this setting, the story is designed to convey a message of an anti-Shīʿī import. Whereas for the Shīʿīs it was important to establish the immaculate state of mind of ʿAlī's father, the Sunnīs insisted that he died an infidel.

Only versions with this unflattering presentation of Abū Ṭālib could gain entrance into some of the *muṣannaf* compilations. Ibn Abī Shayba recorded one of them in the "book" of *Maghāzī*, in the chapter about the Qurashī persecution of Muḥammad.[16] A similar version was recorded by al-Tirmidhī and al-Ḥākim[17] in the sections of *Tafsīr*, where these traditions provide the *asbāb al-nuzūl* of Sūrat Ṣād.

But in most versions found in the *muṣannaf* compilations, Sūrat Ṣād is not mentioned; nor is there any reference to the direct discourse and confrontation between the leaders and Muḥammad, or to Abū Ṭālib's support of Muḥammad in this confrontation. These versions are confined to the request posed by Muḥammad to Abū Ṭālib to profess the *shahāda*, and to the failure of the latter to comply. In response to Muḥammad's demand of Abū Ṭālib, Quran 28:56, as well as 9:113, are said to have been revealed, the latter stating that it is not for the Quranic prophet and the believers to ask pardon for the polytheists. Abū Ṭālib's role as Muḥammad's courageous defender in his struggle for Islam is thus entirely suppressed. Al-Bukhārī and Muslim recorded several versions of

---

15 The *isnād*: Aḥmad ibn al-Mufaḍḍal (Kūfan d. AH 215)←Asbāṭ (Kūfan d. AH 200)←al-Suddī. See Ṭabarī, *Tārīkh*, I, 1176 (II, 323–24).

16 It is the tradition with the *isnād*: ʿAbbād ibn Jaʿfar←Saʿīd ibn Jubayr←Ibn ʿAbbās. See Ibn Abī Shayba, XIV, 299–300 (no. 18413).

17 The tradition with the *isnād*: Yaḥyā ibn ʿUmāra←Saʿīd ibn Jubayr←Ibn ʿAbbās. See Tirmidhī/*Tuḥfa*, IX, 99–100 (*Tafsīr*); *Mustadrak*, II, 432 (*Tafsīr*).

this kind, one of them from the Kūfan Yazīd ibn Kaysān,[18] related on the authority of Abū Hurayra. Here Abū Ṭālib merely refuses to say the *shahāda*. In another version of Abū Hurayra of the same Yazīd ibn Kaysān, Abū Ṭālib explains that he is not saying the *shahāda* lest Quraysh think that he only did so out of fear of death.[19] In other versions he is said to have stressed his attachment to the *milla* ("creed") of his father, 'Abd al-Muṭṭalib. These versions were circulated under the *isnād* of al-Zuhrī (Medinan d. AH 124)←Sa'īd ibn al-Musayyab (Medinan d. AH 94)←his father, the Companion al-Musayyab ibn Ḥazn.[20]

With the suppression of Abū Ṭālib's role as Muḥammad's defender, the story of persecution retained its most dominant aspect—rejection.

Such were the versions which seemed acceptable to the Sunnī compilers of the *muṣannaf* collections. These versions corresponded to the image of Abū Ṭālib as seen by these compilers, which differed considerably from the more heroic one, as reflected in the Shī'ī oriented versions. Outside of these compilations all the other versions of the visit of the leaders may be found, including those in which the visit takes place at the stage of declaration. They are recorded not only in the above-mentioned biographical sources, but also in the Sunnī *tafsīrs*,[21] as well as in the Shī'ī ones,[22] where they provide the *asbāb al-nuzūl* of Sūrat Ṣād. One version may also be found in the commentaries on Quran 6:108, which the commentators thought was also relevant to the same scene. The verse prohibits the cursing of idols by Muslims, so as not to provoke the cursing of God by the polytheists. The exegetes applied to this verse one of the Kūfan traditions which they had borrowed from the exegesis of Sūrat Ṣād. The

[18] The *isnād*: Yazīd ibn Kaysān←Abū Ḥāzim (Salmān) al-Ashja'ī (Kūfan)←Abū Hurayra. Yazīd ibn Kaysān is quoted by Marwān ibn Mu'āwiya (Kūfan d. AH 193). See Muslim, I, 41 (1:41).

[19] This version is quoted from Yazīd ibn Kaysān by Yaḥyā ibn Sa'īd al-Qaṭṭān (Baṣran d. AH 198). See *Ibid.*, I, 41 (1:42). See also Tirmidhī/*Tuḥfa*, IX, 46–47 (44, Sūra 28); Ibn Ḥibbān, XIV, no. 6270.

[20] One of the versions is quoted from al-Zuhrī by Ṣāliḥ ibn Kaysān (Medinan). See Bukhārī, *Ṣaḥīḥ*, II, 119 (23:81); Muslim, I, 40 (1:40). Another version is quoted from al-Zuhrī by Yūnus ibn Yazīd (Egyptian d. AH 159). See Muslim, I, 40 (1:39). And see also the version of Zuhrī's secretary, Shu'ayb ibn Abī Ḥamza (Ḥimṣī d. AH 162), in Bukhārī, *Ṣaḥīḥ*, VI, 141 (65, Sūra 28). There is also a version which is quoted from Zuhrī by Ma'mar ibn Rāshid (d. AH 154). See Bukhārī, *Ṣaḥīḥ*,V, 65–66 (63:40); VI, 87 (65, Sūra 9).

[21] See Muqātil, II, fol. 114b; Huwwārī, IV, 6–7; Ṭabarī, *Tafsīr*, XXIII, 79–81; Zajjāj, IV, 321; Wāḥidī, *Asbāb*, 209–10; Baghawī, *Ma'ālim*, IV, 587–88; Naḥḥās, *I'rāb*, III, 454–55; Ibn 'Aṭiyya, XIV, 9–10; Zamakhsharī, III, 360; Rāzī, XXVI, 177; Qurṭubī, XV, 150.

[22] See Qummī, *Tafsīr*, II, 202; Ṭūsī, *Tabyān*, VIII, 543; Ṭabarsī, *Majma'*, XXIII, 96.

linking words of the *sūra* which the Meccan leaders utter in response to Muḥammad's suggestions were omitted from the borrowed tradition.[23]

Thus the modular structure of the *asbāb al-nuzūl* traditions has once more manifested itself, which demonstrates again the process in which an originally *sīra* material became part of *tafsīr*, being incorporated into the exegesis of various Quranic passages.

---

[23] The tradition is of the Kūfan al-Suddī. See Ṭabarī, *Tafsīr*, VII, 207–208; Wāḥidī, *Asbāb*, 127; Baghawī, *Ma'ālim*, II, 402; Rāzī, XIII, 140; Qurṭubī, VII, 61; Ibn Kathīr, *Tafsīr*, II, 164; Suyūṭī, *Durr*, III, 38.

10

Isolation

The Satanic Verses

A SPECIAL GROUP of traditions elaborates on a specific aspect of persecution, namely, isolation caused by rejection. This theme was linked to some Quranic models as well, which turned the story from one about isolation into one about satanic temptation. The latter theme is also universal by origin, but it seems to have found its way into Muslim tradition via the Quran.

I

The story of isolation emerges in a group of traditions telling about a massive movement of Islamisation which preceded the hostile reaction of the Meccan leaders. The latter only react when their idols are attacked; they then exercise their authority to intimidate the Meccan masses into abandoning Muḥammad. Thus the target of persecution includes the entire Meccan public, and brings about the isolation of Muḥammad. In this manner the evil effect of the leaders' reaction is heightened. One of the traditions is that of al-Zuhrī (Medinan d. AH 124), transmitted from him by Maʿmar ibn Rāshid (d. AH 154). The tradition was recorded by ʿAbd al-Razzāq in the "book" of *Maghāzī*,[1] but the present edition of ʿAbd al-Razzāq's *Muṣannaf* only has it in a distorted form. It can be reconstructed according to a more coherent version preserved in al-Balādhurī, where it is quoted from al-Wāqidī.[2] The tradition of al-Zuhrī says that at first Muḥammad preached Islam secretly (*sirran*), and young people of the lower classes followed him. Eventually the number of Muslims grew large, yet the infidels of Quraysh did not defy the Prophet, and even admitted that he was addressed from Heaven. But when he began to revile their idols in public, and stated that their fathers had died as infidels and were condemned to Hell, the Meccans resented this and persecuted him. The statement that a large number of people embraced Islam prior to the reaction of the Meccans renders the isolation caused by their reaction all the more grievous.

---

[1] Abd al-Razzāq, *Muṣannaf*, V, 324–25.

[2] Balādhurī, *Ansāb*, I, 115–16 (no. 228). And cf. also Ibn Saʿd, I, 199 (Wāqidī).

The story of isolation is also related in a series of three parallel versions attributed to the Medinan ʿUrwa ibn al-Zubayr (d. AH 94), which, taken together, demonstrate the coexistence of non-Quranic and Quranic levels in the story of isolation. Versions 1 and 2 represent the non-Quranic level, whereas Version 3 is Quranic. In Version 1 ʿUrwa is quoted by his son Hishām ibn ʿUrwa (Meccan d. AH 146) from a treatise ʿUrwa wrote for the caliph ʿAbd al-Malik, some extracts from which al-Ṭabarī has recorded in his *Tārīkh*.[3] A more comprehensive version—not yet noticed by Western scholars—is preserved in al-Ṭabarī's *Tafsīr*.[4] In his letter to the caliph, ʿUrwa writes:

> ...at first the Meccans followed Muḥammad willingly and did not reject him. But when he began to attack their idols, and when the Meccan leaders returned from Ṭā'if (where they had looked after their estates—U.R.), some Meccans disliked his attitude and tormented him, and made their own followers resist him, and eventually most people abandoned him. Only a few, whom God protected against their foes, stayed with him. Thereafter, the Meccan leaders decided to persecute those who had joined him from among their own families and clans, in order to force them to abandon God's religion. This was a tormenting tribulation (*fitna*). Some of his followers gave up, but others were protected by God [from surrender]. Then the Prophet ordered the Muslims to set out to Abyssinia, where there was a righteous king who oppressed none of his subjects. Quraysh used to trade there and made profits there. Most of the Muslims set out because of their sufferings in Mecca. The Prophet remained in Mecca for several years, during which the Meccans continued to torment the people who embraced Islam. However, Islam eventually spread in Mecca, and was embraced by Meccan notables and rich persons, which obliged the leaders of opposition to moderate their persecution of the Prophet and his companions. This was the first *fitna*, the one which compelled the Muslims to leave for Abyssinia. When the tribulation eased off, and Islam spread in Mecca, rumours about the improved conditions reached Abyssinia, and the believers who had come there returned to Mecca. The Muslims in Mecca became almost entirely secure there, and their number increased. Moreover, people of Medina also embraced Islam, and it spread in Medina, and the Medinans began coming to the Prophet in Mecca. When the Meccan opponents realized that Muḥammad was regaining power, they renewed their persecution of him more fiercely than ever. This was the second *fitna*....

In this version the isolation is labelled as the first *fitna*, a term signifying a sweeping tribulation. Identified as such, the isolation is only a stage in the long

---

[3] Ṭabarī, *Tārīkh*, I, 1180–81 (II, 328).
[4] Ṭabarī, *Tafsīr*, IX, 162–63 (on 8:39).

course of persecution which leads up to the second *fitna*. The latter occurs after an interval during which Meccan notables convert to Islam, Muslim refugees return from Abyssinia, and many Medinans join the Prophet.

In Version 2 a similar state of affairs is described, but covering only the stage labelled in Version 1 as the first *fitna*. The massive Islamisation which resulted in isolation due to the intervention of the leaders is mentioned explicitly. This version was preserved by al-Ṭabarānī in his great *Mu'jam*,[5] with the *isnād*: Ibn Lahī'a (Egyptian d. AH 174)←Abū l-Aswad (Medinan d. AH 131)←'Urwa. This time 'Urwa relates his story on the authority of a Companion, namely, Makhrama ibn Nawfal, whose son Miswar ibn Makhrama (Medinan Companion d. AH 64) is 'Urwa's immediate source. This version says:

> When Muḥammad announced his message openly, all (!) of the people of Mecca embraced Islam (*aslama ahlu Makka kullahum*). This took place before the daily prayer became obligatory. The Muslims grew so numerous that when they gathered together and wanted to perform prostration during the recitation of the Quran, they could not do so because of the pressing crowds. Such was the state of affairs till the leaders of Quraysh (al-Walīd ibn al-Mughīra, Abū Jahl, and others) returned from Ṭā'if. The leaders reproved the Meccans for having abandoned the religion of their ancestors, and ultimately the people renounced Islam and broke up with Muḥammad.

A new element emerges in Version 2. This is the ceremony of prostration, which in Arabic is *sujūd*. This is a most typical part of Islamic prayer, which in the present context symbolizes the massive spread of Islam in Mecca prior to the Prophet's isolation.

Version 3 of 'Urwa's story of isolation describes the stage labelled in Version 1 as the second *fitna*, using elements of the first *fitna* as well, and shifts the narrative from a non-Quranic to a Quranic level. Quranic ideas and extracts appear in the story, providing a specific reason for the interval of improved conditions for Muḥammad between the first and the second *fitna*. In this setting the theme of isolation is coupled with the theme of temptation. In his desire to improve his situation and break out of isolation (first *fitna* of Version 1), the Prophet is tempted into making concessions; his isolation is eliminated, but this lapse is finally rectified by God, and persecution is renewed (second *fitna* of Version 1). The bottom line of the story is the victory of God over Satan.

---

[5] See Ṭabarānī, *Kabīr*, XX, no. 2. See also *Fatḥ al-bārī*, II, 462.

The idea of temptation which appears in Version 3 is imported from Quran 17:73-74:

> (73) They almost tempted you away from what We have revealed to you, that you might attribute to Us false [words] instead—and then they would have taken you as their friend. (74) Had We not made you firm, you would have tended towards them a bit....

In this passage isolation almost brings about temporary temptation of the Quranic prophet into attributing false words to God; this is finally prevented by God, who makes His prophet "firm" in his heroic combat.

There is yet another Quranic passage which repeats the notion that prophets might be tempted into attributing false words to God. This is 22:52:

> Whenever a messenger or a prophet whom We have sent before you recited (*tamannā*), Satan would throw [words] into his recitation (*umniyyatihi*). But God removes (*yansakhu*) what Satan throws, and God establishes His [own] signs....

This passage became the source of what is known as the story of the "satanic verses".[6] It treats the idea of temptation as a universal one, presenting a model of satanic temptation to which every prophet is subjected. The *sīra* traditions contain an episode of such temptation in which Satan causes some false verses of his to appear as a genuine part of the Quran, verses in which the three major goddesses of the polytheists are recognized as divine deities. These satanic verses are:

> Those are the exalted cranes (*al-gharānīq*[7]); their intercession is to be hoped for.

This text is derived from a pre-Islamic ritual utterance (*talbiya*) of Quraysh, who reportedly uttered it in honour of the three so-called "Daughters of God" (Allāt, Manāt, and al-'Uzzā).[8] When imported from the pre-Islamic into the Islamic sphere of Muḥammad's own life, this *talbiya* became Satan's words. In the *sīra* the satanic verses are linked to the only Quranic passage in which the three goddesses are mentioned by name. This is Sūrat al-Najm (53), verses 19–23 of which read:

---

[6] The various Muslim traditions about the satanic verses were collected and discussed by Nāṣir al-Dīn al-Albānī in his *Naṣb al-majānīq li-nasf qiṣṣat al-gharānīq* (Damascus, 1952).

[7] On the significance of this word, see Ilse Lichtenstaedter, "A Note on the *Gharānīq* and Related Qur'ānic Problems", *Israel Oriental Studies* 5 (1975), 54–61.

[8] Ibn al-Kalbī (d. AH 204), *Aṣnām*, 19. See also Yāqūt, IV, 116.

> (19) Have you seen Allāt and al-'Uzzā (20) and Manāt the third, the other? (21) Is the male [offspring] for you, and the female for Him? (22) This would be an unjust division. (23) They are none but names which you and your ancestors gave them. God invested them with no power....

This outright attack on the three "Daughters of God" provided Sūrat al-Najm with a key role in the story of Muḥammad's campaign against polytheism as related in the *sīra*. In fact, some held that Sūrat al-Najm was the first chapter ever to be declared openly by the Prophet.[9] The satanic verses are said to have been interpolated by Satan into this *sūra*.

Version 3 of 'Urwa's story, which contains all these Quranic materials, was also recorded in al-Ṭabarānī's great *Mu'jam*.[10] Again it has the *isnād*: Ibn Lahī'a←Abū l-Aswad←'Urwa (= Version 2), but no Companion is mentioned this time. The story takes place only after the Prophet is already isolated and some Muslims have fled to Abyssinia due to the persecution of the Meccans (first *fitna* of Version 1). The improvement of conditions in Mecca and the subsequent return of the Muslims from Abyssinia are caused here by the affair of the satanic verses. It runs as follows:

> ...The polytheists of Quraysh said: "If this man only mentioned our idols in a favourable manner, we would have let him and his companions alone, for he has attacked neither the Jews nor the Christians as fiercely as he has attacked our own idols." Afterwards God revealed Sūrat al-Najm, and when the Prophet reached the passage about the three goddesses, Satan introduced his own false words into Muḥammad's recitation. This was the temptation (*fitna*) of Satan, and the polytheists repeated his verses and rejoiced in them, saying: "Muḥammad has reverted to the former religion of his people." When Muḥammad reached the end of the *sūra*, he prostrated himself, and every one prostrated himself along with him, Muslims and polytheists alike. Of the latter only al-Walīd ibn al-Mughīra did not prostrate himself, because he was a very old man. The best he could do was to raise a handful of earth to his forehead. Both parties (i.e. Muslims and polytheists) marvelled at their common prostration with the prophet. The Muslims marvelled at the participation of the polytheists in the *sujūd* ("prostration"), because the latter were unbelievers, and [the Muslims] were not aware of the verses of Satan, which only the polytheists could hear. The polytheists were pleased with what Satan had "thrown into the recitation of the prophet". Satan told them that Muḥammad had recited the verses along with the rest of Sūrat al-Najm, therefore they prostrated themselves in veneration of their own idols. The verses of

[9] Muqātil, II, fol. 255b. See also *Fatḥ al-bārī*, II, 456; VIII, 473.
[10] See Ṭabarānī, *Kabīr*, IX, no. 8316; Albānī, no. 6.

> Satan spread in Mecca, and the news about the participation of the polytheists in the Islamic prayer reached the Muslims who had fled to Abyssinia.... Thereupon they returned to Mecca. These events worried the Prophet, and when Gabriel came to Muḥammad in the evening to review the revelations of the day, Muḥammad told him about his worries. The angel asked him to recite to him Sūrat al-Najm. When the Prophet reached the verses of Satan, Gabriel disclaimed them and said: "Far be it from God to reveal such verses. He has never sent them down, and has never ordered me to bring them to you." When Muḥammad realized what had taken place, he was deeply aggrieved and said: "I have obeyed Satan and spoken his words, and he has taken part in God's authority on me." Thereupon, God abrogated the verses of Satan and revealed the verses about the temptation to which every prophet can be subjected (22:52). When God redeemed the Prophet from Satan's verses and from his temptation, the polytheists reverted to their former erring and enmity....

The effect of isolation (first *fitna* of Version 1) is intensified in Version 3 by adding to it the Quranic idea of temptation which figures as its result. Thus the human *fitna* of the polytheists is reinforced by the *fitna* of Satan. The participation of the entire Meccan population in the *sujūd*, which in Version 2 takes place prior to the first *fitna*, is now the result of the proclamation of the satanic verses, taking place only after the first *fitna* of Version 1. The satanic verses are announced as part of Sūrat al-Najm, which in fact concludes with a command to perform *sujūd* (v. 62). This provided the link to the prostration of the Meccans which is part of the non-Quranic level of the story of isolation (Version 2).

Other similar versions of the story of temptation caused by isolation were circulated by Mūsā ibn ʿUqba (Medinan d. AH 141)[11] and Ibn Isḥāq (d. AH 150). The version of the latter has the *isnād*: Yazīd ibn Ziyād al-Madanī←Muḥammad ibn Kaʿb al-Quraẓī (Medinan d. AH 117).[12] This tradition speaks expressly about the state of isolation which made Muḥammad wish that God would send down to him milder revelations that would draw Quraysh closer to him. Abū Maʿshar al-Sindī (Medinan d. AH 170) transmitted the same story on the authority of Muḥammad ibn Kaʿb al-Quraẓī and Muḥammad ibn Qays (Medinan story-teller).[13] Al-Wāqidī quotes Muḥammad ibn Faḍāla al-Ẓafarī (Companion) and al-Muṭṭalib ibn ʿAbdallāh ibn Ḥanṭab (Medinan).[14]

---

[11] Bayhaqī, *Dalāʾil*, II, 285–91.

[12] See Ṭabarī, *Tārīkh*, I, 1192–94 (II, 338–40). See also Ibn Bukayr, 177–78; Guillaume, "New Light", 38–39. In the recension of Ibn Hishām (II, 3) the story is omitted. And see also Suhaylī, *Rawḍ*, II, 126.

[13] See Ṭabarī, *Tārīkh*, I, 1195–96 (II, 340–41); Albānī, no. 4.

[14] See Ibn Saʿd, I, 205–206; Naḥḥās, *Nāsikh*, 187; Albānī, no. 9.

Some of the above versions have already attracted the attention of modern Islamicists who, as usual, have tried to explain the "history" behind the traditions.[15] Others, like John Burton for instance, have attempted to explain the dogmatic function of the story.[16] It seems, however, that the story only demonstrates once again the process of adaptation of universal prophetic themes to Islamic models such as the Quran. The basic non-Quranic level of the story of isolation was enriched with the Quranic passages of satanic temptation which provided dramatic air to the story of the two *fitna*s suffered by the Prophet in Mecca. As a result of this adaptation, the *fitna*s caused by human rejection were heightened by the *fitna* of Satan.

Finally, short versions of the affair of the satanic verses—detached from the immediate course of *sīra* events—reappear in the exegetic sources. These versions, like those preserved in the biographical sources, are mostly *mursal*, without Companions in their *isnād*s, and they usually function as *asbāb* in the exegesis of the relevant Quranic passages embedded in the story. They are occasionally recorded in the exegesis of Sūrat al-Najm,[17] but more frequently they appear in the exegesis of 22:52,[18] sometimes containing the scene of the participation of the polytheists in the *sujūd* following the recitation of the satanic verses. One such version is of Dāwūd ibn Abī Hind (Baṣran d. AH 139)←Abū l-'Āliya Rufay' ibn Mihrān (Baṣran d. AH 90),[19] and another version is of Sa'īd ibn Jubayr (Kūfan d. AH 95).[20] The *isnād* of this latter version is remarkable because it also appears as a Companion *isnād* ending with Ibn 'Abbās, who is quoted by Ibn Jubayr.[21] Other versions do not refer to the act of *sujūd*, but only note that the polytheists were pleased with what they believed they had heard from the Prophet. One of these versions is again of Sa'īd ibn Jubayr;[22]

---

[15] See e.g. Andræ, *Person*, 129–32; Watt, *M/Mecca*, 101–109.

[16] John Burton, "Those are the High-Flying Cranes", *Journal of Semitic Studies* 15 (1970), 246–65 (an oversimplified view that the traditions were invented merely to provide a Quranic basis for one of the formulas of the *naskh* theories).

[17] Huwwārī, IV, 239–40.

[18] Muqātil, II, fol. 26b; 'Abd al-Razzāq, *Tafsīr*, II, 40; Naḥḥās, *Nāsikh*, 187; Ṭabarī, *Tafsīr*, XVII, 131–33; Wāḥidī, *Asbāb*, 177–78; Suyūṭī, *Durr*, IV, 366–68; Ibn Kathīr, *Tafsīr*, III, 229–30.

[19] Ṭabarī, *Tafsīr*, XVII, 132–33 (nos. 3, 4.); Albānī, no. 3.

[20] Ṭabarī, *Tafsīr*, XVII, 133 (nos. 5, 6); Albānī, no. 1. The *isnād*: Shu'ba (Baṣran d. AH 160)←Abū Bishr (Ja'far ibn Iyās, Baṣran–Wāsiṭī d. AH 123)←Sa'īd ibn Jubayr.

[21] See Ṭabarānī, *Kabīr*, XII, no. 12450. Cf. the discussion in Albānī, 4–9.

[22] Wāḥidī, *Asbāb*, 178. The *isnād*: Yaḥyā ibn Sa'īd al-Qaṭṭān (Baṣran d. AH 198)←'Uthmān ibn al-Aswad (Meccan d. AH 150)←Sa'īd ibn Jubayr.

another is of al-Ḍaḥḥāk ibn Muzāḥim (Khurāsānī d. AH 102).[23] There is also a version of al-Zuhrī←Abū Bakr ibn 'Abd al-Raḥmān ibn al-Ḥārith (Medinan d. AH 93).[24] Another version is of Abū Ṣāliḥ (Bādhām, *mawlā* of Umm Hāni'),[25] and another one is again of Ibn 'Abbās.[26] The tradition of Ma'mar ibn Rāshid (Baṣran d. AH 154) from Qatāda (Baṣran d. AH 117) refers to the act of *naskh*, or "abrogation", stating that the satanic verses were abrogated by the canonical verses of Sūrat al-Najm about the three goddesses.[27]

II

In spite of the firm Quranic links of the story of isolation which turned into temptation, none of the above versions of the story gained access into any of the *muṣannaf* compilations. This is a unique case in which a group of traditions are rejected only after being subjected to Quranic models, and as a direct result of this adjustment. The temporary control taken by Satan over Muḥammad, although hinted at in the Quran itself, made such traditions unacceptable to the compilers. However, some abridged versions which do not mention Satan and his verses do appear in the *muṣannaf* compilations, where they illustrate a ritual issue. This is the topic of *sujūd al-Qur'ān*, the routine of performing prostration during the public recitation of the Quran. The prostration is carried out at certain points in the text of the scripture, either where the imperative (*amr*) *usjud* etc. occurs (e.g. 22:77), or where it is stated (*khabar*) that prostration has taken place (e.g. 22:18). The performance of *sujūd* by the believers at these points of recitation signifies their most earnest participation in the worship of God. This topic is dealt with in many traditions designed to establish the exact verses which demand prostration, and to what extent, if at all, prostration is mandatory. Whole sections named *Sujūd al-Qur'ān*, or, *Sujūd al-tilāwa* may be found in al-Bukhārī (no. 17) and Abū Dāwūd (no. 7). These sections are actually part of the "book" of *Ṣalāt* ("Prayer"), under which heading they are found in other compilations as well. Some compilers recorded them under the heading of *Faḍā'il al-Qur'ān*.[28]

---

[23] Ṭabarī, *Tafsīr*, XVII, 133 (no. 8); Albānī, no. 8. The *isnād*: Abū Mu'ādh (al-Faḍl ibn Khālid, of Marw, d. AH 211)←'Ubayd ibn Sulaymān (of Marw)←al-Ḍaḥḥāk.

[24] Ṭabarī, *Tafsīr*, XVII, 133 (no. 9); Albānī, no. 2.

[25] Suyūṭī, *Durr*, IV, 366; Albānī, no. 7.

[26] Ṭabarī, *Tafsīr*, XVII, 133 (no. 7); Albānī, no. 10; with the family *isnād* of Aṭiyya ibn Sa'd al 'Awfī.

[27] Ṭabarī, *Tafsīr*, XVII, 134; Albānī, no. 5.

[28] Under *Ṣalāt*: Zayd ibn 'Alī, 132–33; Mālik/Zurqānī, *Kitāb* no. 15; Tirmidhī/*Tuḥfa*, *Kitāb* no. 4; Nasā'ī, *Kubrā*, Book no. 10; Ibn Khuzayma, I, 276–80; Ibn Abī Shayba, II, 1–25; Dāraquṭnī, *Sunan*, I, 406–10; Ibn Ḥibbān, *Ṣaḥīḥ*, VI, 465–75; Bayhaqī, *Sunan*, II, 312–

One of the places indicated in the traditions as appropriate for prostration is at the end of Sūrat al-Najm (v. 62), where, as seen above, a command (*amr*) is given to the audience to perform prostration before God. That *sujūd* should be practiced at this point of recitation was endorsed by the jurists of most law schools; they held that Sūrat al-Najm was included in the list of *'azā'im*, i.e. imperative duties, of the *sujūd*. This is confirmed in the sources concerning the Ḥanafīs,[29] the Shāfi'īs[30] and the Ḥanbalīs.[31] The same applies to the Shī'īs—Zaydīs[32] as well as Twelvers.[33] This view is communicated through several traditions.[34]

However, some held that prostration was only to be performed in places of *khabar*, not *amr*, which means that Sūrat al-Najm is not one of them. There are, in fact, traditions to the effect that Sūrat al-Najm is not included in the imperative duties of the *sujūd*.[35] Moreover, there are some traditions implying that the Prophet did not perform *sujūd* at Sūrat al-Najm.[36] Furthermore, there are traditions on the authority of several Companions stating that there is no *sujūd* in the entire *mufaṣṣal*,[37] i.e. the last section of the Quran with the shorter *sūras*, including al-Najm. This view was shared mainly by the scholars of Medina, i.e. the disciples of Mālik ibn Anas.[38]

Those who held that *sujūd* at the end of Sūrat al-Najm was imperative had at their disposal traditions to the effect that this had been the practice of the

26; Ṭaḥāwī, *Sharḥ ma'ānī*, I, 352–62; *Kanz*, VIII, 142–47. Under *Faḍā'il al-Qur'ān*: 'Abd al-Razzāq, *Muṣannaf*, III, 335–57 (Book's heading missing); Bayhaqī, *Shu'ab*, II, 378–79; *Kanz*, II, 57.

[29] Shaybānī, *Ḥujja*, I, 114; Ibn Ḥazm, *Muḥallā*, V, 109.

[30] See Ibn Ḥazm, *Muḥallā*, V, 109.

[31] See Aḥmad, *Masā'il* ('Abdallāh), 104 (no. 369). See also *idem*, *Masā'il* (Isḥāq), 97–98 (no. 488); Ibn Qudāma, *Mughnī*, I, 685 (no. 860).

[32] Zayd ibn 'Alī, 132.

[33] Kulīnī, III, 317–18.

[34] 'Abd al-Razzāq, *Muṣannaf*, III, no. 5863; Ibn Abī Shayba, II, 7, 17; Bayhaqī, *Sunan*, II, 315; Ṭaḥāwī, *Sharḥ ma'ānī*, I, 355.

[35] Ibn Abī Shayba, II, 17.

[36] The most current tradition to the effect that Muḥammad did not make *sujūd* by Sūrat al-Najm is of 'Aṭā' ibn Yasār (Medinan story-teller, d. AH 103)←Zayd ibn Thābit. It is recorded in the following compilations in the chapters about *sujūd al-Qur'ān*: 'Abd al-Razzāq, *Muṣannaf*, III, no. 5899; Bukhārī, *Ṣaḥīḥ*, II, 51; Muslim II, 88; Nasā'ī, *Kubrā*, I, 331–32 (no. 1032 [10:50]); Abū 'Awāna, II, 208; Ibn Khuzayma, I, 285 (no. 568); Abū Dāwūd, I, 324–25; Ibn Abī Shayba, II, 6; Dāraquṭnī, I, 409–10 (no. 15); Ibn Ḥibbān, *Ṣaḥīḥ*, VI, nos. 2762, 2769; Ṭaḥāwī, *Sharḥ ma'ānī*, I, 352.

[37] E.g. 'Abd al-Razzāq, *Muṣannaf*, III, nos. 5900–5903; Ṭaḥāwī, *Sharḥ ma'ānī*, I, 354.

[38] See Shaybānī, *Ḥujja*, I, 106; Mālik/Zurqānī, II, 196; Saḥnūn, *Mudawwana*, I, 105.

Prophet, as well as of prominent Companions of his.[39] The traditions relate that the Prophet once recited Sūrat al-Najm and performed *sujūd* at its end, and all the assembled crowds, Muslims and polytheists (*mushrikūn*) alike, followed suit. One of these traditions has the *isnād*: Ayyūb al-Sakhtiyānī (Baṣran d. AH 131)←'Ikrima (Medinan d. AH 105)←Ibn 'Abbās. It is recorded in the most authoritative *ḥadīth* compilations,[40] and recurs outside the *muṣannaf* compilations as well.[41] There are also less "trustworthy" *isnāds* of the same story, one of Hushaym ibn Bashīr (Wāsiṭī d. AH 183)←Ibn 'Awn (Baṣran d. AH 150)←al-Sha'bī (Kūfan d. AH 103),[42] and another one of Muṣ'ab ibn Thābit (Medinan d. AH 157)←Nāfi' (Medinan d. AH 117)←Ibn 'Umar.[43] The story fits perfectly well into the legal context in which the *muṣannaf* compilers recorded it (*sujūd al-Qur'ān*), and establishes the view that Sūrat al-Najm is indeed included in the list of *sūras* at the recitation of which *sujūd* is warranted. The allusion to the participation of the *mushrikūn* emphasises how overwhelming and intense the effect of this *sūra* was on those attending. The traditions actually state that all cognizant creatures took part in it, humans as well as demons (*jinn*).

Nevertheless, there is something very wrong in the inner logic of the events. The participation of the polytheists in the *sujūd* is inexplicable because it does not fit into the specific *sūra* being recited. The polytheists have no reason to prostrate themselves upon hearing a *sūra* in which their idols are said to be nothing but empty names (v. 24). The inconsistency is partly solved in other versions, recorded in the *muṣannaf* compilations, where only the Muslims perform *sujūd*. Only one polytheist is present, but he does not take part in the ceremony. In some versions he only raises a handful of earth to his forehead, to show his disrespect. This person is said to have been killed later on by the Muslims at war (battle of Badr). The traditions of this kind are far more numerous than those of the former. One has a Kūfan *isnād*: Abū Isḥāq al-Sabī'ī (Kūfan Shī'ī d. AH 126–29)←al-Aswad ibn Yazīd (Kūfan Companion d. AH 75)←'Abdallāh ibn Mas'ūd (Medinan/Kūfan Companion d. AH 32). Like all

---

39 'Umar performs *sujūd* at al-Najm: 'Abd al-Razzāq, *Muṣannaf*, III, nos. 5880, 5882; Shaybānī, *Ḥujja*, I, 113; Bayhaqī, *Sunan*, II, 314; Ṭaḥāwī, *Sharḥ ma'ānī*, I, 355–56. 'Uthmān performs *sujūd* at al-Najm: Ibn Abī Shayba, II, 8; Ṭaḥāwī, *Sharḥ ma'ānī*, I, 355. Ibn 'Umar performs *sujūd* at al-Najm: 'Abd al-Razzāq, *Muṣannaf*, III, nos. 5893, 5897; Ibn Abī Shayba, II, 8, 24; Ṭaḥāwī, *Sharḥ ma'ānī*, I, 356. Ibn Mas'ūd performs *sujūd* at al-Najm: Ibn Abī Shayba, II, 7, 17.

40 Bukhārī, *Ṣaḥīḥ*, II, 51 (17:5); Tirmidhī/*Tuḥfa*, III, 166 (no. 572); Ibn Ḥibbān, *Ṣaḥīḥ*, VI, no. 2763; Dāraquṭnī, I, 409 (no. 12); Bayhaqī, *Sunan*, II, 314.

41 See Ṭabarānī, *Kabīr*, XI, no. 11866; Ibn Kathīr, *Bidāya*, III, 90.

42 See Ibn Abī Shayba, II, 7–8.

43 Ṭaḥāwī, *Sharḥ ma'ānī*, I, 352.

other versions it is recorded in the section *Sujūd al-Qur'ān*,[44] but al-Bukhārī also recorded it in a chapter about the persecution of Muḥammad by Quraysh,[45] as well as in the chapter about the death of Muḥammad's enemies in the battle of Badr.[46] Another has a Ḥijāzī *isnād*: Ibn Ṭāwūs (Yemeni d. AH 132)←'Ikrima ibn Khālid ibn al-'Āṣ al-Qurashī←Ja'far ibn al-Muṭṭalib ibn Abī Wadā'a al-Qurashī←his father al-Muṭṭalib (Medinan Companion).[47] There is also a tradition of al-Ḥārith ibn 'Abd al-Raḥmān al-Qurashī (Medinan d. AH 129)←Abū Salama ibn 'Abd al-Raḥmān ibn 'Awf (Medinan d. AH 94)←Abū Hurayra.[48] Another *isnād* is: Abū Khālid al-Aḥmar (Kūfan d. AH 190)←Dāwūd ibn Abī l-'Āliya.[49] In a tradition of Maymūn ibn Mihrān (Jazarī d. AH 116)←Ibn 'Abbās, only Muḥammad prostrates himself.[50]

But there remains the problem of the versions in which the polytheists do prostrate themselves alongside the Muslims. The only reasonable explanation for these versions is that they contain traces of the story of the satanic verses. In their present form, these versions underwent the following changes which made the story acceptable to the compilers: to begin with, the satanic verses were cut out, the participation of the *mushrikūn* in the *sujūd* of Sūrat al-Najm remaining without a cause, or being simply suppressed. Besides, the story of the single polytheist who raised a handful of earth to his forehead was transformed from a sincere attempt of an old disabled man to participate in Muḥammad's *sujūd* (Version 3 of 'Urwa), into a sarcastic act of an enemy of Muḥammad wishing to dishonour the Islamic prayer. Only such edited versions could gain appropriate *isnād*s acceptable to such compilers as al-Bukhārī and others.

Thus traditions which originally related the dramatic story of temptation became a sterilized anecdote providing prophetic precedent for a ritual practice.

---

44 See Bukhārī, *Ṣaḥīḥ*, II, 50–51 (17:1, 4); Muslim II, 88 (5, *Sujūd al-tilāwa*); Abū Dāwūd, I, 325; Abū 'Awāna, II, 207; Ibn Khuzayma, I, 278 (no. 553); Ibn Ḥibbān, *Ṣaḥīḥ*, VI, no. 2764; Ibn Abī Shayba, II, 7; Bayhaqī, *Sunan*, II, 314; Ṭaḥāwī, *Sharḥ ma'ānī*, I, 353. Outside the *muṣannaf* compilations the tradition is recorded in Aḥmad, *Musnad*, I, 388, 401, 437, 443, 462; Ibn Kathīr, *Bidāya*, III, 90. It is noteworthy that in *Mustadrak*, I, 220–21, the same tradition refers to Sūrat al-Ḥajj (22) instead of al-Najm.

45 See Bukhārī, *Ṣaḥīḥ*, V, 57 (63:29).

46 *Ibid.*, V, 96 (64:8).

47 See 'Abd al-Razzāq, *Muṣannaf*, III, no. 5881; Nasā'ī, *Kubrā*, I, 331 (no. 1030 [10:49]); Bayhaqī, *Sunan*, II, 314; Ṭaḥāwī, *Sharḥ ma'ānī*, I, 353. In this tradition the person who does not participate in the *sujūd* is al-Muṭṭalib himself, when he is still an unbeliever. Outside the *muṣannaf* compilations the tradition recurs in Aḥmad, *Musnad*, III, 420; IV, 215–16; Ibn Kathīr, *Bidāya*, III, 91.

48 Ibn Abī Shayba, II, 8. Other similar traditions of Abū Hurayra: Dāraquṭnī, *Sunan*, I, 409 (no. 11); Ṭaḥāwī, *Sharḥ ma'ānī*, I, 353; And see also Aḥmad, *Musnad*, II, 443.

49 Ibn Abī Shayba, II, 7.

50 Dāraquṭnī, I, 409 (no. 13).

PART V

SALVATION

11

The 'Aqaba Meetings

PERSECUTION IS BROUGHT TO AN END by salvation through emigration. The latter act, called *hijra*, emerges twice in the story of Muḥammad's emergence in Mecca: an emigration of a group of Muslims to Abyssinia, and a more massive emigration of most Meccan Muslims to Medina. The latter emigration forms the finale of the Meccan chapter in Muḥammad's life and brings the Prophet final salvation from persecution.

The story of salvation brings a new group onto the stage, the Anṣār, or the "Helpers", as the Arabs of Medina are called. They belong to the tribes of al-Aws and al-Khazraj, who were of south Arabian descent, and the great pride they took in their title is reflected in a statement attributed to the Baṣran Companion Anas ibn Mālik (d. AH 91–95) saying that God Himself named them Anṣār. This statement alludes to the Quran, where the title Anṣār occurs in a most favourable context alongside the names of other groups of blessed believers (9:100 and 117). Anṣār is, in fact, the very title which the Quran confers on the disciples of Jesus (3:52, 61:14). The statement of Anas was circulated by Baṣran traditionists of a southern descent (Azd), and was recorded by al-Bukhārī in a chapter devoted especially to the virtues (*manāqib*) of the Anṣār.[1] Such chapters about them are, in fact, included in most of the *muṣannaf* compilations.[2]

The Anṣār are the main participants in the story of salvation. Their story begins with a series of meetings between the Prophet and some Medinans at al-'Aqaba. A thorough analysis of the various versions of these meetings was carried out by Gertrud Mélamède.[3] Her aim was to find out "what happened in reality",[4] and later scholars have studied the event with the same purpose in mind.[5] All of them, however, have noticed the existence of tendentious manipu-

[1] Bukhārī, *Ṣaḥīḥ*, V, 37–38 (63:1). The *isnād*: Mahdī ibn Maymūn (Baṣran d. AH 171)←Ghaylān ibn Jarīr (Baṣran d. AH 129)←Anas.

[2] See, for example, 'Abd al-Razzāq, *Muṣannaf*, XI, 59–65; Ibn Abī Shayba, XII, 156–66; Bukhārī, *Ṣaḥīḥ*, Book 63; Muslim, VII, 173–76 (43, *Bāb faḍā'il al-Anṣār*); Tirmidhī/*Tuḥfa*, 46:65 (X, 399–412); Ibn Māja, I, 57–58 (Intro.); *Kashf al-astār*, III, 299–307; *Mustadrak*, IV, 78–81 (*Faḍā'il al-qabā'il*); Ibn Ḥajar, *Maṭālib*, IV, 140–43; *Majma' al-zawā'id*, X, 31–45; *Kanz*, XIV, 56–68.

[3] Gertrud Mélamède, "The Meetings at al-'Aḳaba", *Le Monde Oriental* 28 (1934), 17–58.

[4] *Ibid.*, 17.

[5] See especially Watt, *M/Mecca*, 144–49.

lations of the reports, and have tried to isolate these from the "real" facts. Our concern here, however, is not with the facts of the 'Aqaba meetings *per se*, but rather with the story itself. There is more to be said about this than has hitherto been done, and examination of it will complete our survey of the story of Muḥammad's emergence in Mecca as viewed by the early Muslims.

I

The story of the 'Aqaba meetings is the last link in the chain of persecution, and the meetings themselves mark its last accord and bring about salvation. They take place in Minā, near Mecca. This is one of the stations of the pilgrimage, where the pilgrims perform the "stoning" (*rajm*) of the devil near three stone-heaps, the largest of which is called Jamrat al-'Aqaba. Hence 'Aqaba signifies the place of this stone-heap. The Prophet meets the Anṣār there while looking for supporters in the Meccan fairs,[6] as well as in the stations of the *ḥajj*.

In some versions, emphasis is laid on the role played by God in bringing about salvation through the unification of the Anṣār, which creates conditions of permanent asylum for Muḥammad in Medina. In a tradition recorded by Ibn Sa'd, Muḥammad meets eight Medinans in Minā, and offers them conversion to Islam. They accept, and the Prophet asks whether they are willing to safeguard him, till he accomplishes the mission of his Lord. In response they say that as their people have been enemies to each other since the battle of Bu'āth (thus named after a district in Medina), they are not likely to unite round Muḥammad. Instead they suggest that he wait till next year, and perhaps by then God will have established peace among their people.[7] In this tradition, the unification of the Medinans by God is a precondition for the Prophet's arrival in Medina; without this unity, no shelter could be offered to him by the Medinans.

The topic of the reconciliation of the Medinans by God was applied by Quran exegetes to the *tafsīr* of Quran 8:63. This verse reads:

> He drew their hearts together. If you spent all that is upon earth, you still could not have brought their hearts together. It is God who drew their hearts together....

This verse was said to refer to the establishment of peace between the Aws and the Khazraj, thus ending the pre-Islamic wars between them.[8]

---

[6] For this scene see also above, 141–42.

[7] Ibn Sa'd, I, 218–19.

[8] See Farrā', I, 417. See also Ṭabarī, *Tafsīr*, X, 25, the tradition of Asbāṭ (Kūfan d. AH 200)←al-Suddī (Kūfan d. AH 128), the tradition of Shu'ba (Baṣran d. AH 160)←Bashīr ibn

The same divine act in Medina was read into the exegesis of Quran 3:103:

> ...recall God's blessing upon you, when you were enemies and He drew your hearts together, and you became brothers by His blessing....

The Quran exegetes applied to this verse the story of God's unification of the Medinan Arabs.[9] A specific tradition was also imported into the *tafsīr* of this verse, in which, again, the main role of providing Muḥammad with conditions of shelter in Medina is played by God, whereas the Anṣār are passive—indeed, sceptical—witnesses to the events. The tradition has the *isnād*: 'Abd al-Razzāq←Ma'mar ibn Rāshid (Baṣran d. AH 154)←Ayyūb al-Sakhtiyānī (Baṣran d. AH 131)←'Ikrima (Medinan d. AH 105).[10] Muḥammad meets six Anṣār, and they embrace Islam. He wants to come with them (i.e. to Medina), but they say that as long as the Medinans are at war with each other, he will not achieve his goal. They promise to meet him again the following year, saying that perhaps by then God will have established peace among them. So they leave, not believing that the civil war will ever end. However, God does establish peace among them, so that the following year 70 of the Anṣār can meet the Prophet and pledge allegiance to him. The Prophet appoints 12 leaders (*nuqabā'*) from among the 70 Medinans. The scepticism of the Anṣār as displayed in this tradition renders God's blessing in uniting them all the more wondrous.

In other versions of the 'Aqaba meetings, the role of providing salvation is shifted from God to human beings. It is here that religious notions give way to political considerations. These traditions demonstrate what has already become apparent in the previous chapters, namely, that apart from the urge to convey a dogmatic message concerning the image of Muḥammad as guided and protected by God, political interests of various Islamic groups left their own mark on the stories. The following versions keep telling about the scheme of God, but in a different setting in which the Anṣār are no longer passive and sceptical; in fact, they have become the main factor in providing to Muḥammad salvation from persecution.

These traditions bear certain Quranic elements gleaned from passages believed to refer to the Anṣār. The most notable are 8:72 and 74. In both verses

---

Thābit al-Anṣārī (Baṣran), and the tradition of Salama ibn al-Faḍl al-Anṣārī (d. AH 191)←Ibn Isḥāq.

[9] See Zajjāj, I, 451; Māwardī, *Nukat*, I, 414; Zamakhsharī, I, 451; Ibn al-Jawzī, *Zād al-masīr*, I, 433; Rāzī, VIII, 163–64. Shī'ī *tafsīr*: Qummī, I, 116; Ṭūsī, *Tabyān*, II, 546; Ṭabarsī, *Majma'*, IV, 158.

[10] See 'Abd al-Razzāq, *Tafsīr*, I, 129; Ṭabarī, *Tafsīr*, IV, 24; Suyūṭī, *Durr*, II, 61.

"those who have emigrated" are mentioned, and next to them reference is made to "those who gave shelter and helped" (*āwaw wa-naṣarū*). The verb *āwā*, which the Quran employs for indicating the shelter extended by those who "helped", i.e. the Anṣār, is often repeated in traditions about them, including those about the 'Aqaba meetings. Ibn Sa'd has such a tradition on the authority of al-Wāqidī that depicts Muḥammad's sufferings caused by the infidels, and the shelter the Anṣār finally provided to him. Al-Wāqidī relates that Muḥammad remained in Mecca, summoning the Arab tribes to believe in God, and introducing himself to them in the annual fairs of the pilgrimage, asking them to grant him shelter (*...an yu'wūhu*). None of the tribes agreed; instead they tormented and abused him, till God willed that His religion should triumph and led His Prophet to the Anṣār. He met some of them while they were shaving their heads (i.e. for the ceremonies), called them to believe in God, and recited the Quran to them; they complied and hastened to embrace Islam, and they believed and gave shelter and helped and supported....[11] All references to a delay suggested by the Anṣār till God should unite them have disappeared from this presentation. The Anṣār are rather able to offer support then and there. A similar tradition with the Anṣār as the ultimate origin of shelter was recorded by Aḥmad ibn Ḥanbal, as transmitted on the authority of the Medinan Companion Jābir ibn 'Abdallāh (d. AH 77). Here again God leads the Anṣār to the rejected Prophet, and as soon as some of them are approached by him, they embrace Islam without hesitation and offer shelter without preconditions. When later on they return to Medina, Islam begins to spread in that town till 70 of the newly converted Anṣār decide to go to Mecca, saying to one another: "Till when shall we let Muḥammad be chased away in the mountains of Mecca, and be intimidated?" So they go to Mecca and pledge allegiance to Muḥammad at al-'Aqaba.[12] The tradition recurs in some of the *muṣannaf* compilations.[13]

The theme of salvation extended by the Anṣār to the persecuted Prophet played an important role in the political rivalry between them and Quraysh during the first Islamic decades. Some versions of the story were deliberately attributed to some prominent Companions belonging to Quraysh, thus making them acknowledge the merits of the Anṣār. 'Alī ibn Abī Ṭālib is said to have related the story, stating that he who does not love the Anṣār and does not recognize their merits is not a true believer. According to 'Alī, the Prophet went

[11] Ibn Sa'd, I, 217 (Wāqidī). See also Abū Nu'aym, *Dalā'il*, no. 225 (Wāqidī).

[12] The *isnād*: 'Abdallāh ibn 'Uthmān ibn Khuthaym (Meccan d. AH 132)←Abū l-Zubayr (Muḥammad ibn Muslim ibn Tadrus, Meccan d. AH 126)←Jābir (d. AH 77). See Aḥmad, *Musnad*, III, 322–23, 339–40. See also Fākihī, IV, no. 2539; Bayhaqī, *Dalā'il*, II, 442–44.

[13] Ibn Ḥibbān, XIV, no. 6274; XV, no. 7012 (*Manāqib*); *Mustadrak*, II, 624–25 (*Tārīkh*); Bayhaqī, *Sunan*, IX, 9 (*Siyar*).

out to the markets during the pilgrimage, year after year, summoning the tribes to Islam, but none of them listened. This went on till God decided to implement His plan concerning the Anṣār. So when Muḥammad met them and asked them to embrace Islam, they hastened to accept, and gave shelter and supported....[14]

The Anṣār felt that for their deeds they deserved an appropriate reward, which was never given to them in full. This feeling is reflected in the tradition about 'Umar in which he too relates the story of Muḥammad's first meeting with the Anṣār. Having related it, 'Umar states: "By God, we have not rewarded the Anṣār as we should have; we told them instead: 'We (i.e. Quraysh) are the leaders (*umarā'*) and you are the deputies (*wuzarā'*).' If I am still alive next year, I shall not leave a governor in office who is not of the Anṣār."[15] The tradition implies that 'Umar did not live to fulfil his promise.

Quraysh were no less eager to stress their own important role in Muḥammad's salvation from their own persecution of him. Their viewpoint is reflected in other versions about the 'Aqaba meetings in which their ancestors feature as Muḥammad's great defenders. Again, the role of protection is assigned to a paternal uncle of Muḥammad, this time not to Abū Ṭālib, who is already dead, but to al-'Abbās. The latter was the ancestor of the 'Abbāsids, which explains the political importance of the part he plays. The tendentious nature of the story about him has already been noticed by several Islamicists.[16] The role of the Anṣār is reduced in these versions to that of mere hosts who invite the Prophet to stay with them at his pleasure, not as a persecuted outcast seeking refuge. One such version in the *Sīra* of Ibn Isḥāq[17] contains a lengthy story about the journey of the Anṣār to Mecca and their meeting with Muḥammad, including a speech of al-'Abbās interpolated into the actual meeting. It has the *isnād*: Ma'bad ibn Ka'b ibn Mālik (Medinan)←'Abdallāh ibn Ka'b ibn Mālik←Ka'b ibn Mālik (Medinan Companion d. AH 51). Al-'Abbās appears in what is called the "second" 'Aqaba meeting (with the 70 Medinans). He is still holding the polytheist religion (*'alā dīni qawmihi*), but he is eager to look after the interests of his nephew Muḥammad. He addresses the Anṣār, saying:

---

14 Abū Nu'aym, *Dalā'il*, no. 224 (from al-Wāqidī).

15 Bazzār, I, no. 281. The *isnād*: Usāma ibn Zayd←Zayd ibn Aslam (Medinan d. AH 136)←Aslam, *mawlā* of 'Umar←'Umar.

16 See e.g. Watt, *M/Mecca*, 147; M.J. Kister, "Notes on the Papyrus Account of the 'Aqaba Meeting", *Le Muséon* 76 (1963), 406–11. See also Sellheim, "Prophet, Chalif und Geschichte", 51–52.

17 On the possible relation between Ibn Isḥāq and the 'Abbāsids, see Sellheim, "Prophet, Chalif und Geschichte", 33–36.

> Muḥammad holds among us a position which is very well known to you. We have protected him against our own tribe, people who think about [his religion] the way we do. He therefore enjoys the protection of his people, and is defended in his own town. However, he insists on separating from us and on joining you. If you are confident that you can hold faithful to that for which you have invited him, and can protect him against his rivals, then go ahead with what you have undertaken. But if you think you might surrender him after taking him out with you, leave him now, because he already enjoys the protection and defence of his own people and town.

Afterwards the Anṣār ask the Prophet to promise not to leave them and return to his own people, once God has given him victory. Then they pledge allegiance to him.[18] The speech put into the mouth of al-ʻAbbās tries so hard to absolve Quraysh from the blame of persecution that it paints Muḥammad's stay at Mecca in the rosiest colours. Similar words are uttered by al-ʻAbbās in the version of al-Wāqidī. Here he says that the Anṣār have invited Muḥammad in their own interests, while he is nevertheless the most esteemed person among his own people. He is protected by his followers, as well as by the polytheists (!). The former protect him due to their common faith, whereas the latter protect him because blood relations unite them. But Muḥammad has insisted on joining the Anṣār, al-ʻAbbās adds, therefore they are requested to join forces behind him against the rest of the Arabs.[19] Such presentation of the state of affairs entirely overshadows the theme of persecution which is so fundamental in the former versions of the same events of the ʻAqaba meetings. Thus the honour of Quraysh, who have been turned into Muḥammad's most affectionate supporters, is saved at the expense of that of the Anṣār.

Because the collective virtues of the Anṣār are considerably toned down in the story of al-ʻAbbās, the authors of the *muṣannaf* collections could not use it for the purpose of *faḍā'il*. Only Ibn Ḥibbān and al-Ḥākim recorded Ibn Isḥāq's tradition of Kaʻb ibn Mālik,[20] adducing it for the *faḍā'il* of individual Medinans. The beginning of the tradition contains the story of the journey to Mecca by the Anṣārī al-Barā' ibn Maʻrūr, who is credited with the virtue of being the first Medinan to take the Kaʻba as his direction of prayer (*qibla*). A few commentators of the Quran incorporated the same tradition into the exegesis of 3:103.[21]

---

[18] Ibn Hishām, II, 84–85; Ṭabarī, *Tārīkh*, I, 1220–21 (II, 362–63); Fākihī, IV, no. 2542. There is also a version of Yūnus ibn Bukayr. See Bayhaqī, *Dalā'il*, II, 446–47; Ṭabarānī, *Kabīr*, XIX, no. 174. For another *isnād* from Ibn Isḥāq, see Aḥmad, *Musnad*, III, 460–62.

[19] Ibn Saʻd, I, 221–22. Cf. Balādhurī, *Ansāb*, I, no. 584.

[20] Ibn Ḥibbān, XV, no. 7011; *Mustadrak*, III, 441.

[21] E.g. Thaʻlabī (MS Tel Aviv), 137–39.

But in further versions about al-'Abbās, an Anṣārī reaction is detectable. In a tradition recorded on the authority of the Qurashī Companion 'Aqīl ibn Abī Ṭālib and others, the address of al-'Abbās is answered by one of the Anṣār (Abū Umāma As'ad ibn Zurāra), who says that the Medinans have sacrificed a lot in accepting Muḥammad into their town. They have had to renounce the religion of their fathers, to sever their pacts with their neighbours and blood relations, and to accept the leadership of an outsider whom his own people have driven away.[22] The same Anṣārī response is included in the version of Wahb ibn Munabbih (Yemeni d. AH 110) recorded in a Schott-Reinhardt papyrus.[23] In this particular version the Prophet is accompanied not only by al-'Abbās, but also by Abū Bakr, 'Umar, and 'Alī. The latter three, however, have no lines of their own to speak.

II

In another group of traditions about the 'Aqaba meetings, the political interests of the various Islamic groups give way to the general Islamic veneration of the Prophet. In these traditions the *hijra* of Muḥammad to Medina is not a flight of a persecuted prophet seeking salvation, but rather the triumphant arrival of the long-expected leader and saviour. The reconciliation of the fighting Medinan clans is not a precondition for his arrival, but rather the goal of his appearance and the blessed outcome of the spread of his religion. Thus Muḥammad does not gain salvation, but rather provides it. Such a presentation reads into the story of salvation the state of leadership which marks the entire duration of Muḥammad's stay in Medina.

The shift from the image of Muḥammad as a recipient of salvation to that of a saviour is conspicuous in a variety of traditions in which Muḥammad's authority rests on annunciation. These traditions were circulated by some Medinan traditionists, among them 'Āṣim ibn 'Umar ibn Qatāda (d. AH 120), whose tradition has been recorded in the *Sīra* of Ibn Isḥāq.[24] 'Āṣim relates on the authority of some indigenous informants of his tribe (al-Khazraj) that Muḥammad met in Mecca six Medinans who belonged to the tribe of al-Khazraj and were allies of the Jews who lived in Medina. The tradition says that it was in accordance with God's scheme that the Medinan Arabs and the Jews had been neighbours; the Jews possessed a sacred scripture and knowledge, and whenever a

[22] Abū Nu'aym, *Dalā'il*, no. 226. This tradition was noticed for the first time in Kister, "The 'Aqaba", 411.

[23] See Mélamède, 48–50.

[24] See Ibn Hishām, II, 70–73; Ṭabarī, *Tārīkh*, I, 1209–13 (II, 353–56); Bayhaqī, *Dalā'il*, II, 433–35; Abū Nu'aym, *Dalā'il*, no. 223.

dispute had broken out between them and the Arabs, they used to threaten the latter that within a short while a prophet was to come who would destroy them. When the Medinan Arabs met Muḥammad in Mecca, and when he introduced his religion to them, they realized immediately that he was the prophet whom the Jews had been awaiting. So, deciding to get ahead of the Jews in joining the Prophet, the six Medinans embraced Islam then and there and said to the Prophet: "We have left our people [back at Medina] in a state of hatred and war as has not been suffered by any other people. Perhaps God will unite them through you. We shall return and introduce to them your religion, which we have accepted. If God unites them in it, no one will be mightier than you." So the six Anṣār returned to Medina, told their people about Muḥammad, and Islam spread into every household of the Anṣār. The next year twelve Anṣārīs returned to Mecca and pledged allegiance to Muḥammad at al-'Aqaba, in the so-called "pledge of the women" (*bay'at al-nisā'*). This tradition of 'Āṣim ibn 'Umar was incorporated by al-Ṭabarī into the exegesis of Quran 3:103,[25] and a tradition with a similar setting of the story was related by 'Urwa ibn al-Zubayr (Medinan d. AH 94).[26] Abridged reports about the meeting of Muḥammad with the first group of six Anṣār and their relations with the Jews were also recorded by al-Wāqidī.[27]

The story in its present form is focussed on Muḥammad as fulfilling the messianic hopes of the Jews of Medina, which are shared by their Arab neighbours and rivals. But the image of Muḥammad as a leader bringing salvation to Medina emerges not only in traditions about the 'Aqaba meetings, but also recurs in a general statement about conditions in Medina on the eve of Islam. The statement is contained in a tradition of Hishām ibn 'Urwa (Meccan d. AH 146)←'Urwa ibn al-Zubayr (Medinan d. AH 94)←'Ā'isha. She states that the war of Bu'āth was granted by God as a blessed event to Muḥammad, who came to a divided Medina, where the leaders had either died or been wounded. The battles of Bu'āth were a blessing to Muḥammad, in that they caused the Medinans to embrace Islam. This tradition appears in the *Saḥīḥ* of al-Bukhārī in the chapter about the virtues of the Anṣār, and recurs in other later sources.[28] It implies that the exhausted state of all parties after the "wars of Bu'āth", the discord and the elimination of local leadership, paved the way for Muḥammad,

---

[25] Ṭabarī, *Tafsīr*, IV, 23–24. See also Tha'labī (MS Tel Aviv), 135–36; Baghawī, *Ma'ālim*, I, 520–21; Ibn 'Aṭiyya, III, 183–84.

[26] Abū Nu'aym, *Dalā'il*, no. 227. The *isnād*: Ibn Lahī'a (Egyptian d. AH 174)←Abū l-Aswad (Medinan d. AH 131)←'Urwa. See also *Majma' al-zawā'id*, VI, 43–44.

[27] Ibn Sa'd, I, 219; Balādhurī, *Ansāb*, I, no. 566.

[28] Bukhārī, *Ṣaḥīḥ*, V, 38 (63:1). See also Bayhaqī, *Dalā'il*, II, 421.

who redeemed them from their miserable condition and united them all under the banner of Islam.

Both aspects of Muḥammad's image, as reflected in the story of the 'Aqaba meetings, are also brought out in some of his own statements, said to have been made on other later occasions. One of these events is the division of the spoils of Hawāzin among the Muslims after the battle of Ḥunayn (AH 8). No share is allotted to the Anṣār, which makes them speak some bitter words about Muḥammad. The Prophet is informed of this, and comes to the Anṣār and addresses them. In his speech some Quranic materials are used, especially 3:103, which, as we have seen, was connected in Islamic exegesis with the reconciliation of the Aws and the Khazraj.

In the *Sīra* of Ibn Isḥāq Muḥammad's address to the Anṣār is recorded under the Medinan *isnād* of 'Āṣim ibn 'Umar ibn Qatāda (d. AH 120)←Maḥmūd ibn Labīd (d. AH 96)←Abū Sa'īd al-Khudrī (Anṣārī Companion d. AH 65). In his speech the Prophet reproaches the Anṣār for having criticised him, and says: "Have I not come to you when you were erring (*ḍullāl*), and God guided you, poor, and God enriched you, enemies, and God drew your hearts together?" Apart from 3:103, Quran 93:6–8 seems also to have inspired the stylistic structure of this address, in which Muḥammad appears as the guiding master and the uniting leader. But the tradition goes on to relate that immediately afterwards, the Prophet told the Anṣār that if they wished, they could very well answer him: "Have you not come to us being called a liar, and we believed in you, deserted, and we supported you, expelled, and we gave you shelter, poor, and we assisted you." In the suggested retort of the Anṣār, the Prophet is cast in the other aspect of his image, that of the persecuted outcast in search of protection. The Prophet's address is concluded with the statement that were it not for his *hijra*, which he has already performed (thus becoming one of the Emigrants), the Prophet would have preferred to be one of the Anṣār.[29]

Extracts from Muḥammad's address were also circulated with another Medinan *isnād*, that of the Companion al-Sā'ib ibn Yazīd (d. AH 96).[30] Other versions are recorded with Kūfan *isnād*s which again lead back to the Anṣārī Companion Abū Sa'īd al-Khudrī.[31] There are also Baṣran *isnād*s of the Com-

---

[29] Ibn Hishām, IV, 141–42. See also Ṭabarī, *Tārīkh*, I, 1683–84 (III, 93–94); Aḥmad, *Musnad*, III, 76–77; Wāqidī, III, 957–58.

[30] The *isnād*: Yūnus and 'Aqīl ibn Yazīd←al-Zuhrī (Medinan d. AH 124)←al-Sā'ib ibn Yazīd. See Ṭabarānī, *Kabīr*, VII, no. 6665.

[31] Ma'mar←A'mash (Kūfan d. AH 148)←Abū Ṣāliḥ (Dhakwān, *mawlā* of Juwayriyya, Medinan d. AH 101)←Abū Sa'īd: Aḥmad, *Musnad*, III, 57; 'Abd al-Razzāq, *Muṣannaf*, XI, no. 19918. 'Aṭiyya ibn Sa'd al 'Awfī (Kūfan, Shī'ī d. AH 111)←Abū Sa'īd: Abū Ya'lā, II,

panion Anas ibn Mālik (d. AH 91–95),[32] and versions on the authority of two Companions: Ibn 'Abbās[33] and Jābir ibn 'Abdallāh.[34]

In the most authoritative *muṣannaf* compilations there is one more version; here the suggested answer of the Anṣār has been concealed behind the vague statement that they could say "such and such" (*kadhā wa-kadhā*), leaving only the explicit words of Muḥammad himself, and thus presenting him as the uniting saviour, not the recipient of salvation. This reshaped version was circulated with the *isnād* of 'Amr ibn Yaḥyā ibn 'Umāra (Medinan Anṣārī d. AH 140)←'Abbād ibn Tamīm (Medinan Anṣārī)←'Abdallāh ibn Zayd ibn 'Āṣim (Anṣārī Companion d. AH 63).[35]

The second occasion on which Muḥammad is said to have made a statement concerning his relations with the Anṣār is his last illness. Here he is the recipient of their protection, and is said to have entreated the Muhājirūn to behave kindly towards the Anṣār because they were his closest allies, with whom he found shelter. This tradition was circulated with several *isnād*s of the Medinan Companion Ka'b ibn Mālik (d. AH 51), recorded in early *sīra* sources[36] as well as in the chapters about the merits (*faḍā'il*) of the Anṣār in some *muṣannaf* compilations.[37] There are also versions of 'Ā'isha[38] and Abū Hurayra.[39]

III

The image of Muḥammad as a source of salvation is the main basis of his leadership. The 'Aqaba story includes a specific element which confirms Muḥammad's authority as a saving leader, namely, the pledge of allegiance. However, the traditions about this are intended not so much to elaborate on Muḥammad's leadership, as to supply legal precedents for the administrative practice of the pledge of allegiance. As is usually the case, legal precedents were sought by the Muslims in the utterances and acts of the Prophet, who in this re-

no. 1358; Aḥmad, *Musnad*, III, 89; Ibn Abī Shayba, XII, no. 12407; Tirmidhī/*Tuḥfa*, X, 405 (46:65).

[32] Aḥmad, *Musnad*, III, 104–105: Ibn Abī 'Adī (Muḥammad ibn Ibrāhīm, Baṣran d. AH 194)←Ḥumayd al-Ṭawīl (Baṣran d. AH 142)←Anas ibn Mālik. Aḥmad, *Musnad*, III, 253: Thābit al-Bunānī (Baṣran d. AH 123)←Anas.

[33] *Majma' al-zawā'id*, X, 35 (from Ṭabarānī, *Awsaṭ)*.

[34] *Kanz*, XIV, no. 37932 (Daylamī).

[35] See Bukhārī, *Ṣaḥīḥ*, V, 200 (64:56); Muslim, III, 108 (12, 139). See also Aḥmad, *Musnad*, IV, 42.

[36] Ibn Hishām, IV, 300. See also Aḥmad, *Musnad*, III, 500; V, 224.

[37] 'Abd al-Razzāq, *Muṣannaf*, XI, no. 19917; *Mustadrak*, IV, 78.

[38] *Kashf al-astār*, III, no. 2799.

[39] 'Abd al-Razzāq, *Muṣannaf*, XI, no. 19911. The *isnād*: Thābit al-Bunānī (Baṣran d. AH 123)←Abū Hurayra.

spect is the supreme Islamic law-giver. In some cases the Quran too was taken as a legal model. For the practice of pledging allegiance, known in Arabic as *bayʿa*, the Muslims employed Quran 60:12, which they incorporated into the story of the Anṣār's *bayʿa* at the ʿAqaba meeting. This verse reads:

> Oh Prophet, when the believing women come to you to pledge allegiance to you that they will not associate with God anything else, and that they will not steal, nor commit adultery, nor kill their children, nor cheat....then accept their pledge of allegiance and ask God's forgiveness for them....

This is the only Quranic passage where the actual contents of a *bayʿa* to the leader is provided. Early Muslim tradition did not fail to use this Quranic prescription as a model for the pledge of allegiance taken by the Anṣār during the ʿAqaba meetings.

The most prevalent traditions using the wording of this verse were circulated on the authority of the Syrian Companion ʿUbāda ibn al-Ṣāmit (d. AH 34–45), who belonged to the Anṣār. He describes the *bayʿa* as an eyewitness, speaking in the first person. The earliest available versions of his description are recorded in Ibn Hishām's recension of the *Sīra* of Ibn Isḥāq, and appear under two different *isnāds*. In one of them ʿUbāda is quoted by the Syrian Successor Abū Idrīs al-Khawlānī (ʿĀʾidhullāh ibn ʿAbdallāh, d. AH 80). Ibn Isḥāq's source for this version is al-Zuhrī. In it ʿUbāda is made to say that the *bayʿa* took place on the night of the "first" ʿAqaba. The content of the *bayʿa* as related by him accords with Quran 60:12.[40] In the other version, ʿUbāda is quoted by the Syrian Successor al-Ṣunābiḥī (ʿAbd al-Raḥmān ibn ʿUsayla, Abū ʿAbdallāh).[41] Here ʿUbāda is made to supply some more details: the *bayʿa* takes place during the "first" ʿAqaba, when Muḥammad meets with the twelve Anṣār, before the duty of making war is enjoined (i.e. upon the Muslims), and the people's pledge of allegiance is taken "according to the pledge of the women" (*ʿalā bayʿat al-nisāʾ*), which is an allusion to Quran 60:12.[42]

As already observed by Western scholars,[43] Quran 60:12 and the label "pledge of the women" (*bayʿat al-nisāʾ*) are not part of the basic narrative framework of the ʿAqaba meetings. This is confirmed by the fact that there are versions of

---

[40] Ibn Hishām, II, 76. Cf. Ṭabarī, *Tārīkh*, I, 1213 (II, 356–57).

[41] The *isnād*: Yazīd ibn Abī Ḥabīb (Egyptian d. AH 128)←Marthad ibn ʿAbdallāh, Abū l-Khayr (Egyptian d. AH 90)←al-Ṣunābiḥī←ʿUbāda ibn al-Ṣāmit.

[42] Ibn Hishām, II, 75. See also Ṭabarī, *Tārīkh*, I, 1213 (II, 356); Aḥmad, *Musnad*, V, 323; Bayhaqī, *Dalāʾil*, II, 436; Ibn ʿAbd al-Barr, *Tamhīd*, XXIII, 273.

[43] E.g. Watt, *M/Mecca*, 146.

the 'Aqaba meetings which refer neither to *bay'at al-nisā'* nor to the "first" 'Aqaba meeting during which it supposedly took place. Some of them have already been considered above. Another is of Jābir ibn 'Abdallāh, in which the only meeting which takes place is with the 70 Anṣār who come to Mecca following Muḥammad's preliminary contacts with a few Anṣār. This is also the case in the above tradition of Ayyūb al-Sakhtiyānī←'Ikrima, where the meeting with the 70 Anṣār is the only one after the encounter with the six. No mention is made of a "first" 'Aqaba meeting with twelve Anṣār. The letter of 'Urwa ibn al-Zubayr to 'Abd al-Malik also refers to only one meeting with 70 Anṣār which followed sporadic meetings with Medinans in Mecca.[44] Furthermore, a tradition of Mūsā ibn 'Uqba (Medinan d. AH 141)←al-Zuhrī (Medinan d. AH 124) speaks of only one meeting with eight Anṣār, after which Muṣ'ab ibn 'Umayr is sent to Medina.[45] Only with the introduction of the Quranic model of the "women's pledge" did the story about the "first" 'Aqaba meeting with the 12 Anṣār come into existence, being placed before the one with the 70 Medinans, and after the preliminary one with the 6 (or 8). The Muslims themselves sometimes noticed that the meeting called the "first" 'Aqaba is not part of the original story. For example, 'Abdallāh ibn Abī Bakr (Medinan d. AH 135) declared that he did not know what the "first" 'Aqaba was; Ibn Isḥāq, however, assured him that there were indeed two successive 'Aqaba meetings.[46] Specific lists of participants in the meeting of the twelve Anṣār came also into being, and actually repeat names appearing in the lists of the 6 and the 70 Medinans.[47]

Moreover, the Quranic *bay'a* verse of 60:12 was believed to have been revealed long after the *hijra*,[48] which again indicates that the link between it and the 'Aqaba story is secondary. The verse was regarded as part of a later revelation including the preceding verse as well (60:10), in which the Quranic prophet is ordered to test the women who come to him as *muhājirāt*. Quran 60:12 was perceived as providing the contents of that test. This was asserted in a tradition of 'Ā'isha stating that the Prophet tested the women who came to him at Medina by presenting them with the interdictions of 60:12. This tradition was given

---

[44] Ṭabarī, *Tārīkh*, I, 1224–25 (II, 366). See also Watt, *M/Mecca*, 145–46.

[45] Bayhaqī, *Dalā'il*, II, 430–33.

[46] *Ibid.*, II, 438.

[47] For the list of the six, see Ibn Hishām, II, 71–72; Ibn Sa'd, I, 219 (Wāqidī); Ṭabarī, *Tārīkh*, I, 1210–11 (II, 354–55). The list of the twelve: Ibn Hishām, II, 73–74; Balādhurī, *Ansāb*, I, no. 566; Ṭabarī, *Tārīkh*, I, 1210–11 (II, 354–55). List of twelve *naqībs* from the 70 Medinans: Ibn Hishām, II, 86–87. That the various lists were tampered with was observed by Ibn al-Kalbī. See Balādhurī, *Ansāb*, I, no. 579.

[48] Cf. Mélamède, 34.

prominence in the *muṣannaf* compilations.[49] The Quranic test of the *muhājirāt* was itself linked to the period following the treaty of al-Ḥudaybiyya (AH 6), when Meccan women performed the *hijra* to Medina, staying there against the stipulations of the extradition article of the Ḥudaybiyya agreement. The story about this usually revolves round Umm Kulthūm bint 'Uqba, and the Quranic passage of the women's test was said to have sanctioned her stay at Medina.[50] Furthermore, Muḥammad is said to have performed the test of 60:10–12 with women who embraced Islam not earlier than the conquest of Mecca. Here the main figure is Hind bint 'Utba, Abū Sufyān's wife.[51] But there are also stories about several other emigrating women taking the same test.[52]

Nevertheless, the Quranic *bay'a* verse was dragged into the much earlier 'Aqaba scene, in order to serve as a model for a general *bay'a* applying not only to women, but to men as well. This created a chronological gap between the presumed time of the revelation of the verse (al-Ḥudaybiyya) and the 'Aqaba meetings. Due to this gap, other versions attributed to the Companion 'Ubāda ibn al-Ṣāmit, as recorded by several *muṣannaf* compilers, use the *bay'a* verse with no mention of the 'Aqaba meeting. The dating of the "pledge of the women" was deliberately suppressed in these versions, so as to avoid the chronological gap between the 'Aqaba meetings and al-Ḥudaybiyya. But the higher parts of their *isnāds* remained unchanged. In the version of al-Ṣunābiḥī, as produced by al-Bukhārī and Muslim, 'Ubāda only states that he was one of the *nuqabā'* who pledged allegiance to Muḥammad, swearing that they would not associate anything with God, neither steal, nor....[53] In the version by Abū Idrīs al-Khawlānī of 'Ubāda's statement, as recorded by 'Abd al-Razzāq, the event is not dated.[54] However, in two places in al-Bukhārī's *Ṣaḥīḥ*, "the night of al-'Aqaba" is still mentioned in the version of Abū Idrīs,[55] but in other places in the *Ṣaḥīḥ*, as well as in Muslim and al-Nasā'ī, the same version does not

---

[49] The *isnād*: Zuhrī←'Urwa←'Ā'isha. See 'Abd al-Razzāq, *Muṣannaf*, VI, no. 9820; Bukhārī, *Ṣaḥīḥ*, III, 247 (54:1); V, 162 (64:35); VI, 186–87 (65, Sūra 60); VII, 63–64 (68:20); Muslim, VI, 29 (33, *Bay'at al-nisā'*); Ibn Māja, II, no. 2875 (24:43); Tirmidhī/*Tuḥfa*, IX, 202 (no. 3361 [44, Sūra 60]). And see also Aḥmad, *Musnad*, VI, 163, 270.

[50] See e.g. Ibn Hishām, III, 340–41; Wāqidī, II, 629–33. A similar story was related about Subay'a bint al-Ḥārith. See Muqātil, II, fol. 193b; Wāḥidī, *Asbāb*, 241.

[51] E.g. Muqātil, II, fol. 194a–b.

[52] See e.g. 'Abd al-Razzāq, *Muṣannaf*, VI, nos. 9826–27; Ibn Kathīr, *Tafsīr*, IV, 352–55 (on 60:12).

[53] See Bukhārī, *Ṣaḥīḥ*, V, 70 (63:43); Muslim, V, 127 (29, *al-Ḥudūd kaffārāt....*). See also Aḥmad, *Musnad*, V, 321.

[54] 'Abd al-Razzāq, *Muṣannaf*, VI, no. 9818.

[55] Bukhārī, *Ṣaḥīḥ*, I, 11 (2:10); V, 70 (63:43).

mention the name 'Aqaba at all.[56] In fact, there is one more version of 'Ubāda's tradition, recorded by Muslim, in which he is quoted by a third Syrian Successor, namely, Abū l-Ash'ath al-Ṣan'ānī. Here the date of the *bay'a* is not indicated either.[57]

On the other hand, the presumably late date of the revelation of the *bay'a* verse did leave its mark on another version of 'Ubāda's statement (circulated by al-Zuhrī) in which the women's *bay'a* is said to have taken place at the conquest of Mecca.[58] Alternatively, one finds traditions about the same *bay'at al-nisā'* attributed to another Companion, namely, Jarīr ibn 'Abdallāh al-Bajalī (Yemeni Companion d. AH 51). He too speaks in the first person as an eyewitness, and again, no mention is made of the 'Aqaba.[59] The name of this Companion is not included in any of the lists of the 'Aqaba participants; in fact, he is not an Anṣārī at all. There are traditions attributing to him statements about other *bay'a*s, besides the women's one.[60]

The scene of *bay'at al-'Aqaba* and scenes of later *bay'a*s are indeed overlapping. This is further illustrated through the impact of another Quranic verse in which the act of *bay'a* is mentioned, albeit without a text. This is Quran 48:18:

> God was pleased with the believers when they pledged allegiance to you under the tree....

The locution "under the tree" (*taḥta l-shajara*) became a label usually used in the *sīra* for designating the *bay'a* taken at al-Ḥudaybiyya, but the same Quranic phrase appears in one version of the 'Aqaba story as well. This is contained in a tradition of the Companion Abū Mas'ūd al-Anṣārī ('Uqba ibn 'Amr, d. AH 40), whose name appears in the lists of the 70 Anṣār, being marked as their youngest.[61] There is, in fact, a tradition in which he reports about the *bay'a* of the 70 Medinans.[62] One version of this tradition is remarkable: "The Prophet

---

[56] Bukhārī, *Ṣaḥīḥ*, IX, 99 (93:49); Muslim, V, 127 (29, *al-Ḥudūd kaffārāt....*); Nasā'ī, *Kubrā*, IV, no. 7784, 7801. See also Aḥmad, *Musnad*, V, 314, 320.

[57] Muslim, V, 127 (29, *al-Ḥudūd kaffārāt....*). The *isnād*: Khālid al-Ḥadhdhā' (Baṣran d. AH 141)←Abū Qilāba al-Jarmī (Baṣran d. AH 104)←Abū l-Ash'ath←'Ubāda ibn al-Ṣāmit. See also Aḥmad, *Musnad*, V, 313, 320.

[58] *Fatḥ al-bārī*, I, 63 (from Ṭabarānī). And see also Mélamède, 33 (quoting Diyārbakrī), 34 (quoting Ḥalabī).

[59] The *isnād*: Sayf ibn Hārūn (Kūfan)←Ismā'īl ibn Abī Khālid (Kūfan d. AH 146)←Qays ibn Abī Ḥāzim (Kūfan d. AH 84–98)←Jarīr ibn 'Abdallāh. See Ṭabarānī, *Kabīr*, II, no. 2260.

[60] 'Abd al-Razzāq, *Muṣannaf*, VI, nos. 9819, 9821.

[61] Ibn Hishām, II, 102. See also Ṭabarānī, *Kabīr*, XVII, no. 519 ('Urwa ibn al-Zubayr).

[62] Ibn Abī Shayba, XIV, 598 (no. 18949).

came with al-'Abbās to the 70 Anṣār at the 'Aqaba *under the tree....*"[63] Such a Quranic placement of the meeting is designed to imply that the Anṣār are the very people with whom God was so "pleased", according to 48:18.

The case of "under the tree" is thus another example of the role of the Quran in the *sīra* text. Unlike 60:12, which was incorporated into the story for legal purposes, this locution was added to the description for political purposes, i.e. the *faḍā'il* of the Anṣār. Both excerpts, gleaned from Quranic *bay'a* passages, were incorporated into the *sīra* irrespective of the accepted chronology of the Quranic revelations.

IV

The Quran was not the only source of Islamic law, and probably not even the earliest. Pre-Islamic practices could also become Islamic laws, normally by gaining the sanction of traditions attributed to the Prophet. In the case of the pledge of allegiance, there are further traditions in which a pre-Islamic practice, rather than the Quran, is taken as the model. These too were recorded by Ibn Isḥāq. One of them has already been mentioned above, for the role of al-'Abbās in the meeting with the 70 Medinans. In this story of the Medinan Companion Ka'b ibn Mālik (d. AH 51), after the address of al-'Abbās both sides undertake to defend each other and cooperate in peace and in war. Muḥammad utters a somewhat obscure pre-Islamic slogan of blood solidarity (*al-dam al-dam wa-l-hadm al-hadm*). Then he says: "I am of you and you are of me. I will wage war on those whom you fight, and will make peace with those with whom you make peace."[64] The tradition of 'Āṣim ibn 'Umar (Medinan d. AH 120), which is not related on the authority of a specific eyewitness, also mentions a similar *bay'a* in which the Anṣār undertake to fight all people (*al-aḥmar wa-l-aswad*).[65]

This model of allegiance is a militant one which accords with the pre-Islamic types of tribal pacts. In the *sīra* it was made part of the meeting with the 70 Medinans, whereas the Quranic women's pledge was made part of the meeting with the 12. This order of the two *bay'a* types created a narrative framework in which two successive *bay'as* take place, first *bay'at al-nisā'*, then the *bay'a* of war, or *bay'at al-ḥarb*, as it is usually called. This chronological outlook is reflected in the *Sīra* of Ibn Isḥāq, who in his typical way says that the "first"

[63] Ibn 'Abd al-Barr, *Tamhīd*, XXIII, 273–74. See also Aḥmad, *Musnad*, IV, 119. The *isnād* of the tradition is: Zakariyyā ibn Abī Zā'ida (Kūfan d. AH 148)←al-Sha'bī (Kūfan d. AH 103)←Abū Mas'ūd al-Anṣārī.

[64] Ibn Hishām, II, 84–85; Ṭabarī, *Tārīkh*, I, 1220–21 (II, 362–63).

[65] Ibn Hishām, II, 88–89; Ṭabarī, *Tārīkh*, I, 1221 (II, 363).

'Aqaba, during which the "pledge of the women" was taken, took place "before the duty of making war was enjoined upon them".[66] Thus it is implied that the pledge of war was a separate event which took place later on. Ibn Isḥāq derives this observation from one version of the Companion 'Ubāda ibn al-Ṣāmit about the women's pledge, which, as seen above, was circulated by al-Ṣunābiḥī.[67] But in the other version of the same Companion, as circulated by Abū Idrīs al-Khawlānī, such a chronological observation is entirely missing.[68] Thus, another example is provided for the turning of what were originally two different versions of the same scene into two progressive *sīra* episodes.

The Quranic model (women's pledge) and the pre-Islamic one (pledge of war) were not the only ones considered by the Muslims as precedents by which to run their own state. In further traditions about the 'Aqaba meetings, a third model of *bay'a* comes to light which is neither Quranic nor pre-Islamic; it probably draws on administrative models current in the neighbouring states, either the Byzantine, or the Sasanian, or both. The model is based on the idea of total obedience to the ruler; in Arabic it is the principle of *al-sam' wa-l-ṭā'a*, "to hear and obey [the legitimate ruler]". This principle became part of the 'Aqaba *bay'a* in a version which was once more circulated under the name of the Companion 'Ubāda ibn al-Ṣāmit, disseminated by his own descendants (his son al-Walīd and his grandson 'Ubāda) and recorded by Ibn Isḥāq. In Yūnus ibn Bukayr's recension of Ibn Isḥāq's *Sīra* (as preserved by al-Bayhaqī), 'Ubāda states: "We pledged to the Prophet the allegiance of war (*bay'at al-ḥarb*), that we hear and obey (*'alā l-sam' wa-l-ṭā'a*) in hardship and in ease, in ability and in disability, and even though others may be preferred to us...."[69] In the recension of Ibn Hishām a gloss was inserted into the tradition, saying that 'Ubāda was also the one of the twelve who pledged to Muḥammad the *bay'a* of the women, in the "first" 'Aqaba.[70] It is obvious that in this version of the pledge of war, the obligation of *sam' wa-ṭā'a* is a secondary element which in itself has nothing to do with war. It was only incorporated into *bay'at al-ḥarb* to make it part of the 'Aqaba precedent.

The present version of 'Ubāda ibn al-Ṣāmit appears with the same higher part of the *isnād* not only in Ibn Isḥāq, but also in other biographical compilations. Here, however, the efforts to link the principle of hearing and obeying

---

66 Ibn Hishām, II, 73.
67 *Ibid.*, II, 75.
68 *Ibid.*, II, 76.
69 Bayhaqī, *Dalā'il*, II, 452.
70 Ibn Hishām, II, 97. See also Ṭabarī, *Tārīkh*, I, 1227 (II, 368); Aḥmad, *Musnad*, V, 316; Ibn 'Abd al-Barr, *Tamhīd*, XXIII, 272.

with *bay'at al-ḥarb* of the 'Aqaba have been given up. The *bay'a* to "hear and obey" appears neither named nor dated. In this plain form it has become a more appropriate model for all the Muslims, not just the Anṣār. One such version in which the *bay'a* to "hear and obey" is neither dated nor named is quoted from 'Ubāda's grandson by Yaḥyā ibn Sa'īd ibn Qays al-Anṣārī (Medinan d. AH 144).[71] There are similar versions quoted from the same grandson of 'Ubāda by other traditionists,[72] with the same version reappearing under different *isnāds* of the same Companion. One is of 'Umayr ibn Hāni' (Syrian)←Junāda ibn Abī Umayya (Syrian d. AH 80)←'Ubāda. In this particular version it is the Prophet himself who utters the text of the *bay'a*.[73] Another has the *isnād*: 'Abdallāh ibn 'Uthmān ibn Khuthaym (Meccan d. AH 132)←Ismā'īl ibn 'Ubayd al-Anṣārī←'Ubāda.[74] Several of the same versions, mainly those of 'Ubāda's grandson, recur in the *muṣannaf* compilations, where they illustrate how subjects should pledge allegiance to the ruler.[75] Here one more version is found in which 'Ubāda quotes the *bay'a* on his deathbed, as if this was the most important *ḥadīth* to be remembered.[76]

The legal precedent of the *bay'a* to "hear and obey" was supported by further traditions of another Companion, Ibn 'Umar. He too was said to have heard the Prophet prescribe it to the Muslims, and to have used it himself upon pledging allegiance in writing to the caliph 'Abd al-Malik.[77] The same *bay'a* type was said to have been used by the Prophet for the conversion of the Companion Jarīr ibn 'Abdallāh al-Bajalī.[78]

To conclude the subject of the *bay'a*, the divergency of versions illustrates the role of the *sīra* as a source of Islamic law. In order for a certain legal practice to gain authority, it had to become part of Muḥammad's own utterances or acts. Since there was disagreement on the model to be followed, different utterances and acts were attributed to the Prophet, and all of them became part of the progressive story of his life.

---

[71] Balādhurī, *Ansāb*, I, no. 580; Aḥmad, *Musnad*, III, 441; V, 314.

[72] Aḥmad, *Musnad*, V, 318, 319.

[73] *Ibid.*, V, 321; Ibn 'Abd al-Barr, *Tamhīd*, XXIII, 277.

[74] Aḥmad, *Musnad*, V, 325.

[75] Mālik/Zurqānī, III, 285 (21:5); Bukhārī, *Ṣaḥīḥ*, IX, 96 (93:43); Muslim, VI, 16 (33, *Wujūb ṭā'at al-umarā'*); Nasā'ī, *Kubrā*, IV, nos. 7770–75; Ibn Māja, II, no. 2866 (24:41).

[76] The *isnād*: Busr ibn Sa'īd (Medinan d. AH 100)←Junāda ibn Abī Umayya←'Ubāda. See Bukhārī, *Ṣaḥīḥ*, IX, 59 (92:2); Muslim, VI, 16–17 (33, *Wujūb ṭā'at al-umarā'*).

[77] 'Abd al-Razzāq, *Muṣannaf*, VI, nos. 9822–23; Bukhārī, *Ṣaḥīḥ*, IX, 96, 96–97 (93:43).

[78] Bukhārī, *Ṣaḥīḥ*, IX, 96 (93:43).

EPILOGUE

12

The Chronology of Muḥammad's Life

MUSLIM TRADITION is very much preoccupied with the chronology of Muḥammad's life. The biographical and historiographical sources contain chapters about the chronology of his Meccan and Medinan periods,[1] about the chronology of his first revelation,[2] and about the chronology of his birth and death.[3] Similar chapters are to be found in several *muṣannaf* compilations of *ḥadīth*.[4] Already in previous chapters occasional allusion has been made to the chronology of Muḥammad's life. In what follows we shall discuss further aspects of this theme, which places Muḥammad's Meccan period within a larger framework encompassing his entire life.

Modern Islamicists, like Jones for example, have treated these traditions of chronology with a view to revealing the historical reality that they supposedly preserve.[5] Our goal, however, is different. In accordance with the general attitude followed throughout this book, we shall examine the textual dynamics of the material, rather than the extent to which it reflects the actual chronology of events in the Prophet's life. This material seems to be built upon some basic symbolic numerical patterns. Some general observations concerning the symbolism of numbers in the *sīra* and other Islamic texts have already been made

---

[1] Abū Zur'a, 144–48; Ibn Sa'd, I, 224–25; Ṭabarī, *Tārīkh*, I, 1245–50 (II, 383–87); Bayhaqī, *Dalā'il*, II, 511–15.

[2] Ibn Sa'd, I, 193–94; Ṭabarī, *Tārīkh*, I, 1139–43 (II, 290–94); Bayhaqī, *Dalā'il*, II, 131–34.

[3] Abū Zur'a, 148–53; Khalīfa ibn Khayyāṭ, 58–60; Tirmidhī, *Shamā'il*, 221–31; Ibn Sa'd, II, 272–74; Ṭabarī, *Tārīkh*, I, 1815–20, 1834–37 (III, 199–203, 215–17); Bayhaqī, *Dalā'il*, I, 71–79; VII, 233–41; Ibn 'Asākir (*Mukhtaṣar*), II, 387–90.

[4] Chronology of Meccan and Medinan periods: Muslim, VII, 87–89 (43, *Bāb kam aqāma l-nabiyy (ṣ) bi-Makka wa-l-Madīna*). Birth and death: Tirmidhī/*Tuḥfa*, X, no. 3698 (46:4), 134–37 (46:13); 'Abd al-Razzāq, *Muṣannaf*, III, 598–600; Muslim, VII, 87 (43, *Bāb kam sinn al-nabī*); Dārimī, I, 49–56 (Introduction, 14); Ibn Ḥibbān, *Ṣaḥīḥ*, XIV, 298–300; *Kanz*, VII, 224–25. First revelation: Ibn Abī Shayba, XIV, 289–91; Bukhārī, *Ṣaḥīḥ*, V, 56 (63:28); Muslim, VII, 87 (43, *Bāb ṣifat al-nabī (ṣ) wa-mab'athihi*); Tirmidhī/*Tuḥfa*, X, 94–97 (46:4).

[5] See J.M.B. Jones, "The Chronology of the *Maghāzī*—a Textual Survey", *Bulletin of the School of Oriental and African Studies* 19 (1957), 245–80. For a survey of various other studies of the chronology of Muḥammad's life, beginning with Lammens, see Lawrence I. Conrad, "Theophanes and the Arabic Historical Tradition: Some Indications of Intercultural Transmission", *Byzantinische Forschungen* 15 (1990), 16–20.

by certain scholars,[6] but no comprehensive study of the symbolism of the chronology of Muḥammad's life has yet been attempted. It will be shown here that this material forms part of the theme of attestation.

I

Chronology is a key theme in the *vita* of any prominent biblical king, or patriarch, or prophet; this is frequently based on a harmonic numerical framework, implying the divinely ordained course of the leader's life. In the case of Muḥammad this harmony is reflected in the recurrence of the same date—Monday, 12 Rabīʿ al-awwal—for each and every key event of his life.[7] Tradition asserts that this was the date of his birth, his first revelation, his night journey and ascension to heaven, and his *hijra*, as well as his death.[8] The most prevalent traditions are those indicating this date as that of the Prophet's death.[9]

It may well be that the selection of Rabīʿ al-awwal reflects a Jewish tradition about Moses. This prophet was born and died in the same month, Adar. In the converted Islamic version of this tradition, Adar was replaced by its most natural equivalent in the Arabian calendar, Rabīʿ al-awwal. The term *rabīʿ* does not just stand for a calendar month, but also denotes a season, the very season in which the Hebrew Adar always falls—spring. More specifically, Adar falls on the vernal equinox (21 March), which the Arabs called *al-istiwāʾ al-rabīʿī*. Therefore, Adar actually marks the transition from *shitāʾ* (winter) to *rabīʿ* (spring).[10] As for the Jewish tradition, Adar was probably chosen for the chronology of Moses because it was the last month in the ancient Hebrew calendar, so that the birth of Moses occurred on the verge of a new year. The same seems to apply to Jesus, whose birth was dated to the last month of the Roman calendar. Jewish tradition is not unanimous as to the exact day in Adar on which Moses was born and died. The most prevalent view is that it was 7 Adar,

---

[6] E.g. Sellheim, "Prophet, Chalif und Geschichte", 70–71, 77–78; Lawrence I. Conrad, "Seven and the Tasbīʿ: on the Implications of Numerical Symbolism for the Study of Medieval Islamic History", *Journal of the Economic and Social History of the Orient* 31 (1988), 42–73.

[7] On the function of this date in the *sīra*, see already Sellheim, "Prophet, Chalif und Geschichte", 77–78. See also Conrad, "Theophanes", 17.

[8] As date of *hijra*: e.g., Bayhaqī, *Dalāʾil*, II, 512 (a tradition of ʿUrwa ibn al-Zubayr quoted from Ibn Isḥāq). As the date of all other events: Ibn Kathīr, *Bidāya*, II, 260 (from Ibn Abī Shayba).

[9] E.g. Ibn Saʿd, II, 272–73; Ṭabarī, *Tārīkh*, I, 1815, 1837 (III, 200, 217).

[10] For the Arabic terms applying to the four seasons and their astronomic synchronization, see for example, Quṭrub, *Azmina*, 98–107; Marzūqī, *Azmina*, I, 154–55; also II, 357 (on Adar).

but some say 1 Adar.[11] The Islamic tradition chose for Muḥammad the typological number 12, and also a day in the week based on the same typology, Monday.

The selection of Monday seems also to stem from Jewish tradition, in which Monday and Thursday in particular were known as days of fasting.[12] This is also the case in Islamic traditions anchoring these days to Muḥammad's harmonious life chronology. In one tradition Monday is recommended as a day of fasting because Muḥammad was born on it and was sent as a prophet on it. This is formulated as a statement of the Prophet himself,[13] and is recorded in the biographical sources,[14] as well as in the *muṣannaf* compilations.[15] Another tradition combines the sacredness of Monday as a fast day with that of Thursday. The Syrian Makḥūl (d. AH 112) states that he used to fast on Monday and Thursday; the Prophet was born on a Monday, was sent as a prophet on a Monday, and died on a Monday. The works of man are raised (i.e. to Heaven) on Thursday.[16]

Other traditions naming Monday as the day of Muḥammad's birth, first revelation, *hijra*, and death, as well as of some other events, are traced back to Ibn 'Abbās, one through Ḥanash ibn 'Abdallāh [or 'Alī] al-Ṣan'ānī (African d. AH 100);[17] another through Mujāhid ibn Jabr (Meccan d. AH 104).[18] There is also a similar tradition of Yazīd ibn Abī Ḥabīb (Egyptian d. AH 128).[19] Numerous traditions focus on Monday as the day on which the Prophet died. These are traditions of al-Zuhrī (Medinan d. AH 124), Mālik ibn Anas (Medinan d. AH 180), 'Ikrima (Medinan d. AH 105), 'Uthmān ibn Muḥammad al-Akhnasī

---

11 E.g. *Megilla*, 13b. For 1 Adar see e.g. Josephus Flavius, *Antiquities of the Jews* IV. 49.

12 See *Masekhet Sofrim* (ed. M. Higger), 21:1 (Hebrew).

13 The *isnād*: Ghaylān ibn Jarīr (Baṣran d. AH 129)←'Abdallāh ibn Ma'bad al-Zamānī (Baṣran)←Abū Qatāda al-Anṣārī (Medinan Companion d. AH 54)←Prophet.

14 Ṭabarī, *Tārīkh*, I, 1141 (II, 293); Aḥmad, *Musnad*, V, 297, 299; Bayhaqī, *Dalā'il*, I, 71–73; II, 133.

15 Muslim, III, 168 (13, *Bāb istiḥbāb ṣiyām thalāthat ayyām....*); *Mustadrak*, II, 602; Bayhaqī, *Sunan*, IV, 293.

16 Ibn 'Asākir (*Mukhtaṣar*), II, 34.

17 Ṭabarī, *Tārīkh*, I, 1836 (III, 217); Aḥmad, *Musnad*, I, 277; Ṭabarānī, *Kabīr*, XII, no. 12984; Bayhaqī, *Dalā'il*, VII, 233, 234; Ibn 'Asākir (*Mukhtaṣar*), II, 33 (+*fatḥ* Badr/Mecca, last Quranic revelation). See also Ibn 'Abd al-Barr, *Istī'āb*, I, 31 (+ Badr). Cf. parts of the same tradition in Ibn Sa'd, I, 101, 193; II, 274; Ṭabarī, *Tārīkh*, I, 1142 (II, 293); Bayhaqī, *Dalā'il*, I, 73.

18 Ṭabarānī, *Kabīr*, XI, no. 11124.

19 Ibn 'Asākir (*Mukhtaṣar*), II, 34.

(Ḥijāzī), Sahl ibn Sa'd al-Anṣārī (Medinan Companion d. AH 88),[20] and 'Ā'isha.[21] But the most prevalent tradition, which also gained access into the most authoritative *muṣannaf* compilations, is the one of Anas ibn Mālik (Baṣran Companion d. AH 91–95), describing how Abū Bakr led the public prayer on the Monday on which Muḥammad died.[22] The tradition is also recorded outside the *muṣannaf* compilations.[23] The same Companion also has a tradition about Monday being the day of Muḥammad's first revelation.[24]

Monday was actually made part of the stories of attestation, in which it signals Muḥammad's day of death, as predicted by monotheistic scholars according to their own scriptures. One such story is related by the Yemeni Companion Jarīr ibn 'Abdallāh al-Bajalī (d. AH 51). A Jewish rabbi met him once in Yemen, and said: "If your companion (i.e. Muḥammad) is a true prophet, he must have died on this day [of the week]." Jarīr goes on to say that the Prophet died on a Monday.[25]

There are, however, other sacred days of the week which also became part of the chronology of Muḥammad's life. Friday, for instance, the day of public prayer, is indicated in a tradition of al-Kalbī (Muḥammad ibn al-Sā'ib, Kūfan d. AH 146) as the day of Muḥammad's *hijra* (12 Rabī' al-awwal), and of his arrival at some other stations in Medina.[26] In Shī'ī sources Friday is also the day of the Prophet's birth (12 Rabī' al-awwal).[27] Tuesday is also mentioned as the day of that same event.[28] Saturday has a role too in the Prophet's life, and

---

[20] Zuhrī: Ibn Sa'd, II, 274, 304. Mālik ibn Anas: Mālik/Zurqānī, II, 265 (16:27); Ibn Sa'd, II, 274. 'Ikrima: Dārimī, I, no. 83 (Intro. 14); Ibn Sa'd, II, 273. 'Uthmān ibn Muḥammad al-Akhnasī: Ibn Sa'd, II, 273. Sahl ibn Sa'd al-Anṣārī: *Ibid.*

[21] The *isnād*: Ibn Isḥāq←'Abd al-Raḥmān ibn al-Qāsim (Medinan d. AH 126)←his father, al-Qāsim ibn Muḥammad ibn Abī Bakr (Medinan d. AH 106)←'Ā'isha. See Aḥmad, *Musnad*, VI, 110.

[22] The *isnād*: Zuhrī (Medinan d. AH 124)←Anas. See Bukhārī, *Ṣaḥīḥ*, I, 173 (10:46); II, 80 (21:6); VI, 15 (64:83); Muslim, II, 24 (4, *Bāb istikhlāf al-imām....*); Nasā'ī, *Kubrā*, I, no. 1957 (23:7); Ibn Māja, I, no. 1624 (6:64); Abū 'Awāna, II, 119; Bayhaqī, *Sunan*, III, 75.

[23] Ḥumaydī, *Musnad*, II, no. 1188; Abū Zur'a, 152 (nos. 16–17); Nasā'ī, *Wafāt*, no. 33; Tirmidhī, *Shamā'il*, 223; Abū Ya'lā, VI, no. 3548; Aḥmad, *Musnad*, III, 110, 196, 197.

[24] The *isnād*: 'Alī ibn 'Ābis al-Kūfī←Muslim ibn Kaysān al-Malā'ī al-A'war (Kūfan)←Anas. See Ibn Sa'd, I, 193–94.

[25] Aḥmad, *Musnad*, IV, 364; Bayhaqī, *Dalā'il*, VII, 271. The *isnād*: Zā'ida ibn Qudāma (Kūfan d. AH 161)←Ziyād ibn 'Ilāqa (Kūfan d. AH 153)←Jarīr. Cf. Ibn Abī Shayba, XIV, no. 18869; Bukhārī, *Ṣaḥīḥ*, V, 210 (64:64); Bayhaqī, *Dalā'il*, VII, 270.

[26] Ibn 'Abd al-Barr, *Istī'āb*, I, 41, 42.

[27] Kulīnī, I, 439.

[28] Ya'qūbī, II, 7.

sometimes it is said to have been the day of the *isrā'–mi'rāj* (his nocturnal journey to Jerusalem).[29]

As for the day of the month, not all traditions mentioning Rabī' al-awwal indicate the twelfth day. Other numbers also figure in some less prevalent traditions. To begin with, 1 Rabī' al-awwal (cf. 1 Adar in the Moses chronology) is indicated in a Medinan tradition of Ibn 'Abbās as the time of Muḥammad's first revelation. The day of the week remains Monday, on which all other key events of Muḥammad's career, including his birth and death, are said to have taken place.[30] Monday, 1 Rabī' al-awwal, recurs as the time of Muḥammad's death in a Medinan tradition of Ibn Shihāb al-Zuhrī (Medinan d. AH 124),[31] as well as in a tradition of al-Faḍl ibn Dukayn (Kūfan d. AH 219).[32]

The second day of Rabī' al-awwal is also mentioned. This day of Rabī' al-awwal is indicated by Abū Ma'shar al-Sindī (Medinan d. AH 170) as the date of Muḥammad's birth, which is again a Monday.[33] The same Abū Ma'shar dates Muḥammad's death to the same time, quoting Muḥammad ibn Qays (Medinan story-teller).[34] The same date of Muḥammad's death is repeated by Sulaymān al-Taymī (Baṣran d. AH 143),[35] Sa'd ibn Ibrāhīm al-Zuhrī (Medinan d. AH 125–28),[36] and Abū Mikhnaf (Kūfan d. AH 157).[37]

The date of 8 Rabī' al-awwal also figures in the chronological traditions. It appears as indicating Muḥammad's birth in some Shī'ī sources, but this time it is a Tuesday.[38] As a Monday, 8 Rabī' al-awwal is recorded as the date of Muḥammad's arrival in Medina.[39]

---

[29] Khargūshī (MS Tübingen), 34b (1516). For the various dates suggested for this event see *Fatḥ al-bārī*, VII, 154–55.

[30] The *isnād*: Zuhrī (Medinan d. AH 124)←'Ubaydallāh ibn 'Abdallāh ibn 'Utba (Medinan d. AH 98)←Ibn 'Abbās. See Ibn 'Asākir (*Mukhtaṣar*), II, 33; Ibn Kathīr, *Bidāya*, II, 260–61 (Ibn 'Asākir).

[31] The *isnād*: Mūsā ibn 'Uqba (Medinan d. AH 141)←al-Zuhrī. See Bayhaqī, *Dalā'il*, VII, 234.

[32] Ibn 'Asākir (*Mukhtaṣar*), II, 387.

[33] Ibn Sa'd, I, 101; Ibn Kathīr, *Bidāya*, II, 260.

[34] Ibn Sa'd, II, 272; Bayhaqī, *Dalā'il*, VII, 234–35; Ibn 'Asākir (*Mukhtaṣar*), II, 387.

[35] Bayhaqī, *Dalā'il*, VII, 234; Ibn Kathīr, *Bidāya*, V, 255. The *isnād*: al-Mu'tamir ibn Sulaymān (Baṣran d. AH 187)←Sulaymān al-Taymī.

[36] Ibn Kathīr, *Bidāya*, V, 255 (from Ibn 'Asākir).

[37] The *isnād*: Abū Mikhnaf←al-Ṣaq'ab ibn Zuhayr (Kūfan)←*fuqahā'* of Ḥijāz. See Ṭabarī, *Tārīkh*, I, 1815 (III, 200).

[38] Ya'qūbī, II, 7.

[39] Ibn 'Abd al-Barr, *Istī'āb*, I, 32, 41.

Finally, Monday, 10 Rabīʻ al-awwal is also mentioned (in a tradition of Ibn ʻAbbās[40]), signaling Muḥammad's death.[41]

II

The model of Moses on which the traditions about Rabīʻ al-awwal seem to be based did not remain the only one employed by the Muslims for the harmonic chronology of their prophet's life. Genuine Islamic patterns were also sought. Thus a phenomenon already revealed in previous cases in this book presents itself once more: that of biblical or Jewish models giving way to Islamic ones. The aim of the Muslims was to anchor Muḥammad's life in the most genuine Islamic source of attestation, the Quran. This scripture mentions the month of Ramaḍān as the time at which the Quran was revealed (2:185);[42] consequently, traditions were circulated in which Rabīʻ al-awwal was replaced by Ramaḍān as the date of Muḥammad's first revelation, as well as of his birth.

Ramaḍān appears already in the *Sīra* of Ibn Isḥāq (d. AH 150) as marking the first revelation. The day in this month is not stated by Ibn Isḥāq, but he nevertheless adds that the victory of the Muslims at Badr occurred on Friday, 17 Ramaḍān.[43] Indeed, this became the date of the first revelation as well. Al-Ṭabarī states that the first revelation was believed by some to have taken place on 17 Ramaḍān, and that these authorities relied on the fact that this was the date of the victory at Badr.[44] The textual link for such a deduction was the Quranic word *furqān*, which describes both the revelation of the Quran in Ramaḍān (2:185) and the victory at war over the infidels (8:41). 17 Ramaḍān is also the date of the first revelation in a tradition of the Medinan imām Abū Jaʻfar Muḥammad al-Bāqir (d. AH 114). In this particular tradition the day in the week remains unchanged, compared with the above traditions about Rabīʻ al-awwal; it is again a Monday.[45]

Other days in Ramaḍān, besides 17, were also indicated in some Baṣran traditions as the date of the first revelation. One of them has the *isnād*: al-Ḥasan ibn Dīnār (Baṣran)←Ayyūb al-Sakhtiyānī (Baṣran d. AH 131)←Abū Qilāba al-Jarmī (Baṣran d. AH 104), and fixes the first revelation of the *furqān* as 18

40 The *isnād*: Muḥammad ibn ʻUbaydallāh al-ʻArzamī (Kūfan d. AH 155)←al-Ḥakam ibn ʻUtayba (Kūfan d. AH 115)←Miqsam ibn Bujra [Najda] (Meccan d. AH 101)←Ibn ʻAbbās.

41 See Ibn Kathīr, *Bidāya*, V, 256.

42 On Ramaḍān in the Quran, see e.g. Kees Wagtendonk, *Fasting in the Koran* (Leiden, 1968), 47–81.

43 Ibn Hishām, I, 256. See also Bayhaqī, *Dalāʼil*, II, 133–34 (Ibn Bukayr).

44 Ṭabarī, *Tārīkh*, I, 1142–43 (II, 294).

45 Ibn Saʻd, I, 194; Balādhurī, *Ansāb*, I, 104 (no. 188). The *isnād*: Abū Bakr ibn ʻAbdallāh ibn Abī Sabra (d. AH 162)←Isḥāq ibn ʻAbdallāh ibn Abī Farwa (d. AH 144)←Abū Jaʻfar.

Ramaḍān.[46] The same event is dated to 24 Ramaḍān in a tradition of Sa'īd ibn Abī 'Arūba (Baṣran d. AH 156)←Qatāda (Baṣran d. AH 117)←Abū l-Jald al-Jawnī (Baṣran).[47]

In a few traditions, Ramaḍān replaces Rabī' al-awwal as the date of Muḥammad's birth. The day of the week (Monday) and of the month (12) remain the same.[48] However, sometimes Monday too was changed, being replaced by Friday.[49] Finally, the *isrā'–mi'rāj* was also an event whose date was sometimes fixed to Ramaḍān. It was said to have taken place on Saturday, 17 Ramaḍān.[50]

Ramaḍān actually became a month of universal sacredness, marking the time of revelation not only of the Quran, but of other scriptures as well. Thus a tradition of the Syrian Wāthila ibn al-Asqa' (d. AH 83) states that the scriptures of Abraham were sent down on 1 Ramaḍān, the Torah was revealed (to Moses) on 6 Ramaḍān, the *Injīl* was sent (to Jesus) on 13 Ramaḍān; the *furqān* was sent down (to Muḥammad) on 24 Ramaḍān.[51] A similar tradition is available on the authority of the Medinan Companion Jābir ibn 'Abdallāh (d. AH 77), in which the revelation of the *Zabūr* (Psalms) to David is mentioned as well (on 11 Ramaḍān).[52]

In less current traditions a local Arabian pre-Islamic model of sacredness is adopted, instead of the Quranic one. This is the month of Rajab, whose pre-Islamic sacredness and position in Islam have already been surveyed by Kister.[53] As shown by him, Muḥammad was said to have been born in this month;[54] the day picked for this event was 27 Rajab.[55] This day was of special pre-Islamic sacredness, and on it the *'umra* (lesser pilgrimage) used to be

---

[46] Ṭabarī, *Tārīkh*, I, 1142 (II, 293–94).

[47] *Ibid.* (II, 294).

[48] See Ibn 'Abd al-Barr, *Istī'āb*, I, 30 (Zubayr ibn Bakkār); Ibn Kathīr, *Bidāya*, II, 260. And see also the Syrian tradition of Shu'ayb ibn Shu'ayb (d. AH 264)←his father Shu'ayb ibn Isḥāq (d. AH 189)←his grandfather Isḥāq ibn 'Abd al-Raḥmān: Ibn 'Asākir (*Mukhtaṣar*), II, 33; Ibn Kathīr, *Bidāya*, II, 261 (Ibn 'Asākir).

[49] Ya'qūbī, II, 7.

[50] Khargūshī (MS Tübingen), 34b (1516). For the various other dates suggested for this event, see *Fatḥ al-bārī*, VII, 154–55.

[51] Aḥmad, *Musnad*, IV, 107; Ṭabarānī, *Kabīr*, XXII, no. 185. The *isnād*: Qatāda (Baṣran d. AH 117)←Abū l-Mulayḥ ibn Usāma (Baṣran d. AH 112)←Wāthila ibn al-Asqa'.

[52] Abū Ya'lā, IV, no. 2190. The *isnād*: 'Ubaydallāh ibn Abī Ḥumayd (Baṣran)←Abū Mulayḥ ibn Usāma al-Hudhalī (Baṣran d. AH 112)←Jābir.

[53] M.J. Kister, "Rajab is the Month of God....", *Israel Oriental Studies* 1 (1971), 191–223.

[54] *Ibid.*, 197.

[55] *Fatḥ al-bārī*, VI, 414 (from the *Tārīkh* of Abū 'Abd al-Raḥmān al-'Ataqī).

performed.[56] It was also turned into the date of Muḥammad's first revelation,[57] as well as of his *isrā'–mi'rāj*.[58]

III

But the chronological harmony of Muḥammad's life is based on more complex numerical patterns, other than just a recurrent day and month. They too reflect the chronology of the life of Moses, which is based on the typology of the number 40 and its multiples.[59] Moses began his mission at the age of 80 (Exodus 7:7), and died at the age of 120 (Deuteronomy 31:2). Muslim tradition is well aware of this biblical tradition.[60] Muḥammad's own prophetic chronology is symmetrical to that of Moses, decreased by half. The Islamic prophet is said to have started his prophetic activity at the age of 40, and to have died at the age of 60. A tradition to this effect was transmitted by 'Amr ibn Dīnār (Meccan d. AH 126) on the authority of 'Urwa ibn al-Zubayr (Medinan d. AH 94).[61]

Muslim tradition is indeed aware of the symmetry decreased by half linking the life of the Islamic prophet to those of his predecessors. There is a tradition of the same 'Amr ibn Dīnār fixing the numerical relation between the life of Muḥammad and that of Jesus. The Prophet is said to have addressed his daughter Fāṭima, saying:

> Oh Fāṭima, every prophet reaches half the age reached by his predecessor. Jesus son of Mary was sent to act as a prophet for 40 years, and I was sent to be a prophet for 20 years.[62]

This prophetic statement was transmitted by 'Amr ibn Dīnār on the authority of the Qurashī Successor Yaḥyā ibn Ja'da. Since a Companion is missing from the chain of transmission, the isnād is *mursal*. A similar statement of the Prophet was transmitted by al-A'mash (Kūfan d. AH 148) on the authority of Ibrāhīm al-Nakha'ī (Kūfan d. AH 96), again with no Companion.[63] Of course, these

---

[56] Kister, "Rajab", 219.

[57] *Ibid.*, 200. See also Ṭabarsī, *A'lām al-warā*, 15.

[58] Kister, "Rajab", 197, 221.

[59] See *Encyclopaedia Biblica*, V, 184, s.v. *Mispar* (in Hebrew).

[60] See Ṭabarī, *Tārīkh*, I, 444 (I, 386).

[61] Ibn Sa'd, II, 308; Ṭabarī, *Tārīkh*, I, 1836 (III, 216). Some versions of this tradition mention either his age at his first revelation or at his death. See Khalīfa ibn Khayyāṭ, 60 (only death); Ṭabarī, *Tārīkh*, I, 1140 (II, 291, *mab'ath* only).

[62] Ibn Sa'd, II, 308; Ṭabarī, *Tārīkh*, I, 1140 (II, 291).

[63] Ibn Sa'd, II, 308–309.

statements refer to Jesus, not to Moses, but the principle of the numerical link is the same.

Nevertheless, implicit in the age limits of Muḥammad's prophetic activity is also another ancient symbolic type, the age of 40 as marking the peak of man's physical and intellectual powers.[64] This topos may even be the basic point of departure, upon which the complete Mosaic pattern of 40–60 was eventually built.

Parallel to the pattern of 40–60 marking the age limits of Muḥammad's prophetic activity, there is yet another pattern determining the geographical dimension of these twenty years. This is a pattern of 10–10, signifying the duration of Muḥammad's prophetic activity in Mecca and in Medina, respectively. Unlike the former pattern, which to all appearances reflects biblical models (Moses, decreased by half), the latter is purely Quranic. The Islamic scripture in its canonical structure is composed of Meccan and Medinan revelations, and the pattern 10–10 creates harmonic symmetry between the two periods of Quranic revelation.[65]

Muslim tradition contains explicit statements with the 10–10 model. One is of the Baṣran Qatāda (d. AH 117) which simply confirms that Muḥammad spent ten years of revelation in Mecca and ten in Medina.[66] The most current statement to the same effect has a complete Companion *isnād*: Yaḥyā ibn Abī Kathīr (d. AH 129)←Abū Salama ibn 'Abd al-Raḥmān ibn 'Awf (Medinan d. AH 94)←'Ā'isha and Ibn 'Abbās (Medinan d. AH 68). The tradition was recorded in biographical sources,[67] as well as in some *muṣannaf* compilations, including al-Bukhārī.[68] Sometimes the event which separates the two periods from each other, i.e. the *hijra*, is added to the 10–10 formula with its own typological date, i.e. Monday, 12 Rabī' al-awwal.[69]

---

[64] See Lawrence I. Conrad, "Abraha and Muḥammad: Some Observations Apropos of Chronology and Literary *Topoi* in the Early Arabic Historical Tradition", *Bulletin of the School of Oriental and African Studies* 50 (1987), 230–34.

[65] Cf. Conrad, "Theophanes", 18.

[66] The *isnād*: Yazīd ibn Zuray' (Baṣran d. AH 182)←Sa'īd ibn Abī 'Arūba (Baṣran d. AH 156)←Qatāda. See Khalīfa ibn Khayyāṭ, 10.

[67] Abū Zur'a, 147–48 (no. 9); Ibn Sa'd, I, 224; Bukhārī, *Tārīkh kabīr*, I, 8; Khalīfa ibn Khayyāṭ, 10; Ṭabarī, *Tārīkh*, I, 1245, 1836 (II, 383–84; III, 216); Ibn 'Abd al-Barr, *Tamhīd*, III, 16–17.

[68] Ibn Abī Shayba, XIV, no. 18395; Bukhārī, *Ṣaḥīḥ*, VI, 19 (64:85).

[69] E.g. Ibn Sa'd, I, 224, the tradition of Ibn Lahī'a ('Abdallāh, Egyptian d. AH 174)←Yazīd ibn Abī Ḥabīb (Egyptian d. AH 128). And see also the tradition of Abū l-Baddāḥ ibn 'Āṣim ibn 'Adī (Medinan d. AH 117)←his father 'Āṣim ibn 'Adī (Medinan Companion d. AH 40) in Bayhaqī, *Dalā'il*, II, 511.

The date of the Prophet's death is also part of the same Meccan–Medinan 10–10 scheme. Some traditions related on the authority of al-Zuhrī (Medinan d. AH 124) and referring to Muḥammad's death, assert that this took place at the end of his tenth year in Medina. The date is again Monday, 12 Rabī' al-awwal.[70] In a tradition of al-Layth ibn Sa'd (Egyptian d. AH 175), which likewise dates Muḥammad's death to his tenth Medinan year, the date is Monday, 1, or 2 Rabī' al-awwal.[71]

In further traditions the age boundaries 40–60 and the Meccan–Medinan pattern of 10–10 are combined. The most prevalent tradition with this combined structure is that of the Baṣran Companion Anas ibn Mālik (d. AH 91–95), as quoted by Rabī'a ibn Abī 'Abd al-Raḥmān (Medinan d. AH 136). Anas' statement is embodied in a description of the Prophet's outer appearance. He states that Muḥammad was sent as a prophet at the age of 40, then spent ten years in Mecca, ten in Medina, and died at the age of 60. The tradition appears in several biographical sources,[72] and is prevalent in the various *muṣannaf* compilations.[73] There are also less current versions of the same statement of Anas which appear only in the biographical sources,[74] and a rare version to the same effect on the authority of the Companion Abū Hurayra.[75] A similar statement is available on the authority of al-Ḥasan al-Baṣrī (d. AH 110), who is quoted by

[70] E.g. the tradition of Ibn Isḥāq←Ṣāliḥ ibn Kaysān (Medinan)←Zuhrī←'Ubaydallāh ibn 'Abdallāh ibn 'Utba (Medinan d. AH 98)←'Ā'isha. See Ṭabarī, *Tārīkh*, I, 1834 (III, 214–15). Cf. Bayhaqī, *Dalā'il*, VII, 235. See also the tradition of Layth ibn Sa'd (Egyptian d. AH 175)←'Uqayl ibn Khālid ibn 'Uqayl (*mawlā* of 'Uthmān from Ayla d. AH 141, Zuhrī's disciple)←Zuhrī in Bayhaqī, *Dalā'il*, II, 511.

[71] Ibn 'Asākir (*Mukhtaṣar*), II, 387; Ibn Kathīr, *Bidāya*, V, 255.

[72] Abū Zur'a, 146–47 (no. 6–8); Tirmidhī, *Shamā'il*, 222–23; Ṭabarī, *Tārīkh*, I, 1245 (II, 383, Medinan period missing); Aḥmad, *Musnad*, III, 240; Ibn 'Abd al-Barr, *Tamhīd*, III, 7; Bayhaqī, *Dalā'il*, I, 201, 203; VII, 236. Some versions provide only some of the data: Abū Zur'a, 150 (nos. 12–14, death only); Ibn Sa'd, I, 190 (*mab'ath* only); II, 308 (death only); Khalīfa ibn Khayyāṭ, 60 (death only); Ṭabarī, *Tārīkh*, I, 1139–40 (II, 291, *mab'ath* only); Aḥmad, *Musnad*, III, 130 (death only).

[73] 'Abd al-Razzāq, *Muṣannaf*, III, no. 6786; Ibn Abī Shayba, XIII, no. 15737; XIV, no. 18401; Mālik/Zurqānī, V, 284 (49:1); Bukhārī, *Ṣaḥīḥ*, IV, 227–28 (61:23); Muslim, VII, 87 (43, *Bāb ṣifat al-nabī wa-mab'athihi*); Ibn Ḥibbān, *Ṣaḥīḥ*, XIV, no. 6387; Tirmidhī/*Tuḥfa*, X, no. 3702 (46:4).

[74] One with the *isnād*: Qurra ibn 'Abd al-Raḥmān (Zuhrī's disciple, Egyptian, d. AH 147)←Ibn Shihāb al-Zuhrī (Medinan d. AH 124)←Anas. See Ibn Sa'd, II, 308; Ibn 'Abd al-Barr, *Tamhīd*, III, 12, 16. And see another version of Abū Ghālib al-Bāhilī (Nāfi', Baṣran) from Anas, in Ibn Sa'd, I, 190; II, 308 (death only); Ibn 'Abd al-Barr, *Tamhīd*, III, 12 (Meccan period only); Bayhaqī, *Dalā'il*, VII, 237.

[75] Ibn 'Abd al-Barr, *Tamhīd*, III, 13.

Hishām ibn Ḥassān (Baṣran d. AH 147).[76] There is also a statement of the same al-Ḥasan al-Baṣrī referring only to Muḥammad's death-age, i.e. 60.[77]

IV

The typological figures of Muḥammad's prophetic career (10–10 built into 40–60) appear in some other traditions where they are linked to a pre-Islamic Arabian chronological tradition, thus adding local colouring to the divinely ordained course of the Prophet's life.

The local Arabian calendar used as a starting point what is known in the sources as *'ām al-fīl*, the "Year of the Elephant" (hereafter: AF), which marked the year in which Abraha's troops and elephants were said to have been defeated at the outskirts of Mecca. The Elephant chronology was used to reckon the date of some key events in the pre-Islamic history of Mecca. The traditions refer mainly to two pre-Islamic events, separated from each other by fifteen years, that were given AF dates: the war of the Fijār, which was dated to AF 40, and the building of the Ka'ba, dated to AF 55. The prophetic chronology of Muḥammad's life was reckoned according to these dates, always preserving its basic typology of first revelation at the age of 40.

A tradition synchronizing Muḥammad's life with the local Meccan chronology is that of the *maghāzī* expert Mūsā ibn 'Uqba (Medinan d. AH 141). To begin with, in a tradition of his nephew Ismā'īl ibn Ibrāhīm ibn 'Uqba, Mūsā states that the Ka'ba was built by Quraysh fifteen years after the Fijār.[78] The same Mūsā ibn 'Uqba also states on the authority of al-Zuhrī that Muḥammad was sent as a prophet fifteen years after the building of the Ka'ba, in the year AF 70.[79] This means that in the chronological tradition known to Ibn 'Uqba, the building of the Ka'ba was dated to AF 55, and the Fijār to AF 40. Muḥammad's age at his first revelation (AF 70) is not stated by Mūsā ibn 'Uqba, but it must be 40, because in another tradition Mūsā states that Muḥammad was born in AF 30.[80] From these traditions of Ibn 'Uqba a coherent AF chronology of Muḥammad's Meccan period emerges: birth in AF 30; wars of the Fijār when he is ten years old (AF 40); building of the Ka'ba when he is 25 (AF 55); first revelation at the age of 40 (AF 70). Precisely this chronology is reflected in reports of other traditionists, apart from Ibn 'Uqba. 'Umar ibn Abī Bakr al-Mu'ammilī,

[76] Ibn Abī Shayba, XIV, no. 18394. See also Khalīfa ibn Khayyāṭ, 11, 60 (death only).

[77] Khalīfa ibn Khayyāṭ, 60. The *isnād*: Wuhayb ibn Khālid (Baṣran d. AH 165)←Yūnus ibn 'Ubayd (Baṣran d. AH 140)←al-Ḥasan al-Baṣrī.

[78] Bayhaqī, *Dalā'il*, II, 58.

[79] *Ibid*., I, 78.

[80] Khalīfa ibn Khayyāṭ, 9.

for example, states that he heard from quite a few sources that Muḥammad was 25 years old when Quraysh built the Ka'ba.[81]

The basis of this synchronization between the local and the prophetic chronology is the setting of the first revelation to fifteen years after the building of the Ka'ba. Such a formula of Ka'ba + 15 was designed to achieve symbolism through the typology of the number 70. Since the building of the Ka'ba was dated to AF 55 in the local chronology as known to Mūsā ibn 'Uqba, the formula Ka'ba + 15 made the first revelation fall on AF 70, a date stated explicitly by Ibn 'Uqba. Thus, the event is made part of a harmoniously designed scheme of God. This method of calculation was shared by quite a few traditionists (e.g. Mujāhid and 'Urwa ibn al-Zubayr), who stated that the Ka'ba was built fifteen years before Muḥammad's first revelation.[82]

The symbolism of 70 achieved through the formula Ka'ba + 15 was never limited to the first revelation. A no less important event in Muḥammad's career was his *hijra* from Mecca to Medina, and the same formula was applied to its dating. This is demonstrated in a tradition with the *isnād*: 'Umar ibn Abī Bakr al-Mu'ammilī←Zakariyyā ibn Abī 'Īsā←Ibn Shihāb al-Zuhrī (Medinan d. AH 124). The tradition has already been discussed by Kister,[83] but in spite of what is implied in his study concerning its historical value, the tradition is just another manifestation of widely current conventions of chronological synchronization, designed to produce the symbolism of 70; the local events are reckoned in it in exactly the same manner pursued in the traditions mentioned above. The Fijār and the building of the Ka'ba are again said to have taken place at AF 40 and AF 55, respectively. The tradition also adds the date of the death of a local Meccan leader, Hishām ibn al-Mughīra (AF 46). The building of the Ka'ba is said to have been followed by fifteen years, at the end of which the *hijra* took place, which makes the latter event fall on exactly AF 70. The tradition adds that Muḥammad's first revelation took place five years after the building of the Ka'ba (= AF 60), which means that he remained in Mecca ten years as a prophet before performing the *hijra*. This tradition as well seems to be based on the convention that the first revelation took place when Muḥammad was 40 years old, though there is no explicit statement to that effect. Assuming that this be really the case, the following chronology emerges: birth of Muḥammad in AF 20, Fijār when he is 20 years old (AF 40); building of the Ka'ba when he is 35 (AF 55); first revelation at the age of 40 (AF 60), *hijra* at 50 (AF 70). Such dat-

[81] Bayhaqī, *Dalā'il*, II, 72.

[82] *Ibid.*, II, 62.

[83] M.J. Kister, "The Campaign of Ḥulubān: a New Light on the Expedition of Abraha", *Le Muséon* 78 (1965), 427–28. Cf. Ibn 'Asākir (*Mukhtaṣar*), I, 29. See also Conrad, "Abraha and Muḥammad", 238–39.

ing of the major events of Muḥammad's Meccan period is clearly reflected elsewhere in the sources. As seen above, the convention that ten years elapsed between the first revelation and the *hijra* is well known. Equally current is the view that Muḥammad was 20 at the Fijār,[84] and that he was 35 when the Ka'ba was built.[85]

Symbolic value was sought not only for the AF dating of the first revelation and the *hijra*, but also for that of Muḥammad's birth. The numerical symbolism of the latter event was achieved by simply fixing its date to the very Year of the Elephant, i.e. the first year of the Meccan local calendar. This meant the removal of the symbolic date AF 70 from either the first revelation or the *hijra*. It also meant the invalidation of any AF dating of his birth, other than to the Year of the Elephant itself. There were, in fact, several typological AF dates of this event.[86] There is also a tradition of al-Kalbī (Muḥammad ibn al-Sā'ib, Kūfan d. AH 146) dating Muḥammad's birth to fifteen years *before* the Elephant.[87]

Indeed, the symbolism of birth in the Year of the Elephant itself won the strongest support in Islam. It was circulated in numerous traditions, one with the *isnād* of Yūnus ibn Abī Isḥāq (Kūfan d. AH 152)←his father Abū Isḥāq al-Sabī'ī (Kūfan Shī'ī d. AH 126–29)←Sa'īd ibn Jubayr (Kūfan d. AH 95)←Ibn 'Abbās. This tradition, which simply states that Muḥammad was born in the Year of the Elephant, was recorded in biographical and historiographical sources,[88] and was included by al-Ḥākim in his *Mustadrak*.[89] Other traditions to the same effect also contain some of the above models of days and months. Already Ibn Isḥāq states that the Prophet was born on Monday, 12 Rabī' al-awwal, in the Year of the Elephant.[90] Al-Ḥākim recorded this statement in his *Mustadrak*.[91] Ibn Sa'd has a tradition with a similar date, except for the day in Rabī' al-awwal, which is 10 rather than 12. It also states that his birth took

---

[84] E.g. Ibn Hishām, I, 198.

[85] *Ibid*., I, 204; Ibn Bukayr, 109; Bayhaqī, *Dalā'il*, II, 62 (Yūnus from Ibn Isḥāq).

[86] AF 40: Khalīfa ibn Khayyāṭ, 9 (from Abū Zakariyyā al-'Ijlānī); AF 23: Ibn 'Asākir (*Mukhtaṣar*), II, 33; Ibn Kathīr, *Bidāya*, II, 261 (Ibn 'Asākir); AF 10: Bayhaqī, *Dalā'il*, I, 79 (the *isnād*: Ya'qūb al-Qummī←Ja'far ibn Abī l-Mughīra al-Qummī←the Kūfan Sa'īd ibn 'Abd al-Raḥmān ibn Abzā).

[87] Khalīfa ibn Khayyāṭ, 9–10. The *isnād*: al-Kalbī←Abū Ṣāliḥ (Bādhām, *mawlā* of Umm Hāni')←Ibn 'Abbās. See also Ibn 'Asākir (*Mukhtaṣar*), II, 34; Ibn Kathīr, *Bidāya*, II, 262. For further dates of Muḥammad's birth, see Conrad, "Abraha and Muḥammad", 234–35.

[88] Abū Zur'a, 141–42 (no. 1); Ibn Sa'd, I, 101; Ṭabarī, *Tārīkh*, I, 967 (II, 155); Ṭabarānī, *Kabīr*, XII, no. 12432; Bayhaqī, *Dalā'il*, I, 75.

[89] *Mustadrak*, II, 603.

[90] Ibn Hishām, I, 167. See also Ṭabarī, *Tārīkh*, I, 967–68 (II, 156); Bayhaqī, *Dalā'il*, I, 74.

[91] *Mustadrak*, II, 603.

place 55 days after the arrival of the elephant in Mecca. This tradition is of the Medinan imām Abū Ja'far Muḥammad al-Bāqir (d. AH 114).[92] In still other traditions dating Muḥammad's birth to the same year, the day is either 2 or 8 Rabī' al-awwal.[93] The latter day was said to have also been that of his first revelation.[94] Friday sometimes replaces Monday, being fixed to 17 Rabī' al-awwal of the Year of the Elephant.[95]

Given the dating of Muḥammad's birth to the Year of the Elephant, the first revelation was to be dated to AF 40, and the *hijra* to AF 50. In this manner, the AF dating of the latter events became identical with Muḥammad's typological age, and thus the harmony was completed between the local calendar and Muḥammad's prophetic biography. There are in fact traditions with such dating. One of them preserves the period of fifteen years between the Fijār and the building of the Ka'ba, as well as the interval of five years between the building of the Ka'ba and the first revelation. This accords with the formula of Ka'ba + 15 adding up to the date of the *hijra*. The typology of the age of 40 marking the first revelation is also maintained, which leaves unchanged the age of Muḥammad at the events indicated, compared with the above traditions with the same basis of Ka'ba + 15 for the date of the *hijra*. This tradition, circulated by the Medinan *sīra* expert Ibn Isḥāq on the authority of a descendant of the Meccan Companion Qays ibn Makhrama says that the Prophet was born in the Year of the Elephant; the Fijār took place 20 years after that year, and the Ka'ba was built fifteen years afterwards. Five years after the building of the Ka'ba, Muḥammad was sent as a prophet; this took place when he was 40 years old.[96]

Another tradition with the same symbolism of birth in the Year of the Elephant preserves the formula of Ka'ba + 15 signaling the date of the first revelation. However, it does not mention the Fijār, referring instead to a different event called "'Ukāẓ". It has the *isnād*: 'Uthmān ibn Abī Sulaymān al-Nawfalī←Muḥammad ibn Jubayr ibn Muṭ'im, and says that Muḥammad was born in the Year of the Elephant, 'Ukāẓ was (established?[97]) fifteen years

[92] Ibn Sa'd, I, 100–101. Cf. Ibn Kathīr, *Bidāya*, II, 260. The *isnād*: Abū Bakr ibn 'Abdallāh ibn Abī Sabra (d. AH 162)←Isḥāq ibn 'Abdallāh ibn Abī Farwa (d. AH 144)←Abū Ja'far.

[93] Ibn 'Abd al-Barr, *Istī'āb*, I, 30, 31; Ibn Kathīr, *Bidāya*, II, 260.

[94] Ibn 'Abd al-Barr, *Istī'āb*, I, 31; Ibn Kathīr, *Bidāya*, II, 260 (Khwārizmī).

[95] Ṭabarsī, *A'lām al-warā*, 13; Ibn Kathīr, *Bidāya*, II, 260.

[96] Khalīfa ibn Khayyāṭ, 9. See also Ibn Kathīr, *Bidāya*, II, 261.

[97] That the market of 'Ukāẓ was established in AF 15 is maintained by some Muslim scholars quoted in M.J. Kister, "Some Reports Concerning Mecca", *Journal of the Economic and Social History of the Orient* 15 (1972), 76. See also Uri Rubin, "The *Īlāf* of Quraysh: a Study of Sūra CVI", *Arabica* 31 (1984), 177. However, it may well be that the reference to 'Ukāẓ here does not stand for its establishment, but rather refers to some battles of the Fijār

afterwards, the Ka'ba was built in AF 25, and Muḥammad became a prophet in AF 40.[98] The basic formula, Ka'ba + 15, originally designed to apply the symbolism of 70 to the AF dating of the first revelation, was here preserved in a stagnant status, the number 70 being no longer attainable, as the Year of the Elephant became the year of Muḥammad's birth. The latter dating indeed superseded all other methods of calculation.

V

The model 10–10 indicating the equal length of Muḥammad's Meccan and Medinan periods was not always retained in the chronological traditions, as the symmetry was sometimes disturbed. Whereas the Medinan term almost always remains a ten-year period of successive post-*hijra* prophetic revelations, the Meccan one appears in other traditions as consisting of sub-stages of different degrees of success, and of various kinds of revelations. These traditions actually absorbed details from the stories about Muḥammad's first steps as a prophet in Mecca. These stories, in which prophetic revelation is not always Quranic, infiltrated into the chronological material, together with some early poetic verses which also had their own significant impact on the chronological data.

Let us begin with the poetry. The *Sīra* of Ibn Isḥāq contains verses attributed to the Medinan poet and *ḥanīf*, Abū Qays Ṣirma ibn Abī Anas.[99] In them he praises the Anṣār for having extended their support to the Prophet. The first verse contains a statement to the effect that the Prophet spent "some ten years" (*biḍ'a 'ashrata ḥijjatan*) among the Quraysh, preaching to them and hoping in vain to find a friend and supporter (i.e. before finding shelter in Medina).[100] This verse reappears in Islamic *ḥadīth*, where it is said to have been adduced by the Medinan Ibn 'Abbās. Although, as seen above, the latter was invoked as authority for the model of 10–10, there are traditions in which he rejects this model and explicitly holds that Muḥammad's Meccan period of prophetic preaching lasted more than just ten years. His evidence is the said poetic verse. In one of these traditions he is seen by an anonymous old Medinan woman

---

which took place in that market. For these battles, see Ella Landau-Tasseron, "The Sinful Wars: Religious, Social and Historical Aspects of *Ḥurūb al-Fijār*", *Jerusalem Studies in Arabic and Islam* 8 (1986), 37–60.

[98] Bayhaqī, *Dalā'il*, I, 78; Ibn Kathīr, *Bidāya*, II, 261.

[99] See on him Uri Rubin, "*Ḥanīfiyya* and Ka'ba: an Inquiry into the Arabian Pre-Islamic Background of *Dīn Ibrāhīm*", *Jerusalem Studies in Arabic and Islam* 13 (1990), 98.

[100] Ibn Hishām, II, 158; See also Ṭabarī, *Tārīkh*, I, 1247 (II, 385).

visiting the poet Ṣirma, from whom he heard the verse.[101] In another tradition, 'Amr ibn Dīnār (Meccan d. AH 126) asks his master 'Urwa ibn al-Zubayr (Medinan d. AH 94) about the view held by Ibn 'Abbās, according to which the Meccan period lasted "some ten years". As seen above, 'Urwa is said to have transmitted to this 'Amr ibn Dīnār the figures 40–60 marking the age boundaries of Muḥammad's prophetic activity. In the present tradition he confirms to 'Amr that the Prophet spent ten years in Mecca, and states that Ibn 'Abbās was wrong in relying on the above poetic verse. This discourse between 'Urwa and 'Amr ibn Dīnār is recorded in some *muṣannaf* compilations,[102] as well as in other sources.[103]

In fact, Ibn 'Abbās is presented in yet another tradition as a fiery opponent of the 10–10 model. His disciple Sa'īd ibn Jubayr (Kūfan d. AH 95) relates that someone once asked Ibn 'Abbās whether the Prophet had revelations for ten years in Mecca and ten years in Medina. Ibn 'Abbās retorted angrily: "Who says so? The Prophet had revelations in Mecca for ten years and for five [more] years, or even for more!"[104] Another disciple of Ibn 'Abbās, namely, 'Ikrima (Medinan d. AH 105), says that his master used to adduce the verse of Ṣirma in support of his view. This time the verse reads "fifteen years" (*khamsa 'ashrata ḥijjatan*) instead of "some ten years" *(biḍ'a 'ashrata ḥijjatan)*, thus raising Muḥammad's Meccan period to a specific number of years higher than ten.[105]

The number 15 is the total of 5 added to the basic 10 of the symmetric Meccan–Medinan model. The breaking of this symmetry in favour of Mecca seems to reflect the tension between the *faḍā'il* (virtues) of various sacred cities in early Islam. 15 is in fact the figure marking the Meccan period in yet another tradition about Ibn 'Abbās, who this time communicates his view to 'Ammār ibn Abī 'Ammār (Meccan d. *ca.* AH 105). Ibn 'Abbās' message now includes further details about Muḥammad's Meccan period, gleaned from the early *sīra* stories and designed to fill in the extended period with adequate events. In some of the *sīra* stories mentioned in previous chapters of this book, reference is made to a hiding period which preceded Muḥammad's public preaching.[106]

---

[101] Bayhaqī, *Dalā'il*, II, 513–14; Ibn 'Abd al-Barr, *Istī'āb*, I, 33. The *isnād*: Sufyān ibn 'Uyayna (Meccan d. AH 196)←Yaḥyā ibn Sa'īd ibn Qays al-Anṣārī (Medinan d. AH 144)←old Medinan woman.

[102] 'Abd al-Razzāq, *Muṣannaf*, III, no. 6787; Muslim, VII, 87–88 (43, *Bāb kam aqāma l-nabiyy (ṣ) bi-Makka wa-l-Madīna*).

[103] Abū Zur'a, 144–46 (nos. 4–5); Ibn 'Abd al-Barr, *Tamhīd*, III, 17; Bayhaqī, *Dalā'il*, II, 514.

[104] Ibn Sa'd, I, 224–25. See also Ibn Abī Shayba, XIV, no. 18399; Aḥmad, *Musnad*, I, 230; Ibn 'Asākir (*Mukhtaṣar*), II, 390; Ibn 'Abd al-Barr, *Tamhīd*, III, 19.

[105] Ṭabarī, *Tārīkh*, I, 1248 (II, 386).

[106] For these stories, see above, 127–29, 156.

This period is adduced in the discourse between Ibn 'Abbās and 'Ammār to stand for the first five years of Muḥammad's fifteen years of activity in Mecca. Ibn 'Abbās is made to say to 'Ammār: "The messenger of God was sent as a prophet at the age of 40; he spent five years in Mecca, in hiding, ten years in public preaching, and ten more years in Medina." This specific statement of Ibn 'Abbās to 'Ammār was transmitted by the Baṣran Yūnus ibn 'Ubayd (d. AH 140).[107] Muslim included a similar version of Yūnus ibn 'Ubayd in his *Ṣaḥīḥ*, but in it the Meccan period is just fifteen years of hiding and public preaching, with no specific subdivision of these two stages.[108] But the same Muslim has yet another version of the discourse between Ibn 'Abbās and 'Ammār, in which the symbolic number 7 is used instead of the number 5, for the first stage of the fifteen years of the extended Meccan period. The first stage of this period is this time a reflection of another kind of *sīra* stories, also mentioned in previous chapters. These stories refer to a non-Quranic stage of Muḥammad's prophetic revelations in which he did not receive proper Quranic text, but merely heard voices and saw light.[109] In the present version of Ibn 'Abbās' statement, transmitted by the Baṣran Ḥammād ibn Salama (d. AH 167), this has become the contents of the first seven years of the Meccan period. Ibn 'Abbās is said to have told 'Ammār that the messenger of God stayed fifteen years in Mecca, during which he "heard voices and saw light" (*yasma'u l-ṣawta wa-yarā l-ḍaw'a*) for seven years, and received proper revelations for eight years; then he spent ten more years in Medina.[110]

The various versions of the statement made by Ibn 'Abbās to 'Ammār ibn Abī 'Ammār raise the death-age of the Prophet from 60 to 65, and this is stated explicitly in yet further versions of the same statement which were likewise circulated by Baṣrans, among them Khālid al-Ḥadhdhā' (d. AH 141), as well as by some of the above mentioned traditionists. The traditions appear in some *muṣannaf* compilations,[111] as well as in quite a few biographical sources.[112] In fact, there are more Baṣran traditions fixing Muḥammad's death to the age of

---

[107] Khalīfa ibn Khayyāṭ, 10.

[108] Muslim, VII, 88–89 (43, *Bāb kam aqāma l-nabiyy (ṣ) bi-Makka wa-l-Madīna*). And see also Ibn Sa'd, II, 310; Aḥmad, *Musnad*, I, 290.

[109] For the traditions about this kind of revelations, see above, 108–109.

[110] Muslim, VII, 89 (43, *Bāb kam aqāma l-nabiyy (ṣ) bi-Makka wa-l-Madīna*). And see also Ibn Sa'd, I, 224; Aḥmad, *Musnad*, I, 266, 279, 294, 312; Ṭabarānī, *Kabīr*, XII, no. 12840; Bayhaqī, *Dalā'il*, VII, 240.

[111] See Ibn Abī Shayba, XIV, nos. 18396, 18398; Tirmidhī/*Tuḥfa*, X, 134 (nos. 3730–31 [46:13]).

[112] Ibn Sa'd, II, 310; Khalīfa ibn Khayyāṭ, 60; Tirmidhī, *Shamā'il*, 222; Aḥmad, *Musnad*, I, 223, 359; Ṭabarānī, *Kabīr*, XII, nos. 12843, 12844; Bayhaqī, *Dalā'il*, VII, 240.

65. They are of the Companion Anas ibn Mālik (d. AH 91–95),[113] and of Daghfal ibn Ḥanẓala, the expert on genealogy.[114] There are also Baṣran versions with the death-age 65, which are again traced back to Ibn ʻAbbās.[115]

In another cluster of traditions, mostly Meccan, the Meccan period of ten years is extended not by 5, but rather by 3, which is again a symbolic enough figure.[116] These traditions gained wider circulation in the *muṣannaf* sources than the former.

To begin with, the addition of the number 3 to the basic 10 appears in yet another version of the discourse between ʻAmr ibn Dīnār and his master ʻUrwa ibn al-Zubayr. As in the former version mentioned above, ʻAmr asks ʻUrwa to comment on Ibn ʻAbbās' view concerning the length of the Meccan period. But this time ʻAmr claims that Ibn ʻAbbās thinks that it lasted thirteen, not "some ten" years. The present version was circulated by Sufyān ibn ʻUyayna (Meccan d. AH 196), and was recorded by Muslim.[117] The same ʻAmr ibn Dīnār figures in the *isnād* of one more tradition attributing to Ibn ʻAbbās the number 13 as marking the duration of the Meccan period of Muḥammad's prophetic activity. It also contains the Prophet's befitting death-age, which should now rise from the basic 60 to 63. This version, circulated by the Meccan Zakariyyā ibn Isḥāq, was also recorded by Muslim in his *Ṣaḥīḥ*,[118] as well as by al-Tirmidhī.[119] Muslim's *Ṣaḥīḥ* contains yet another tradition with a similar statement of Ibn ʻAbbās, this time attributed to him by Abū Jamra al-Ḍubaʻī (Naṣr ibn ʻImrān, Baṣran d. AH 128). The latter relates that Ibn ʻAbbās said that the Prophet received revelations in Mecca for thirteen years, and in Medina for ten years, and

---

[113] One *isnād* is: Bishr ibn al-Mufaḍḍal (Baṣran d. AH 186)←Ḥumayd al-Ṭawīl (Baṣran d. AH 142)←Anas. See Ibn ʻAbd al-Barr, *Tamhīd*, III, 18, 22. Another *isnād* is: Hishām ibn ʻAbdallāh al-Dustuwāʼī (Baṣran d. AH 152)←Qatāda (Baṣran d. AH 117)←Anas. See Ibn ʻAbd al-Barr, *Tamhīd*, III, 22.

[114] The *isnād*: Qatāda (Baṣran d. AH 117)←al-Ḥasan al-Baṣrī (d. AH 110)←Daghfal. See Abū Zurʻa, 151 (no. 15); Khalīfa ibn Khayyāṭ, 60; Tirmidhī, *Shamāʼil*, 222; Ṭabarī, *Tārīkh*, I, 1835 (III, 216); Bayhaqī, *Dalāʼil*, VII, 241; Ibn ʻAbd al-Barr, *Tamhīd*, III, 18, 22.

[115] One *isnād* is: ʻAlī ibn Zayd ibn ʻAbdallāh ibn Abī Mulayka (Baṣran d. AH 131)←Yūsuf ibn Mihrān (Baṣran)←Ibn ʻAbbās. See Ibn Saʻd, II, 310; Ṭabarī, *Tārīkh*, I, 1835 (III, 216); Aḥmad, *Musnad*, I, 215; Ṭabarānī, *Kabīr*, XII, no. 12845; Bayhaqī, *Dalāʼil*, VII, 240. Another *isnād* is: Ibn Abī ʻAdī (Muḥammad ibn Ibrāhīm, Baṣran d. AH 194)←Hishām ibn Ḥassān (Baṣran d. AH 147)–ʻIkrima (Medinan d. AH 105)←Ibn ʻAbbās. See Tirmidhī/*Tuḥfa*, X, no. 3701 (46:4).

[116] See Sellheim, "Prophet, Chalif und Geschichte", 70.

[117] Muslim, VII, 87 (43, *Bāb kam aqāma l-nabiyy (ṣ) bi-Makka wa-l-Madīna*).

[118] *Ibid.*, 88 (43, *Bāb kam aqāma l-nabiyy (ṣ) bi-Makka wa-l-Madīna*).

[119] See Tirmidhī/*Tuḥfa*, X, 135 (no. 3732 [46:13]). And see Bukhārī, *Tārīkh kabīr*, I, 10; Tirmidhī, *Shamāʼil*, 221; Ṭabarī, *Tārīkh*, I, 1246 (II, 385); Aḥmad, *Musnad*, I, 370, 371; Bayhaqī, *Dalāʼil*, II, 512; VII, 238.

he died at the age of 63.[120] Sometimes the same Abū Jamra attributes to Ibn 'Abbās the statement about Muḥammad's age at his first revelation, which is, of course, 40.[121] The same chronology (13–10 for the Meccan–Medinan periods, and 40–63 for the age boundaries) was also attributed to Ibn 'Abbās by Hishām ibn 'Urwa (Meccan d. AH 146),[122] by Ibn Sīrīn (Muḥammad, Baṣran d. AH 110),[123] by Abū Ḥamza (al-Qaṣṣāb, al-Wāsiṭī, Baṣran),[124] and by 'Ikrima (Medinan d. AH 105).[125] The version of the latter appears in quite a few *muṣannaf* compilations,[126] as well as in the biographical sources.[127] The formula 13–10 was also adopted by Ibn Isḥāq.[128]

The extra three years added to the basic 10 of the Meccan period were again filled in with *sīra* material dealing with the non-Quranic revelations, discussed previously in this book. These revelations are said to have been delivered to Muḥammad between the ages of 40 and 43 by an angel whose name is either Michael or Isrāfīl. When the Prophet was 43, it is related, Gabriel took over. He brought to Muḥammad the proper Quranic revelations for ten years in Mecca, and ten more years in Medina. The Prophet died at the age of 63. The traditions to this effect were circulated with the *isnād*: Dāwūd ibn Abī Hind (Baṣran d. AH 139)←'Āmir al-Sha'bī (Kūfan d. AH 103).[129] In this chronology the age boundaries of Muḥammad's Quranic revelations are 43–63, while the Meccan–Medinan model is restored to 10–10, as far as the proper Quranic revelations are concerned. These are indeed the figures indicated in one more version traced back to Ibn 'Abbās through 'Ikrima.[130] They are also stated in

---

120 Muslim, VII, 88 (43, *Bāb kam aqāma l-nabiyy (ṣ) bi-Makka wa-l-Madīna*). See the same tradition in Ibn Sa'd, II, 310–11; Khalīfa ibn Khayyāṭ, 10, 59; Ṭabarī, *Tārīkh*, I, 1246, 1834, 1835 (II, 384; III, 215, 215–16); Bukhārī, *Tārīkh kabīr*, I, 8; Aḥmad, *Musnad*, I, 363; Bayhaqī, *Dalā'il*, VII, 239.

121 Ṭabarī, *Tārīkh*, I, 1139 (II, 290).

122 Ibn Abī Shayba, XIV, no. 18393.

123 'Abd al-Razzāq, *Muṣannaf*, III, no. 6784; Ibn Ḥibbān, *Ṣaḥīḥ*, XIV, no. 6390; Ṭabarānī, *Kabīr*, XII, no 12870.

124 Ibn Sa'd, I, 225. And cf. *Majma' al-zawā'id*, I, 202: Abū Ḥamza←his father←Ibn 'Abbās.

125 The *isnād*: Hishām ibn Ḥassān (Baṣran d. AH 147)←'Ikrima←Ibn 'Abbās.

126 Ibn Abī Shayba, XIII, no. 15735; XIV, no. 18400; Bukhārī, *Ṣaḥīḥ*, V, 56 (63:28), 72–73 (63:45); Tirmidhī/*Tuḥfa*, X, no. 3700 (46:4).

127 Khalīfa ibn Khayyāṭ, 10–11, 59–60; Bukhārī, *Tārīkh kabīr*, I, 8, 10; Ibn Sa'd, I, 190, 225; Ṭabarī, *Tārīkh*, I, 1140, 1246 (II, 292, 385); Aḥmad, *Musnad*, I, 249; Bayhaqī, *Dalā'il*, II, 131; VII, 239.

128 Ibn Bukayr, 109. See also Ibn Hishām, I, 168: Ibn Isḥāq holds that the Prophet left Mecca at the age of 53. And see Bayhaqī, *Dalā'il*, II, 511–12.

129 For references, see above, 111, nn. 30–31.

130 Ṭabarī, *Tārīkh*, I, 1141, 1246 (II, 292, 384); Aḥmad, *Musnad*, I, 228; Ibn 'Abd al-Barr, *Tamhīd*, III, 14–15.

traditions of Sa'īd ibn al-Musayyab (Medinan d. AH 94).[131] A Medinan tradition related on the authority of 'Ā'isha[132] only states that Muḥammad died at 63, and considering the above tradition of the same person, it may be assumed that here the Meccan/Medinan model of 10–10 is being followed as well. The present tradition of Ā'isha was recorded in several authoritative *muṣannaf* sources,[133] as well as in the historiographical and biographical compilations.[134]

The tension between Mecca and Medina is reflected in the breaking of the 10–10 symmetry not only in favour of the former, but also in favour of the latter. The extra number of years is now 2. There are Baṣran traditions of authorities who, as seen above, are usually invoked in support of the model 10–10 combined with the age boundaries 40–60. In the present statements, which did not gain wide circulation, the Medinan period appears longer than the Meccan one by two years. Thus Qatāda (Baṣran d. AH 117) reportedly stated that the Quran was revealed to the Prophet for eight years in Mecca and ten years in Medina.[135] In a parallel version Qatāda states this on the authority of al-Ḥasan al-Baṣrī (d. AH 110).[136] It may well be that the age boundaries implicit in this case are 44–62. There is, in fact, one more tradition of Qatāda in which he states that the Prophet died at the age of 62.[137] But al-Ḥasan al-Baṣrī was also made to declare the opposite, namely, that the Prophet spent ten years of Quranic revelations in Mecca and only eight such years in Medina. Muḥammad's age bound-

131 'Abd al-Razzāq, *Muṣannaf*, III, no. 6782. The *isnād*: Ma'mar ibn Rāshid (Baṣran, lived in Yemen, d. AH 154)←Qatāda (Baṣran d. AH 117)←Sa'īd ibn al-Musayyab. Another *isnād*: Yaḥyā ibn Sa'īd ibn Qays al-Anṣārī (Medinan d. AH 144)←Sa'īd ibn al-Musayyab. See Ibn Abī Shayba, XIV, no. 18397; Ibn Sa'd, I, 224; Ṭabarī, *Tārīkh*, I, 1141, 1245–46, 1835 (II, 292, 384; III, 215); Bayhaqī, *Dalā'il*, II, 132; Ibn 'Abd al-Barr, *Tamhīd*, III, 15. Cf. Khalīfa ibn Khayyāṭ, 59. But see the same *isnād* in Ibn 'Abd al-Barr, *Tamhīd*, III, 26, where the Meccan period is again 13 years, not 10, and the age boundaries are 40–63.

132 The *isnād*: Zuhrī←'Urwa←'Ā'isha.

133 Bukhārī, *Ṣaḥīḥ*, IV, 226 (61:19); VI, 19 (64:85); Muslim, VII, 87 (43, *Bāb kam sinn al-nabī*); Tirmidhī/*Tuḥfa*, X, no. 3734 (46:13); Ibn Ḥibbān, *Ṣaḥīḥ*, XIV, no. 6388.

134 Abū Zur'a, 149 (no. 11); Ibn Sa'd, II, 309; Khalīfa ibn Khayyāṭ, 59; Tirmidhī, *Shamā'il*, 222; Bukhārī, *Tārīkh kabīr*, I, 8–9; Ṭabarī, *Tārīkh*, I, 1835 (III, 216); Aḥmad, *Musnad*, VI, 93; Ṭabarānī, *Kabīr*, I, no. 27; Bayhaqī, *Dalā'il*, VII, 238; Ibn 'Abd al-Barr, *Tamhīd*, III, 23–24.

135 Ṭabarī, *Tārīkh*, I, 1250 (II, 387). The *isnād*: Sa'īd ibn Abī 'Arūba (Baṣran d. AH 156)←Qatāda.

136 Khalīfa ibn Khayyāṭ, 10; Ibn Kathīr, *Bidāya*, V, 259 (Aḥmad). And see also Ibn Sa'd, I, 225, the same statement with the *isnād*: Abū Rajā'←al-Ḥasan al-Baṣrī.

137 The *isnād*: Hishām ibn 'Abdallāh al-Dustuwā'ī (Baṣran d. AH 152)←Qatāda. See Khalīfa ibn Khayyāṭ, 60; Ibn Kathīr, *Bidāya*, V, 259.

aries in this case are said to have been 45–63.[138] Thus the superiority of Mecca over Medina was restored.

The number 2 is the axis round which one more tradition rotates, which adds to the structure the befitting day of the week, Monday. It restores, however, the Meccan–Medinan model to its basic 10–10 formula. The tradition is of Makḥūl (Syrian d. AH 112), who states that Muḥammad was born on a Monday, received his first revelation on a Monday, made his *hijra* on a Monday, and died on a Monday, at the age of 62 (and a half). He was 42 at his first revelation, and spent ten years in secret preaching in Mecca, and ten (and a half) more in Medina.[139]

VI

In our consideration above of the theme of attestation (Chapter 2), it has been demonstrated that many traditions about the Prophet's life were shaped so as to highlight the virtues (*faḍā'il*) of groups and individuals who played an active part in his career. The traditions about the chronology of Muḥammad's life were also moulded with the same view in mind. Some chronological details of his life were linked in these traditions to the lives of some of his most prominent Companions, so as to imply that their lives were also part of the same divinely decreed course of sacred history.

Most characteristic are the traditions asserting the correspondence of Muḥammad's death-age with that of Abū Bakr and 'Umar. These were circulated with Kūfan *isnāds*, and the compilers of the *muṣannaf* collections recorded them quite readily, because of their message of ideal harmony. One tradition of this kind, recorded by Muslim and al-Tirmidhī, is traced back to none other than Mu'āwiya. The latter is said to have stated that the Prophet died at the age of 63, Abū Bakr died at 63, and 'Umar was assassinated at the same age.[140] Muslim has one more tradition attributing the same statement to

[138] Khalīfa ibn Khayyāṭ, 10, 60; Ibn 'Asākir (*Mukhtaṣar*), II, 389; Ibn Kathīr, *Bidāya*, V, 259–60. The *isnād*: Abū 'Āṣim←Ash'ath←al-Ḥasan.

[139] Ibn 'Asākir (*Mukhtaṣar*), II, 388. Cf. *Fatḥ al-bārī*, VI, 414; Ibn Kathīr, *Bidāya*, V, 259.

[140] See Muslim, VII, 88 (43, *Bāb kam aqāma l-nabiyy (ṣ) bi-Makka wa-l-Madīna*); Tirmidhī/*Tuḥfa*, X, 136 (no. 3733 [46:13]). The *isnād*: Abū Isḥāq al-Sabī'ī (Kūfan Shī'ī d. AH 126–29)←'Āmir ibn Sa'd al-Bajalī (Kūfan)←Jarīr ibn 'Abdallāh al-Bajalī (Yemeni Companion d. AH 51)←Mu'āwiya. The tradition is also recorded in Tirmidhī, *Shamā'il*, 221; Aḥmad, *Musnad*, IV, 96; Ṭabarānī, *Kabīr*, I, nos. 29, 31–33; Bayhaqī, *Dalā'il*, VII, 239. The tradition is also available with a slightly different *isnād*: Abū l-Safar (Sa'īd ibn Yaḥmad, Kūfan d. AH 112)←al-Sha'bī ('Āmir ibn Shurāḥīl, Kūfan d. AH 103)←Jarīr←Mu'āwiya. See

'Abdallāh ibn 'Utba ibn Mas'ūd (Medinan/Kūfan d. AH 73).[141] Muslim also recorded a Kūfan tradition attributing the same statement to the Companion Anas ibn Mālik.[142] A statement asserting the correspondence of Muḥammad's death-age with that of 'Umar was also interpolated into one of the Iraqi versions of the above traditions about the three years in Mecca which preceded Muḥammad's proper Quranic revelations. This is the tradition mentioning Michael as the angel who preceded Gabriel, which concludes with the statement that Muḥammad died at the age of 63, and so did 'Umar.[143]

In some Medinan traditions the correspondence of death-age is only between Muḥammad and Abū Bakr, without reference to 'Umar. This is the case in some rare versions of the above tradition of Sa'īd ibn al-Musayyab with the Meccan/Medinan model of 10–10 and the age boundaries of 43–63. In some versions of this tradition it is stated that Abū Bakr died at the same age (63).[144] There is also a similarly rare version of the above Medinan tradition of 'Ā'isha to the effect that the Prophet died at 63, in which an addition is again included to the effect that Abū Bakr also died at 63. In this particular version, it is likewise stated by al-Zuhrī that 'Umar died at 55, which leaves him outside the numerical harmony.[145]

The same idea of correspondence was also applied to the traditions setting Muḥammad's death-age to 65. As seen above, these traditions were circulated mainly by Baṣran traditionists. There is one more such Baṣran tradition, this time of Qatāda (d. AH 117), which although not referring explicitly to Muḥammad's death-age, nevertheless states that Abū Bakr died at 65. 'Umar,

---

Abū Zur'a, 148–49 (no. 10); Khalīfa ibn Khayyāṭ, 59; Aḥmad, *Musnad*, IV, 97; Ṭabarānī, *Kabīr*, I, no. 30, 66.

141 The *isnād*: Abū Isḥāq al-Sabī'ī (Kūfan Shī'ī d. AH 126–29)←'Abdallāh ibn 'Utba. See Muslim, VII, 88 (43, *Bāb kam aqāma l-nabiyy (ṣ) bi-Makka wa-l-Madīna*); See also Ibn Abī Shayba, XIII, no. 15730.

142 The *isnād*: 'Uthmān ibn Zā'ida (Kūfan)←al-Zubayr ibn 'Adī (Kūfan d. AH 131)←Anas. See Muslim, VII, 87 (43, *Bāb kam sinn al-nabī*); Ibn Ḥibbān, *Ṣaḥīḥ*, XIV, no. 6389. See also Ibn 'Abd al-Barr, *Tamhīd*, III, 9–10; Bayhaqī, *Dalā'il*, VII, 237–38.

143 'Abd al-Razzāq, *Muṣannaf*, III, no. 6785. The *isnād*: Dāwūd ibn Abī Hind (Baṣran d. AH 139)←'Āmir al-Sha'bī (Kūfan d. AH 103). But cf. Ṭabarānī, *Kabīr*, I, no. 34, where a shortened version with the same *isnād* is quoted from 'Abd al-Razzāq, mentioning Abū Bakr instead of 'Umar.

144 'Abd al-Razzāq, *Muṣannaf*, III, no. 6783; Ibn Abī Shayba, XIII, no. 15770. The *isnād*: Yaḥyā ibn Sa'īd ibn Qays al-Anṣārī (Medinan d. AH 144)←Sa'īd ibn al-Musayyab. See also Ṭabarānī, *Kabīr*, I, no. 35.

145 'Abd al-Razzāq, *Muṣannaf*, III, no. 6791. The *isnād*: Ibn Shihāb al-Zuhrī (Medinan d. AH 124)←'Urwa ibn al-Zubayr (Medinan d. AH 94)←'Ā'isha. And see the same tradition without the remark about 'Umar in Ṭabarānī, *Kabīr*, I, nos. 26, 28.

however, is said to have been assassinated when he was 51 years old.[146] A more explicit formulation is contained in a Ḥijāzī tradition of Ibn 'Abbās, stating that Muḥammad died at the age of 65, and so did Abū Bakr. 'Umar, however, died at 56.[147]

It seems that the reluctance to include 'Umar's death in the harmonic chronological system was caused by the fact that he did not die of natural causes. The act of assassination could not be regarded by all traditionists as a predestined event in an ideal course of history. Among the scholars who nevertheless included his death in the numerical harmony was the Medinan Mālik ibn Anas (d. AH 180), who insisted that 'Umar died at the same age as Muḥammad: 63. But this scholar was opposed by others who claimed that 'Umar died at the ages of 59, 53, 55, or 54.[148] In the same vein, Abū Ḥafṣ 'Amr ibn 'Alī (Baṣran d. AH 249) stated that people claimed that 'Umar died at the age of 63, but the truth was that he was assassinated at the age of 58.[149]

Correspondence was sought not only for age at death, but also for day of death. It is again Abū Bakr who has this in common with the Prophet. In a tradition of 'Urwa ibn al-Zubayr, it is related that on his last day Abū Bakr asked his daughter 'Ā'isha what day it was. When she told him that it was Monday, and that the Prophet had died on the same day, he expressed his wish to die before the night was over. Indeed, he died that very night. The tradition appears in *muṣannaf* compilations,[150] as well as in other sources.[151]

Apart from traditions asserting numerical biographical correspondence between some Companions and the Prophet, there are also traditions which are merely designed to prove that a given Companion was indeed Muḥammad's contemporary. These traditions were designed to corroborate the Companion's claim to the rank of *ṣaḥābī*, which is achieved by reporting the Companion's age at Muḥammad's *hijra* or death. These traditions are usually formulated as the Companion's own first-person statement.

Some such traditions concern the Egyptian governor Maslama ibn Mukhallad al-Anṣārī (d. AH 62). There are two versions of a tradition of 'Alī ibn Rabāḥ

---

[146] Ibn Abī Shayba, XIII, no. 15745. The *isnād*: Abū Hilāl al-Rāsibī (Baṣran d. AH 167)←Qatāda.

[147] 'Abd al-Razzāq, *Muṣannaf*, III, no. 6790. The *isnād*: Ibn Jurayj (Meccan d. AH 150)←Abū l-Ḥuwayrith ('Abd al-Raḥmān ibn Mu'āwiya, Medinan d. AH 128)←Ibn 'Abbās. And see also Ṭabarānī, *Kabīr*, I, no. 36 (without the remark about 'Umar).

[148] Ṭabarānī, *Kabīr*, I, no. 73.

[149] *Ibid.*, I, no. 75.

[150] Bukhārī, *Ṣaḥīḥ*, II, 127 (23:94); Ibn Ḥibbān, *Ṣaḥīḥ*, XIV, no. 6615.

[151] Tirmidhī, *Shamā'il*, 226; Aḥmad, *Musnad*, VI, 45, 118, 132; Bayhaqī, *Dalā'il*, VII, 233.

(Egyptian d. AH 117), who communicates Maslama's statement concerning his own age at the *hijra* and at the Prophet's death. In one version he claims to have been born when Muḥammad came to Medina, and to have been ten years old when the Prophet died.[152] In another version he is older by four years, which brings him closer to the age of majority (fifteen)[153] at the Prophet's death.[154]

A more pressing problem was that of Anas ibn Mālik, who died as late as AH 91, or even later, and is said to have been the last Companion who died in Baṣra.[155] To authenticate his status as a Companion, a tradition was circulated in which Anas states that he was ten years old when Muḥammad came to Medina, and 20 when he died.[156]

The last living Companion in Medina was Sahl ibn Sa'd al-Anṣārī who died there in AH 88.[157] To assert his status as a Companion, there is a tradition attributing to him the statement that he was fifteen when the Prophet died.[158]

Abū Umāma al-Bāhilī was the last Companion in Syria, and died in AH 86.[159] He too appears in a tradition, stating that he was 33 when Muḥammad died.[160]

There are similar traditions about Ibn 'Abbās, who was said to have died in AH 68.[161] His Companionship was also asserted through some chronological synchronizations. There is a Kūfan tradition in which he states that he was fifteen years old when the Prophet died.[162] In another version, his age at that time is only ten, but it is added that he was already able to read the *muḥkam*, i.e. the Quran.[163]

---

[152] Ibn Abī Shayba, XIII, no. 15705; XIV, no. 18468; Ṭabarānī, *Kabīr*, XIX, no. 1060.

[153] For references on the age of majority, see e.g. Conrad, "Abraha and Muḥammad", 238 n. 94.

[154] Ibn Sa'd, VII, 504; Ṭabarānī, *Kabīr*, XIX, no. 1061.

[155] Marzūqī, *Azmina*, II, 342.

[156] Ibn Abī Shayba, XIII, no. 15704; XIV, no. 18469. The *isnād*: Sufyān ibn 'Uyayna (Meccan d. AH 196)←Zuhrī (Medinan d. AH 124)←Anas.

[157] Ibn 'Abd al-Barr, *Istī'āb*, II, 665; Ibn Ḥajar, *Tahdhīb*, IV, 222; Marzūqī, *Azmina*, II, 342.

[158] Ibn 'Abd al-Barr, *Istī'āb*, II, 664. The *isnād*: Shu'ayb ibn Abī Ḥamza (Zuhrī's secretary, Ḥimṣī d. AH 162)←Zuhrī←Sahl ibn Sa'd.

[159] Marzūqī, *Azmina*, II, 342.

[160] Ibn Ḥajar, *Iṣāba*, III, 421.

[161] For other dates, see Noth/Conrad, 44.

[162] Aḥmad, *Musnad*, I, 373. The *isnād*: Abū Isḥāq al-Sabī'ī (Kūfan Shī'ī d. AH 126–29)←Sa'īd ibn Jubayr (Kūfan d. AH 95)←Ibn 'Abbās.

[163] *Ibid.*, I, 253, 357. The *isnād*: Abū Bishr (Ja'far ibn Iyās, Baṣran–Wāsiṭī, d. AH 123)←Sa'īd ibn Jubayr←Ibn 'Abbās.

Of special interest is the case of 'Alī. This Shī'ī hero was regarded by his followers as the first male Muslim; to prove this, chronological synchronization was employed which at the same time joined 'Alī to the harmonic numerical system of the Prophet's life. One tradition rotating round the symbolism of the number 7 states that 'Alī embraced Islam at the age of 7, the Prophet died when he was 27, and 'Umar died when he was 57.[164] Another tradition adjusts 'Alī's death-age to that of the Prophet—63—and accordingly resets his age of conversion to thirteen.[165]

The day of 'Alī's death was actually linked to the global history of some prominent prophets beside Muḥammad. In a statement attributed to his son al-Ḥasan, the latter states that 'Alī died on the day on which Moses' *waṣiyy*, Joshua, died, and on which Jesus ascended, and on which the Quran was revealed.[166]

In a special group of traditions some Companions are credited with being born in the Year of the Elephant, and even to have been eyewitnesses to the actual event of the Elephant's arrival. Thus the Meccan Companion Qays ibn Makhrama was made to state that he and Muḥammad were born in the same year, i.e. the Year of the Elephant. His tradition was circulated by his own descendants, and was recorded in several early biographical sources,[167] as well as in some *muṣannaf* compilations.[168] A similar statement was attributed to the Companion Suwayd ibn Ghafala, who died in Kūfa at the age of 128.[169] His statement is far less current than the one made by Qays ibn Makhrama, and is only recorded in a few biographical sources.[170] In fact, the same Suwayd was also reported to have stated that he was two years younger than the Prophet.[171]

For older Companions it was possible to circulate traditions containing their own personal memories from the year in which Muḥammad was born. Thus Qubāth ibn Ashyam is said to have told the caliph 'Abd al-Malik that he was born some years before Muḥammad, and in the year Muḥammad was born he and his mother saw the faeces of the elephant in Mecca.[172] In another version

---

[164] Ibn Abī Shayba, XIII, no. 15731.

[165] Ibn 'Asākir (*Mukhtaṣar*), XVIII, 96. For this death–age of 'Alī, see also Kulīnī, I, 452.

[166] Kulīnī, I, 457.

[167] Ibn Hishām, I, 167; Ibn Sa'd, I, 101; Ṭabarī, *Tārīkh*, I, 966–67 (II, 155); Aḥmad, *Musnad*, IV, 215; Bayhaqī, *Dalā'il*, I, 76–77.

[168] Tirmidhī/*Tuḥfa*, X, no. 3698 (46:2); *Mustadrak*, II, 603.

[169] See on him Ibn Sa'd, VI, 68–70.

[170] Bayhaqī, *Dalā'il*, I, 79.

[171] Bukhārī, *Tārīkh kabīr*, IV, 142.

[172] Khalīfa ibn Khayyāṭ, 8; Ṭabarī, *Tārīkh*, I, 967 (II, 155–56); Bayhaqī, *Dalā'il*, I, 77–78, II, 131.

recorded by al-Tirmidhī he tells the caliph ʻUthmān that he remembers the droppings of the birds (i.e. the ones that attacked Abraha's army).[173]

The memories of the Medinan poet Ḥassān ibn Thābit from the same year are different. Being a Medinan he could not have witnessed the elephant. Instead, he is made to speak about the reaction of the local Medinan Jews on the night of Muḥammad's birth. His story reflects the numerous traditions of attestation about the messianic expectations of the Jews of Arabia, mentioned in this book. He relates that when he was seven or eight years old, he heard a Jew call out to his brethren from the top of his stronghold: "The star of Aḥmad which marks his birth has just arisen."[174] Ḥassān reportedly died at the age of 120, and was 60 at the time of the *hijra*.[175] This subtle chronology divided his lifetime equally between Jāhiliyya and Islam.

Thus, chronology appears to be just one more universal theme which was accommodated to local Arabian as well as to Quranic models, in a process designed to provide Muḥammad with a proper prophetic *vita*. Tensions within medieval Islamic society also left their mark on the shape of the material.

[173] Tirmidhī/*Tuḥfa*, X, no. 3698 (46:2).
[174] Ibn Hishām, I, 168.
[175] *Ibid.*; Ibn ʻAbd al-Barr, *Istīʻāb*, I, 351.

CONCLUSIONS

13

General Summary

THE PREVIOUS CHAPTERS have demonstrated that the image of Muḥammad as reflected in Muslim tradition is actually the reflection of the communal self-image of the Muslims who related the story of their Prophet's life. The medieval Muslims saw themselves as heirs to previous civilizations which came under their control, and this was how they shaped the story of their own prophet, turning him into the most excellent successor to the previous prophets of God. The foregoing chapters have scrutinized the specific ways in which Muslim tradition applied to the story of Muḥammad's prophetic emergence in Mecca biographical themes known also from the lives of other prophets. But the present study has not just aimed to demonstrate the well-known fact of the biblical origin of basic themes in Muḥammad's biography, but rather to elucidate their textual dynamics within the immediate Islamic context. It has been shown that the Muslims themselves were aware of the presence of biblical elements in the early traditions, and felt that these elements had to be adapted to genuine Islamic models. It is to the study of the transition from biblical to Islamic-Arabian models that the previous chapters are actually dedicated.

The presence of biblical elements in the story of Muḥammad's prophetic emergence in Mecca is demonstrated by the mere themes of which this story consists, which form the five parts of the present book: attestation, preparation, revelation, persecution, salvation. The process of adaptation of these themes, as well as the extent of the success of this process with respect to each theme, has been analyzed. The impact of political tensions within medieval Islamic society on the traditions was also elucidated. Let us take our findings, theme by theme.

Attestation

This theme, so well known from Christian statements about Jesus, was applied by Islamic tradition to Muḥammad. It has been shown (Chapter 1) that the traditions adduce explicit biblical quotations aimed at providing the divine annunciation of Muḥammad's emergence. The traditions quote from the New Testament passages about the "Comforter" (Fāraqlīṭ), applying them to the Islamic "Aḥmad", use biblical passages announcing the future emergence of a great "nation" (*goy*) for the annunciation of the Prophet as *al-nabī al-ummī*, and apply to Muḥammad biblical prophecies about the servant of god, e.g. Isaiah 42:2 (the "streets" passage).

The inner textual dynamics of this material reveal that direct quotations from the Bible became unpopular among the Muslims, who strove to accommodate the tool of attestation to more Islamic and Arabian models. Instead of biblical quotations, versions of traditions were pointed out in which the Islamic scripture, the Quran, emerges as a source of attestation which gradually replaced the Bible. This was quite easily accomplished, because the Quran itself already relies on previous scriptures for the annunciation of the Quranic prophet as Aḥmad and as *nabī ummī*, so that it was quite simple to dispose of direct biblical quotations and concentrate on the Quran instead. Apart from the Quran, the theme of attestation was also adapted to a second genuinely Islamic source of legitimization, namely, the model of the Prophet himself. His precedent is documented in a special type of tradition equipped with a chain of transmitters (*isnād*) reaching back to the Prophet himself. Traditions with such prophetic *isnād*s were employed as a source of Muslim law, but were also used in non-legal contexts. Muḥammad was thus turned into a source for his own self-attestation. This has been illustrated in traditions in which the Prophet utters statements in the first person about his own Quranic annunciation (Abraham's prayer in 2:129, and Jesus' announcement in 61:6). Most typical are the traditions in which the Prophet enumerates lists of his names and appellations gleaned from the Quran. The latter type won the greatest recognition in Islam and was included in the most authoritative *ḥadīth* compilations.

There are also versions which illustrate adaptation to local Arabian models (Chapter 2). The theme of attestation is projected in these traditions into the history of Arabia before Islam. In these traditions Muḥammad features not as a Quranic prophet deriving his attestation from that scripture, but first and foremost as an Arab whose attestation is rooted in local Arabian history. All the stories take place in pre-Islamic Arabia, and the heroes are well-known pre-Islamic figures who foretell the emergence of Muḥammad. This type of the traditions of attestation reflects the competition among various Arab groups (especially the Anṣār and Quraysh) and individual Companions for recognition as a dominant element in medieval Islamic society. The traditions elaborate on the role of each of these groups in the annunciation of the Prophet. But this type of text was not so successful in terms of circulation. It has been shown that the scriptural model, not the Arabian pre-Islamic one, remained the one favoured by compilers of mainstream *ḥadīth*.

Preparation

This theme, which takes us from pre-Islamic times to Muḥammad's childhood, abounds with elements known from the lives of several biblical prophets. The chapters dealing with this theme analyze in particular the stories of initiation (Chapter 3) and guidance (Chapter 4). The traditions about Muḥammad's initiation tell the story of the opening and cleansing of his breast. The scene is known from stories about non-Islamic personalities, and its initially non-Islamic nature seems to be one of the reasons why most of its versions remained outside the authoritative *ḥadīth* compilations. These versions tell the story of the opening and cleansing of Muḥammad's breast as part of his infancy legends. In them Muḥammad is no different from any other prophet who is elected, purified, and initiated into his future prophetic office.

But the inner textual dynamics of the story have revealed a process of adaptation to more specific Islamic models designed to turn it into a legitimate component of the life of the prophet. To begin with, versions were indicated in which the scene emerges as a part of prophetic statements uttered by Muḥammad himself to provide his own self-attestation. The scene was thus awarded the same authority as that of the Quranic passages of attestation adduced by the Prophet in his statement of self-attestation. A further step towards adapting the scene to genuine Islamic models was taken by linking the story to another event that has firm Quranic links, the *isrā'–mi'rāj*, i.e. Muḥammad's nocturnal journey to al-Masjid al-Aqṣā (Quran 17:1). It has been shown that in many versions the opening of Muḥammad's breast emerges as a prelude to this event, thus being entirely detached from the context of infancy legends. The latter versions were the ones accepted into the more authoritative *ḥadīth* compilations. And finally, Quranic models found their way into the very text of the scene of the opening. There are versions in which the act is not indicated as *shaqq baṭn*, "cutting open of the belly", but rather as *sharḥ ṣadr*, "opening of the breast", a formulation that comes directly from Quran 94:1. Thus the textual analysis of the story of the opening of Muḥammad's breast has exposed one more example of universal and originally non-Islamic models being applied to Muḥammad's life, and becoming an acceptable part of his biography only after having been adapted to Islamic and Quranic models.

But there were also attempts at adaptation which ended in total failure. This applies to the idea of God's guidance of Muḥammad from polytheism to monotheism. The theme is treated in many traditions (Chapter 4) forming part of the dogma of Muḥammad's *'iṣma*, i.e. his protection from sin and error. Again, in themselves these stories bear nothing unique compared to tales of other prophets who are said to have been guided to the right path. Muslims circulated them in order to provide Muḥammad with an adequate sacred biography, like that of other prophets. But the attempt to adapt this universal idea of guidance to the image of the Islamic prophet proved unsuccessful. Most versions of these traditions remained outside the authoritative *ḥadīth* compilations, surviving mainly in various biographical and historiographical sources. Mainstream Muslim opinion in particular found it difficult to absorb them, because of the insinuation that Muḥammad was once an ordinary human being holding the same religion as his fellow tribesmen (*dīn qawmihi*). For them, Muḥammad's *'iṣma* did not mean guidance from paganism to monotheism, but rather eternal immunity from the former.

The textual history of the stories of guidance has revealed that only a few of these gained access into the canonical *ḥadīth* compilations, thanks to significant changes in their purport. The story of Muḥammad's meeting with Zayd ibn 'Amr, from whom he learnt that sacrificing to the idols was forbidden, was accepted by al-Bukhārī only in a reshaped form denying the story its basic sense of guidance. Even traditions with self-guidance, i.e. in which the Prophet himself utters his own experience of transition from polytheism to monotheism, were rejected in spite of their prophetic *isnād*s, which in their turn indicate their original popularity. It has been indicated that sometimes the story of guidance is told as an event of pre-prophetic revelation (when Muḥammad walks naked), but again, this only gained limited circulation for the story.

Moreover, the idea of guidance was even read into the Quran, especially into 93:7 (the *ḍāll* passage, with the interpretation of al-Suddī), as well as into 94:2 (*wizr*). But this Quranic link did not prevail either. The Muslims deployed the tool of exegesis (*tafsīr*) to suppress the notion of guidance, in favour of that of total immunity. Thus, what began as an innocent attempt to apply to the Islamic Prophet the universal idea of God's guidance ended with total rejection of this idea in the canonical *ḥadīth* and later *tafsīr*. The personality of the Prophet thus became devoid of drama, static and monolithic, with no wonderful transformation from a human being into a prophet of God.

Revelation

The universal theme of revelation emerges in two types of traditions (Chapter 5). In one group it is adapted to Arabian surroundings and to Muḥammad's own private conditions. The plot revolves round two of Muḥammad's closest supporters, his wife Khadīja and her cousin Waraqa ibn Nawfal. The former provides the Prophet with moral assistance, the latter with attestation. The theme of revelation is represented in these traditions through its well-known universal (biblical) components, such as visions of voices and light, the startling appearance of an angel, fear of the inexperienced prophet, etc. In another cluster of traditions, the theme of revelation is adapted to Quranic models as well. But there was no uniformity in the manner of adaptation. In some traditions the revelation becomes Sūrat al-Fātiḥa (1); in others it is the *iqra'* passage (96:1–5). The latter versions gained the widest circulation in the most authoritative *ḥadīth* compilations.

The link between God and man through prophetic revelation may sometimes be interrupted, which causes the recipient of revelation a serious crisis and loss of confidence. The Bible has some examples of such crisis caused by the departure of the spirit of God. This traumatic aspect of revelation emerges also in the life of Muḥammad (Chapter 6), functioning as a dramatic illustration of his first faltering steps as a prophet. But again, its adaptation to Muḥammad caused serious dogmatic problems. In Muslim tradition it was turned into the anti-climax of Muḥammad's meeting with Waraqa, and is referred to in the sources as *fatrat al-waḥy*, "the lapse of prophetic revelation". The *fatra* lasts until terminated by the renewed appearance of the angel which marks confirmation of the God–prophet link. The textual dynamics of this event in the sources reveal an attempted process of adaptation to Quranic models, which again proved unsuccessful. The Quranic passages linked to the episode of the *fatra* are the Muddaththir passage (74:1–2) and the *mā wadda'aka* passage (93:3), the revelation of which redeems the Prophet from his distress. The basic tradition with the latter passage elaborates on the mental crisis experienced by Muḥammad, who thinks that his Lord has forsaken him, till he is redeemed from his despair when the reassuring *mā wadda'aka* passage is revealed to him. But in spite of the Quranic link, the story in this specific setting was denied wide circulation, and was never recorded in any of the *ḥadīth* compilations. Again, what was meant to be a dramatic presentation of Muḥammad's road to prophethood did not conform to the rigid concept of the Prophet's *'iṣma* as an eternal immunity from error or disbelief, and hence from lack of confidence in his Lord. The versions preferred by the compilers suppressed Muḥammad's lack of confidence during the *fatra*, attributing it to other persons like Khadīja, but mainly to his polytheistic foes. Thus the story was transformed from one about personal prophetic agony into one of persecution.

Persecution

The universal theme of persecution, known especially from Christian contexts, was made in Islam the leading theme of the story of Muḥammad's emergence in Mecca. The role of the tormenting foes, as well as of the few supporters, was assigned to members of the local Meccan tribe, Quraysh. The selection of the figures for the various roles at times reflects political tensions within medieval Islamic society which were read back into the conditions of Muḥammad's Mecca. But the theme of persecution was adapted not only to Meccan surroundings, but also to Islamic textual models, i.e. to the Quran. This was quite an easy and successful task, because the Quran itself already contains detailed descriptions of persecution suffered by the Quranic prophet. The process of adaptation to this scripture can be followed from its very beginning, in traditions in which the Quranic element is still absent, through traditions dominated by such models.

In the story about Muḥammad's hiding period, the non-Quranic stratum is focussed on the figure of ʻUmar as Muḥammad's most energetic supporter, at whose encouragement the hiding period is brought to an end. The Quranic level of the same episode links the transition from hiding to public preaching to the Quranic *iṣdaʻ* passage (15:94) and especially to the *ʻashīra* passage (26:214).

The traditions elaborate on the contents of the *ʻashīra* address (Chapter 7). Its various versions reflect dogmatic concepts such as free will, and political situations, such as the Shīʻī attempts to prove ʻAlī's right to leadership of the Islamic community after Muḥammad. The theme of persecution comes forth mainly in the reaction of the Meccans to the *ʻashīra* address. They are represented by Abū Lahab, whose name was selected due to its occurrence in the Quran as standing for a person who is condemned to Hell. In fact, the story of the revelation of Sūrat al-Masad (111), which contains his name, was incorporated into the narrative of the *ʻashīra* address, as well as into other scenes of persecution (Chapter 8).

The person who was assigned the role of Muḥammad's supporter is Abū Ṭālib, ʻAlī's father (Chapter 9). There is a certain symmetry between him and Abū Lahab, both being paternal uncles of the Prophet. Abū Ṭālib features in several versions of the *ʻashīra* address as defending Muḥammad against Abū

Lahab's abuses, and his image is certainly a reflection of a Shīʿī attitude. Abū Ṭālib's support for the Prophet is also described in another scene which was also linked to the Quran. In it he is approached by the leaders of Quraysh, whose lines of protest against his support for the Prophet consist of verses from Sūrat Ṣād (38). The latter scene remained outside the mainstream *ḥadīth* compilations, which only contain versions in which Abū Ṭālib's image has changed from Muḥammad's sponsor into an old Meccan clinging to the paganism of his ancestors. In these versions the basic Shīʿī bias has been neutralized.

A special group of traditions (Chapter 10) elaborates on a specific aspect of persecution, namely, isolation caused by rejection. This theme was linked to some Quranic models as well, which turned the story from one about isolation into one about satanic temptation. The latter theme is also universal by origin, but it seems to have found its way into Muslim tradition via the Quran. The Quranic passages about the temptation of prophets by men and Satan (17:73–74, 22:52) were applied to the story of human torment, thus heightening the drama, but this did not gain the story any wider circulation. In spite of the firm Quranic link, the story was rejected by all compilers of *ḥadīth* due to the insinuation that the prophet might be placed under temporary satanic control. This is a unique case in which a group of traditions are rejected only after having been subjected to Quranic models, and as direct result of this adjustment. What was accepted was merely a sterilized version adduced for a legal issue of prostration (*sujūd*) during the recitation of the Quran.

Salvation

The theme of salvation in the context of Muḥammad's life brings persecution to an end through emigration (*hijra*). Muḥammad's emigration to Medina forms the finale of the Meccan chapter in the Prophet's life, and brings him definite salvation from persecution.

Two kinds of traditions applied the notion of salvation to Muḥammad's biography. In one of them the Prophet is the recipient of salvation, whereas in the other he figures as its source. Both types tell the story of the negotiations between Muḥammad and the Anṣār during the meetings at al-ʿAqaba, which paved the way for Muḥammad's *hijra*. As a recipient of salvation, the Prophet is the rejected Meccan outcast who seeks shelter in Medina. Some traditions emphasize God's blessing in bringing salvation to the rejected Muḥammad through the unification of the Anṣār under the banner of Islam. Quranic links were easily provided to this group through verses glorifying God's role in bringing together the hearts of the believers (8:63, 3:103). Other versions shift the focus to the

Anṣār as the immediate source of salvation. Here Quranic links were again easily established through verses glorifying the Anṣār as a source of asylum (8:72 and 74).

As an origin of salvation, the Prophet emerges as the messianic saviour whose leadership results in redemption of the local Medinan inhabitants from their miserable situation. A sub-group of these traditions are those which describe the various types of pledge of allegiance (*bay'a*), thus confirming Muḥammad's position as a leader. Some of them incorporate into the story the Quranic model of *bay'a* as formulated in 60:12.

Most versions of the 'Aqaba meetings recur in the *muṣannaf* compilations, where they serve either the purpose of *faḍā'il* (of the Anṣār), or the purpose of legal precedent (the *bay'a*).

In sum, our study of the above universal (biblical) themes has revealed some basic patterns of adaptation to Islamic models which, when successful, gained these themes entrance into the canonical *ḥadīth* compilations. Such adaptation proceeded on two levels: that of the literary structure of the themes, and that of their dogmatic and political message.

On the level of literary structure, the themes were converted to Arabian (which is to say, Meccan) scenery: leading parts in the story were assigned to Meccan figures, and events were told against the Meccan environment and surroundings. On the same level of literary structure, adaptation to Quranic models also took place: extracts from the Quran were made part of the basically non-Quranic narrative framework.

On the level of dogmatic message, the universal themes were adapted to the image of Muhammad as the immaculate prophet and the ideal leader. On the level of political message, they were adapted to the *faḍā'il*, or "virtues", of prominent Companions and tribal/factional groups, in particular the Muhājirūn and the Anṣār.

The most crucial element in this process of adaptation proved to be the dogmatic one; the extent to which the dogmatic message of the universal themes was adapted to the gradually emerging and increasingly dominant image of the Prophet, determined their circulation in the sources. Themes which failed to conform to this idealized perception of the Prophet Muhammad as the most perfect man on earth were denied wide circulation, especially in the canonical *muṣannaf* collections of *ḥadīth*. As it was these collections, more than other types of literary compilations, which served as the venue for the authoritative formulation of an Islamic sense of spiritual and legal identity in Umayyad and early 'Abbāsid times, the on-going process of selection represented by these collections was of crucial importance. Themes, motifs, and ideas rejected by these collections did not become part of mainstream Islamic thinking.

On the whole, the process of adaptation reflects the self-image of medieval Islamic society, which perceived the Islamic heritage as the most ideal substitute for the older monotheistic dispensations—civilisations and cultures which, by divine will and plan, were now superseded.

14

Asbāb al-nuzūl

I

THE FOREGOING CHAPTERS have shown that the text of the Quran plays a dominant role in the traditions about the Prophet's life. A closer examination of this role will reveal that the usual approach of Islamicists towards the function of the Quran in the *sīra* calls for modification. As a rule, these scholars are of the conviction that the *sīra* stories were designed to provide *asbāb al-nuzūl*, the "occasions of revelation" of the Quran.[1] These stories represent, in their view, no more than an exegetic elaboration on the often-obscure text of the Quran. Watt, for instance, in his study of the materials of which the early biography of Muḥammad consists, states: "The Quranic allusions had to be elaborated into complete stories and the background filled in if the main ideas were to be impressed on the minds of simple men."[2] Wansbrough has a similar view. He is able to detect in the early biographies of Muḥammad an "exegetic" narrative technique "in which extracts (serial and isolated) from scripture provided the framework for extended *narratio*...."[3] A similar observation has been made by Rippin, who declares: "Narrative expansion of a Qur'ānic verse is a more frequent feature in the *sabab*, ranging from the most simple setting of the scene to a full elaboration, spinning an entire narrative structure around a Qur'ānic verse."[4] Following Wansbrough, Rippin is particularly certain of the exegetic nature of those *asbāb* which deal with pre-Islamic conditions in Arabia, the *ḥums*, for example. He says that this type of information "is totally exegetic: what has been 'preserved' is only what is relevant to understanding the Qur'ān and *ḥadīth*."[5]

The view that what came to be known as the *asbāb al-nuzūl* material is merely the product of an exegetic elaboration on the Quranic text, actually repre-

---

[1]On this kind of material, see Andrew Rippin, "The Exegetical Genre *Asbāb al-Nuzūl*: a Bibliographical and Terminological Survey", *Bulletin of the School of Oriental and African Studies* 48 (1985), 1–15.

[2] W. Montgomery Watt, "The Materials Used by Ibn Isḥāq", in Bernard Lewis *et al.*, eds., *Historians of the Middle East* (London, 1962), 25.

[3] See Wansbrough, *Sectarian Milieu*, 2.

[4] Andrew Rippin, "The Function of *Asbāb al-Nuzūl* in Qur'ānic Exegesis", *Bulletin of the School of Oriental and African Studies* 51 (1988), 4.

[5] *Ibid.*, 9.

sents the consensus among Western Islamicists.[6] This would imply that all traditions in the *sīra* alluding to the Quran had their origin in the Quranic verse itself, round which they were supposedly built as an exegetic expansion.

But there is much that is misleading in this outlook. To begin with, one should bear in mind that although the traditions known as *asbāb al-nuzūl* occur in the collections of *tafsīr*—for example, al-Ṭabarī's—their birthplace is in the *sīra,* where they do not yet function as *asbāb*. These traditions only became *asbāb* when the Quran exegetes gleaned them from the *sīra* and recorded them in the *tafsīr* of the Quran. Within the realm of the *sīra*, these traditions are still without an exegetic function, because none of them is built round the Quranic verses which occur in it. This has become clear in the course of the preceding chapters. It has been demonstrated that none of the Quranic verses which appear in the biography of Muḥammad can be regarded as the primary source of the story. The basic narrative framework is always independent of Quranic verses and ideas; the Quranic data seem to have been incorporated into the *sīra* story secondarily, for the sake of embellishment and authorization. In other words, no process of spinning a narrative framework round a Quranic verse seems to have taken place. Hence, the material known as *asbāb al-nuzūl* actually consists of independent non-Quranic *sīra* material which gained its Quranic links at a secondary stage, and only then became appropriately exegetic data which the exegetes could use for their own *tafsīr* purposes.

The Quran does not belong to the literary hard core of *sīra* material, which means that the holy scripture was not considered an appropriate tool for the literary refining of the earliest *sīra* traditions. It is significant that early Islamic poetry was also quite independent of Quranic patterns, being influenced more by the pre-Islamic *qaṣīda* than by anything else.[7] The *qaṣīda*, not the Quran, is indeed utilized sweepingly in the early *sīra* reports.[8] Quranic materials only began to be applied to the non-Quranic basic narrative framework when the sacred scripture became a standard source of guidance. At this stage, the story-tellers could promote the Islamic status of their traditions (originally suspect of biblical

---

[6] See also Peters, "The Quest of the Historical Muhammad", 301: "...medieval Muslim scholars were re-creating the 'occasion' by working backwards out of the Qur'ānic verses themselves...."

[7] See A.M. Zubaydi, "The Impact of the Qur'ān and Ḥadīth on Medieval Arabic Literature", in A.F.L. Beeston *et al.*, eds., *Arabic Literature to the End of the Umayyad Period* (Cambridge, 1983), 322.

[8] On the poetry in the *sīra*, see already Josef Horovitz, "Die poetischen Einlagen der *Sīra*", *Islamica* 2 (1926–27), 308–12. And see also Walid 'Arafat, "Early Critics of the Authenticity of the Poetry of the *Sīra*", *Bulletin of the School of Oriental and African Studies* 21 (1958), 453–63; M.J. Kister, "On a New Edition of the *Dīwān* of Ḥassān b. Thābit", *Bulletin of the School of Oriental and African Studies* 39 (1976), 265–68.

influence) by extending to them the divine authority of the Quran. This was achieved by dragging various passages from the scripture into the narrative. The same Quranic extract could actually be installed in different scenes of Muḥammad's life.

However, although the passages from the canon were imported to the *sīra* in a non-exegetic process, their new setting did produce exegesis. The clear *sīra* context in which the Quranic verses were embedded eventually provided them with what the exegetes considered their *asbāb*. Some of the *asbāb*, but not necessarily all of them, were later gleaned from the *sīra* and incorporated into the specialized *tafsīr* and *asbāb al-nuzūl* compilations.

A scrutiny of the evidence in each and every one of the foregoing chapters will confirm the non-Quranic origin of the early *sīra* material, and clarify that the conventional view about the constitution of the *asbāb al-nuzūl* traditions should be abandoned once and for all.

1. The Biblical Annunciation

In this chapter, the most typical case of a Quranic passage being interpolated into an originally non-Quranic basic framework is that of 33:45. This passage appears in Medinan traditions as a part of the "biblical" description of Muḥammad (based on Isaiah 42:2), while it is not included in parallel versions of the same description in Syrian and Iraqi traditions. The Quranic passage was added so as to bestow Quranic authority upon the biblical attestation of Muḥammad, and as soon as the passage was interpolated into the description, the latter became suitable exegetic material. As we have seen, it reappears in some commentaries on 33:45. The Quranic passage itself does not belong to the basic framework of the Prophet's biblical annunciation, and the traditions were certainly not built round it.

The same applies to the rest of the Quranic verses appearing in the *sīra* in the context of attestation. The idea of the *ummī* prophet is basically non-Quranic, and features in independent Iraqi and Ḥijāzī traditions which do not allude to the relevant Quranic passage (7:157). They rather draw directly on the biblical *goy* passages. The Quranic *ummī* passage itself is only adduced for the purpose of Quranic confirmation (Ibn Isḥāq), never forming part of the traditions themselves.

Similarly, the various traditions in which Quran 2:89 is alluded to, are not built round the verse. They use the verse as a Quranic illustration of the independent theme of the messianic expectations of the Jews and their conflict with their Arab neighbours. The traditions came into being in the realm of the

Prophet's biography, and as usual were eventually picked up by the exegetes, who recorded them as *asbāb* in the *tafsīr* of this Quranic verse.

Quran 2:129, in which Abraham beseeches God to send a messenger to act among his descendants, was only added to prophetic statements of self-attestation, never forming a starting point for exegetic elaborations. But again, this did not prevent the exegetes from including the traditions employing 2:129 in the *tafsīr* of this verse.

2. The Arabian Annunciation

In the traditions discussed in this chapter no Quranic allusions are found, and the entire chapter reveals the basic non-Quranic level of the theme of annunciation. Its origins are sacred scriptures of monotheistic scholars, dreams, or demonic sources, and the various anecdotes are bereft of Quranic allusions. The story-tellers seem to have discovered no relevant passages in the canon which could be fitted into the narrative. Occasionally, however, the theme of the annunciation of Aḥmad is inserted into the predictions of some hermits, where it provides the story with an indirect Quranic link.

3. Initiation: the Opening of Muḥammad's Breast

The story of the opening of Muḥammad's breast was not built round the first verse of Sūrat al-Sharḥ (94). The vocabulary of this verse was merely applied to some Iraqi versions of the existing story of the opening, thus subjecting the tale to Quranic models. The Quranic link caused the episode to become one of the suggested interpretations of Quran 94:1, and from the third century AH onwards, the episode began to appear in the *tafsīr*s of this verse.

4. Guidance: from Polytheism to Monotheism

This chapter provides a most vivid example of the transition of material from the *sīra* into Quranic exegesis. In this case it is the idea of "the religion of his people" (*dīn qawmihi*) and the divine guidance of Muḥammad to monotheism. In the *sīra* this occurs in a clearly non-Quranic context (Ibn Isḥāq, etc.), and from the *sīra* it was imported into the exegesis of Quran 93:7 (the *ḍāll* verse) and 94:2 (*wizr*), where, however, it was denied wide circulation due to dogmatic problems.

5. The Khadīja–Waraqa Story

In the Khadīja–Waraqa story two different Quranic passages, Sūrat al-Fātiḥa (1), and the *iqra'* passage (96:1–5), were secondarily incorporated into the basic non-Quranic narrative framework. The former appears in a Kūfan tradition, the latter in several Medinan and Meccan traditions; the non-Quranic story was preserved in other Ḥijāzī traditions. The incorporation of the *iqra'* passage into the story was done by means of the device of the linking word (*iqra'*). The Khadīja–Waraqa tale, with these Quranic passages built into it, became apt material for the Quran exegetes in their ceaseless quest for *asbāb*. For the exegetes, these traditions reflect what really happened when the relevant Quranic verses were revealed to Muḥammad. In fact, even modern Islamicists have taken these traditions for historical records. Watt, for example, refers to the traditions with the *iqra'* passage, stating: "There are no effective objections to the almost universal view of Muslim scholars that this is the first part of the Qur'ān to be revealed."[9] In making such a statement Watt follows the historical approach already established in Nöldeke–Schwally's *Geschichte des Qorans*. In making such a historical statement these scholars seem to have forgotten their own (wrong) hypothesis that *asbāb* are no more than exegetic expansions on the Quran.

6. The Lapse of Revelation (*Fatrat al-waḥy*)

Some of the Medinan traditions of the Khadīja–Waraqa story contain the *Muddaththir* passage (74:1–2), which, once fitted into the tale, began marking the end of the interval of revelations, the *fatra*. However, in other Medinan as well as Iraqi traditions, it is rather the *mā wadda'aka* passage (93:3) that brings the *fatra* to its end. Both passages were added to the basic non-Quranic framework by means of some linking words. When this was accomplished, these passages acquired a concrete context which eventually was used as a *sabab* by the exegetes, who recorded various versions of the story in the *tafsīr* of these Quranic passages.

7. Declaration: the *'Ashīra* Scene

The Quranic passage which was fitted into the narrative of the declaration of the mission is the *'ashīra* verse (26:214). It is employed in Iraqi traditions, and more elaborate traditions with the same verse are Ḥijāzī and Syrian, as well as

---

[9] Watt, *M/Mecca*, 47.

Iraqi. Again, the story was not built round the verse, which was only added to the existing non-Quranic story. The latter was circulated in Meccan, Medinan, and Baṣran traditions dealing with Dār al-Arqam and with 'Umar's conversion. The same basic story received another Quranic passage which was fitted into it, namely, the *iṣda'* verse (15:94). The interpolation of these verses into the story of declaration created suitable material for the Quran exegetes, who recorded the traditions in the commentary on these passages.

8. The Reaction of Abū Lahab

The case of Sūrat al-Masad (111) is perhaps the most enlightening example of the interpolation of a Quranic passage into various disparate scenes which originally did not contain it. The story of the revelation of this *sūra* was applied in most cases to the *'ashīra* scene (in Kūfan and Medinan traditions), in order to illustrate the enmity with which Muḥammad's call was met. But the same *sūra* reappears in other scenes, all with a basic non-Quranic setting. One is the markets scene where Abū Lahab mocks the Prophet in front of his audience. Some of the traditions with this setting (Kūfan and Medinan) do not allude to the revelation of the *sūra*, but nevertheless reappear in some commentaries on it. In other versions (Medinan) the actual revelation of the *sūra* is added to the same scene by means of linking words derived from the Quranic *tabbat*.

Another scene, originally non-Quranic, is the test to which Muḥammad is put by Abū Lahab, in which the Prophet discloses his opinion about the fate of his grandfather 'Abd al-Muṭṭalib. Again, linking words from *tabbat* make the revelation of the *sūra* part of this event.

Abū Lahab's personal name, 'Abd al-'Uzzā, caused the *sūra* to be connected with originally non-Quranic episodes about the goddess al-'Uzzā and her custodian; the linking words in this case were derived from *yadā*. There is also a story in which the same *sūra* is connected to the boycott of Banū Hāshim by Quraysh, again with *yadā* as the origin of the linking words.

9. The Reaction of Abū Ṭālib

The visit the leaders of Quraysh pay to Abū Ṭālib to protest against Muḥammad's attack on their ancestors and idols demonstrates another typical case of a basic narrative framework into which various Quranic passages were incorporated. Apart from versions (Syrian and Ḥijāzī) in which the visit retains its plain form, with no Quranic links, there are versions (Kūfan and Medinan) where the story is associated with the revelation of Sūrat Ṣād (38). The opening passage of this *sūra* became the lines uttered by the leaders.

10. Isolation: the Satanic Verses

The story of isolation is revealed in both its non-Quranic and Quranic levels in the three versions of ʻUrwa. The basic narrative framework refers to what is labelled in Version 1 as the first and second *fitna*. After massive Islamisation of the Meccans (their *sujūd* with the Prophet in Version 2), isolation occurs due to the instigation of the non-Muslim Meccan leaders. This brings about the *hijra* to Abyssinia (first *fitna*). After a temporary improvement of conditions in Mecca and the return of the refugees from Abyssinia, persecution is renewed (second *fitna*). Into this framework, Quranic verses and ideas were incorporated which turned the story into one of temptation (Version 3). The verses are 17:73–74 and 22:52. These are coupled with the satanic verses (originally a pre-Islamic *talbiya*), which in turn are linked to the verses about the "Daughters of God" (53:19–23). All these Quranic references, including the satanic verses, were built into the basic non-Quranic narrative framework of the two *fitna*s. In the combined setting, the affair of Satan's temptation became the outcome of isolation (first *fitna*), and the abrogation of the satanic verses became the reason of renewed isolation (second *fitna*).

Whereas both the Quranic and non-Quranic levels of the story are represented in Medinan traditions of ʻUrwa and others, the Quranic level is exhibited also in Baṣran and Kūfan traditions.

11. The ʻAqaba Meetings

In the story of the ʻAqaba meetings, the line between the Quranic and non-Quranic levels is very clear. The Quranic versions with the women's pledge (adduced from 60:12) are distinct from the non-Quranic versions with the other types of *bayʻa*. Unlike all former cases, the present one represents an interpolation of Quranic ideas into the *sīra* for purposes connected not so much to the image of Muḥammad, as to Islamic law.

This chapter contains an example indicating that the Quran exegetes did not limit themselves to gleaning from the *sīra* passages which already had Quranic extracts built into them. Sometimes they extracted from the story of the Prophet's life traditions which had no built-in Quranic link, but otherwise fitted the exegetic needs of the commentators. Such is the case of Quran 8:63 and 3:103. These verses were never given any particular role in the *sīra*, but *sīra* episodes were nevertheless incorporated into their exegesis. These verses remind the believers that God has drawn their hearts together, and the exegetes found the (non-Quranic) *sīra* traditions about the ʻAqaba meetings most suitable for the exegesis of these verses. Here again, the stories were definitely not built round the Quranic verses: they were imported intact from the *sīra* and incorporated into Quranic exegesis.

In sum, nothing in the early biographies of Muḥammad seems to corroborate the belief that the material which came to be known as *asbāb al-nuzūl* had its origin in the exegetic expansion of Quranic verses. Its real birthplace is the non-Quranic narrative framework of the *sīra*. This framework consists of biblical materials, pre-Islamic epics, and genuinely Islamic traditions about the Prophet and his Companions, all of which were interwoven within a complex biography which gained its final authorization through its Quranic attire.

15

The Evidence of the *Isnāds*

THE HISTORICAL APPROACH of traditional orientalism has long provided the critical foundations for the study of the contents of Muslim traditions, as well as of their *isnāds*. Islamicists have always concerned themselves with the problem of the "authenticity" of the *isnāds*, i.e. whether or not the Prophet or the Companions "really" transmitted what is attributed to them.[1] But an *isnād*, like its *matn* (the text itself), seems only to form part of the literary structure of the tradition. The *isnād* is always designed to make the tradition look authentic, and going into the question of whether or not the *isnād* is really authentic seems futile.

Those Islamicists who were convinced that *isnāds* contained fabrications formulated a neat theory about their supposed development. The theory gained wide popularity among scholars believing to be able to decide by it what in the *isnāds* is authentic and what is not. This chapter sets out to refute this theory, not in order to prove the authenticity of *isnāds*, but rather to show that they could have come into existence much earlier than is usually presumed.

Let us begin with the theory. Its first manifestation is found in Goldziher's *Muslim Studies*. Here he states:

> It is not at all rare in the literature of traditions that sayings are ascribed to the Prophet which for a long time circulated in Islam under the authority of another name. So-called *aḥādīth mawqūfa*, i.e. sayings traced back to companions or even successors, were very easily transformed into *aḥādīth marfū'a*, i.e. sayings traced back to the Prophet, by simply adding without much scruple a few names at random which were necessary to complete the chain.[2]

Goldziher's observation implies that as a rule *aḥādīth mawqūfa* are earlier than *aḥādīth marfū'a*. Schacht developed this approach into a whole system based on the conviction that *isnāds* grow backwards, from the original creator of the tradition (the "common link"[3]) back to higher authorities, i.e. Successors,

[1] For a vivid demonstration of the debate over the authenticity of prophetic *isnāds*, see Patricia Crone, *Roman, Provincial and Islamic Law* (Cambridge, 1987), 29–34.

[2] Goldziher, *Muslim Studies*, II, 148.

[3] Joseph Schacht, *The Origins of Muhammadan Jurisprudence* (repr. Oxford, 1979), 171.

Companions, and finally, the Prophet himself. In the chapter "The Evidence of *Isnāds*" in his *Origins*, Schacht says:

> ...the backwards growth of *isnāds* in particular is identical with the projection of doctrines back to higher authorities. Generally speaking, we can say that the most perfect and complete *isnāds* are the latest.[4]

Schacht's theory stipulates that the latest traditions are those equipped with complete prophetic *isnāds*, i.e. those uninterrupted chains which end with the Prophet himself. In Schacht's own words: "We shall have to conclude that, generally and broadly speaking, traditions from Companions and Successors are earlier than those from the Prophet."[5] Prophetic traditions, according to Schacht, came into being as late as "towards the middle of the second century, in opposition to the slightly earlier traditions from Companions and other authorities."[6] Although Schacht spoke mainly of legal *ḥadīth*, he was convinced that his findings held good for traditions "relating to history" as well.[7]

The hypothesis of the backwards growth of *isnāds* has been taken up without much hesitation by more recent Islamicists (including myself[8]), who have elaborated on Schacht's theories.[9] Even scholars who do not consider themselves members of the Schachtian school have adopted it. For instance, Michael Cook, a critic of Schacht, says nevertheless that "...as everyone knows, *isnāds* grow backwards."[10] For Cook, the supposed backwards growth is a reliable dating tool. He says: "Where one *isnād* reaches only to A and a second goes back through him to his teacher, then given the values of the system we are entitled to suspect that the higher *isnād* is secondary, rather than the other way round."[11]

However, the supposed backwards growth of *isnāds* does not seem to be corroborated by textual evidence. The material assembled by Schacht only demonstrates that incomplete *isnāds* coexist with complete ones, but there is no

---

[4] *Ibid.*, 165.
[5] *Ibid.*, 3.
[6] *Ibid.*, 4–5.
[7] *Ibid.*, 175.
[8] See my "Exegesis and Ḥadīth: the Case of the Seven Mathānī", in G.R. Hawting and Abdul-Kader A. Shareef, eds., *Approaches to the Qur'ān* (London and New York, 1993), 152.
[9] Special notice should be taken of the numerous works of G.H.A. Juynboll, who in the field of "common link" theories, stands as the clear successor to Schacht. See especially his *Muslim Tradition: Studies in Chronology, Provenance and Authorship of Early Ḥadīth* (Cambridge, 1983).
[10] Michael Cook, *Early Muslim Dogma* (Cambridge, 1981), 108.
[11] *Ibid.*

positive evidence that the complete ones grew backwards out of the incomplete ones. Supposedly positive evidence of the backwards growth of *isnād*s has been adduced by Cook, but in fact, the case proves nothing of the sort. Cook's example consists of an anecdote in which the attribution of a certain legal tradition to the Companion Ibn 'Abbās by the Successor Ṭāwūs ibn Kaysān (Yemeni d. AH 101) is doubted by some other traditionists.[12] This does not indicate backwards growth of *isnād*s as assumed by Cook: it only shows that traditions attributed to Companions were now and then suspected by other Muslims of being the Successor's own invention. Even if the suspicion is justified, the fact remains that the tradition itself could have been circulated from the very outset on the authority of a Companion, in our case, Ibn 'Abbās. In fact, the name of Ibn 'Abbās always formed part of the *isnād*s of all parallel versions of the tradition at hand.[13] The critics tried to censor the *isnād* and omit Ibn 'Abbās from it. If anything, the anecdote adduced by Cook indicates potential shrinking of *isnād*s, not their growth.[14]

Neither does the supposed backwards growth of *isnād*s seem to be evinced by the material discussed in the present book. The most striking fact that leaps to the eye is that most *isnād*s occurring in the preceding chapters contain a Companion. Some of them are prophetic and some are not, but neither type indicates a history of backwards growth. The prophetic *isnād*s do not seem to have grown backwards out of the non-prophetic ones, because in either type the Companion (as well as Successor) is usually different. In other words, there is no evidence that the name of the Prophet was merely added—to use Goldziher's terminology—to an already existing Companion *isnād*. The name of the Prophet seems rather to have been part of the hard core of the *isnād* in which it occurs.

Likewise, there is no evidence that the Companion's name was merely added to an already existing Successor *isnād*. In the preceding chapters there is no

---

[12] *Ibid.* The anecdote is found in Aḥmad, *'Ilal*, II, no. 1934 (Cook has used an older edition).

[13] The editor of Aḥmad's *'Ilal* refers the reader to Bayhaqī, *Sunan*, V, 171.

[14] Cook has put the theories of Schacht to the test in his article "Eschatology and the Dating of Traditions", *Princeton Papers in Near Eastern Studies* 1 (1992), 25–47. The diagrams attached to the article do not seem to exhibit even one clear case of the backwards growth of *isnād*s. The higher parts of the prophetic strand in the diagram on p. 31 exists parallel to the non-prophetic ones, and they only meet in relatively late "common links" which could be regarded as the origin of either type. Note especially the diagram of the prophetic tradition on p. 34. Cook himself has admitted (p. 33) that this tradition is "never found ascribed to any other authority", which means that there is no evidence that it ever grew backwards out of a non-prophetic tradition.

case of two parallel *isnād*s of the same tradition, with the same Successor in both, and the Companion only in one. The absence of such cases means that the name of the Companion was never simply added to an existing Successor *isnād*, but rather was part of the original hard core of the *isnād* in which it occurs. Even if one could find incomplete versions in which the Companion is missing, the equally logical possibility would always remain that his name was omitted from the "perfect" *isnād*, rather than added to the "imperfect" *isnād*.

Since the names of the Prophet and the Companions seem to form part of the hard core of the *isnād*s in which they appear, there is no reliable evidence to indicate that these *isnād*s came into being only towards the middle of the second century, as proposed by Schacht. There is nothing to exclude the possibility that the bulk of traditions with prophetic and Companion *isnād*s were put into circulation during the generation of the Companion to which a given tradition is attributed, i.e. already during the first century AH.

But even if a given tradition came into being as early as the Companion's own generation, the tradition itself is not necessarily "authentic", as assumed by some critics of Schacht.[15] The Companion himself may have nothing to do with the prophetic traditions transmitted on his authority, or alternatively, he may have approved of whatever sayings people circulated on his authority. But the question of authenticity of *isnād*s is not our focus of interest; our aim is rather to refute the theory of their backwards growth. Once this is fulfilled, prophetic and Companion *isnād*s can no longer be automatically considered to be later than the less complete ones.

In fact, incomplete *isnād*s are not necessarily earlier than the complete ones. For example, the *mursal* type of prophetic *isnād* (that in which the name of a Companion is missing) must not be considered earlier than the complete sort. The *mursal* type may sometimes indicate a later stage of transmission, well after the extinction of the Companions. By that time, traditions about the Prophet could be related with no Companion's name as intermediate authority, due to lack of personal contact with the Companions. The incomplete *isnād*s may also reflect an individual approach in which the Successor expresses his own independent knowledge (or opinion) about the Prophet.

In sum, the Companion forms part of the hard core of the *isnād* in which he appears. That this should be the case is quite natural. Any informant anywhere will attempt to base his information on contemporary evidence, and preferably

---

[15] Attempts at refuting Schacht and at proving the authenticity of traditions from Companions, and even from the Prophet himself, have been made in the various studies of Harald Motzki. See e.g. his "The *Muṣannaf* of ʻAbd al-Razzāq al-Ṣanʻānī as a Source of Authentic *Aḥādīh* of the First Century A.H.", *Journal of Near Eastern Studies* 50 (1991), 1–21.

on the evidence of the acquaintances of the hero about whom he speaks. The biography of Muḥammad forms no exception to this rule. His Companions were, from the very beginning, the most obvious persons on whose authority the traditions about the Prophet could be circulated. Again, this is only a literary, not a historical observation. The Companions themselves may have had nothing to do with the traditions with which the biographers of Muḥammad credited them, even if this process of attribution had begun as early as their own lifetimes.

However, our observations do not mean that backwards growth of *isnād*s never took place. Muslim critics of *ḥadīth* do refer to traditionists who might turn a *mursal isnād* into a *marfū'* one. But the "raising" of the *isnād*s is not the normal way in which complete *isnād*s came into being, as argued by Goldziher and Schacht. This was rather an exceptional deed condemned by the critics as the work of dishonest traditionists.[16] The honest traditionist was the one who never tampered with the higher parts of the *isnād*s of traditions he transmitted to his own disciples.

To corroborate the above observations, let us take the evidence of the preceding chapters one by one.

1. The Biblical Annunciation

Most traditions about the biblical annunciation are of Companions, who always seem to belong to the hard core of their *isnād*s.

The "streets" traditions constitute the most composite group of traditions of biblical attestation. Among them are such which are not of Companions, but only of Successors. The latter are:

Ka'b al-Aḥbār (regarded by some as a Companion).

Wahb ibn Munabbih.

Qatāda.

None of these names appears elsewhere in the Companion *isnād*s, which excludes any possibility of backwards growth. In other words, there is no evi-

[16] Ibn Ḥibbān, *Ṣaḥīḥ*, I, 152.

dence that names of Companions were merely added to existing *isnād*s of Successors.

The Companion traditions of the "streets" group are far more numerous, and are mostly non-prophetic. They bear the names of the following Companions:

'Ā'isha (quoted by 'Ayzār ibn Ḥurayth).

'Abdallāh ibn Salām (quoted in one variant by Zayd ibn Aslam, and in another by 'Aṭā' ibn Yasār. Sometimes the name of Ka'b al-Aḥbār appears in this version as a confirming party, but he is not part of the *isnād*, only of the *matn*).

'Abdallāh ibn 'Amr ibn al-'Āṣ (quoted by 'Aṭā' ibn Yasār).

Abū Hurayra (quoted by Abū Ṣāliḥ).

'Abdallāh ibn 'Amr. His *isnād* is identical with one of the *isnād*s of 'Abdallāh ibn Salām; both Companions are quoted by the same Successor ('Aṭā' ibn Yasār), who in turn is also quoted by the same traditionist (Hilāl). In this case as well there is no evidence of backwards growth of *isnād*s, merely of the replacement of one Companion by another.

'Abdallāh ibn Mas'ūd (quoted by 'Alqama ibn Qays). His tradition is prophetic, and contains the biblical description of Muḥammad without labelling it as such. This *isnād* is not the result of the supposed backwards growth of any of the former non-prophetic *isnād*s of Companions, for the simple reason that the name of 'Abdallāh ibn Mas'ūd does not appear among the Companions of the non-prophetic versions.

Among the traditions about the prediction of the *ummī* prophet, there is one with a prophetic *isnād* (of the Companion Abū Umāma al-Bāhilī). But most of these traditions are non-prophetic. Some have a Companion *isnād* of Ibn 'Abbās (quoted at one instance by 'Aṭā' ibn Abī Rabāḥ, at another by Sa'īd ibn Jubayr), but most non-prophetic *isnād*s stop at the Successor level ('Āṣim ibn 'Umar ibn Qatāda, Wahb ibn Munabbih, Muqātil ibn Ḥayyān, al-Sha'bī, Muḥammad ibn Ka'b al-Quraẓī, Ka'b al-Aḥbār). The names of the Successors do not recur in the Companion *isnād*s (prophetic and non-prophetic), which again excludes backwards growth.

In the group of traditions of self-attestation, the presence of prophetic traditions increases considerably. Their content seems to reflect an advanced stage of development, since the Bible has been replaced in them by the Quran as the basic document of attestation. But again, the *isnād*s of these prophetic traditions do not seem to be the result of any process of backwards growth. All of them seem to have been prophetic from the first moment the traditions were put into circulation.

Let us take, for instance, the traditions where the Prophet identifies himself in the Quranic prayer of Abraham. The *isnād*s of these traditions are all prophetic from the very outset, and they are all independent of one other, i.e. each of them is circulated through its own Companion. They fall into two groups: complete and *mursal*. The complete *isnād*s contain two Syrian Companions and one Medinan:

Abū Umāma al-Bāhilī.

ʿIrbāḍ ibn Sāriya.

Shaddād ibn Aws (his tradition has been discussed in Chapter 3, apropos of the opening of Muḥammad's breast).

These versions are complete not only in their *isnād*s, but also in their *matn*s. Besides Muḥammad's statement about the prayer of Abraham, they have his statement about the good tidings of Jesus and the vision of his mother, including sometimes the opening of his breast, as well as his statement about Adam's clay. The *mursal* cases of the same statement of the Prophet which lack a Companion's name are lacking in their *matn* as well. They only convey Muḥammad's statement about the prayer of Abraham, and occasionally also his statement about Jesus. One has a Kūfan *isnād* ending with Ḍaḥḥāk ibn Muzāḥim; another is related by al-Wāqidī on the authority of some Medinan Successors.

But there is one exception to this neat correspondence of *isnād* and *matn*. In the version recorded by Ibn Isḥāq (his tradition is also discussed in the chapter about the opening of Muḥammad's breast), a complete *matn* has an incomplete *isnād*, ending with the Syrian Successor Khālid ibn Maʿdān, who only relies on an anonymous group of Muḥammad's Companions. The *matn*, however, is complete: it includes the prayer of Abraham, the good tidings of Jesus, and the vision of the mother, as well as the opening of Muḥammad's breast.

No backwards growth of *isnād*s can be detected in the various *isnād*s of this tradition, for the simple reason that they all end with the Prophet. Besides, there is no clear indication that the incomplete *isnād*s are earlier than the complete ones. Although most of the *mursal*s are attached to incomplete *matn*s, one of them does precede a complete *matn*. Therefore, "complete" and "incomplete" must remain a literary observation, without immediate chronological implications. It should also be noted that none of the Successors of the *mursal* type reappears in the Companion *isnād*s, which again excludes backwards growth.

The greatest number of prophetic traditions of self-attestation contain lists of Muḥammad's names and appellations. These were circulated on the authority of the following Companions:

'Awf ibn Mālik al-Ashja'ī (quoted by Jubayr ibn Nufayr).

Ḥudhayfa ibn al-Yamān (quoted by Zirr ibn Ḥubaysh).

Jubayr ibn Muṭ'im (quoted by Nāfi' ibn Jubayr and by Muḥammad ibn Jubayr).

Abū Mūsā al-Ash'arī (quoted by Abū 'Ubayda ibn 'Abdallāh ibn Mas'ūd).

Jābir ibn 'Abdallāh (quoted by 'Abdallāh ibn Muḥammad ibn 'Aqīl).

Ibn 'Umar.

Ibn 'Abbās (quoted by al-Ḍaḥḥāk ibn Muzāḥim).

Abū l-Ṭufayl 'Āmir ibn Wāthila (quoted by Sayf ibn Wahb).

These lists of Muḥammad's names and appellations seem to have had the form of prophetic statements from the very outset. No non-prophetic utterance with the same lists seems ever to have been in circulation, which again means that these prophetic traditions could not have been produced by the backwards growth of *isnād*s. There is only one Successor version of Mujāhid, who does not mention a Companion as his source.

The group of traditions in which Muḥammad is described as Riding a Camel, etc., demonstrates the coexistence of the same data in the form of an ordinary narrative report (*khabar*) as well as in the form of a prophetic *ḥadīth*. This description appears, as we have seen, in Muḥammad's early biographies as an outright biblical text, common among the Jews of the tribe of Banū l-Naḍīr. In a tradition of the Companion Ubayy ibn Ka'b (quoted by Ibn 'Abbās), the same description is said to have been known to the Jews of Medina. In later sources this description emerges as a prophetic *ḥadīth*, which Ibn 'Abbās quotes from the Prophet. Since we do not have the full *isnād* of the prophetic *ḥadīth*, we cannot tell whether or not it grew backwards out of the *isnād* of Ubayy ibn Ka'b. At any rate, the "highest" Companion is not the same in both traditions, although Ibn 'Abbās is present in both.

To conclude our survey of the traditions of attestation, the prominence of Companion *isnād*s, including prophetic ones, is evident. Since no backwards growth of *isnād*s has proved to be the process which brought them into being, there is nothing to make us believe in their late date of origin. Admittedly, prophetic utterances have been shown to reflect more mainstream trends (reliance on the Quran), which were opposed to other less conventional trends (reliance on the Bible). However, the prophetic utterances, even when reflecting an advanced stage of dogmatic development, may still be dated to a much earlier time than that proposed by Schacht. Nothing dictates against their emergence already in the lifetime of the Companions to whom they were attributed, i.e. more or less towards the middle of the first century AH. Incomplete *isnād*s in which the names of Companions are obscured or entirely missing may reflect a later stage of transmission, when the possibility of pretending to quote directly from Companions was diminished.

2. The Arabian Annunciation

The role of the Companions is especially conspicuous in the traditions with an Arabian setting of attestation. These traditions include no prophetic versions, presumably because their legendary character was only too obvious. Most of them do not contain statements, but rather bear epic stories about various people hearing prophecies about the emergence of Muḥammad. Such traditions, which were never anchored to any Quranic basis, do not seem to have gained the support of mainstream Islamic circles, and therefore stood little chance of passing under decent prophetic *isnād*s.

Apart from the fabulous stories, like those about various soothsayers, as well as about remote mythological forefathers (Sayf ibn Dhī Yazan, 'Abd al-Muṭṭalib, Ka'b ibn Lu'ayy), there are non-prophetic Companion traditions which were circulated mainly to promote the virtues of the Companions themselves. The Companions are presented in them as obtaining knowledge about the future emergence of Muḥammad, either from monotheistic scholars (*ḥanīf*s, Christians, etc.) or from their own dreams. These traditions were designed to uphold claims to status on the part of the descendants and political supporters of those Companions. Such are the traditions about the Companions 'Āmir ibn

Rabīʻa, Abū Bakr, Khadīja, Ṭalḥa ibn ʻUbaydallāh, ʻAmr ibn ʻAbasa, Jubayr ibn Muṭʻim, Khālid ibn Saʻīd, and Abū Umāma Asʻad ibn Zurāra. None of these traditions exhibits a process of backwards growth in its *isnād*, because none of the *isnād*s is available in a less complete form. The lack of proof of backwards growth allows, at least, for the possibility that the traditions were put into circulation already by the earliest Successor appearing in each respective *isnād*.

3. Initiation: the Opening of Muḥammad's Breast

The traditions about the opening of Muḥammad's breast are both prophetic and non-prophetic. In the versions where the event precedes the *isrā'–miʻrāj*, most *isnād*s are prophetic. This is not surprising. The ascension is firmly rooted in the Quran, so traditions about it could very easily be circulated under the name of the Prophet himself.

All relevant *isnād*s are Baṣran. One of them is of the Companion Abū Hurayra, whereas all the others are of the Companion Anas ibn Mālik. In the *isnād*s of the latter, some evidence of minor backwards growth does seem to present itself, but only at the highest end of the *isnād*s. While all *isnād*s extend to Anas, some of them proceed to a yet older Companion who figures as the source of Anas. Anas was indeed underage when the *isrā'* took place (before the *hijra*), so the prophetic *isnād*s bearing his name are actually *mursal*. With the addition of an older Companion, the *isnād*s become complete. The traditions with the additional Companions are all related by Muḥammad himself, in the first person, as proper prophetic *ḥadīth*s. The Companions whom Anas quotes are:

> Mālik ibn Ṣaʻṣaʻa. The *isnād*s bearing his name belong to the Qatāda group (Baṣran). There are several versions, going back as far as this Companion, which differ from each other; the differences may be accounted for by the fact that each of the versions was circulated by a different Baṣran disciple of Qatāda (Hishām al-Dustuwā'ī, Hammām ibn Yaḥyā, and Saʻīd ibn Abī ʻArūba).
>
> Ubayy ibn Kaʻb.
>
> Abū Dharr. Anas quotes the latter two in alternate versions of al-Zuhrī.

In the incomplete *isnād*s of Anas, in which no additional Companion is mentioned beyond himself, Anas is quoted by the following Successors:

Thābit al-Bunānī. In one version this Successor is quoted by Sulaymān ibn al-Mughīra; it does not exhibit any particularly earlier features than the versions with the additional Companion. The tradition is related in the first person, just like the traditions with the complete *isnād*s. It also exhibits the impact of the Quranic vocabulary of Sūrat al-Sharḥ (94), which rather indicates an advanced stage of literary elaboration, present also in one of the traditions with the complete *isnād*s of the Qatāda group. However, two other *mursal isnād*s of Anas belonging to the Bunānī group do precede versions preserving less cultivated features. They are devoid of Quranic vocabulary, and are related in the third person. Their content too is only loosely connected to the ascent, which is not mentioned explicitly. They are quoted from al-Bunānī by Ḥammād ibn Salama (in his version the Prophet is still a young boy) and by 'Abd Rabbihi ibn Sa'īd.

Sharīk ibn 'Abdallāh ibn Abī Namir.

Maymūn ibn Siyāh.

The name of Anas himself does not seem to have appeared in the *isnād*s in a backwards growth process. It seems to have been there from the very outset, because it is never absent from any of the relevant *isnād*s.

Prophetic *isnād*s are attached to the episode of the opening of the Prophet's breast, even when not prefacing the *isrā'–mi'rāj*. To begin with, prophetic *isnād*s occur when the opening is adduced in the context of self-attestation. The Prophet mentions it as an antecedent sign—in fact, as the very first sign—of his prophetic vocation. None of the *isnād*s of these versions seems to evince backwards growth. The Companions quoting the Prophet here are:

Abū Dharr (cited by 'Urwa ibn al-Zubayr).

Abū Hurayra (quoted by Ubayy ibn Ka'b).

'Ā'isha. In her version the opening is followed by the actual first Quranic revelation.

Prophetic *isnād*s are attached to other traditions of self-attestation. In them, the opening is part of a series of events (Abraham's Quranic prayer, etc.) predicting Muḥammad's prophetic mission. In these traditions, which Ibn Isḥāq already included in his *Sīra*, the Syrian Successor Khālid ibn Ma'dān quotes some unnamed Companions of Muḥammad; in another version, he has his prophetic report from the Companion 'Utba ibn 'Abd. All these *isnāds* seem to have been prophetic from the beginning. Their significance of self-attestation actually determines that they should always be prophetic.

There is, however, one more prophetic *isnād* which is *mursal*, lacking a Companion; in it the Prophet is quoted by the Successor Yaḥyā ibn Ja'da al-Qurashī. In spite of the incomplete *isnād*, the *matn* is rather advanced, referring to the opening as *sharḥ ṣadr*, in accordance with the Quranic vocabulary. Again, a *mursal isnād* does not necessarily indicate an early *matn*.

Apart from the strictly prophetic traditions, there are non-prophetic versions of the opening. Nonetheless, some of these were also circulated on the authority of a Companion, namely, Muḥammad's wet-nurse, Ḥalīma. We cannot regard her versions as "prophetic" because Muḥammad is still underage; her tale reflects her own point of view as an eyewitness. In the various traditions recorded on her authority Ḥalīma is cited by the following figures:

'Abdallāh ibn Ja'far ibn Abī Ṭālib. In this version the episode is entirely isolated, not combined with any other event of Muḥammad's life. It also lacks any traces of the vocabulary of Sūrat al-Sharḥ (94). In this respect it is not as refined as the other versions of the same episode, in which it is already part of a wider perspective of Muḥammad's life.

Ibn 'Abbās. This version gives the impression of literary embellishment in accordance with advanced views about Muḥammad's immunity from error and sin, his *'iṣma*.

But whatever the nature of the *matn*, the *isnāds* of the prophetic and non-prophetic versions of the episode of the opening of Muḥammad's breast do not reveal backwards growth; none of the prophetic versions grew out of the Ḥalīma versions. As we have just seen, the latter have their own particular *isnāds*, which have nothing in common with the *isnāds* of the prophetic versions.

Again, in the absence of backwards growth of *isnāds*, one may assume that the various types of traditions about the opening of Muḥammad's breast could have come into existence more or less simultaneously, at a relatively early date, well before the Schachtian "common link". Changes in the *matn* could have been introduced by later transmitters over the ages (as is clear in the case of the various versions of the Qatāda group, etc.).

4. Guidance: from Polytheism to Monotheism

The cases discussed in the chapter on guidance also lead to the conclusion that no systematic backwards growth of *isnād* took place in Islamic *ḥadīth*.

The first theme studied in that chapter was Muḥammad's meeting with the *ḥanīf* Zayd ibn 'Amr. All traditions dealing with this scene have Companions in their *isnād*s, and these figures are part of their original unchanging hard core. One of them has an *isnād* of the descendants of Zayd ibn 'Amr, ending with the son of this *ḥanīf*, Sa'īd ibn Zayd, who was a Companion. Another ends with Zayd ibn Ḥāritha, who relates the story in the first person as an eyewitness. There are prophetic *isnād*s as well, in one of which the Companion is Ibn 'Umar. The story is quoted from the Prophet in the third person. There are even two versions in which Muḥammad himself relates the story in the first person. One has the *isnād*: 'Urwa←'Ā'isha; another is recorded without an *isnād* already by Ibn Isḥāq. The prophetic *isnād*s do not seem to have grown out of the non-prophetic; neither type has anything in common with the other. The prophetic as well as the non-prophetic are static in all cases, their higher parts never growing backwards, which means that from the beginning the *isnād*s included the names of Muḥammad's contemporaries. Therefore, they could very well have come into existence already when these contemporaries were still alive, though this does not mean that those contemporaries really related what was attributed to them.

The case of the prophetic tradition of the Companion Ibn 'Umar is noteworthy. This tradition, circulated by Mūsā ibn 'Uqba, exhibits some changes which were introduced in the *matn* in accordance with the more advanced concept of the *'iṣma*. Nevertheless, the higher part of the *isnād* is always the same in all sources, which means that over the ages only the *matn* was tampered with, while the *isnād* remained static, being complete from the very outset.

The higher parts of the *isnād*s in the traditions about the deliverance of the Prophet from direct physical contact with idols are consistently static. All of them contain names of Companions:

Ibn 'Abbās (quoted by 'Aṭā' ibn Abī Rabāḥ).

Jābir ibn 'Abdallāh (quoted by 'Abdallāh ibn Muḥammad ibn 'Aqīl).

Umm Ayman (quoted by Ibn 'Abbās→'Ikrima). She gives her own story as an eyewitness.

'Ā'isha. This is a strictly prophetic tradition in which Muḥammad himself tells the story in the first person. In this case, however, the full *isnād* is not recorded, and only the Companion's name is mentioned.

There are prophetic *isnāds* attached to statements of Muḥammad about his own aversion to idolatry. They did not grow backwards out of any of the *isnāds* of the former versions; in fact, in themselves they are not entirely complete, but rather *mursal*. One of them, in which Muḥammad's statement is announced in the presence of Khadīja, is related by 'Urwa ibn al-Zubayr on the authority of an anonymous neighbour of hers. Another statement of Muḥammad in which he describes his long since abandoned worship of al-'Uzzā is recorded by Ibn al-Kalbī.

All the traditions about Muḥammad being seen unclothed in public are also circulated under various names of Muḥammad's contemporaries. These Companion *isnāds* are all *mursal*, because none of the Companions could have attended the event; they were all either too young, or still non-Muslims. But the fact remains that even in this form the *isnāds* are already attributed to Companions, without any manifest indication of backwards growth. The Companions whose names appear in the various versions are:

Jābir ibn 'Abdallāh (quoted by 'Amr ibn Dīnār). There is also another version which is no longer *mursal*. In it Jābir states that the Prophet himself told him the story, which, of course, could have been done some considerable time after the actual event. This particular prophetic *ḥadīth* was circulated by Abū l-Zubayr.

Abū l-Ṭufayl (quoted by 'Abdallāh ibn 'Uthmān ibn Khuthaym).

Ibn 'Abbās (quoted by 'Ikrima). In this case, an attempt was made to transform the *isnād* into a complete one by adding an older Companion, namely, the father of Ibn 'Abbās, who acts as an eyewitness and relates the story to his son in the first person. Here, again, only a minor backwards growth has occurred, by the addition of a second Companion. The *mursal* 'Ikrima←Ibn 'Abbās version was circulated by al-Naḍr Abū 'Umar ibn 'Abd al-Raḥmān al-Khazzāz, whereas the version with the complete *isnād* was circulated by Simāk ibn Ḥarb. The *matns* of both versions differ in some details.

Companion unspecified. This is a yet another version, a proper prophetic one, in which Muḥammad tells the story in the first person. This was already recorded by Ibn Isḥāq, who, as usual, does not provide the full *isnād*. The *matn* reveals the dogma of the *'iṣma* only in its primitive form (Muḥammad takes off his clothes of his own accord). This again indicates that contrary to Goldziher and Schacht, a prophetic version of a certain tradition is not necessarily the latest and most elaborate one.

In fact, Ibn Isḥāq has another prophetic tradition of 'Alī ibn Abī Ṭālib in which Muḥammad relates in the first person the story of his quest for unlawful nightly entertainment in Mecca. This again demonstrates how prophetic *isnād*s cannot be a reliable sign for dating traditions. In our particular case, it precedes a quite undeveloped tradition occurring in one of Muḥammad's earliest biographies.

The group of traditions dealing with Muḥammad's participation in the rites of 'Arafa is, again, most revealing. All the traditions seem to have had a Companion *isnād* from the very first moment. All *isnād*s end with Jubayr ibn Muṭ'im, who acts as an eyewitness relating the story in the first person. In each specific version of his story he is quoted by a different Successor:

Muḥammad ibn Jubayr ibn Muṭ'im.

Ibn Jurayj's father.

Nāfi' ibn Jubayr. This version, recorded by Ibn Isḥāq, is most noteworthy; in various sources it is quoted from Ibn Isḥāq with dogmatic textual changes of the contents, designed to avoid the statement about the Prophet's part in "the religion of his people" (*dīn qawmihi*), as recorded in the original text of Ibn Isḥāq. In spite of the dogmatic elaboration of the contents, the same *isnād* is always fully retained in all of the variants. Again, this does not indicate backwards growth over the ages, only introduction of changes in the *matn*, the *isnād* being static in its highest level, containing a Companion from the very outset, i.e. from Ibn Isḥāq at the latest. Nothing prevents us from assuming that the story came into circulation under the name of the Companion Jubayr ibn Muṭ'im when he was still alive.

5. The Khadīja–Waraqa Story

The traditions about the first prophetic revelation of Muḥammad exhibit no history of backwards growth in their *isnāds*. Most of them have a Companion who seems to be part of the hard core of the *isnād*, not a secondary addition. They also show that complete as well as incomplete *isnāds* may precede all types of *matns*.

Companions occur in the *isnāds* of traditions with Quranic allusions. The tradition with Sūrat al-Fātiḥa (1) is of the Companion Abū Maysara ʻAmr ibn Shuraḥbīl, who does not appear to be a later addition to the *isnād*. The same applies to names of Companions appearing in the traditions about the revelation of the *iqra'* passage. These traditions are attached with the following *isnāds*:

Zuhrī←ʻUrwa←ʻĀ'isha. There is a whole group of traditions bearing this *isnād*, and as Ā'isha's name occurs in all variants, it does not appear to be a secondary addition. Since she was underage at the time of the event, the *isnād* is technically *mursal*. Various disciples of al-Zuhrī circulated the tradition, and although the higher part of the *isnād* is always the same, the *matn* does change from one version to another. Some versions only have the part with the revelation of the *iqra'* passage, others add the Prophet's attempted suicide, while still others include the episode of the *fatra*. This means that time may have had its effect on the *matn*, but not on the *isnād*, which has remained as high as ever from the very outset. In other words, contrary to what is implied by Schacht's observations, the condition of the higher parts of *isnāds* is a very poor tool for dating *matns*. In this specific case, in which no backwards growth can be proved, one may assume that the tradition was indeed circulated from the very outset with the *isnād* of Zuhrī←ʻUrwa←ʻĀ'isha. Nothing excludes the possibility that already during ʻUrwa's own lifetime (d. AH 94), the various versions attributed to his aunt ʻĀ'isha, whom he used to frequent, began to circulate in his name. He himself may or may not have been responsible for any of them. Changes in the *matn* may have continued to be introduced by al-Zuhrī, as well as by his disciples, but we cannot know who is responsible for each nuance.

Jābir ibn ʻAbdallāh. The tradition of this Companion (transmitted again by al-Zuhrī) is a prophetic tradition in the first person, dealing with the revelation of the Muddaththir passage following the lapse of revelation. In spite of the fact that the tradition is prophetic and cited from the Prophet by a Companion, there is no evidence here of any history of backwards growth.

'Ubayd ibn 'Umayr. The tradition of this Meccan story-teller deals with the revelation of the *iqra'* passage. The *isnād* is incomplete, because 'Ubayd is not a Companion; nevertheless, the *matn* is most elaborate, part of it being related by the Prophet himself in the first person. By Schachtian measures, this "late" feature does not fit the incomplete *isnād*, which according to Schacht is rather an early sign. Contrary to Schacht, we again are at liberty to hold that an interrupted *isnād* may rather precede a *matn* with already advanced literary features. The contents of the story of 'Ubayd is indeed elaborate, being loaded with Quranic allusions.

But the appearance of Companions is not limited to the *isnād*s of elaborate traditions with Quranic allusions. The traditions which lack Quranic allusions and seem to have preserved the basic narrative framework of the first revelations are traced back to the Companion Ibn 'Abbās. In one case Ibn 'Abbās is quoted by 'Ammār ibn Abī 'Ammār, in another by 'Ikrima. Admittedly, there is also a "non-Quranic" tradition with an *isnād* going only as high as the Successor 'Urwa ibn al-Zubayr (quoted by his son Hishām), but it does not seem to be any earlier than the versions of Ibn 'Abbās. 'Urwa's version is less elaborate than the "Quranic" versions he quotes from 'Ā'isha, but the latter belong to a different group quoted from 'Urwa by al-Zuhrī, not by Hishām, so that again, the occurrence of 'Ā'isha's name does not indicate backwards growth.

6. The Lapse of Revelation (*Fatrat al-waḥy*)

Many traditions focus on the affair of *fatrat al-waḥy* and the revelation of the *mā wadda'aka* passage. They are transmitted on the authority of the following figures:

The Companion Zayd ibn Arqam (quoted by Abū Isḥāq al-Sabī'ī). His version refers to Umm Jamīl as the one who offended the Prophet, thus causing the revelation of the *mā wadda'aka* passage.

The Successors Ma'mar ibn Rāshid, Qatāda, and Ḍaḥḥāk ibn Muzāḥim. However, the *matn*s of these less complete *isnād*s, which revolve round the "polytheists" (*mushrikūn*) as the offending party, do not exhibit any particularly early features, but rather represent the already resolved consensus.

The Companion Ibn 'Abbās (through the 'Awfī family *isnād*). His version likewise indicates the polytheists as the offending party, according to the consensus, and its *isnād* certainly did not grow backwards out of any of the Successors' *isnāds*.

The Successor 'Urwa ibn al-Zubayr (quoted by his son Hishām). This version may be in accordance with Schacht's theory, because it seems less conventional according to its *matn* (referring to Khadīja as doubting Muḥammad's integrity) and equipped with an incomplete *isnād*, lacking a Companion. However, none of the extant Companion *isnāds* grew backwards out of this one.

The Successor 'Abdallāh ibn Shaddād, (quoted by Abū Isḥāq al-Shaybānī). His tradition too refers to Khadīja, and is likewise lacking a Companion. It is noteworthy that it survives in several versions, all with the same *isnād* of Abū Isḥāq←'Abdallāh ibn Shaddād. Some tendentious changes have been introduced in the *matn*. While in one version (circulated by 'Abd al-Wāḥid ibn Ziyād) the offending party is still Khadīja, in another (circulated by Ḥafṣ ibn Ghiyāth) she is replaced by the "unbelievers of Quraysh" (*kuffār Quraysh*), according to the consensus. However, in spite of the emendation, the *isnād* remains static and does not extend any higher than the Successor 'Abdallāh ibn Shaddād. Thus, although the correlation between incomplete *isnāds* and unconventional *matns* might corroborate Schacht's theories, no backwards growth is indicated in the *isnāds* of the more conventional *matns*.

The Companion Jundab ibn 'Abdallāh al-Bajalī (quoted by al-Aswad ibn Qays al-'Abdī). This is the largest group of traditions about *fatrat al-waḥy* and the revelation of the *mā wadda'aka* passage. Again, the only noticeable development takes place in the ever-changing *matn*, not in the *isnād*, which remains static in its higher part, being as high as ever from the very outset. In all versions of the group, Jundab is always there, and he is always quoted by al-Aswad. This part of the *isnād* forms its hard core. Changes in the *isnād* only occur as low as the level of Aswad's disciples, which means that the tradition with the Aswad←Jundab *isnād* gained wide circulation in the generation following Aswad. This does not mean that it came into being during that generation, as Schacht would hold, but rather that in earlier generations only one traditionist, namely, Aswad, transmitted the tradition of Jundab about *fatrat al-waḥy*. Unlike the static higher part of the *isnād*, the *matn* keeps changing from one version to another. Some versions have a woman as the offending party, but sometimes the situation is not the *fatra* itself, only the illness of the Prophet. In still other versions, the foes are the polytheists. In another version about the polytheists, the Companion speaks in the first person, and the episode of the recitation of a poetic verse by Muḥammad has been added to the scene. These changes mean that the traditionists tampered with the contents of the original *matn* over the ages. We cannot know when this began (Aswad himself could have authorized some changes on different occasions), nor be sure of the original text of the tradition which Aswad circulated under the name of the Companion Jundab. We can only assume that the version with the polytheists corresponds to the advanced model of persecution, according to which they are the sole source of evil.

The Prophet himself (?). This is the most outstanding version of the *fatra* episode, and in it Muḥammad himself is the doubting party, whose disbelief in himself causes the revelation of the passage. This tradition, which does not yet reflect the conventions of persecution or the advanced dogma of the *'iṣma*, was preserved in the recension of Yūnus ibn Bukayr of the *Sīra* of Ibn Isḥāq. Again, Ibn Isḥāq has failed to record the *isnād*, so that we cannot know what its type was. From what we see throughout our exploration, the *isnād* could very well be prophetic. In fact, the *matn* is fairly prophetic, as the Prophet's sceptical view of himself is quoted as his own words, in the first person. This would mean that prophetic *isnād*s might indeed be attached to *matn*s not yet shaped according to the more mainstream conventions.

Thus, the various versions of the *fatra* and the revelation of the *mā wadda'aka* passage do not exhibit any history of the backwards growth of *isnād*s. Complete and incomplete *isnād*s simultaneously precede conventional ("late") and unconventional ("early") *matn*s, and neither type seems to have grown backwards out of the other.

7. Declaration: the *'Ashīra* Scene

In the chapter of declaration, most traditions deal with the *'ashīra* scene, and those in which the Prophet warns his audience of an approaching disaster have Companions in their *isnād*s. They are:

Qabīṣa ibn al-Mukhāriq.

Zuhayr ibn ʻAmr al-Hilālī.

Abū Mūsā al-Ashʻarī.

ʻAmr ibn Murra al-Juhanī.

The one *mursal* version with an *isnād* reaching only as high as a Successor (al-Ḥasan al-Baṣrī) was not an origin for any of the Companion *isnāds*, because the name of al-Ḥasan al-Baṣrī does not recur in any of them. Therefore any assumption of backwards growth is precluded straightaway.

Among the traditions incorporating the idea of individual judgement into the *ʻashīra* scene, there are some with incomplete *isnāds* of al-Zuhrī and Qatāda and others with complete *isnāds* containing the following Companions:

ʻĀ'isha.

Abū Hurayra.

Abū Umāma al-Bāhilī.

The two types have nothing in common on the Successor level, so the Companion *isnāds* could not have grown backwards out of the Successor ones.

Furthermore, the traditions in which the idea of free will is expressed independently of the *ʻashīra* scene have their own *isnāds* which have nothing in common with the *isnāds* of the *ʻashīra* scene. Almost all the Companions are different:

Ibn ʻAbbās.

ʻImrān ibn Ḥuṣayn.

al-Ḥakam ibn Mīnā'.

Abū Hurayra.

Only Abū Hurayra features in the former type as well. But his *isnād* has its own names of Successors, who do not recur in any of the other *isnāds*.

There is one *isnād* which is *mursal*, ending with the Successor ʻUbayd ibn ʻUmayr. His name does not recur in any of the relevant Companion *isnāds*, which means that none of the latter ever grew backwards. The impression is again that all the *isnāds* came into being with their higher parts already built in and stable, containing—or lacking—names of Companions from the very beginning.

In the traditions of the *'ashīra* scene where the position of 'Alī as Muḥammad's successor is highlighted, all *isnād*s have Companions. In this case as well, they seem to form the hard core of the *isnād*s. In most instances it is 'Alī himself, who speaks in the first person; in one case, it is al-Barā' ibn 'Āzib. In the versions in which the episode with 'Alī takes place independent of the *'ashīra* scene, all the *isnād*s are again with 'Alī himself as Companion, but with entirely different Successors.

8. The Reaction of Abū Lahab

The traditions about Abū Lahab's reaction to Muḥammad's call do not exhibit backwards growth of *isnād*s. Many of them are of Companions, who seem to form their hard core. The versions in which the revelation of Sūrat al-Masad (111) is made part of the *'ashīra* scene are all circulated under the name of Ibn 'Abbās, who is quoted in each version by a different successor (Sa'īd ibn Jubayr, Abū Ṣāliḥ, and 'Ikrima). These *isnād*s did not grow backwards out of any less complete *isnād*s of other traditions of the same scene.

The *isnād*s of the traditions describing Abū Lahab's persecution of the Prophet, when the latter tried to preach in the markets of Mecca, are also of Companions:

Ṭāriq ibn 'Abdallāh al-Muḥāribī (quoted by Jāmi' ibn Shaddād).

Rabī'a ibn 'Ibād (cited by several disparate Successors: Sa'īd ibn Khālid al-Qāriẓī, Muḥammad ibn al-Munkadir, Abū l-Zinād, Ḥusayn ibn 'Abdallāh ibn 'Ubaydallāh ibn al-'Abbās, Zayd ibn Aslam, and Bukayr ibn 'Abdallāh ibn al-Ashajj).

There is also a *mursal* version, of the Successor 'Abd al-Raḥmān ibn Kaysān. None of the Companion *isnād*s seems to have grown backwards out of this *isnād*.

In the traditions about the reaction of Abū Lahab's wife (Umm Jamīl) to the revelation of Sūrat al-Masad, all the *isnād*s are of Companions:

Asmā' bint Abī Bakr.

Ibn 'Abbās.

No evidence of backwards growth is provided here either. Therefore, all the traditions seem to have been circulated from the very first moment under the names of the highest authorities mentioned in their respective *isnāds*. Some of them may even have been first put into circulation during the lifetime of the Companions on whose authority they were related.

9. The Reaction of Abū Ṭālib

Most traditions in this chapter deal with the visit paid to Abū Ṭālib by the leaders of Quraysh, and a comparison of the various *isnāds* fails to reveal any traces of backwards growth. There are a few incomplete *isnāds*, but these do not seem to have formed the origin for the numerous higher *isnāds*. The incomplete ones reach only as high as the following Successors:

Ya'qūb ibn 'Utba ibn al-Mughīra ibn al-Akhnas.

'Āṣim ibn 'Umar.

al-Suddī.

None of these names appears in the *isnāds* reaching the level of the Companions, who are:

'Iyāḍ ibn Ḥimār al-Mujāshi'ī.

'Aqīl ibn Abī Ṭālib.

Ibn 'Abbās. This Companion appears in a relatively large number of *isnāds* of various versions of the story of the visit. The Successors citing him are Mujāhid, Abū Ṣāliḥ, Sa'īd ibn Jubayr, and al-'Abbās ibn 'Abdallāh ibn Ma'bad ibn 'Abbās. Although Ibn 'Abbās is apparently not the source of any of the versions, his name forms part of the hard core of the *isnāds* in which he is included, since there are no parallel incomplete variants of the same *isnāds* in which his name is not already included. This means that the originator of each version already circulated his story on the authority of Ibn 'Abbās. Again, it is not clear who the originator of each version was, but nothing seems to preclude the possibility that in some cases it was already the first Successor mentioned after Ibn 'Abbās.

In a special group of traditions the visit of the leaders is not mentioned; only Abū Ṭālib's last illness is described. In this group as well, all the *isnād*s have Companions in their hard core:

Musayyab ibn Ḥazn.

Abū Hurayra. This Companion is quoted by the Successor Abū Ḥāzim al-Ashja'ī. There are two versions with this *isnād*, both circulated by Yazīd ibn Kaysān, which are slightly different from each other. The differences imply what has already been seen on previous occasions, namely, that the original *matn* of a tradition may be exposed to changes during later generations, while the higher part of its *isnād* remains unaltered.

10. Isolation: the Satanic Verses

The case of the traditions about the satanic verses is most remarkable. There is one *isnād* here which exists in two parallel forms, *mursal* and complete (*muttaṣil*). The *mursal* form is Shu'ba←Abū Bishr←Sa'īd ibn Jubayr, and is the most prevalent one in the sources. The *muttaṣil* form continues to Ibn 'Abbās, but only survives in a few sources. Now, according to Schacht, we have here a clear case of backwards growth. However, one may assume with equal likelihood that the process was the other way round. The name of Ibn 'Abbās could have been deliberately omitted from the originally complete *isnād*, because of the problematic *matn* alluding to the satanic verses. As a result of the omission, the embarrassing *matn* was deprived of its "sound" (*ṣaḥīḥ*) *isnād* and could be discredited. In other words, complete and sound *isnād*s attached to overly provocative *matn*s could have been subjected to deliberate distortion which made them shrink, so that disapproving traditionists could dismiss the whole *ḥadīth* on the ground of defective transmission. In fact, the complete *isnād* with Ibn 'Abbās, when it is recorded, is always followed by sceptical comments of some traditionists, for whom such an implausible tradition could not have come out of Ibn 'Abbās' mouth.[17] Therefore, backwards growth—that is to say, improvement of the *isnād*—could not have taken place in this case. No one was interested in improving the chances of this tradition gaining wide circulation. In conclusion, the name of Ibn 'Abbās must have been part of the original *isnād*. This does not mean that the historical Ibn 'Abbās had anything to do with the tradition, only that its first prompter circulated it under his name. Of course, there remains the question, if the tradition was so provoca-

[17] See the discussion of Albānī in his *Naṣb al-majānīq li-nasf qiṣṣat al-gharānīq*, 4–9.

tive, how did it gain its sound *isnād* in the first place? This may be explained by assuming that at the time the tradition was first put into circulation, its provocative aspects were not yet noticed, since the dogma of the *'iṣma* had not yet reached its extreme and most rigid stage of development.

Other Companion *isnād*s precede other versions of the satanic verses story, none of which exists in a less complete (*mursal*) version. This means that the higher parts of these *isnād*s constitute their hard core. The Companions are:

Muḥammad ibn Faḍāla al-Ẓafarī.

Ibn 'Abbās (this time in the well-known family *isnād* of al-'Awfī).

Further versions of the satanic verses story have *isnād*s from which the Companion is absent (*mursal*), and none of them exists in a more complete version. The Successors are:

Muḥammad ibn Ka'b al-Quraẓī.

Abū l-'Āliya Rufay' ibn Mihrān.

al-Ḍaḥḥāk ibn Muzāḥim.

Abū Bakr ibn 'Abd al-Raḥmān ibn al-Ḥārith.

Sa'īd ibn Jubayr. This Successor appears in an entirely different *isnād* from the one mentioned above, which goes as high as Ibn 'Abbās.

'Urwa ibn al-Zubayr. His three parallel versions deserve special attention. Version 3 has the *isnād* Ibn Lahī'a←Abū l-Aswad←'Urwa, which is *mursal* because no Companion is mentioned. The same *isnād* has a complete version including a Companion (Version 2). This is Makhrama ibn Nawfal, whose son Miswar is 'Urwa's ultimate source. Again, according to Schacht this must signify backwards growth: the earlier version would be the *mursal* one (no. 3). Now, the two versions differ in their *matn*s. The *mursal* one (no. 3) contains the Quranic materials of temptation. The *matn* with the Companion *isnād* (no. 2) is entirely non-Quranic. Since, according to our analysis, the non-Quranic version (no. 2) is probably the one closer to the basic narrative framework, and since it is the one equipped with the complete Companion *isnād*, Schacht's theory is once again refuted. What seems to have happened is again a process of shrinking of an *isnād*: the Companion was omitted from the chain preceding the version with the Quranic allusions because of the reference to the satanic verses. The *isnād* was thus sullied, so as to discredit the *matn* and reduce its chances of circulation. 'Urwa himself seems to have had little to do with either of the versions, both of which were circulated under his name by Ibn Lahī'a through Abū l-Aswad. The original version of 'Urwa himself, if there was one, seems rather to have been preserved with a third *isnād* (no. 1) in which he is quoted by his son Hishām. It is entirely non-Quranic, and is not a *ḥadīth* at all, but rather is quoted from the treatise 'Urwa wrote to the caliph 'Abd al-Malik providing his own individual account.

Other versions of the same episode do not mention the satanic verses, and shift the focus of the story to the theme of *sujūd al-Qur'ān*. These are equipped with complete Companion *isnād*s with which no one had reason to tamper; the Companions are:

'Abdallāh ibn Mas'ūd (quoted by al-Aswad ibn Yazīd).

al-Muṭṭalib ibn Abī Wadā'a (quoted by Ja'far ibn al-Muṭṭalib ibn Abī Wadā'a).

Abū Hurayra (quoted by Abū Salama ibn 'Abd al-Raḥmān).

Ibn 'Abbās (quoted by Maymūn ibn Mihrān and by 'Ikrima).

Ibn 'Umar (quoted by Nāfi').

There are similar *mursal* versions ending with Successors, none of whom reappearing in the complete Companion *isnād*s, which again excludes any evidence of backwards growth. The Successors are:

Dāwūd ibn Abī l-'Āliya.

al-Sha'bī.

11. The 'Aqaba Meetings

In the traditions about the 'Aqaba meetings no Companion *isnād*s seem to have grown backwards out of Successors *isnād*s. The versions in which Muḥammad appears as the messianic saviour and uniting leader are equipped with a Companion *isnād* of 'Urwa ibn al-Zubayr←'Ā'isha. In this case 'Urwa is quoted by his son Hishām, but another similar version of 'Urwa is quoted from him by Abū l-Aswad. In the latter no Companion appears as 'Urwa's source. This might indicate backwards growth in the version with 'Ā'isha, but it is equally conceivable that her name was omitted from Abū l-Aswad's version, for some reason now obscure. There are other traditions of this kind with incomplete *isnāds* lacking Companions. They are of 'Āṣim ibn 'Umar ibn Qatāda and al-Zuhrī, and the *isnāds* with these names never grew backwards into Companion *isnāds*.

In the traditions in which the Anṣār appear as providing the Prophet with shelter from his Meccan adversaries, most *isnāds* are of Companions. There is no evidence that they ever grew backwards out of less complete *isnāds*. The Companions on whose authority the traditions are related are:

Jābir ibn 'Abdallāh.

'Alī ibn Abī Ṭālib.

'Umar ibn al-Khaṭṭāb.

There is one Successor *isnād* of 'Ikrima. Here again, no backwards growth took place.

The traditions in which al-'Abbās states the Meccan point of view are of Companions (the papyrus version of Wahb ibn Munabbih of the same scene is recorded without an *isnād* at all). They are:

Ka'b ibn Mālik.

'Aqīl ibn Abī Ṭālib.

Numerous versions are available of the discourse between Muḥammad and the Anṣār following the division of the spoils of Ḥunayn, and all of them have Companion *isnāds*:

Abū Sa'īd al-Khudrī (several versions).

al-Sā'ib ibn Yazīd.

Anas ibn Mālik.

Ibn 'Abbās.

Jābir ibn ʻAbdallāh.

ʻAbdallāh ibn Zayd ibn ʻĀṣim.

None of these *isnāds* seems to have grown backwards out of a *mursal* one.

Traditions of Companions who actually figure as eyewitnesses to the ʻAqaba meetings are also available. They all provide the contents of the *bayʻa*, and most of them are of the Syrian ʻUbāda ibn al-Ṣāmit. There are two main groups here, Quranic and non-Quranic. The Quranic versions with the passage about *bayʻat al-nisā'* (Quran 60:12) built into them were circulated under the name of ʻUbāda by the Syrian Successors Abū Idrīs al-Khawlānī and al-Ṣunābiḥī. The non-Quranic versions, with only a pledge of *al-samʻ wa-l-ṭāʻa*, were circulated on the authority of the same Companion by his son and grandson. Each type is available in dated and undated versions, i.e. with and without explicit reference to the ʻAqaba scene. These changes in the *matn* never affected the higher *isnāds* in either type. This means that these parts constitute the hard core of the *isnāds*, so that any assumption of backwards growth is once more precluded. Other undated versions of ʻUbāda about the *bayʻa* were circulated on his authority by the Successors Junāda ibn Abī Umayya and Ismāʻīl ibn ʻUbayd.

To sum up, the evidence of lack of backwards growth of *isnāds* deprives the Schachtian theory of one of its basic dating tools. From what we have seen, traditions with complete *isnāds*, including a Companion, could have come into being as early as the generation of the Companion himself. In later generations, the higher parts of the *isnāds* either remained static or shrank, sometimes with the introduction of changes in the *matn*.

Bibliography of Works Cited

In the arrangement adopted here, the Arabic definite article *al-* at the beginning of a personal name or book title, the transliteration symbols for the Arabic letters *hamza* (') and *'ayn* ('), and distinctions between letters of the same basic Latin form (e.g. *d* and *ḍ*) are disregarded for purposes of alphabetization.

'Abd al-Razzāq, Abū Bakr ibn Hammām al-Ṣan'ānī. *Al-Muṣannaf*. Ed. Ḥabīb al-Raḥmān al-A'ẓamī. 11 vols. Beirut, 1970.

_______. *Tafsīr al-Qur'ān*. Ed. Muṣṭafā Muslim Muḥammad. 3 vols. Riyad, 1989.

Abū 'Awāna, Ya'qūb ibn Isḥāq. *Al-Musnad*. 2 vols. Hyderabad, 1362/1943, repr. Beirut, n.d.

Abū Dāwūd, Sulaymān ibn al-Ash'ath al-Sijistānī. *Al-Sunan*. 2 vols. Cairo, 1952.

Abū Nu'aym, Aḥmad ibn 'Abdallāh al-Iṣbahānī. *Dalā'il al-nubuwwa*. Ed. Muḥammad Qal'ajī and 'Abd al-Barr 'Abbās. Beirut, 1986.

_______. *Ḥilyat al-awliyā'*. 10 vols. Cairo, 1357/1938, repr. Beirut, 1967.

_______. *Ma'rifat al-ṣaḥāba*. Ed. Muḥammad Rāḍī ibn Ḥājj 'Uthmān. 3 vols. Medina and Riyad, 1988.

Abū 'Ubayda, Ma'mar ibn al-Muthannā. *Majāz al-Qur'ān*. Ed. Muḥammad Fu'ād Sezgin. 2 vols. Cairo, 1962.

Abū Ya'lā, Aḥmad ibn 'Alī al-Mawṣilī. *Al-Musnad*. Ed. Ḥusayn Salīm Asad. 13 vols. Damascus and Beirut, 1984–90.

Abū Zur'a, 'Abd al-Raḥmān al-Dimashqī. *Tārīkh*. Ed. Shukrullāh al-Qawjānī. 2 vols. Damascus, 1480/1980.

Adang, Camilla. *Muslim Writers on Judaism and the Hebrew Bible from Ibn Rabban to Ibn Hazm*. Ph.D. Thesis. Nijmegen, 1993.

Aghānī = Abū l-Faraj 'Alī ibn al-Ḥusayn al-Iṣfahānī. *Kitāb al-aghānī*. 20 vols. Cairo, 1285/1868, repr. Beirut, 1970.

Aḥmad ibn Ḥanbal. *Al-'Ilal wa-ma'rifat al-rijāl*. Ed. Waṣiyyullāh ibn Muḥammad 'Abbās. 3 vols. Riyad and Beirut, 1988.

_______. *Al-Masā'il, riwāyat 'Abdallāh ibn Aḥmad*. Ed. Zuhayr al-Shāwīsh. Beirut, 1988.

_______. *Al-Masā'il, riwāyat Isḥāq ibn Ibrāhīm*. Ed. Zuhayr al-Shāwīsh. 2 vols. Beirut, 1979.

_______. *Al-Musnad*. 6 vols. Cairo, 1313/1895, repr. Beirut n.d.

al-Albānī, Nāṣir al-Dīn. *Naṣb al-majānīq li-nasf qiṣṣat al-gharānīq*. Damascus, 1952.

Andræ, Tor. *Die Person Muhammeds in Lehre und Glauben seiner Gemeinde*. Uppsala, 1917.

'Arafat, Walid. "Early Critics of the Authenticity of the Poetry of the *Sīra*", *Bulletin of the School of Oriental and African Studies* 21 (1958), 453–63.

'Athamina, Khalil. "*Al-Nabiyy al-Umiyy* [sic.]...", *Der Islam* 69 (1992), 61–81.

al-Azraqī, Abū l-Walīd Aḥmad ibn Muḥammad. *Akhbār Makka*, in Ferdinand Wüstenfeld, ed., *Die Chroniken der Stadt Mekka*. 3 vols. Göttingen, 1858, repr. Beirut, n.d.

al-Baghawī, al-Ḥusayn ibn Mas'ūd *Al-Anwār fī shamā'il al-nabiyy al-mukhtār*. Ed. Ibrāhīm al-Ya'qūbī. 2 vols. Beirut, 1989.

_______. *Ma'ālim al-tanzīl fī l-tafsīr wa-l-ta'wīl*. 5 vols. Beirut, 1985.

_______. *Maṣābīḥ al-sunna*. Ed. Yūsuf al-Mar'ashlī, Muḥammad Samāra, and Jamāl al-

Dhahabī. 4 vols. Beirut, 1987.
al-Balādhurī, Aḥmad ibn Yaḥyā. *Ansāb al-ashrāf,* I. Ed. Muḥammad Hamīdullāh. Cairo, 1959.
_______. *Ansāb al-ashrāf,* IVb. Ed. Max Schloessinger. Jerusalem, 1938.
_______. *Al-Shaykhān Abū Bakr wa-'Umar wa-wulduhumā*, extracted from *Ansāb al-ashrāf.* Ed. Iḥsān Ṣidqī al-'Amad. Kuwait, 1989.
Bashear, Suliman. "Riding Beasts on Divine Missions: an Examination of the Ass and Camel Traditions", *Journal of Semitic Studies* 36 (1991), 37–75.
al-Bayhaqī, Aḥmad ibn al-Ḥusayn. *Dalā'il al-nubuwwa.* Ed. 'Abd al-Mu'ṭī Qal'ajī. 7 vols. Beirut, 1988.
_______. *Shu'ab al-īmān.* Ed. Basyūnī Zaghlūl. 7 vols. Beirut, 1990.
_______. *Al-Sunan al-kubrā.* 10 vols. Hyderabad, 1355/1936, repr. Beirut, n.d.
al-Bazzār, Abū Bakr Aḥmad ibn 'Amr. *Al-Baḥr al-zakhkhār.* Ed. Maḥfūẓ al-Raḥmān Zaynullāh. 3 vols. to date. Medina, 1988–proceeding.
Bell, Richard. "Mohammed's Call", *The Muslim World* 24 (1934), 13–19.
_______. "Muhammad's Visions", *The Muslim World* 24 (1934), 145–54.
Biḥār al-anwār = al-Majlisī, Muḥammad Bāqir. *Biḥār al-anwār.* 110 vols. Tehran, repr. Beirut, 1983.
Birkeland, Harris. *The Legend of the Opening of Muhammed's Breast.* Oslo, 1955.
_______. *The Lord Guideth.* Uppsala, 1956.
Bonner, Michael. "Some Observations Concerning the Early Development of *Jihād* on the Arab–Byzantine Frontier", *Studia Islamica* 75 (1992), 5–31.
Bravmann, Meir M. *The Spiritual Background of Early Islam.* Leiden, 1972.
Buhl, Frants. *Das Leben Muhammeds.* Trans. Hans H. Schaeder. Heidelberg, 1961.
Bukhārī, *Adab mufrad* = Faḍlullāh al-Jaylānī. *Faḍlullāh al-ṣamad fī tawḍīḥ al-adab al-mufrad li-l-Bukhārī.* 2 vols. Homs, 1969.
al-Bukhārī, Muḥammad ibn Ismā'īl. *Al-Ṣaḥīḥ.* 9 vols. Cairo, 1958.
_______. *Al-Tārīkh al-kabīr.* 8 vols. Hyderabad, 1360/1941, repr. Beirut, 1986.
_______. *Al-Tārīkh al-ṣaghīr.* Ed. Maḥmūd Ibrāhīm Zāyid. 2 vols. Beirut, 1986.
Burton, John. "Those are the High-Flying Cranes", *Journal of Semitic Studies* 15 (1970), 246–65.
Calder, Norman. "*Ḥinth, birr*...: an Inquiry into the Arabic Vocabulary of Vows", *Bulletin of the School of Oriental and African Studies* 51 (1988), 214–39.
_______. "The *Ummī* in Early Islamic Juridic Literature", *Der Islam* 67 (1990), 111–23.
Carr, E.H. *What is History.* Repr. Penguin Books, 1980.
Conrad, Lawrence I. "Abraha and Muḥammad: Some Observations Apropos of Chronology and Literary *Topoi* in the Early Arabic Historical Tradition, *Bulletin of the School of Oriental and African Studies* 50 (1987), 225–40.
_______. "The Conquest of Arwād: a Source-Critical Study in the Historiography of the Early Medieval Near East", in Averil Cameron and Lawrence I. Conrad, eds., *The Byzantine and Early Islamic Near East I: Problems in the Literary Source Material* (Princeton, 1992), 317–401.
_______. "Seven and the Tasbī': on the Implications of Numerical Symbolism for the Study of Medieval Islamic History", *Journal of the Economic and Social History of the Orient* 31 (1988), 42–73.
_______. "Theophanes and the Arabic Historical Tradition: Some Indications of Intercultural Transmission", *Byzantinische Forschungen* 15 (1990), 1–44.
Cook, Michael. *Early Muslim Dogma.* Cambridge, 1981.
_______. "Eschatology and the Dating of Traditions", *Princeton Papers in Near Eastern Studies* 1 (1992), 25–47.

Crone, Patricia. *Roman, Provincial and Islamic Law*. Cambridge, 1987.
Crone, Patricia and Martin Hinds. *God's Caliph: Religious Authority in the First Centuries of Islam*. Cambridge, 1986.
al-Damīrī, Kamāl al-Dīn Muḥammad ibn Mūsā. *Ḥayāt al-ḥayawān*. 2 vols. Cairo, 1970.
al-Dāraquṭnī, 'Alī ibn 'Umar. *Al-Sunan*. Ed. Yamānī al-Madanī. 4 vols. Medina, 1966.
al-Dārimī, 'Abdallāh ibn 'Abd al-Raḥmān. *Al-Sunan*. Ed. Fawāz Zimirlī and Khālid al-'Alamī. 2 vols. Beirut, 1987.
al-Daylamī, Abū Shujā' Ilkiyā. *Al-Firdaws bi-ma'thūr al-khiṭāb*. Ed. Basyūnī Zaghlūl. 5 vols. Beirut, 1986.
al-Dhahabī, Muḥammad ibn Aḥmad. *Al-Sīra al-nabawiyya*. Ed. Ḥusām al-Dīn al-Qudsī. Beirut, 1981.
EI^2 = *The Encyclopaedia of Islam* (New Edition). Leiden, 1960–proceeding.
al-Fākihī, Muḥammad ibn Isḥāq. *Akhbār Makka*. Ed. 'Abd al-Malik ibn Dehish. 6 vols. Mecca, 1986–88.
al-Farrā', Yaḥyā ibn Ziyād. *Ma'ānī l-Qur'ān*. Ed. Aḥmad Yūsuf Najātī, Muḥammad 'Alī al-Najjār, and 'Abd al-Fattāḥ Ismā'īl Shalabī. 3 vols. Repr. Beirut, n.d.
Fatḥ al-bārī = Shihāb al-Dīn Aḥmad ibn Ḥajar al-'Asqalānī. *Fatḥ al-bārī sharḥ Ṣaḥīḥ al-Bukhārī*. 13 vols. Būlāq, 1310/1892, repr. Beirut, n.d.
Goldfeld, Isaiah. "The Illiterate Prophet (*nabī ummī*): an Inquiry into the Development of a Dogma in Islamic Tradition", *Der Islam* 57 (1980), 58–67.
Goldziher, Ignaz. *Muslim Studies*. 2 vols. London, 1967–71.
_______. "Ueber muhammadanische Polemik gegen Ahl al-kitāb", *Zeitschrift der Deutschen Morgenländischen Gesellschaft* 32 (1878), 341–87. Reprinted in his *Gesammelte Schriften*, II (Hildesheim, 1968), 1–47.
Guillaume, Alfred. *The Life of Muhammad*: a *Translation of Ibn Isḥāq's Sīrat Rasūl Allāh*. Oxford, 1974.
_______. "New Light on the Life of Muhammad", *Journal of Semitic Studies*, Monograph no. 1. Manchester, n.d.
Guthrie, A., and E.F.F. Bishop. "The Paraclete, Almunhamanna and Aḥmad", *The Muslim World* 41 (1951), 251–56.
al-Ḥalabī, 'Alī ibn Burhān al-Dīn. *Al-Sīra al-ḥalabiyya*. 3 vols. Cairo, 1320/1902, repr. Beirut, n.d.
Ḥassān ibn Thābit. *Dīwān*. Ed. Walīd N. 'Arafāt. 2 vols. London, 1971.
Hawting, Gerald R. "The Disappearance and Rediscovery of Zamzam and the 'Well of the Ka'ba'", *Bulletin of the School of Oriental and African Studies* 43 (1980), 44–54.
al-Ḥibarī, Abū 'Abdallāh al-Ḥusayn ibn al-Ḥakam. *Tafsīr*. Ed. Muḥammad Riḍā al-Ḥusaynī. Beirut, 1987.
Horovitz, Josef. "Biblische Nachwirkungen in der Sira", *Der Islam* 12 (1922), 184–89.
_______. "Muhammeds Himmelfahrt", *Der Islam* 9 (1918), 159–83.
_______. "Die poetischen Einlagen der *Sīra*", *Islamica* 2 (1926–27), 308–12.
_______. "Zur Muḥammadlegende", *Der Islam* 5 (1914), 41–53.
al-Ḥumaydī, Abū Bakr 'Abdallāh ibn al-Zubayr. *Al-Musnad*. Ed. Ḥabīb al-Raḥmān al-A'ẓamī. 2 vols. Medina, n.d.
al-Huwwārī, Hūd ibn Muḥakkam. *Tafsīr kitāb Allāh al-'Azīz*. Ed. Belḥāj Sharīfī. 4 vols. Beirut, 1990.
Ibn 'Abd al-Barr, Yūsuf ibn 'Abdallāh. *Al-Istī'āb fī ma'rifat al-aṣḥāb*. Ed. 'Alī Muḥammad al-Bijāwī. 4 vols. Cairo, 1960.
_______. *Al-Tamhīd li-mā fī l-Muwaṭṭa' min al-ma'ānī wa-l-asānīd*. Various editors, 22 vols. Rabat, 1967–90.
Ibn Abī 'Āṣim, Aḥmad ibn 'Amr al-Shaybānī. *Al-Awā'il*. Ed. Maḥmūd Naṣṣār. Beirut, 1991.

Ibn Abī l-Dunyā, ʿAbdallāh ibn Muḥammad. *Al-Ṣamt wa-ḥifẓ al-lisān*. Ed. Muḥammad Aḥmad ʿĀshūr. Cairo, 1988.
Ibn Abī Shayba, ʿAbdallāh ibn Muḥammad. *Al-Muṣannaf fī l-aḥādīth wa-l-āthār*. Ed. ʿAbd al-Khāliq al-Afghānī. 15 vols. Bombay, 1979–83.
Ibn Abī Zayd al-Qayrawānī, ʿAbdallāh. *Al-Jāmiʿ fī l-sunan wa-l-ādāb wa-l-maghāzī wa-l-tārīkh*. Tunis, 1982.
Ibn al-ʿArabī, Muḥammad ibn ʿAbdallāh. *Aḥkām al-Qur'ān*. Ed. ʿAlī Muḥammad al-Bijāwī. 4 vols. Beirut, 1987.
Ibn ʿAsākir (*Mukhtaṣar*) = Ibn Manẓūr Muḥammad ibn Mukarram. *Mukhtaṣar Tārīkh Dimashq li-Ibn ʿAsākir*. 29 vols. Damascus, 1984–88.
Ibn ʿAṭiyya, Abū Muḥammad ʿAbd al-Ḥaqq. *Al-Muḥarrar al-wajīz fī tafsīr al-kitāb al-ʿazīz*. 16 vols. Muḥammadiyya [Morocco], 1975–91.
Ibn Bukayr, Yūnus. *Kitāb al-siyar wa-l-maghāzī li-Muḥammad Ibn Isḥāq*. Ed. Suhayl Zakkār. Damascus, 1978.
Ibn al-Ḍurays, Muḥammad ibn Ayyūb. *Faḍā'il al-Qur'ān*. Ed. Ghazwat Budayr. Damascus, 1987.
Ibn Ḥajar, Shihāb al-Dīn Aḥmad al-ʿAsqalānī. *Al-Iṣāba fī maʿrifat al-ṣaḥāba*. Ed. ʿAlī Muḥammad al-Bijāwī. 8 vols. Cairo, 1970.
_______. *Al-Maṭālib al-ʿāliya bi-zawā'id al-masānīd al-thamāniya*. Ed. Ḥabīb al-Raḥmān al-Aʿẓamī. 4 vols. Beirut, 1987.
Ibn Ḥazm, ʿAlī ibn Aḥmad. *Al-Muḥallā*. 11 vols. Cairo, 1352/1933.
Ibn Ḥibbān, Muḥammad ibn Aḥmad al-Bustī. *Al-Iḥsān fī taqrīb Ṣaḥīḥ Ibn Ḥibbān, tartīb ʿAlā' al-Dīn al-Fārisī*. Ed. Shuʿayb al-Arna'ūṭ. 16 vols. Beirut, 1988.
Ibn Hishām, ʿAbd al-Malik. *Al-Sīra al-nabawiyya*. Ed. Muṣṭafā al-Saqqā, Ibrāhīm al-Abyārī, and ʿAbd al-Ḥāfiẓ Shalabī. 4 vols. Repr. Beirut, 1971.
Ibn al-Jawzī, ʿAbd al-Raḥmān. *Al-Wafā bi-aḥwāl al-Muṣṭafā*. Ed. Muṣṭafā ʿAbd al-Wāḥid. Cairo, 1966.
_______. *Zād al-masīr fī ʿilm al-tafsīr*. 9 vols. Beirut, 1984.
Ibn al-Kalbī, Hishām ibn Muḥammad. *Kitāb al-aṣnām*. Ed. Aḥmad Zakī. Cairo, 1924, repr. Cairo, n.d.
Ibn Kathīr, Ismāʿīl ibn ʿUmar. *Al-Bidāya wa-l-nihāya*. 14 vols. Repr. Beirut, 1974.
_______. *Tafsīr al-Qur'ān al-aẓīm*. 4 vols. Cairo, n.d.
Ibn Khuzayma, Abū Bakr Muḥammad ibn Isḥāq. *Al-Ṣaḥīḥ*. Ed. Muḥammad Muṣṭafā al-Aʿẓamī. 4 vols. Beirut, 1975.
Ibn Māja, Muḥammad ibn Yazīd. *Al-Sunan*. Ed. Muḥammad Fu'ād ʿAbd al-Bāqī. 2 vols. Cairo, 1952.
Ibn al-Mubārak, ʿAbdallāh. *Al-Musnad*. Ed. Ṣubḥī al-Badrī al-al-Sāmarrā'ī. Riyad, 1987.
Ibn Qudāma, ʿAbdallāh ibn Aḥmad. *Al-Mughnī*, with *al-Sharḥ al-kabīr* by ʿAbd al-Raḥmān ibn Qudāma. 12 vols. Beirut, 1984.
Ibn Qutayba, ʿAbdallāh ibn Muslim. *Kitāb al-maʿārif*. Ed. Muḥammad Ismāʿīl ʿAbdallāh al-Ṣāwī. Repr. Beirut, 1970.
_______. *Tafsīr gharīb al-Qur'ān*. Ed. Aḥmad Ṣaqr. Beirut, 1978.
_______. *Ta'wīl mushkil al-Qur'ān*. Ed. Aḥmad Ṣaqr. Cairo, 1973.
Ibn Rabban, ʿAlī al-Ṭabarī. *Al-Dīn wa-l-dawla fī ithbāt nubuwwat al-nabiyy Muḥammad*. Ed. ʿĀdil Nuwayhiḍ. Beirut, 1973.
Ibn Saʿd, Muḥammad. *Kitāb al-ṭabaqāt*. 8 vols. Beirut, 1960.
Ibn Sayyid al-Nās, Muḥammad ibn Abī Bakr.*ʿUyūn al-athar*. 2 vols. Repr. Beirut, n.d.
Ibn Shabba, Abū Zayd ʿUmar. *Tārīkh al-Madīna al-Munawwara*. Ed. Fuhaym Muḥammad Shaltūt. 4 vols. Mecca, 1979.
Ibn Shahrāshūb, Muḥammad ibn ʿAlī. *Manāqib āl Abī Ṭālib*. 3 vols. Najaf, 1956.

Jeffery, Arthur. "Was Muhammad a Prophet from his Infancy?", *The Muslim World* 20 (1930), 226–34.
Jones, M.B. "The Chronology of the *Maghāzī*—a Textual Survey", *Bulletin of the School of Oriental and African Studies* 19 (1957), 245–80.
Juynboll, G.H.A. *Muslim Tradition: Studies in Chronology, Provenance and Authorship of Early Ḥadīth.* Cambridge, 1983.
_______. "Some New Ideas on the Development of *Sunna* as a Technical Term in Early Islam", *Jerusalem Studies in Arabic and Islam* 10 (1987), 97–118.
Kanz = 'Alā' al-Dīn al-Muttaqī ibn Ḥusām al-Dīn al-Hindī. *Kanz al-'ummāl fī sunan al-aqwāl wa-l-af'āl.* Ed. Ṣafwat al-Saqqā and Bakrī Ḥayyānī. 16 vols. Beirut, 1979.
Kashf al-astār = al-Haythamī, Nūr al-Dīn. *Kashf al-astār 'an zawā'id al-Bazzār* Ed. Ḥabīb al-Raḥmān al-A'ẓamī.. 4 vols. Beirut, 1979.
al-Khafājī. Shihāb al-Dīn. *Nasīm al-riyāḍ fī sharḥ Shifā' al-Qāḍī 'Iyāḍ.* Ed. Ibrāhīm al-Ṭāhirī. 4 vols. Cairo, 1327/1909, repr. Medina, n.d.
Khalīfa ibn Khayyāṭ. *Tārīkh.* Ed. Akram Ḍiyā' al-'Umarī. Baghdad, 1967.
al-Kharā'iṭī, Abū Bakr Muḥammad ibn Ja'far. *Hawātif al-jinnān.* In *Nawādir al-rasā'il.* Ed. Ibrāhīm Ṣāliḥ (Beirut, 1986), 123–210.
al-Khargūshī, Abū Sa'd 'Abd al-Malik ibn Abī 'Uthmān. *Sharaf al-nabiyy.* MS Br. Lib., Or. 3014.
_______. *op. cit.*, MS Tübingen, M. a. VI, 12.
Kinberg, Leah. *Morality in the Guise of Dreams.* Leiden, 1994.
Kister, M.J. "A Bag of Meat", *Bulletin of the School of Oriental and African Studies* 33 (1970), 267–75.
_______. "The Campaign of Ḥulubān: a New Light on the Expedition of Abraha", *Le Muséon* 78 (1965), 425–36.
_______. " 'God will Never Disgrace Thee' ", *Journal of the Royal Asiatic Society*, 1965, 27–32.
_______. "*Ḥaddithū 'an banī isrā'īla wa-lā ḥaraja*", *Israel Oriental Studies* 2 (1972), 222–25.
_______. "The Interpretation of Dreams", *Israel Oriental Studies* 4 (1974), 67–103.
_______. "Mecca and Tamīm", *Journal of the Economic and Social History of the Orient* 8 (1965), 113–63.
_______. "Notes on the Papyrus Account of the 'Aqaba Meeting", *Le Muséon* 76 (1963), 403–17.
_______. "On a New Edition of the *Dīwān* of Ḥassān ibn Thābit", *Bulletin of the School of Oriental and African Studies* 39 (1976), 265–68.
_______. "Pare your Nails: a Study of an Early Tradition", *Near Eastern Studies in Memory of M.M. Bravmann, The Journal of The Ancient Near Eastern Society of Columbia University* 11 (1979), 63–70.
_______. "Rajab is the Month of God...", *Israel Oriental Studies* 1 (1971), 191–223.
_______. "Some Reports Concerning Mecca", *Journal of the Economic and Social History of the Orient* 15 (1972), 61–91.
_______. "The Sons of Khadīja", *Jerusalem Studies in Arabic and Islam* 16 (1993), 59–95.
_______. " '*Al-Taḥannuth*': an Inquiry into the Meaning of a Term", *Bulletin of the School of Oriental and African Studies* 31 (1968), 223–36.
al-Kulīnī, Abū Ja'far Muḥammad ibn Ya'qūb. *Al-Uṣūl wa-l-furū' min al-Kafī.* Ed. 'Alī Akbar al-Ghaffārī. 8 vols. Beirut, 1980.
Landau-Tasseron, Ella. "The Sinful Wars: Religious, Social and Historical Aspects of *Ḥurūb al-Fijār*", *Jerusalem Studies in Arabic and Islam* 8 (1986), 37–60.
Lecker, Michael. *The Banū Sulaym.* Jerusalem, 1989.

Lichtenstaedter, Ilse. "A Note on the *Gharānīq* and Related Qur'ānic Problems", *Israel Oriental Studies* 5 (1975), 54–61.
Lisān = Ibn Manẓūr Muḥammad ibn Mukarram. *Lisān al-'arab*. 6 vols. Cairo, n.d.
Lohmann, Theodor. "Sure 96 und die Berufung Muḥammeds", *Mitteilungen des Instituts für Orientforschung*, 14 (1968), 249–302, 416–69.
Majma' al-zawā'id = al-Haythamī, Nūr al-Dīn. *Majma' al-zawā'id wa-manba' al-fawā'id*. 10 vols. Repr. Beirut, 1987.
Mālik/Zurqānī = al-Zurqānī, Muḥammad ibn 'Abd al-Bāqī. *Sharḥ Muwaṭṭa' al-imām Mālik*. Ed. Ibrāhīm 'Aṭwa 'Iwaḍ. 5 vols. Cairo, 1961.
al-Marzūqī, Abū 'Alī Aḥmad ibn Muḥammad. *Al-Azmina wa-l-amkina*. 2 vols. Qatar, 1968.
(pseudo-) al-Mas'ūdī, 'Alī ibn al-Ḥusayn. *Ithbāt al-waṣiyya li-l-imām 'Alī ibn Abī Ṭālib*. Najaf, 1955.
_______. *Murūj al-dhahab*. Ed. Muḥammad Muḥyī l-Dīn 'Abd al-Ḥamīd. 4 vols. Cairo, 1965.
al-Māwardī, 'Alī ibn Muḥammad. *Al-Nukat wa-l-'uyūn fī tafsīr al-Qur'ān*. Ed. 'Abd al-Maqṣūd ibn 'Abd al-Raḥīm. 6 vols. Beirut, 1992.
Mélamède, Gertrud. "The Meetings at al-'Aḳaba", *Le Monde Oriental* 28 (1934), 17–58.
Motzki, Harald. "The *Muṣannaf* of 'Abd al-Razzāq al-Ṣan'ānī as a Source of Authentic *Aḥādīh* of the First Century A.H.", *Journal of Near Eastern Studies* 50 (1991), 1–21.
Mughulṭāy, 'Alā' al-Dīn ibn Qillīj. *Al-Zahr al-bāsim*. MS Leiden, Or. 370.
Muḥibb al-Dīn Aḥmad ibn 'Abdallāh al-Ṭabarī. *Dhakhā'ir al-'uqbā fī manāqib dhawī l-qurbā*. Beirut, 1981.
Mujāhid ibn Jabr. *Tafsīr*. Ed. 'Abd al-Raḥmān al-Sūratī. 2 vols. Islamabad, n.d.
Muqātil ibn Sulaymān. *Tafsīr al-Qur'ān*. MS Istanbul, Ahmet III, 74/I–II. Ed. 'Abdallāh Maḥmūd Shiḥāta. 5 vols. Cairo, 1979.
Muranyi, Miklos. "Die ersten Muslime von Mekka—soziale Basis einer neuen Religion?", *Jerusalem Studies in Arabic and Islam* 8 (1986), 25–36.
_______. "Ibn Isḥāq's *Kitāb al-Maġāzī* in der *Riwāya* von Yūnus b. Bukayr", *Jerusalem Studies in Arabic and Islam* 14 (1991), 214–75.
Muslim ibn al-Ḥajjāj. *Al-Ṣaḥīḥ*. 8 vols. Cairo, 1334/1915, repr. Cairo, n.d.
Mustadrak = al-Ḥākim Muḥammad ibn 'Abdallāh al-Naysābūrī. *Al-Mustadrak 'alā l-Ṣaḥīḥayn*. 4 vols. Hyderabad, 1342/1923.
al-Naḥḥās, Aḥmad ibn Muḥammad. *I'rāb al-Qur'ān*. Ed. Zuhayr Ghāzī Zāhid. 5 vols. Cairo, 1985.
_______. *Al-Nāsikh wa-l-mansūkh*. Beirut, 1989.
al-Nasā'ī, Aḥmad b. Shu'ayb. *Kitāb wafāt al-nabiyy*. Ed. Muḥammad al-Sa'īd Zaghlūl. Cairo, 1988.
_______. *Al-Sunan al-kubrā*. Ed. 'Abd al-Ghaffār al-Bandārī, and Sayyid Ḥasan. 6 vols. Beirut, 1991.
Nöldeke–Schwally = Nöldeke, Theodor. *Geschichte des Qorans*. Zweite Auflage, bearbeitet von Friedrich Schwally. 3 vols. Leipzig, 1909–38, repr. Hildesheim and New York, 1970.
Noth, Albrecht, and Conrad, Lawrence I. *The Early Islamic Historical Tradition: a Source Critical Study*. Princeton, 1994.
Paret, Rudi. *Mohammed und der Koran*. Stuttgart. 1966.
Parrinder, Geoffrey. *Jesus in the Qur'ān*. London, 1977.
Peters, F.E. "The Quest of the Historical Muhammad", *International Journal of Middle East Studies* 23 (1991), 291–315.
al-Qazwīnī, Zakariyyā ibn Muḥammad. *'Ajā'ib al-makhlūqāt*. Cairo, 1970.
Qiwām al-Sunna, Abū l-Qāsim Ismā'īl ibn Muḥammad al-Taymī al-Iṣfahānī. *Dalā'il al-nubuwwa*. Ed. al-Rāshid al-Ḥamīd. 4 vols. Riyad, 1992.

al-Qummī, 'Alī ibn Ibrāhīm. *Al-Tafsīr*. 2 vols. Beirut, 1991.
al-Qurṭubī, Muḥammad ibn Aḥmad. *Al-Jāmi' li-aḥkām al-Qur'ān*. 20 vols. Cairo, 1967.
Quṭrub, Abū 'Alī Muḥamad ibn al-Mustanīr. *Al-Azmina wa-talbiyat al-jāhiliyya*. Ed. Ḥannā Jamīl Ḥaddād. Zarqa, 1985.
al-Rāzī, Fakhr al-Dīn Abū 'Abdallāh Muḥammad ibn 'Umar. *Al-Tafsīr al-kabīr*. 32 vols. Cairo n.d., repr. Tehran, n.d.
Rippin, Andrew. "The Exegetical Genre *Asbāb al-Nuzūl*: a Bibliographical and Terminological Survey", *Bulletin of the School of Oriental and African Studies* 48 (1985), 1–15.
______. "The Function of *Asbāb al-Nuzūl* in Qur'ānic Exegesis", *Bulletin of the School of Oriental and African Studies* 51 (1988), 1–20.
Rubin, Uri. "Abū Lahab and *Sūra* CXI", *Bulletin of the School of Oriental and African Studies* 42 (1979), 13–28.
______. "The Assassination of Ka'b b. al-Ashraf", *Oriens* 32 (1990), 65–71.
______. "Exegesis and Ḥadīth: the Case of the Seven Mathānī", in G.R. Hawting and Abdul-Kader A. Shareef, eds., *Approaches to the Qur'ān* (London and New York, 1993), 141–56.
______. "*Ḥanīfiyya* and Ka'ba: an Inquiry into the Arabian Pre-Islamic Background of *Dīn Ibrāhīm*", *Jerusalem Studies in Arabic and Islam* 13 (1990), 85–112.
______. "The *Īlāf* of Quraysh: a Study of *Sūra* CVI", *Arabica* 31 (1984), 165–88.
______. "*Iqra' bi-smi rabbika*", *Israel Oriental Studies* 13 (1993), 213–30.
______. "The Ka'ba: Aspects of its Ritual Functions", *Jerusalem Studies in Arabic and Islam* 8 (1986), 97–131.
______. "Muḥammad's Curse of Muḍar and the Boycott of Mecca", *Journal of the Economic and Social History of the Orient* 31 (1988), 249–64.
______. "Pre-Existence and Light: Aspects of the Concept of Nūr Muḥammad", *Israel Oriental Studies* 5 (1975), 62–119.
______. "Prophets and Progenitors in the Early Shī'a Tradition", *Jerusalem Studies in Arabic and Islam* 1 (1979), 41–65.
______. "The Shrouded Messenger: On the Interpretation of *al-Muzzammil* and *al-Muddaththir*", *Jerusalem Studies in Arabic and Islam* 16 (1993), 96–107.
al-Ṣafūrī, 'Abd al-Raḥmān. *Nuzhat al-majālis wa-muntakhab al-nafā'is*. Cairo, 1346/1927, repr. Beirut, n.d.
Saḥnūn ibn Sa'īd al-Tanūkhī. *Al-Mudawwana al-kubrā*. 4 vols. Beirut, 1986.
Sa'īd ibn Manṣūr. *Al-Sunan*. Ed. Ḥabīb al-Raḥmān al-A'ẓamī. 2 vols. Beirut, 1985.
al-Samarqandī, Abū l-Layth Naṣr ibn Muḥammad. *Tafsīr al-Qur'ān*. Ed. 'Alī Mu'awwaḍ, 'Ādil 'Abd al-Mawjūd, and Zakariyyā al-Nawtī. 3 vols. Beirut, 1993.
al-Sarakhsī, Muḥammad ibn Aḥmad. *Kitāb al-mabsūṭ*. 30 vols. Repr. Beirut, 1986.
Schacht, Joseph. *The Origins of Muhammadan Jurisprudence*. Repr. Oxford, 1979.
Schimmel, Annemarie. *And Muhammad is His Messenger: the Veneration of the Prophet in Islamic Piety*. Chapel Hill, 1985.
Sellheim, Rudolf. "Muḥammeds erste Offenbarungserlebnis", *Jerusalem Studies in Arabic and Islam* 10 (1987), 1–16.
______. "Prophet, Chalif und Geschichte", *Oriens* 18–19 (1965–66), 33–91.
Sezgin, Fuat. *Geschichte des arabischen Schrifttums*. 9 vols. to date. Leiden, 1967–proceeding.
al-Shāmī, Muḥammad ibn Yūsuf. *Subul al-hudā wa-l-rashād fī sīrat khayr al-'ibād*. Ed. Muṣṭafā 'Abd al-Wāḥid. 8 vols. Cairo, 1990.
al-Shaybānī, Muḥammad ibn al-Ḥasan. *Al-Ḥujja 'alā ahl al-Madīna*. Ed. Mahdī Ḥasan al-Kaylānī al-Qādirī. 4 vols. Beirut, 1983.

al-Shaykh al-Ṣadūq, Abū Ja'far Muḥammad ibn 'Alī ibn Bābūya. *Man lā yaḥḍuruhu l-faqīh.* Ed. Ḥusayn al-A'lamī. 4 vols. Beirut, 1986.

al-Suhaylī, 'Abd al-Raḥmān ibn 'Abdallāh. *Al-Rawḍ al-unuf.* Ed. 'Abd al-Ra'ūf Sa'd. 4 vols. Cairo, 1971.

al-Suyūṭī, Jalāl al-Dīn. *Al-Durr al-manthūr fī l-tafsīr bi-l-ma'thūr.* 6 vols. Cairo, 1314/1869, repr. Beirut, n.d.

_______. *Al-Khaṣā'iṣ al-kubrā.* Ed. Muḥammad Khalīl Harās. 3 vols. Cairo, 1967.

_______. *Al-Wasā'il ilā ma'rifat al-awā'il.* Ed. Ibrāhīm al-'Adawī and 'Alī 'Umar. Cairo, 1980.

al-Ṭabarānī, Sulaymān ibn Aḥmad. *Al-Mu'jam al-awsaṭ.* Ed. Maḥmūd al-Ṭaḥḥān. 3 vols. to date. Riyad, 1985–proceeding.

_______. *Al-Mu'jam al-kabīr.* Ed. Ḥamdī 'Abd al-Majīd al-Salafī. 25 vols. Baghdad, 1980–85.

_______. *Al-Mu'jam al-ṣaghīr.* Ed. 'Abd al-Raḥmān Muḥammad 'Uthmān. Cairo, 1981–83.

al-Ṭabarī, Muḥammad ibn Jarīr. *Jāmi' al-bayān fī tafsīr al-Qur'ān.* 30 vols. Būlāq, 1323/1905, repr. Beirut, 1972.

_______. *Tahdhīb al-āthār.* Ed. Maḥmūd Muḥammad Shākir. 6 vols. Cairo, 1982.

_______. *Tārīkh al-rusul wa-l-mulūk.* Ed. M.J. De Goeje. 15 vols. Leiden, 1879–1901 (Ed. Muḥammad Abū l-Faḍl Ibrāhīm. 10 vols. Repr. Cairo, 1987).

al-Ṭabarsī, al-Faḍl ibn al-Ḥasan. *A'lām al-warā bi-a'lām al-hudā.* Ed. 'Alī Akbar al-Ghaffārī. Repr. Beirut, 1979.

_______. *Majma' al-bayān fī tafsīr al-Qur'ān.* 30 vols. Beirut, 1957.

al-Ṭaḥāwī, Abū Ja'far Aḥmad ibn Muḥammad. *Mushkil al-āthār.* 4 vols. Hyderabad, 1333/1914, repr. Beirut, n.d.

_______. *Sharḥ ma'ānī l-āthār.* Ed. Muḥammad Zuhrī al-Najjār. 4 vols. Repr. Beirut, 1987.

al-Ṭayālisī, Abū Dāwūd Sulaymān ibn Dāwūd. *Al-Musnad.* Hyderabad, 1321/1903.

al-Tha'ālibī, 'Abd al-Raḥmān ibn Muḥammad. *Jawāhir al-ḥisan fī tafsīr al-Qur'ān.* 4 vols. Algiers, 1372/1909, repr. Beirut, n.d.

Tha'lab, Abū l-'Abbās Aḥmad ibn Yaḥyā. *Majālis.* Ed. 'Abd al-Salām Muḥammad Hārūn. Cairo, 1960.

al-Tha'labī, Aḥmad ibn Ibrāhīm. *Al-Kashf wa-l-bayān 'an tafsīr āy al-Qur'ān* (second volume). MS Tel Aviv University, no. 508750.

al-Tirmidhī, Muḥammad ibn 'Īsā. *Al-Shamā'il al-muḥammadiyya* [with commentary of al-Bājūrī]. Cairo, 1344/1925.

Tirmidhī/*Tuḥfa* = 'Abd al-Raḥmān al-Mubārkafūrī. *Tuḥfat al-aḥwadhī sharḥ Jāmi' al-Tirmidhī.* Ed. 'Abd al-Raḥmān Muḥammad 'Uthmān. 10 vols. Cairo, 1979.

al-Ṭūsī, Muḥammad ibn al-Ḥasan. *Al-Tabyān fī tafsīr al-Qur'ān.* Ed. Aḥmad al-'Āmilī. 10 vols. Beirut, n.d.

Wagtendonk, Kees. *Fasting in the Koran.* Leiden, 1968.

al-Wāḥidī, 'Alī ibn Aḥmad. *Asbāb al-nuzūl.* Cairo, 1968.

_______. *Al-Wasīṭ bayna l-maqbūḍ wa-l-basīṭ.* MS Br. Lib., Or. 8249.

Wakī' ibn al-Jarrāḥ. *Kitāb al-zuhd.* Ed. 'Abd al-Raḥmān al-Faryawā'ī. 3 vols. Medina, 1984.

Wansbrough, John. *Quranic Studies.* Oxford, 1977.

_______. *The Sectarian Milieu.* Oxford, 1978.

al-Wāqidī, Muḥammad ibn 'Umar. *Kitāb al-maghāzī.* Ed. Marsden Jones. 3 vols. London, 1966.

Watt, W. Montgomery. "His Name is Aḥmad", *The Muslim World* 43 (1953), 110–17.

_______. "The Materials Used by Ibn Isḥāq", in Bernard Lewis *et al.*, eds., *Historians of the Middle East* (London, 1962), 23–34.

_______. *Muhammad at Mecca.* Oxford, 1953.

_______. *Muhammad at Medina*. Oxford, 1956.

Wellhausen, Julius. *Reste arabischen Heidentums*. 3rd ed. Berlin, 1961.

Wensinck, A.J. "Muhammed und die Propheten", *Acta Orientalia* 2 (1924), 168–98.

Yaḥyā ibn Sallām. *Mukhtasar al-tafsīr, ikhtiṣār Abī 'Abdallāh ibn Abī Zamanīn*. MS Fès, Qar. 34.

al-Ya'qūbī, Aḥmad ibn Abī Ya'qūb ibn Wāḍiḥ. *Al-Tārīkh*. 2 vols. Beirut, 1960.

Yāqūt al-Ḥamawī, Shihāb al-Dīn Abū 'Abdallāh. *Mu'jam al-buldān*. 5 vols. Beirut, 1957.

al-Zajjāj, Abū Isḥāq. *Ma'ānī l-Qur'ān wa-i'rābuhu*. Ed. 'Abd al-Jalīl Shalabī. 5 vols. Beirut, 1988.

al-Zamakhsharī, Jārullāh Maḥmūd ibn 'Umar. *Al-Kashshāf 'an ḥaqā'iq al-tanzīl*. 4 vols. Cairo, 1966.

Zayd ibn 'Alī ibn al-Ḥusayn. *Al-Musnad*. Beirut, 1983.

Zubaydi, A.M. "The Impact of the Qur'ān and Ḥadīth on Medieval Arabic Literature", in A.F.L. Beeston *et al.*, eds., *Arabic Literature to the End of the Umayyad Period* (Cambridge, 1983), 322–43.

al-Zurqānī, Muḥammad ibn 'Abd al-Bāqī. *Sharḥ 'alā l-mawāhib al-laduniyya li-l-Qasṭallānī*. 8 vols. Cairo, 1329/1911, repr. Beirut, 1973.

General Index

On conventions adopted for alphabetization, see the introductory note to the Bibliography. Names of tribes should be looked up under "Banū...." Persons whose writings are quoted in this book are indicated as "author".

Index of Quranic References

Index of Biblical References